STUDIA MISSIONALIA

Publication of the Faculty of Missiology, Gregorian University.
Publication de la Faculté de Missiologie de l'Université Grégorienne.

MARIASUSAI DHAVAMONY, S.J., *Director.*

NEW EVANGELIZATION IN THE THIRD MILLENNIUM

NOUVELLE ÉVANGÉLISATION AU TROISIÈME MILLÉNAIRE

EDITRICE PONTIFICIA UNIVERSITÀ GREGORIANA
ROMA 1999

IMPRIMI POTEST
Romae, die 14 iulii 1999

R.P. Francisco J. Egaña, S.J.
Vice Rector Universitatis

IMPRIMATUR
Dal Vicariato di Roma, 30 settembre 1999

Mons. Luigi Moretti, *Vescovo tit. di Mopta*
Segretario Generale

© 1999 – E.P.U.G. – Roma
ISBN 88-7652-838-5

Editrice Pontificia Università Gregoriana
Piazza della Pilotta, 35 - 00187 Roma, Italia

CONTENTS — SOMMAIRE

New Evangelization in the third Millennium
Nouvelle Évangélisation au Troisième Millénaire

Claude Tassin, Annoncer le Christ: l'expérience multiforme des Actes des Apôtres 1

Raimondo Riva, L'evangelizzazione «nuova» di Gesù nella tradizione sinottica 17

Jean Galot, La bonne nouvelle du Père. 47

Mariasusai Dhavamony, The absoluteness of Jesus Christ and of Christianity 71

Earl Muller, The Holy Spirit, the Principal Agent of Evangelization. 123

Avery Dulles, John Paul II and the New Evangelization 165

Juan Esquerda-Bifet, Nueva Evangelización y espiritualidad misionera (en el inicio del tercer milenio) 181

Francis Card. Arinze, Interreligious Dialogue in the Third Millennium 203

A. Dupré La Tour, Théologie des religions non-Chrétiennes et l'Islam 215

Javier García, Los rostros de Cristo en el Sínodo de América 231

John Paul II, Message to the VI FABC Plenary Assembly. 259

PETER C. PHAN, Catechesis as an instrument of Evangelization: reflections from the perspective of Asia 289

FRANCIS X. CLARK, Asian Saints and Blessed, and the New Evangelization 313

PHILIP GIBBS, The Transformation of Culture as New Evangelization (for the Third Millennium in Oceania) 327

PETER K. SARPONG, The African Synod and the powerful word of God in evangelization at the threshold of the Third Millennium........... 347

RENÉ LUNEAU, Les Eglises d'Afrique et la «nouvelle Evangélisation»........................ 369

J. JOBLIN, Les organisations internationales catholiques et les défis de la nouvelle évangélisation au troisième millénaire................... 383

CONTRIBUTORS – COLLABORATEURS

FRANCIS CARD. ARINZE, Prefect of the Pontifical Council for Interreligious Dialogue, Vatican City.

FRANCIS X. CLARK, Professor of Theology, St John Vianney Seminary, Cagayan de Oro City, Philippines.

MARIASUSAI DHAVAMONY, Professor of Theology and Phenomenology of Religions, Pontifical Gregorian University, Rome.

AVERY DULLES, Lawrence J. McGinley Professor, Fordham University, New York.

AUGUSTIN DUPRÉ LA TOUR, Communauté St Jean Chrysostome, Beyrouth, Liban.

JUAN ESQUERDA-BIFET, Professor of Missiology, Università Urbaniana, Rome.

JEAN GALOT, Professor of Dogmatic Theology, Pontifical Gregorian University, Rome.

PHILIP GIBBS, Divine Word College, Boroko, Papua New Guinea.

JOSEPH JOBLIN, Segretario Commissione: Storia dei movimenti sociali e delle strutture sociali, Roma.

JAVIER GARCÍA GONZALES, Professor of Dogmatic Theology, Pontifical Gregorian University, Rome.

RENÉ LUNEAU, Africanist, Paris.

EARL MULLER, Professor of Dogmatic Theology, St Louis University, St Louis.

PETER C. PHAN, Professor of Theology, Catholic University of America, Washington D.C.

RAIMONDO RIVA, Professor of New Testament Exegesis, Pontifical Gregorian University of Rome.

BISHOP SARPONG, Anthropologist and theologian, Kumasi, Ghana.

CLAUDE TASSIN, Professor of New Testament Exegesis, L'Institut Catholique, Paris.

Annoncer le Christ:
l'expérience multiforme des Actes des Apôtres

CLAUDE TASSIN

Au seuil de l'an 2000, l'Église relit volontiers les sources bibliques de l'annonce du Christ, en particulier les *Actes des Apôtres*[1]. Mais les Actes n'offrent pas de stratégie pour l'avenir de la mission chrétienne car l'histoire ne se répète pas. Dans les années 80, Luc rebâtit l'histoire du christianisme primitif comme une mobilisation des croyants ayant abouti à l'évangélisation de l'Empire et accomplissant l'ordre du Ressuscité: «Vous serez mes témoins à Jérusalem, dans toute la Judée et la Samarie et jusqu'à l'extrémité de la terre» (Ac 1, 8). *L'extrémité de la terre*, vue de Jérusalem, c'est Rome. Paul ayant atteint Rome (Ac 28), le plan est réalisé: Si Rome est évangélisée, le monde est *évangélisé*. Luc céderait-il là à une *mondialisation*[2] illusoire?

---

[1] Les grands commentaires modernes des Actes sont les suivants: E. HAENCHEN, *Die Apostelgeschichte*, Göttingen, [14]1965 (= *The Acts of the Apostles*, Oxford, 1971); G. SCHNEIDER, *Die Apostelgeschichte*, Freiburg-Basel-Wien, 2 vol., 1980-82; F. F. BRUCE, *The Book of the Acts*, Grand Rapids [2]1988. Signalons un bon ouvrage de vulgarisation: A. WEISER, *Die Apostelgeschichte*, 2 vol., Würzburg, 1981-1985. En français: C. L'ÉPLATTENIER, *Le Livre des Actes*, Paris, 1994.

[2] Nuancer cette boutade par l'analyse de D. MARGUERAT, «Luc-Actes entre Jérusalem et Rome. Un procédé lucanien de double signification», *NTS* 45 (1999), p. 70-87. «l'inculturation du christianisme dans l'Empire comportait, selon Luc, deux conditions que l'histoire a fort mal respectées: l'une est l'ouverture du christianisme à sa patrie religieuse, Israël; l'autre est l'acceptation critique du monde, faite de cette liberté de parole (la *parrhèsia*), qui constitue d'après Luc la marque des témoins conduits par l'Esprit» (p. 85).

En réalité, il pratique une relecture spirituelle de l'histoire[3]. Tout *aujourd'hui* se nourrissant d'un hier à réinventer, il s'emploie à discerner par quels chemins l'Esprit Saint a conduit l'expansion de l'Évangile jusqu'à sa propre époque. Or il distingue deux périodes. La première est l'âge d'or dans lequel l'Esprit s'emparait des témoins[4], pour les assister, ou s'imposait en force dans les événements[5]. La dernière intervention directe de l'Esprit empêche l'équipe paulinienne de s'enfoncer en Asie et la propulse ainsi vers l'Europe (Ac 16, 6-7). Cette ère, semble dire l'auteur, ne reviendra plus. Il n'y a plus à attendre de manifestations extraordinaires de l'Esprit. La seconde période, celle de Paul, fait le pont entre les origines et l'actualité de l'Église de Luc. Et, du point de vue statistique, l'Esprit n'intervient quasiment pas dans la mission de Paul (cf. Ac 9, 17; 13, 9). Bref, si les Actes des Apôtres inspirent la mission chrétienne, ils disent aussi que certaines expériences ont fait leur temps, que chaque siècle doit redécouvrir à nouveaux frais l'agir de Dieu.

L'irénisme notoire de Luc sert une *lectio divina* des voies providentielles qui ont accompli, à la fin du 1er siècle, le projet du Ressuscité. Mais le mandat énoncé en Ac 1, 8 sort de la plume du seul Luc, de la découverte, aussi critique qu'émerveillée, d'un plan du Christ qui fit passer l'Évangile de Jérusalem à la Judée, à la Samarie et jusqu'à Rome. Il revient aux Églises ultérieures de mettre sous les mots d'Ac 1, 8 d'autres topographies politiques et socioreligieuses de l'annonce du Christ. Il leur revient aussi de découvrir, sous le vernis consensuel des Actes, une diversité qui ne se laisse réduire à aucune stratégie préméditée. Selon Luc, la première évangélisation releva de groupes chrétiens aux horizons différents, voire opposés, les lieux du témoignage furent fort divers et l'annonce de Jésus Christ s'enrichit de cette diversité. Telles sont les trois approches synthétiques ici proposées.

---

[3] Voir dans les Actes un théologien et un auteur spirituel convient sans doute mieux que l'expression «écrivain édifiant» (*Erbauungsschriftsteller*, E. HAENCHEN, *Die Apg*, p. 93).
[4] Ainsi Ac 3, 8; 4, 31; 6, 3.5. 10; 7, 55; 11, 24.
[5] Cf. Ac 2, 4; 8, 29.39; 10, 19.44-46; 11, 15; 13, 2; 19, 6.

I. Diversité des témoins

A. *Les milieux chrétiens*

Si Luc plaide pour une Église unie, dans ses sommaires (Ac 2, 42-47; 4, 32-35; 5, 12-16), il ne masque pas les tensions. Contre l'idée reçue d'une Église dont l'unité originelle se serait ensuite effritée, on constate plutôt une pluralité de courants qui contribuèrent à la richesse de l'annonce de l'Évangile[6]. Pierre apparaît comme le porte-parole du groupe des Douze, d'un christianisme galiléen fidèle aux pratiques missionnaires de Jésus (cf. Mc 6, 6b-12) et proche des familles païennes sympathisantes du judaïsme, les «craignant-Dieu» (cf. Ac 10, 1-11, 18; comparer Lc 10, 5-8). Pierre ne dirigea sans doute jamais l'Église de Jérusalem[7]. Ce rôle échut à Jacques, le frère du Seigneur. Ce dernier représente un christianisme qui, proche du pharisaïsme, voit en Jésus le Restaurateur d'un Israël chrétien désormais ouvert aux païens, pourvu que ces derniers, quoique non circoncis, observent quelques règles rituelles manifestant leur lien juridique avec le Peuple élu (cf. Ac 15, 19-21)[8].

Face à Jacques, résolument tourné vers une restauration d'Israël, face à un Pierre prêt à concilier différents courants (cf. Ga 2, 11-13), il faut situer le groupe dont Étienne est le chef de file (Ac 6, 1-15). Le réquisitoire du martyr devant le sanhédrin (Ac 7, 1-53), le discours le plus long des Actes, constitue la

---

[6] Pour un panorama commode des premières communautés chrétiennes, voir C. PERROT, *Jésus, Christ et Seigneur des premiers chrétiens*, Paris, 1997, p. 65-124. Plus complexe, F. VOUGA, *Les premiers pas du christianisme*, Genève, 1997.

[7] La délivrance pascale de Pierre en Ac 12, 1-17 salue la fin de l'activité de l'Apôtre à Jérusalem et confirme l'autorité de Jacques (Ac 12, 17b). Cf. J. DUPONT, «Pierre délivré de prison (Ac 12, 1-11)», *Nouvelles études sur les Actes des Apôtres*, Paris, 1984 (LeDiv 118), p. 329-342.

[8] Voir C. PERROT, «Les décisions de l'Assemblée de Jérusalem», *RSR* 69 (198 1), p. 195-208. Ce sont les pharisiens qui protestèrent contre l'exécution de Jacques sur l'ordre du grand prêtre Anan en 62 (cf Josèphe, Ant. 20, 200). En Mc 3, 31-35, certains lisent une protestation contre les «frères de Jésus» qui ne se sont guère manifestés durant le ministère du Seigneur. Au reste, l'épisode matthéen de la Cananéenne peut être un dialogue critique avec le courant de Jacques, cf. J.-F. BAUDOZ, *Les Miettes de la Table*, Paris, 1995, p. 400.

charte et le manifeste du cercle des chrétiens hellénistes des judéochrétiens de langue et de culture grecques[9]. Selon eux, Dieu n'a pas voulu le Temple de Salomon (cf. Ac 7, 47-50), d'autant que la première expérience cultuelle d'Israël fut l'idolâtrie (cf. Ac 7, 40-43). D'autre part, l'appel divin adressé à Abraham. fit de lui un étranger (Ac 7, 2-7), si bien que la promesse d'un lieu saint n'a pas encore trouvé son accomplissement. Que le Temple de Jérusalem, ne soit pas le centre du monde et que la Judée n'ait rien d'une Terre Sainte, voilà les idées subversives qui obligèrent les Hellénistes á fuir Jérusalem, tandis que le christianisme des Douze ne trempait pas dans ce conflit (cf. Ac 8, 1). Voilà aussi pourquoi ce furent les Hellénistes qui conduisirent à la foi chrétienne les Samaritains (cf. Ac 8) hostiles au Temple de Jérusalem et à la Judée revendiquant le statut de Terre Sainte. L'Église des Douze ne fit que moissonner ce que les Hellénistes avaient semé (cf. Jn 4, 35-38)[10]. Forts de leur liberté par rapport aux institutions juives, ce sont les Hellénistes qui fondèrent à Antioche une Église composée de païens (cf. Ac 11, 19-21). Barnabé, autre helléniste, un Chypriote (cf. Ac 4, 36), comprit que Saul donnerait là toute la mesure (cf. Ac 11, 35-36) de ce qu'il n'avait pas pu réaliser à Jérusalem (cf. Ac 9, 26-30).

On ne s'étendra pas davantage sur la diversité des courants chrétiens primitifs qui évangélisèrent le monde romain. Retenons que les premières Églises se distinguaient les unes des autres en fonction de leur identité socioculturelle et que, préci-

---

[9] Sur le cercle chrétien helléniste, cf. l'article classique de M. HENGEL, «Between Jesus and Paul: The "Hellenists" the "Seven" and Stephen (Ac 6, 1-15; 7, 54-8, 3)», dans *Between Jesus and Paul*, Londres, 1983, p. 1-29. Du point de vue missiologique, C. TASSIN, «Un tournant missionnaire: le témoignage d'Étienne», *Spiritus* 108 (1987), p. 153-168. On regrettera les perspectives minimalistes de S. LEGASSE, *Stéphanos. Histoire et Discours d'Étienne dans les Actes des Apôtres*, Paris, 1992 (LeDiv 147).

[10] Sur le rapport entre ce texte johannique et Ac 8, 14 ss., voir O. CULLMANN, «La Samarie et les origines de la mission chrétienne. Qui sont les ALLOI en Jean 4, 38?», *École Pratique des Hautes Études. Annuaire*, 1954, p. 3-12. Hérode Agrippa 1er (41-44) persécuta les mouvements déviants, dont les chrétiens (cf. Ac 12). En Samarie, il semble avoir défendu les intérêts juifs contre ceux des autochtones (cf. Josèphe, *Ant* XIX, 356). Les chrétiens hellénistes se trouvaient ainsi dans le même camp que les Samaritains.

sément, les témoins de l'Évangile qu'elles avaient écoutés étaient en consonance avec cette identité.

B. *Paul*

Les Douze restent les témoins privilégiés du Christ. Eux seuls ont le titre d'apôtres, puisque, pour Luc, l'apostolat suppose un compagnonnage avec Jésus durant sa mission terrestre (cf. Ac 1, 21-22; 10, 39). Dans ce cadre, Paul n'est pas un apôtre[11]. En revanche, les témoins se multiplient pour autant qu'ils ont connu les apôtres. Si Paul a peu fréquenté les Douze, il a œuvré avec Barnabé qui sert de relais avec ces derniers et, aux yeux de Luc, qui lui consacre la seconde partie des Actes, il est le témoin par excellence[12].

Ainsi, du point de vue théologique, Luc souligne la continuité historique de l'annonce du Christ, et son portrait de Paul s'en ressent. Ce dernier est un Juif fidèle, obéissant à la ligne de Jacques (cf. Ac 21, 17-26)[13]. Mais l'auteur des Actes avoue implicitement que les Judéochrétiens des années 80 gardent rancune à un missionnaire qui, en son zèle pour l'accès des païens à la foi en Jésus Christ, semblait avoir ruiné les valeurs de la Torah mosaïque. Aussi la version lucanienne de l'assemblée de Jérusalem (Ac 15) déborde-t-elle d'ironie. Paul (est-ce possible?) ne tient dans ce colloque que des propos doxologiques (cf. Ac 15, 4.12). C'est Pierre que Luc propulse comme porte-parole des thèses pauliniennes (cf. 15, 9-11). Bref, les lecteurs, judéochrétiens des Actes ne pouvaient admettre les orientations de Paul que si celles-ci avaient reçu l'aval de Pierre – et de Jacques (cf. Ac 15, 13 ss.)[14].

---

[11] Sur ce problème, voir la synthèse de G. SCHNEIDER, *Die Apg*, «Die zwölf Apostel als "Zeugen"» (Exkurs 2), p. 221-232. Paul, quant à lui, revendique le titre d'apôtre (cf. 1 Co 9, 1-2).

[12] Sur le vocabulaire du témoignage appliqué à Paul: Ac 22, 15.20 (*martus*); 22, 18 (*marturia*); 14, 3; 23, 12; 26, 22 (*martureô/marturomai*); 18, 5; 20, 21.24; 23, 11; 28, 23 (*diamarturomai*).

[13] Voir aussi Ac 22, 2; 23, 1-10. Cf. J. JERVELL, «Paulus in der Apostelgeschichte und die Geschichte des Urchristentums», *NTS* 32 (1986), p. 378-392.

[14] Ce subterfuge lucanien a fait l'objet d'un article de F. REFOULE, «Le Discours de Pierre à l'assemblée de Jérusalem», *RB* 100 (1993), pp. 239-251.

Les Actes cultivent un autre moyen de valoriser le témoignage de Paul, selon le procédé des annales soulignant que les héros de la mission d'hier étaient en avance sur leur temps. Certes, Paul s'efforce d'être «tout à tous», Juifs ou Grecs (cf. 1 Co 9, 19-23), mais jamais il ne revendique une citoyenneté romaine qui conforterait la dimension universelle de son apostolat. Au contraire, les Actes jouent sur ce statut civique, fictif ou réel[15] pour montrer que Paul, contesté par certains, est un homme d'aujourd'hui:

«Luc a dépeint Paul comme un homme au statut social élevé et de grande moralité. En d'autres termes, le Paul de Luc possède une assise sociale considérable et incarne ce qui pouvait être reconnu par les premiers lecteurs ou auditeurs des Actes comme les vertus cardinales classiques»[16].

Luc voit en Paul le témoin adapté à son temps et capable, par sa personnalité, d'attirer au Christ non seulement les humbles, mais aussi les élites. Il change nettement de pinceau entre le portrait des témoins de naguère, Pierre, Étienne ou Jacques, et celui du héros appelé à comparaître devant César. À partir du milieu de ce siècle, l'exégèse a largement exploré les grands axes théologiques des Actes[17]. Aujourd'hui, la recherche se polarise davantage sur les rapports entre la rédaction lucanienne et son environnement gréco-romain, sur le projet de l'auteur d'inscrire l'Évangile dans la diversité culturelle de son temps. Cette orientation se constate aussi dans l'évocation des lieux de l'annonce de Jésus Christ.

---

[15] Cf. Ac 16, 37; 22, 25-29; 23, 27; 25, 10-12.21.25; 26, 32. «Luc a mis en valeur, s'il ne l'a pas créé, le statut social élevé et la vertu supérieure de Paul. À la fin des Actes, le Paul qui a été décrit est, franchement, trop beau pour être vrai», J. C. LENTZ, *Le Portrait de Paul selon Luc dans les Actes des Apôtres*, Paris, 1998 (LeDiv 172), p. 225.

[16] J. C. LENTZ, *op. cit.*, p. 10.

[17] Voir encore, récemment, le point de vue pentecôtiste de J.M. PENNEY, *The Missionary Emphasis of Lukan Pneumatology*, Sheffield, 1997. L'auteur ignore des travaux antérieurs importants: G. HAYA-PRATS, *L'Esprit force de l'Église*, Paris, 1975 (LeDiv 81) et A. GEORGE (posthume), «L'Esprit Saint dans l'œuvre de Luc», *RB* 85 (1978), p. 500-542.

II. Les lieux de l'annonce de Jesus Christ

L'importance des voyages dans les Actes des Apôtres a toujours frappé les lecteurs. Mais l'étude plus serrée des récits de voyages dans l'Antiquité en dévoile mieux l'effet théologique. Le souci documentaire des Actes

«signale un rapport positif à la société romaine, qui se traduit par une confiance (non dénuée de critique) envers ses institutions, un savoir sur l'efficacité de son réseau de communication et sur les possibilités de mobilité qu'il offre. Luc se plaît à dresser le tableau d'un univers où voyager est possible, où paroles et hommes circulent, où malgré les risques et grâce au Dieu-providence les missionnaires parviennent à bon port»[18].

Paul se trouve ainsi investi du motif de l'universalité attaché aux philosophes thaumaturges de l'Antiquité, et autres sages nomades qui se disent citoyens du monde[19]. En schématisant son évangile comme une route vers Jérusalem, à partir de Lc 9, 51, le rédacteur fait déjà de Jésus un sage itinérant, mais sans grande attention aux étapes du voyage[20]. À l'évidence, les missions des Actes se situent dans un nouveau contexte socioculturel.

Outre ce cadre général, relevons la diversité des lieux de l'annonce du Christ, à savoir les synagogues, les tribunaux et aux maisons. Mais toute rencontre devient occasion de témoignage[21].

1. École, tribunal, hôtellerie, la synagogue est le centre local de la vie juive, partout dans l'Empire. Le jour du sabbat[22],

---

[18] D. MARGUERAT, «Voyages et voyageurs dans le Livre des Actes et la culture gréco-romaine», *RHPR* 78 (1998), p. 33-59; citation p. 51.

[19] Ainsi Appolonius de Tyane (fin du Ier siècle). Cf. PHILOSTRATE, «Vie d'Apollonios de Tyane» dans P. GRIMAL, *Romans Grecs et Latins*, Paris (La Pléiade), 1958, p. 1025-1338.

[20] Les commentaires situent d'ordinaire en Lc 19, 28 l'aboutissement de l'itinéraire. Mais Luc évite de dire que Jésus entre dans Jérusalem (cf. 19. 28.37.41). Grammaticalement, la fin du voyage est l'entrée dans le Temple en 19, 45.

[21] Je reprends ici mon article «L'Annonce de Jésus Christ dans les Actes des Apôtres», *Cahiers de l'Atelier* 467, 1996, p. 65-73.

[22] Voir C. PERROT, «La lecture de la Bible dans les synagogues du Ier siècle de notre ère», *La Maison-Dieu* 126 (1976), p. 24-41; «La lecture de la Bible dans la Diaspora hellénistique», in R. KUNTZMANN & J. SCHLOSSER (éd.), *Études sur le judaïsme hellénistique*, Paris, 1984 (LeDiv 119), p. 109-145.

on y lit la loi de Moïse (cf. Ac 15, 21), illustrée par un passage des prophètes. Puis vient l'homélie que l'on pouvait confier à un invité (cf. Lc 4, 16-21; Ac 13, 15). Les synagogues ouvraient leurs portes aux païens sympathisants, les craignant-Dieu dont le centurion Corneille est le modèle (cf. Ac 10, 2.22). Jésus avait fait de la synagogue une tribune. Ce sont surtout les Hellénistes qui continuèrent d'intervenir dans ce cadre. Étienne[23], leur *leader*, débattait dans les synagogues hellénophones de Jérusalem (cf. Ac 6, 8-10). Paul commença son apostolat dans leurs rangs, et on le trouve, deux sabbats de suite, dans la synagogue d'Antioche de Pisidie (Ac 13. 14-52).

Ces interventions ont une double visée. D'une part, à partir des lectures du sabbat, il s'agit de situer Jésus comme l'aboutissement des Écritures et de montrer qu'en lui seul se reçoit le salut espéré. D'autre part, il s'agit d'atteindre, dans leur langue, une frange de païens déjà acquis au message biblique. En prêchant dans la synagogue, les missionnaires hellénistes rejoignent le lieu central d'expression de l'expérience religieuse des gens. Cette expérience synagogale devient le terreau de la découverte du Christ et de la fondation de communautés nouvelles (cf. Ac 11, 19-21).

2. Luc ponctue l'histoire de la communauté de Jérusalem par trois comparutions devant le Sanhédrin[24]. La seconde partie du livre fait de Paul un habitué des tribunaux romains et juifs[25], et son appel à César doit lui permettre de témoigner du Christ à Rome (cf. Ac 23, 11). Les discours des accusés livrent, en fait, les tensions entre le christianisme et la société: l'aristocratie conservatrice de Jérusalem a contré l'Évangile, tandis qu'une aile du pharisaïsme (cf. Ac 5, 34-39), l'autorité romaine (18, 12-17), et même Agrippa II (26, 30-32) ont admis que l'annonce de Jésus Christ n'était pas un délit.

---

[23] Même le discours de Pierre (Ac 2, 25-31) ou de Jacques (15, 17) suppose, en réalité, des milieux où on lisait la Bible en grec.

[24] On note le *crescendo* dramatique: Pierre et Jean (Ac 4, 1-22) sont menacés; Les apôtres (5, 27-41) sont battus de verges; Étienne (6, 12-7, 60) est exécuté.

[25] Devant les politarques de Thessalonique (17, 5-8); devant le proconsul Gallion (18, 12-17); devant le Sanhédrin (22, 30-23, 11); devant les procurateurs Félix (24, 1-23) et Festus (25, 6-12); devant le roi juif Agrippa II.

L'insistance sur les tribunaux poursuit un double objectif. Étienne apparaît en Ac 6-7 comme le témoin idéal («Étienne, ton témoin [*martus*], Ac 22, 20). Sa comparution devant le Sanhédrin, l'accusation de blasphème (cf. Mc 14, 58), l'ultime prière (Ac 7, SO, cf. Lc 23, 46) et l'intercession pour les bourreaux, tout cela fait de son martyre une actualisation de la passion de Jésus[26]. Le dernier voyage de Paul vers Jérusalem s'orne d'une orientation analogue (cf. Ac 20, 23-24; 21, 11-13). Ces deux figures concrétisent une conviction omniprésente dans le NT, depuis 1 Th 2, 12-15 jusqu'à Mt 10, 24-25. Elles ne cherchent pas simplement à émouvoir. Elles rappellent plutôt que l'épreuve identifiant le chrétien aux souffrances du Seigneur reste la loi fondamentale qui authentifie le témoignage.

Mais la persécution n'est pas le lot des lecteurs de *l'Ad Theophilum*. Ils cèdent plutôt à la tiédeur, l'inconstance, l'apostasie, le manque d'ouverture et la suffisance[27]. L'auteur ne demande à ses destinataires qu'un sursaut de courage. Il constate surtout que les tribunaux ont été pour la première génération chrétienne une tribune inattendue offrant à l'annonce du Christ l'audience qu'elle méritait. Par là, second objectif, il suggère que le croyant aura souvent à s'expliquer sur la place publique. En ce sens, Luc suit d'abord la tradition lorsqu'il promet aux témoins l'assistance défensive de l'Esprit Saint devant les tribunaux (cf. Lc 12, 11-12). Mais, au vu des expériences, il ajoute une interprétation plus personnelle et plus combative: «Cela vous donnera une occasion de témoignage» (Lc 21, 13).

3. Les premiers missionnaires cultivèrent aussi les relations domestiques, la maison, comme lieu privilégié de l'annonce de l'Évangile. Une fois décodé l'appareil théophanique du récit, l'épisode de Corneille (Ac 10, 1-11, 18) tient en ceci:

---

[26] Cf. S. LEGASSE, *Stephanos*, p. 147-148.
[27] Voir les commentaires de passages propres à Luc tels que Lc 8, 15; 10, 36; 15, 32; 18, 1.9; 21, 19 comme allusions aux difficultés de cette Église. Cf. J.A. FITZMYER, *The Gospel According to Luke I-IX*, Garden City, 1981 (Anchor Bible 28), p. 235-257.

un païen judaïsant invite en sa maison un chrétien de renom pour l'entendre parler de Jésus Christ[28]. Pierre reste quelques jours chez lui, mangeant avec lui, au mépris des règles juives (cf. Ac 11, 2-3). Lydie, première baptisée à Philippes, recevra Paul en sa demeure (16, 15), comme le fera aussi le geôlier converti (16, 25-34)[29].

Ce type de mission remonte à Jésus et à ses consignes données en Galilée[30]. L'envoyé, depouillé de tout, se livre à l'accueil de familles disponibles au message du Royaume (cf. Lc 9, 1-6). En ses ambassadeurs, c'est au Christ que ces maisons ouvrent leurs portes (cf. Mt 10, 40-42). Elles reçoivent en retour la paix du Règne divin (Lc 10. 5-6), puisque Jésus a partagé aux siens ses pouvoirs sur les forces du mal (Mt 10, 1). L'ordre de «ne pas passer de maison en maison» (Mc 6, 9 et par.) suppose que la maison d'accueil sera un relais de l'annonce de l'Évangile.

L'apostolat galiléen posera deux problèmes. D'abord, que fera le missionnaire d'origine juive lorsqu'une maison païenne l'invitera? Au nom de l'Évangile, il transgressera les signes identitaires qui lui semblaient sacrés. En Ac 11, 3, Luc salue Pierre comme le premier à abattre cette barrière, et son instruction évangélique confirme la nécessité, pour le missionnaire, de manger ce qu'on lui servira (Lc 10, 7-8).

En second lieu, l'ordre de n'emporter «ni pain ni besace ni monnaie» (Mc 6, 8) avait son sens. Nourrir les envoyés de Jésus, c'était payer de soi pour accueillir le Royaume. Mais ce jeu de l'hospitalité, naturel dans la Galilée rurale, devenait un fléau pour les prolétaires des villes grecques. Paul a donc refusé

---

[28] Cf. C. TASSIN, «Conversion de Corneille et conversion de Pierre», *Spiritus* 141 (1995), p. 465-474.

[29] Même stratégie de Paul, selon Luc, à Corinthe et à Éphèse: Ac 18, 1-8; 19, 8-10.

[30] Ces instructions, assorties de modifications dues à la diversité des expériences missionnaires, ont deux sources: Mc 6, 7-11 et la Source Q. Luc, non sans les contaminer l'un par l'autre, distingue ces deux documents comme un envoi des Douze (Lc 9, 1-6) et un envoi des Soixante-Douze (Lc 10, 1-11). Mt 10, 5-42 préfère fondre les deux sources en un seul discours. Sur les problèmes posés dans la mission ultérieure par les premières expériences galiléennes, voir C. TASSIN, «Finances et Mission selon saint Paul», *Spiritus* 129 (1992), p. 452-467.

de se faire entretenir par les maisons corinthiennes (cf. 1 Co 9, 4-7), tout en sachant qu'il contrevenait à la consigne de Jésus (1 Co 9, 14). Les apôtres important en Achaïe les mœurs missionnaires galiléennes n'etaient à ses yeux que des exploiteurs (cf. 2 Co 11, 7-12; 12, 14-18. L'épisode de Marthe et Marie (Lc 10, 38-42) suggère aussi qu'à la suite de Jésus, le missionnaire s'estimera accueilli lorsqu'on s'assiéra à ses pieds pour écouter la parole du Seigneur, et non lorsqu'on lui aura préparé un festin.

4. Privées de statut officiel, les premières Églises s'infiltrent dans les réseaux de la communication socioreligieuse (la synagogue), politique (les tribunaux) et domestique (la maison). Mais toute rencontre conduit le disciple à partager sa foi. Voici l'Éthiopien priant Philippe de lui expliquer l'Écriture (Ac 8, 26-40), ou le proconsul recevant Paul en audience (Ac 13, 6-12).

Jean Baptiste lançait cette prédiction: «Toute chair verra le salut de Dieu»[31]. Luc retient dès lors les épisodes propres à montrer que l'annonce du Christ rejoint toutes les couches sociales. Évangéliste des pauvres, il se plaît aussi à souligner l'impact de l'Évangile sur les classes aisées, du centurion Corneille au proconsul de Chypre, de Lydie, la négociante de pourpre (Ac 16, 14), aux dames de qualité de Thessalonique (17, 4). L'expression *toute chair* embrasse les cultures; et les Actes de saluer l'épopée des Hellénistes qui atteignent les Grecs d'Antioche (11, 20). Les rencontres s'entachent parfois d'équivoques: Paul et Barnabé devront dissuader les Lycaoniens de voir en eux des dieux descendus de l'Olympe (cf. Ac 14, 8-12)[32].

Certes, les Églises du 1er siècle participent à la compétition des mouvements religieux de l'époque. Plus profondément, Luc voit dans l'expansion chrétienne un projet guidé par

---

[31] Lc 3, 6 = Is 40, 5. La citation fait inclusion avec la fin de l'œuvre lucanienne: «C'est aux païens qu'a été envoyé ce salut de Dieu; et eux, ils écouteront» (Ac 28, 28).
[32] Sur cet épisode, voir D. GEORGI, «Socioeconomic Reasons for the "Divine Man" as a Propagandistic Pattern», in E. SCHÜSSLER FIORENZA éd.), *Aspects of Religious Propaganda in Judaism and Early Christianity*, Notre Dame-Londres, 1976, p. 33-34.

l'Esprit Saint. Mais ce plan ne s'est concrétisé que grâce à l'obéissance des témoins à des faits et à des rencontres qu'ils étaient bien incapables de planifier. Leur soumission à l'Esprit et aux rencontres les a aussi conduits à une annonce diversifiée de l'unique Sauveur.

III. L'ANNONCE MULTIFORME DE JESUS CHRIST

Les discours de Pierre, Étienne et Paul, objet de maintes études[33], tiennent une place considérable dans les Actes. Y brille ce que l'exégèse anglophone appelle *the Lukan versatility*, qui joue, dans ces textes, sur la variété des traditions primitives de la prédication chrétienne, tandis que la rédaction révèle une fine sensibilité à l'intéraction entre l'événement et le témoignage, à l'écoute de l'autre et à la confrontation ecclésiale.

1. «Nous ne pouvons pas, quant à nous, ne pas publier ce que nous avons vu et entendu», s'écrie Pierre devant le sanhédrin (Ac 4, 20). E. Haenchen interprète ainsi le verset: «Ce que les Apôtres ont vu et entendu, ce sont les paroles et les actes de Jésus (cf. 10, 39), mais avant tout la Résurrection ici mise en question». C'est, concrètement, la guérison d'un impotent (3, 1-10) qui manifeste la puissance actuelle du Ressuscité (Ac 3, 12-16; 4, 9-10). Ainsi, l'événement commande le témoignage, et l'exorde des discours[34] a pour fonction d'établir le lien entre les deux. De même, le sermon de la Pentecôte interprète l'irruption insolite de l'Esprit qui intrigue les pèlerins (2, 12-16). L'explication de Pierre culmine en ceci: l'Esprit ne peut venir que du Messie. S'il est maintenant répandu, c'est que Dieu a couronné comme Messie et Seigneur ce Jésus contesté par Jérusalem (1, 33-36).

---

[33] L'ouvrage de référence est celui de U. WILCKENS, *Die Missionsreden der Apostelgeschichte*, Neukirchen-Vluyn, ³1974. Voir aussi J. DUPONT, «Les discours missionnaires des Actes des Apôtres», *Études sur les Actes des Apôtres*, Paris, 1967 (LeDiv 45), p. 393-419, et plusieurs articles dans *Nouvelles Études sur les Actes des Apôtres*, Paris, 1984 (LeDiv 118).

[34] Voir J. DUPONT, «Les discours de Pierre», dans *Nouvelles Études sur les Actes des Apôtres*, spécialement p. 62-65.

Le Christ s'annonce en personne dans les événements, à travers ses témoins. Quand ces derniers s'en expliquent, ils se précisent à eux-mêmes quelle puissance les fait agir. Mais sur quelle base s'expliquer?

2. Les discours missionnaires des Actes présentent sensiblement le même schéma[35]. L'histoire de Jésus (cf. Ac 2, 22) y tient peu de place, l'actualité du Christ important davantage aux témoins que le passé. On s'attarde sur la croix [a]: échec apparent, elle est pourtant conforme au «dessein arrêté et à la prescience de Dieu» (2, 23), c'est-à-dire aux Écritures (13, 27) [b]. On proclame surtout la résurrection du Crucifié comme un acte de Dieu [c], annoncé par les Écritures (2, 24-32a) [d] et dont les Apôtres sont les témoins (2, 32b) [e]. Leur témoignage tisse une continuité entre la vie terrestre de Jésus (10, 39-41) et la puissance actuelle du Ressuscité 4, 10b). Jusqu'à ce point, ce schéma oratoire s'appuie sur un credo traditionnel des premières Églises, recopié par Paul en 1 Co 15, 3b-5[36]:

Christ mourut [a] pour nos péchés selon les Écritures [b], il fut enseveli, il est ressuscité [c] le troisième jour selon les Écritures [d] et il se fit voir à Céphas, puis aux Douze [e].

Les prédicateurs nourrissent aussi leur message par le patrimoine liturgique, comme l'indique la résurgence de titres tels *que le Saint, le Juste, le Prince de la vie* (Ac 3, 14) ou ceux de *Christ* et de *Seigneur*.

Pourtant, il ne s'agit pas d'une répétition mécanique du credo, mais d'une réinterprétation de celui-ci pour le temps présent. Voilà pourquoi les discours s'achèvent par un vibrant appel au repentir (3, 26) ou à la foi (13, 38-39). En effet la puissance du Christ, expérimentée par les croyants, est destinée à toutes celles et à tous ceux qui savent lire dans l'événement un appel à vivre autrement, à se dégager de solidarités perverses (2, 38-40).

---

[35] Sur ce schéma, inspiré de M. DIBELIUS, cf. J. DUPONT, «Les discours de Pierre», p. 61-80.

[36] J. DUPONT, «Les discours de Pierre», p. 91-96, retient cette hypothèse classique et la nuance par l'apport d'autres méthodes.

3. Un discours tel que celui d'Ac 2, 14-40 suppose un auditoire composé de Juifs et de païens sympathisants, habitués aux homélies synagogales truffées de références à l'AT. Mais les témoins savent entrer dans l'expérience de l'autre et, grâce à cet autre, découvrir eux-mêmes un nouveau visage du Christ. Déjà, disais-je, Étienne tient, sur les rapports entre Jésus et les institutions juives, un discours critique plus acceptable des Samaritains que des Judéens. À Corneille, Pierre présente un Jésus «qui a passé *en faisant le bien*» (10, 38). L'expression était parlante pour un officier romain connaissant le titre de *Bienfaiteur* (Évergète) donné à certains souverains païens.

Quand ils s'adressaient à des païens étrangers à la tradition d'Israël, les prédicateurs ne commençaient point par une annonce directe de Jésus Christ. Il fallait d'abord s'entendre sur le sens du mot «Dieu» avant de révéler l'Envoyé de Dieu[37]. La mésaventure, déjà évoquée, de Barnabé et Paul en Lycaonie (Ac 14, 8-18) est significative. Certaines cités rendaient des honneurs divins à des thaumaturges comme à l'épiphanie terrestre d'un dieu. Partant de cette religiosité déviante Paul se situe comme un simple humain et entreprend de faire connaître l'unique Créateur.

Mais Luc laisse la harangue en suspens. Il en réserve la suite pour la prestation de Paul devant l'Aréopage[38]. Le missionnaire frémit à la vue des idoles d'Athènes et converse avec les philosophes du lieu (17, 16-17). Et s'il en arrive à l'annonce du Christ (17, 31), c'est comme conclusion d'un dialogue entre la quête de

---

[37] Au kérygme pascal de 1 Co 15, 3b-5, évoqué ci-dessus, s'ajoute un kérygme à l'adresse des païens. On en trouve l'écho en 1 Th 1, 9b-10, un texte étudié par P.E. LANGEVIN, «Le Seigneur Jésus dans un texte prépaulinien (1 Th 1, 9-10)», *Sciences ecclésiastiques* 18 (1965), p. 263-282. Avec raison, L. LEGRAND estime que ce kérygme charpente le discours d'Athènes en Ac 17, 22-31, «The Areopagus Speech; its theological kerygma and its missionary significance», dans J. COPPENS (éd.), *La Notion biblique de Dieu*, Gembloux, 1976 (BETL 41), p. 337-350 (p. 343).

[38] Voir J. DUPONT, «Le Discours de l'Aréopage (Ac 17, 22-3 1), lieu de rencontre entre christianisme et hellénisme», *Nouvelles Études sur les Actes*, p. 380-423, et L. LEGRAND, «Aratos est-il aussi parmi les prophètes?», *La Vie selon la Parole. Mélanges P. Grelot*, Paris, 1987, p. 241-258.

Dieu chez les Grecs et la figure juive et chrétienne du Créateur[39]. Au reste, cette page éblouissante se nourrit des deux siècles pendant lesquels les Juifs avaient déjà entretenu ce dialogue[40].

4. Luc insiste peu sur la dimension communautaire de la prédication. Écrivant une épopée, il peint des héros, aussi stimulants qu'inimitables. Cependant, son livre bâtit des convergences progressives qui supposent une concertation ecclésiale, parfois conflictuelle. En se compromettant chez Corneille, Pierre a soulevé des remous (Ac 11, 1-3). Sans se couvrir en rien de son autorité, il s'est expliqué humblement, et – d'après Luc – on l'a compris (11, 18). On n'a tiré de l'affaire aucune stratégie conquérante. Plus tard, l'assemblée de Jérusalem (15, 1-29) confronte différentes manières d'annoncer le Christ et de respecter l'identité socioculturelle des nouveaux croyants. On est parvenu à un compromis que Paul rompra bientôt[41].

Les actes des apotres Aujourd'hui

Cette synthèse sur l'annonce du Christ dans les Actes consistait à lire, au 20ᵉ siècle, à l'aide d'outils scientifiques, un texte fondateur du 1° siècle. Faibles de cette ambiguïté, les trois derniers propos n'engagent que moi.

1. L'écriture de Luc est *doxologique*. Elle glorifie Dieu pour l'achèvement d'une phase capitale de la mission. La ruine de Jéru-

---

[39] D. MARGUERAT (*NTS* 45 [1999]) relève finement le procédé lucanien d'ambivalence sémantique. Selon l'adjectif employé en Ac 17, 22, les Athéniens «sont-ils très religieux ou très superstitieux? Le mot supporte les deux nuances dans la koinè, et je crois que Luc veut laisser le lecteur choisir son appréciation» (p. 75). Il y a une «double entrée» de compréhension, une entrée juive ou une entrée judéochrétienne. C'est dans cette ambiguïté même que commence le dialogue interreligieux.

[40] On songe ici à tout un pan de la littérature «intertestamentaire» de langue grecque dialoguant avec le stoicisme. Par exemple, *Pseudo-Phocylide. Sentences*, présenté par P. DERRON, Paris, 1986 (Les Belles Lettres). Dans le patrimoine canonique, relevons Sg 13, 1-9.

[41] La restructuration des équipes en Ac 15, 36-40 recouvre des enjeux autres que de simples fictions entre personnes. Jacques (Ac 15, 13-21) défend la conception d'une Église en deux peuples, Juifs et païens, associés par quatre règles rituelles communes. Paul, lui, a opté pour une Église en laquelle il n'y a plus ni Juifs ni Grecs (Ga 3, 27-28); d'où l'incident d'Antioche en Ga 2, 11-14.

salem perturba moins les Églises que la disparition des premiers témoins[42], une frontière que Luc situe à la disparition de Paul. Par connivence culturelle, les chrétiens salueront l'an 2000, mais pour quelle raison? Seulement, selon les Actes, au prix d'une relecture de l'histoire récente, pour saisir ce que le Christ attend des siens. Et Luc évite toute prospective, sauf par allusions.

2. La tradition voit dans le Livre des Actes *l'Évangile du Saint Esprit*. Certes, l'Esprit y est le guide de la mission[43], mais en des événements qui conduisirent les témoins à des rencontres imprévues. Luc n'ignore pas le ministère des prophètes (cf. Ac 12, 27; 13, 1; 15, 32; 21, 10), mais il ne les met pas à l'avant-scène de la mission. Peut-être connaît-il déjà les abus de prophètes itinérants dénoncés par la *Didachè* (ch. 11) et qui aboutirent à l'extinction de ce ministère. Pour l'auteur des Actes, l'Esprit est conféré à tout baptisé (2, 38) et peut faire de lui le témoin dont il a besoin. Son action a toujours quelque chose d'imprévisible par quoi la mission ne se réduit jamais au mandat officiel d'un magistère. Surtout, une mission fidèle à l'Esprit se veut respectueuse de la diversité des situations, des milieux et des témoins.

3. Une *lectio divina* fructueuse des Actes s'enrichit d'une mise à distance historique et sociologique sans laquelle on reproduirait des modèles missionnaires obsolètes. Lire les Actes, c'est les réécrire, à l'écoute de la pédagogie de Luc qui se résumerait ainsi: L'annonce du Christ naît de l'expérience du croyant qui voit sa vie transformée par sa foi. Or les événements le somment d'expliquer cette transformation. Il revient alors à son credo. Mais ce credo risque de rester opaque à ceux qui l'interpellent. Il écoute donc les autres et leur partage, en leur langage, l'originalité de sa foi. Puis, pour que cette originalité ne soit pas trahison, il se réfère au discernement ecclésial.

---

[42] Saluons ici la pédagogie de R.E. BROWN, *L'Église héritée des Apôtres*, Paris, (Le Cerf) 1987. Titre originel: *The Churches The Apostles left behind*.
[43] Cf. ci-dessus note 17. Voir aussi C. Tassin, «L'Esprit, guide de la mission, dans les Actes des Apôtres», *Mission de l'Église* 119 (1998), p. 3-8.

L'evangelizzazione «nuova» di Gesù nella tradizione sinottica

RAIMONDO RIVA

1. L'EVENTO NUOVO DELL'ANNUNCIO

Gesù inizia il suo ministero «predicando il vangelo di Dio: il tempo è compiuto ed è giunto il regno di Dio», Mc 1,14. Il regno di Dio è l'annuncio delle parabole, che sono proclamazione delle caratteristiche e della storia del regno. Il regno di Dio è la realtà che si rivela nella sua azione taumaturgica; esso è la situazione nuova che esige la conversione e costituisce l'orientamento di tutta la vita; per il regno Gesù sceglie i dodici, perché condividano il suo ministero e siano essi pure gli annunciatori. L'annuncio del regno di Dio è prerogativa del suo ministero, e si qualifica per il rapporto inscindibile con la sua persona[1].

Al tempo di Gesù, la speranza di Israele assommava le molteplici esperienze che il popolo aveva fatto nella sua storia, guidata dal Signore verso il compimento del suo disegno di salvezza per tutta l'umanità[2]. Per la storia del regno di Davide e

---

[1] Cf. J. GNILKA, *Jesus von Nazaret. Botschaft und Geschichte*, Freiburg, Herder, p. 87. J.P. MEIER, *A Marginal Jew. Rethinking the historical Jesus*, Vol. 2, New York, Doubleday 1994, p. 237, cita N. Perrin: "The central aspect of the teaching of Jesus was that concerning the Kingdom of God. On this there can be no doubt and today no scholar does, in fact, doubt it. Jesus appeared as one who proclaimed the Kingdom; all else in his message and ministry serves a function in relation to that proclamation and derives its meaning from it", e commenta: "This last point, in particular needs to be tested rather than taken for granted. It is one thing to say that the kingdom of God was *a* central or at least *a* major part of Jesus' message. It is quite another to claim that it was *the* central element from which every other part of his message derives its meaning".

[2] Cf. P. GRELOT, *L'espérance juive à l'heure de Jesus*, Paris, Desclée 1979.

dei suoi discendenti, la fede nella sovranità creatrice e salvatrice di Dio ha configurato la speranza di Israele, specialmente dopo la catastrofe della distruzione e della deportazione da parte dei babilonesi, anche come attesa del regno di Dio[3]. E proprio per l'esperienza della storia, l'attesa del regno si specificava anche come attesa messianica, che, pure essa, si esprimeva in forme differenti[4]. Si attendeva la manifestazione della sovranità di Dio nella restaurazione del regno, che fosse la condizione della vita indipendente del popolo, che, così, potesse vivere, in modo compiuto, la sua realtà di popolo di Dio, cf. Is 32,1; Gr 23,5-6; 33,14-16; Ez 37, 24-25; Dn 7,13-14.18. Ai tempi dell'esilio la liberazione ha avuto inizio con l'annuncio gioioso del messaggero di Dio: «Consolate, consolate il mio popolo, dice il vostro Dio. Parlate al cuore di Gerusalemme e annunziatele che la sua schiavitù è finita», Is. 40,1-2. Allora è stupore gioioso la vista dell'arrivo del messaggero: «Come sono belli sulle montagne i piedi del messaggero – εὐαγγελιζόμενος – che annuncia la pace, che reca una buona notizia, che annuncia la salvezza, che dice a Sion; «Il tuo Dio regna!», Is 52,7 cf. Is 40,9. E il messaggero proclama l'origine e il contenuto della sua missione: «Lo spirito del Signore è su di me, perché il Signore mi unse, ad evangelizzare i poveri mi inviò – εὐαγγελίσασθαι πτωχοῖς ἀπέσταλκέν με», Is 61,1. È «la buona notizia»: τὸ εὐαγγελιον τῆς βασλείας *il vangelo del regno*[5]. Nella ignoranza dei tempi e dei modi nei quali Dio avrebbe manifestato la sua regalità, Israele ne attendeva l'annuncio. Nella situazione del popolo giudaico al tempo di Gesù, sotto il dominio di Roma, l'attesa della manifestazione del regno e della venuta del messia esprimeva in modo particolare la speranza di Israele.

---

[3] Cf. K.L. SCHIMIDT, βασιλεία, ThWbNT 1(1933) 579-590. R. SCHNACKENBURG, *Gottes Herschaft und Reich*, Freiburg i.B., Herder, 4 Aufl. 1965. E. SCHÜRER, *The History of the Jewish People in the Age of Jesus Christ* (175 B.C.-A.D. 135). Version revides and edited by G. VERMES, F. MILLAR, M. BLACK, Vol. II, Edinburg, T.&T. Clark 1979, pp. 531-533.

[4] Cf. M.J. LAGRANGE, *Le messianisme chez les juifs*, Paris, Gabalda 1909. A. GELIN, *Messianisme*, in SBD 5, coll. 1166-1212. AA.VV., *La Venue du Messie* (Sources Bibliques VI) Bruges-Paris, Desclée de Bouwer 1962. E. SCHÜRER, *o.c.* a n. 3, pp. 488-554.

[5] G. FRIEDRICH, εὐαγγελίζομαι, εὐαγγέλιον, κ.τ.λ., ThWbNT II (1935) 705-735.

Gesù, nelle molteplici configurazioni di questa speranza, inizia il suo ministero annunciando appunto l'avvento del regno di Dio: egli è il κηρύσσων τὸ εὐαγγέλιον τῆς βασλείας. È la scelta che Gesù fa[6]. Con essa egli non solo si collocava nella storia del suo popolo, ne cui svolgimento doveva essere compreso il suo ministero, ma assumeva quell'aspetto della speranza che più era vivo allora nel popolo e che, secondo l'interpretazione più diffusa, includeva l'attesa anche del messia, e convergeva, quindi, l'interesse del popolo pure sulla persona di questi. E, ancora, il suo annuncio era la proclamazione dell'evento decisivo della storia millenaria della volontà sovrana salvifica universale di Dio, realizzantesi con la elezione del suo popolo. L'annuncio che Israele attendeva, ora è proclamato; quanto la fede di Israele sperava, ora è avverato. È questo annuncio del compimento del tempo per la venuta del regno la novità dell'inizio del ministero di Gesù. La sua parola è innanzitutto quella del profeta che rivela gli eventi dell'azione salvifica di Dio.

L'annuncio è fatto ad un popolo che vive una relazione particolare con Dio, che informa tutta la sua storia. È una concezione del mondo e della storia che contrasta con la concezione della natura come totalità di realtà dell'esperienza retta dalle regole che la costituiscono, e che la scienza, col suo progresso, scopre. Anche se si crede all'esistenza di Dio, egli di fatto, una volta che ha creato il mondo, è ininfluente. La vita di Gesù come annuncio della venuta del regno di Dio nella storia è la realtà che contraddice la predetta visione del mondo; allora l'evangelizzazione per se stessa avviene come critica, per una concezione adeguata della realtà della storia, nella quale Dio è sempre presente come il creatore e salvatore.

Con l'annuncio nuovo della presenza del regno di Dio all'uomo è proposta la visione della storia che si evolve non solo per il libero gioco delle volontà umane, bensì che si svolge con mutamenti fondamentali, perché le libere azioni dell'uomo

---

[6] J.P. MEIER, *o.c.* a n. 1, p. 265 scrive: "as only one symbol (cioè; the symbol of God's rule) among many, it was not something imposed on Jesus as the necessary way in which he had to present his message. His choice of it as a key theme is just that: a conscious, personal choice, and for that reason the symbol is a privileged way of entering into Jesus' message".

sono le situazioni degli interventi di Dio per la realizzazione del suo disegno di salvezza misericordiosa.

La novità dell'annuncio sconvolge tutte le altre concezioni religiose. Con gli uomini che le possiedono necessariamente dialoga, per la sua stessa natura di annuncio di salvezza per tutti, ma, proprio per questo, non può amalgamarsi con esse, e però rilevare in esse quanto, nel disegno universale di Dio, può essere suo preannuncio o anche solo anelito ad esso.

2. La novità della manifestazione del regno

Gesù, ancora in continuità con la predicazione profetica, proclama la beatitudine dei «poveri», di coloro che sono nella situazione di «abbattimento», senza la effettiva possibilità della vita degna dell'uomo nella parità, sofferenti, facili bersagli di soprusi e di violenze, trascurati, la cui unica risorsa è la certezza dell'aiuto di Dio. Egli, salvatore, salva tutti coloro che sono bisognosi di salvezza, come Israele in Egitto, e il povero è la presenza simbolica di chi è salvato, dell'uomo povero nella sua storia di sofferenza e peccato[7]. E il bambino che vive con la spontaneità e la semplicità senza interrogativi nell'amore dei genitori, è, col povero, il destinatario del regno, Mt 18,2-4; 19,13-15.

L'annuncio di Gesù di questo intervento salvifico, vertice e compimento di tutti gli interventi di Dio nella storia di Israele, non è accompagnato dalla minaccia di un fuoco divino distruttore e purificatore per l'avvento del regno di Dio della giustizia e della pace. Il suo annuncio non è la predicazione per la conversione come quella di Giovanni, l'austero abitatore del deserto, amministratore del battesimo di penitenza in preparazione dell'evento escatologico. Gesù richiede pure la conversione, ma non per essere pronti per la venuta del Dio giudice; bensì perché la venuta del Dio misericordioso è la situazione nuova che esige il cambiamento radicale. Egli intrattiene rapporti amichevoli con i peccatori, cf. Mc 2,15-16; Lc 19,5-7; tan-

---

[7] Cf. J. Dupont, *Le Beatitudini*, Vol. I, Roma, Ed. Paoline 1971, pp. 521-945.

to da essere considerato «amico di pubblicani e peccatori», Mt 11,9; la sua presenza suscita il pentimento e l'omaggio della donna peccatrice, Lc 7,36-50; e i suoi rimproveri aspri sono indirizzati a coloro che non vogliono capire che i peccatori sono gli ammalati, per i quali è necessario che il medico misericordioso li visiti, Mc 2,17. E Gesù cercherà di far comprendere il suo comportamento con i peccatori anche con le parabole: del pastore della pecora smarrita, della donna alla ricerca della moneta perduta, del padre amorevole del figlio prodigo. Lc 15,1-32, del re che condona il debito enorme per misericordia, che è in contrasto con la scandalosa durezza di cuore, per un piccolo debito, di chi ne è stato beneficiario, Mt 18,23-35; quella ancora del signore della vigna, che, perché è «buono», è generoso nel distribuire i suoi doni, senza far torto a nessuno, Mt 20,1-16. Le parabole della misericordia sono la proclamazione della venuta del regno della salvezza perché, inseparabili dal suo comportamento, di cui sono la «parola», nel ministero di Gesù hanno il loro riferimento di senso[8].

Manifestazione della verità del suo annuncio della venuta del regno della sovranità salvifica di Dio è la sua azione verso i sofferenti. Egli è il taumaturgo che fa ricordare eventi ammirabili compiuti da profeti, ma le sue azioni suscitano una meraviglia eccezionale. Sempre interventi in situazioni particolari, esse sono le più differenti e sono una minaccia limite, da cui l'uomo di fatto è salvato solo per il suo aiuto. Gesù salva in tutte le condizioni di sofferenza nella vita dell'uomo, malattie del corpo e dello spirito, situazioni di pericolo dipendenti da condizioni esterne o da fenomeni naturali, fino all'annullamento della morte. I suoi comandi sono la $\delta\acute{\upsilon}\nu\alpha\mu\iota\varsigma$ – cf. Mc 5,30; 6,2.5; *passim* – della sovranità assoluta, sicché tutti sono stupefatti e «lodavano Do dicendo: «Non abbiamo mai visto nulla di simile!», Mc 2,12. La parola imperativa efficace di Gesù è per-

---

[8] Cf. J. GNILKA, *o.c.* a n. 1, p. 99; "Die Zusage der neuen Ordnung empfängt ihre Gültigkeit dadurch, daß es Jesus ist, der sie zusagt. Trennt man das Wort von seiner Person, löst man das Gleichnis von seinem Wirken ab, indem man es zu einer 'absoluten' Größe verselbständigt, macht man es zu einer nichtssagenden Metapher".

cepita come l'intervento del Dio misericordioso per il popolo. E il ministero benefico di Gesù è talmente sovrano nuovo e personale che si incomincia a porre la domanda: «Chi è dunque costui?», Mc 4,41.

Il regno presente annunciato da Gesù, manifestato nella sua vita, mette in rapporto con una esperienza di Dio impensata e impensabile prima di lui. La promulgazione del vangelo di Gesù è la comprensione sempre più intima della novità della sua stessa vita, che diventa fascino e consuetudine d'ascolto, che fa suoi discepoli.

3. Il regno di Dio nella storia quotidiana

«Se io scaccio i demoni in virtù dello spirito di Dio, è dunque giunto a voi il regno di Dio», Mt 12,28. «Allora incominciò ad incolpare le città, nelle quali fu compiuta la maggior parte delle sue δυνάμεις, perché non si convertirono», Mt 11,20. Egli annuncia la venuta del regno di Dio e le sue azioni sono manifestazione dello spirito potente di Dio nella salvezza del suo popolo. Ma i «segni attesi», che rendano evidente la presenza del regno? "I farisei gli domandarono: «Quando viene il regno di Dio?». Egli rispose: «Il regno di Dio non viene in modo che si possa osservare. Nessuno potrà dire: «Eccolo quì o Eccolo là». Ecco, infatti, il regno di Dio è tra voi»", Lc 17,20-21. Gesù allora racconta le parabole: la parola «del mistero del regno», cf. Mc 4,11[9]. Una difficoltà a riconoscere nel ministero di Gesù la venuta del regno è appunto l'incertezza, anzi persino il rifiuto, tra quelli che conoscono il suo ministero: il regno di Dio è l'intervento atteso per la promessa al popolo, e quindi il suo avvento deve essere tale che tutto il popolo e soprattutto i capi lo avvertano con chiarezza e vivano la nuova era che Dio instaura. Ma

---

[9] W.S. Kissinger, *The Parables of Jesus*. A History of Interpretation and Bibliography (ATLA Bibliography Series, No. 4), Metuchen N.J. & London, The Scarecrow Press and The American Theological Library Association 1979. Per la valenza specifica delle parabole e il loro rapporto col regno, cf. V. Fusco, *Oltre la parabola*. Introduzione alle parabole di Gesù, Roma, Borla 1983.

non è questa la situazione che si sta determinando con la presenza di Gesù. Ed egli, allora, narra: avviene per il regno quello che avviene per la seminagione: il seminatore semina e il seme cade in terreni diversi, per cui ci saranno perdite e rese diverse; ma questa è appunto la storia normale di ogni seminagione; l'infruttuosità o la resa scarsa non dipendono dalla assenza del seme o dalla sua incapacità a dare frutto, bensì dalle condizioni del terreno, il seminatore lo sa bene, ma non per questo si astiene dal suo lavoro, perché sa pure che il frutto sarà abbondante, cf. Mc 4,3-9. Dunque non è prova della inconsistenza del seme del regno seminato da Gesù se esso non fruttifica in tutti; piuttosto questa storia del seme del regno diventa un richiamo perché ciascuno sia il terreno adatto che faccia fruttificare il seme, cf. Mc 4,13-20. E non bisogna aspettarsi di vedere germogliare il seme: avviene per il regno di Dio come quando «un uomo abbia gettato il seme in terra, e poi dorme e veglia, di notte e di giorno, mentre il seme germina e si sviluppa, senza che egli sappia come», Mc 4,26-27. Il seme può anche essere piccolo come il granello di senapa, ma «cresce e diventa più grande di tutti gli erbaggi», Mc 4,32. Ancora avviene per il campo del regno di Dio che accanto al buon seme cresca anche la zizzania, seminata dal nemico, Mt 13,24-28; o accade per il regno quanto avviene nella pesca, quando la rete raccoglie ogni genere di pesci, buoni e cattivi, Mt 13,47. Solo quando il disegno di misericordia del Padre avrà raggiunto la sua compiutezza ci sarà la fine, con la separazione tra i buoni e i cattivi, e perciò con il pieno godimento dei beni del regno per i primi e con la esclusione dei secondi, Mt 13,30.37-43.48-49. Il regno di Dio è realtà storica, ma non l'evento storico che sia, nello stesso tempo, la fine di questa nostra storia; la storia del regno di Dio, del regno «dei cieli», è storia che assume le dimensioni della nostra storia, e che, perciò, dopo la instaurazione di esso con la presenza di Gesù, avrà il compimento della sua venuta nel futuro, che il Padre conosce, cf. Mc 13,32 e per la quale il discepolo di Gesù prega il Padre: «Venga il tuo regno», Mt 6,10: Lc 11,2: allora sarà il termine della storia con la compiuta realizzazione della signoria di Dio su tutti. La storia, per la presenza del regno, è perciò «diversa», «nuova» nel suo svolgimento delle interazioni libere degli uomini, nelle quali Dio è presente nel modo definitivo da lui stabilito per la realizzazione della sua sovranità di misericordia nella storia. È, appunto, il mistero del regno, che è donato; come è donata la parabola, che è la «parola» che partecipa della trascendenza del mistero che «dice», e che, per la sua valenza argomentativa per dire qualcosa d'altro, è anche pedagogia di apertura al mistero e alla sua accettazione. Il regno non è la realtà che succede alla nostra storia, secondo attese escatologiche di ambienti palestinesi; e neppure è la attesa restaurazione, quand'anche in forme diverse e con caratteristiche ideali, di un regno terreno di piena libertà per Israele, che viva nella perfetta fedeltà al suo Dio, nella giustizia e nel godimento di tutti i beni espressi nel desiderio della «pace»[10].

L'evangelizzazione del regno di Dio non proclama una realtà trascendente perché ultrastorica. Il regno è trascendente perché è presenza della sovranità salvifica di Dio; non ha la sua compiutezza nei singoli momenti della storia, perché si estende a tutta la storia; e tuttavia è già la realtà *escatologica*, la realtà del fine e della fine, perché in Gesù vi è la pienezza del dono di salvezza del Padre. E Gesù è quell'uomo di Nazaret, che ha rivelato i benefici di amore e di misericordia della sovranità del Padre presenti nella storia e mediante la sua opera. L'evangelizzazione è pure scoperta dei beni del regno presenti in questa nostra storia, fiducia certa della continua premura del padre, speranza sicura del Bene appagante: di Lui.

4. LA NOVITÀ DELL'INSEGNAMENTO

Nuovo e di tanta autorevolezza incomparabile da suscitare uguale stupore è anche l'insegnamento di Gesù: «Che è questo? διδαχὴ καινὴ κατ' ἐξουσίαν», Mc 1,27. Egli insegna come un *rab*, ma non come i *rabbin* che il popolo ben conosce. Non è stato discepolo di nessun *rab*, dal quale abbia appreso quell'insegnamento tradizionale che è la garanzia stessa della sua validità:

---

[10] Cf. R. SCHNACKENBURG, *o.c.* a n. 3, Cf. Anche B. KLAPPERT, *Regno/βασιλεία in Dizionario dei Concetti biblici del Nuovo Testamento*, a cura di L. COENEN, E. BEYREUTHER, H. BIETENHARD, Bologna, Ed. Dehoniane 1976, pp. 1528-1538. J. SCHLOSSER, *Le règne de Dieu dans les dits de Jésus*, I-II, Paris, Gabalda 1980.

«È sufficiente per il discepolo diventare come il suo maestro», Mt 10,25. Oltre le parabole e l'insegnamento che si riferiscono ai suoi comportamenti di bontà misericordiosa, Gesù esprime con chiarezza le sue convinzioni circa le tradizioni che regolano la vita del pio giudeo, rappresentato soprattutto dal fariseo. La tradizione, con i suoi minuziosi precetti, era considerata come la «siepe della Legge», *Abot* 3,13: difesa e custodia per la sua osservanza, e come essa prescrittiva[11]. Quando queste prescrizioni diventano una casuistica, che, con l'intento di rendere praticabile la Legge nelle diverse e mutevoli circostanze, ne contraddicono l'intento originario, Gesù non teme di condannare queste interpretazioni e di opporsi in modo deciso ai maestri e ai praticanti. La attenzione al precetto in se stesso, sia pur nell'atteggiamento religioso della fedeltà alla Legge di Dio, induceva il pericolo di una osservanza che si riducesse alla esecuzione esteriore, trascurando le disposizioni interiori che dovevano esserne la sorgente: «Non c'è nulla di esterno all'uomo che, entrando in lui, possa contaminarlo. Piuttosto sono le cose che escono dall'uomo quelle che contaminano l'uomo», Mc 7,15.21.23. Il fedele osservante dei numerosi precetti si ritiene giusto e pretende di farsi così valere davanti a Dio: «O Dio ti ringrazio perché non sono come gli altri uomini, rapaci, ingiusti, adulteri, e neppure come questo pubblicano. Io digiuno due volte alla settimana e offro la decima parte di quello che possiedo», Lc 18,11-12. L'autocompiacimento si accompagna al disprezzo e alla condanna di chi è ritenuto ignorante e, quindi, inosservante: «Ma questa folla che non conosce la legge è maledetta», Gv 7,49. La stima di sé genera la cura per il riconoscimento della propria pietà e per l'ossequio al proprio ruolo: «Fanno tutto per essere visti dagli uomini... amano i primi posti nei conviti e le prime file nelle sinagoghe; amano essere salutati nelle piazze ed essere chiamati dalla gente 'Rabbì'», Mt 23,5-6. La preoccupazione della fedeltà legalistica alla tradizione finisce anche col contraddire la stessa funzione della tradizione e porta alla violazione della legge, e

---

[11] Cf. E. SCHÜRER, *o.c.* a n. 3, vol. II, pp. 337-355: "Halakhah and Haggadah". J. NEUSNER, *The Mishnah: An Introduction*, J. Aronson Inc., Northvale, New Jersey, London 1989, pp. 200-229: "The Mishnah and the Torah".

provoca la condanna di Gesù: «Così annullate la parola di Dio per la tradizione che voi stessi vi siete tramandata», Mc 7,13. Ed egli prende posizione anche a riguardo della pratica del sabato, quando l'osservanza della precettistica diventava impedimento per l'aiuto al sofferente, cf. Mc 3,4 e per la comprensione delle necessità degli altri, cf. M 2,24-26, e afferma il valore proprio del riposo sabbatico proclamando che «il Sabato è fatto per l'uomo e non l'uomo per il sabato», Mc 2,27. La stessa pratica del culto nel tempio con la moltiplicazione di offerte e sacrifici è riprovata da Gesù, ingenerando facilmente il sentimento di una sicurezza della protezione divina per il gesto rituale compiuto, senza l'impegno di dedizione alla volontà di Dio; il tempio diventa allora un luogo di riparo simile alla spelonca, in cui il rapinatore pensa di trovare riparo sicuro, cf. Mc 11,15-17. Gesù condanna una concezione della legge e della osservanza che finisce con l'essere oppressione dell'uomo: «Legano infatti pesi opprimenti, difficili a portarsi e li impongono sulle spalle degli uomini; mentre essi non li vogliono nemmeno smuovere con un dito» Mt 23,4. Nella discrepanza tra l'esigenza della fedeltà esigita dagli altri e la rilassatezza personale si manifesta, oltre la «ipocrisia», l'autoritarismo del potere religioso-magisteriale.

Al contrario Gesù maestro afferma: «Venite a me, voi tutti che siete affaticati sotto il carico, ed io vi darò sollievo. Prendete su di voi il mio giogo, e prendete ammaestramento da me, che sono mite ed umile di cuore, e troverete sollievo per le vostre anime. Infatti il mio giogo è soave e il mio peso leggero», Mt 11,28-30. A chi, rivolgendosi a lui come «maestro buono», gli chiede che cosa fare per avere la vita eterna, Gesù risponde innanzitutto che «buono» è solo Dio, e di questo Dio buono egli enumera i comandamenti che riguardano i rapporti con il prossimo, Mc 10,17-19. Quando poi un dottore della legge lo interroga: «qual'è il primo di tutti i comandamenti?», Gesù risponde citando dapprima il testo di Dt 6,4-5: «Ascolta Israele. Il Signore nostro Dio è il Signore l'unico...», poi aggiunge: «Il secondo è questo: «Amerai il prossimo tuo come te stesso». Non c'è altro comandamento maggiore di questi». Al commento dello scriba che amare Dio e amare il prossimo come se stessi «vale più di tutti gli olocausti e i sacrifici», Gesù conclude: «Non sei lontano dal regno di Dio», Cf. Mc 12,28-34. Per Gesù l'amore di Dio consiste nel riconoscere la sua sovranità esclusiva e osservare i suoi comandamenti, che sono tutti a beneficio dell'uomo. Egli non dichiara decaduta la legge, anzi ne esige l'osservanza nella situazione stessa di vigenza delle tradizioni come vogliono i farisei, ma con una pratica ben diversa da quella dei farisei, Cf. Mt 23,23. Come egli intendesse l'amore del prossimo, appare in tutto il suo ministero di maestro, che con autorità interpreta la legge, e nella sua azione di taumaturgo benefico. La sua dedizione al prossimo, nella negazione di ogni domanda su chi sia «il mio prossimo», che già suppone una distinzione tra chi amare e non amare, ha la illustrazione nella parabola del buon samaritano, Lc 10,25-37. E il superamento di ogni distinzione ed esclusione nell'amore del prossimo ha la sua affermazione suprema nella esigenza di rispondere col bene a chi ci fa violenza, dell'amore del nemico, in un amore di totale comprensività, come quello di Dio, del Padre, di cui tutti siamo figli, e in una iniziativa di illimitata generosità di dono, che imiti quella del Padre, per fare agli altri quel bene, che ciascuno vorrebbe fosse fatto proprio a sé, cf. Lc 6,27-39; Mt 5,21-48; 7,1-12[12]. «Chiunque all'epoca ascoltava con attenzione la predicazione di Gesù sull'amore, poteva facilmente esserne conquiso, quand'anche Gesù non facesse che esprimere il pensiero di molti. Tuttavia la purezza di tono, caratteristico della predicazione di Gesù, dovette fare intravedere che si trattava di qualcosa molto speciale. Senza aver assunto tutto quanto si insegnava e si pensava nel giudaismo contemporaneo, Gesù era, se non propriamente fariseo, certamente molto vicino a quei farisei usciti dalla scuola di Hillel, che amavano Dio più di quanto lo temessero. Ma Gesù andava più lontano sulla strada che quelli avevano preparato. Solo egli predicava l'amore incondizionato, segnatamente l'amore del nemico e del peccatore. E non si trattava di un amore sentimentale»[13].

---

[12] La storia di formazione e redazione di questi testi è tracciata secondo percorsi diversi; cf. J. DUPONT, *o.c.* a n. 7, pp. 67-292. H.D. BETZ, *The sermon on the Mount*, Minneapolis, Fortress press 1995, pp. 24-44.

[13] D. FLUSSER, *Jésus*, trad. Par M. MARSCH en collaboration avec H. ROCHAIS et l'Auteur, Paris, Seuil 1970, p. 81. Il dotto conoscitore delle tradizioni del suo popolo così conclude le sue considerazioni sull'amore predicato da Gesù nel clima spirituale del tempo. Come un Rabbi d'oggi giudichi l'insegnamento di Gesù, cf. J. NEUSNER, *A Rabbi talks with Jesus. An Intermillennial, Interfaith Exchange*, New York, Doubleday 1993.

Gesù richiede ancora altro: a chi lo interrogava su quanto dovesse fare per entrare nella vita eterna, dopo avere ricordato la legge, aggiunge, con uno sguardo d'amore, che gli manca ancora qualcosa: deve dare tutto ai poveri e seguire lui, Mc 10,21. Seguire lui nella sua missione di annunciatore del «vangelo». Come egli aveva richiesto ai dodici discepoli, che hanno lasciato ogni cosa e l'hanno seguito, cf. Mc 10,28. E la richiesta di seguire lui, Gesù la rivolge a chiunque voglia essere suo discepolo, cf. Mc 8,34. Con le ripetute affermazioni solenni: ἀμὴν λέγω ὑμῖν, la sua è la parola della Parola divina e della azione di Dio nella storia; la sua vita è la fedeltà esemplare di compimento della volontà del Padre. Nel Dt 30,15-16 si legge: «Vedi, oggi ti ho posto davanti la vita e la felicità, la morte e la sventura; perciò ti ordino oggi di amare il Signore tuo Dio, di camminare per le sue vie e di osservare i suoi precetti, i suoi ordini e i suoi decreti; allora tu vivrai». Solo nel compimento della volontà di Dio, espressa nei suoi comandamenti, soprattutto nell'adesione d'amore a Lui, che è il Signore della vita, si ha la vita. Gesù dice: «Chi vuol salvare la sua vita, la perderà; ma chi perderà la propria vita, la salverà», Mc 8,35[14]. Egli esprime la condizione della salvezza nella formulazione paradossale, nella quale proprio chi ricerca la vita, la perde, mentre chi la perde, la salva: nel paradosso è affermata la *radicalità* della condizione ineludibile della salvezza nell'abbandono incondizionato al Padre, nel cui amore si estingue ogni vana preoccupazione per la propria sussistenza, ricercando invece solo il suo regno e il compimento della sua volontà, seguendo il suo insegnamento e conformandosi alla sua vita, cf. Mt 6,24-34.

Le richieste di Gesù non sono un codice di norme morali; sono la formulazione delle esigenze della novità di vita nel regno presente. L'evangelizzazione propone queste esigenze di vita come annuncio della novità del regno, non per formare l'uomo onesto, compiaciuto della sua rettitudine. Per questo le

---

[14] Per la composizione dei detti in Mc 8,34-34 e particolarmente per l'espressione: ἕνεκεν ἐμοῦ καὶ τοῦ εὐαγγελίου, cf. R. PESCH, *Il vangelo di Marco*, II, Brescia, Paideia 1982, pp. 100-114. Anche Mt 25,31-46, nella scena del giudizio finale, fa dipendere la salvezza escatologica, con il godimento della gioia e della gloria del regno, dal rapporto personale con lui; per la formazione di questo testo, cf. J. GNILKA, *Il Vangelo di Matteo*, II, Brescia, Paideia 1991, pp. 537-541.

richieste di Gesù appaiono «impossibili». Ma esse sono espressione del vangelo, quindi della novità di vita per il dono di Dio, al quale tutto è possibile. Il pericolo per l'evangelizzatore è di trasformare le richieste di vita nuova in norme che valgano per se stesse, perché sono considerate garanti della rettitudine. Una tale evangelizzazione diverrebbe il peso gravoso della legge.

5. LA NOVITÀ GESÙ

Il suo annuncio è la novità della venuta del regno, attesa da Israele; la sua è διδαχή καινή κατ' ἐξουσίαν, Mc 1,27; egli conosce il «mistero» del regno, che proclama e di cui rivela le condizioni di realizzazione con le parabole. Queste, la parola del regno di Dio, hanno tutta la loro valenza solo nelle circostanze della loro enunciazione, cioè nel ministero di Gesù e in relazione con la sua persona; egli rivela se stesso con le parabole del regno di Dio; esse sono la parola che parla di lui stesso, sicché egli stesso è «la parabola del regno di Dio»[15]. La sua attività è presenza della misericordia del Padre per i «poveri» sofferenti e peccatori. Egli si denomina «Figlio dell'uomo»: è l'uomo di Nazaret, di cui si conosce la famiglia, Mc 6,3; ma, per quello che fa e che dice, la denominazione evoca la figura escatologica di Dn 7,13-14[16]. Egli ha la pretesa di conoscere il segreto esclusivo di Dio riguardante il perdono dei peccati, cf. Mc 2,5-12. Ancora egli si rivolge al Signore del cielo e della terra chiamandolo «Papà», Mt 11,25-26[17]; Mc 14,36; e così insegna a pregare ai suoi discepoli, Lc 11,2. Del Padre egli conosce le preferenze per gli umili. In tutta la sua azione si esprime una

---

[15] Cf. E. SCHWEIWER, *Jesus, das Gleichnis Gottes. Was wissen wir wirklich vom Leben Jesu?* (Kleine Vandenhoeck-Reihe; 1572). Göttingen, Vandenhoeck und Ruprecht, 2, Aufl. 1996, pp. 26-40.

[16] Cf. F. HAHN, *Christologische Hoheitstiel*. Ihre Geschichte im frühen Christentum, Göttingen, Vandenhoeck & Ruprecht, 1. Aufl. 1963; 5. Erweiterte Aufl. 1995, pp. 1-53. G. SCHNEIDE, *Die Frage nach Jesus. Christus-Aussagen des Neuen Testaments*, Essen, Ludgerus Verlag Hubert Wingen 1971. R. PENNA, *I ritratti originali di Gesù il Cristo. Inizi e sviluppi della cristologia neotestamentaria*. I. Gli inizi, Cinisello Balsamo, Edizioni S. Paolo 2. ed. 1997, pp. 33-195.

[17] Cf. J. GNILKA, *Il Vangelo di Matteo*, cit. a n. 14, pp. 628-635; 640-642.

tale sicurezza e sovranità, da far pensare ad una particolare relazione con Dio e all'esercizio del potere divino[18]. Mentre i suoi discepoli si interrogano, Mc 4,41, sono stupefatti e non riescono a capire, Mc 6,50-51, i «pii» farisei, con sospetto e diffidenza, gli chiedono un segno «dal cielo», ed egli non accetterà la sfida, Mc 8,11-12[19]. La ragione è che essi sono in uno stato d'animo tale per cui, mentre sanno riconoscere il «tempo presente», Mt 16,1-3[20], non sanno riconoscere che la sua presenza segna il tempo della venuta della sovranità divina che esige la decisione. I suoi discepoli incominciano a riconoscerlo diverso da tutti i protagonisti della storia di Israele, fino a ritenerlo il personaggio «cristo» atteso, Mc 8,27-30. Anche tra le gente sorgono domande e si formano opinioni al riguardo, cf. Gv 7,26-27.31.41-43; 10,24. Tuttavia egli evita una risposta diretta alla domanda della gente, e, pure avallando il riconoscimento dei discepoli, proibisce loro di parlarne; anzi egli qualifica la sua missione, quella del Figlio dell'uomo, come servizio, richiamando la figura del «servo di IHWH» dei carmi di Isaia, e preannuncia per sé sofferenza, riprovazione, uccisione da parte dei capi, e poi risurrezione, Mc 8,31; 9,31; 10,45[21]. Avverte che il suo ministero crea troppi guai per i capi politici e religiosi, che hanno ormai deciso di troncare quell'avventura, anche con la uccisione. Gesù allora prende alcune precauzioni ma non vuole sottrarsi ai suoi doveri di buon giudeo, quindi decide, nonostante il pericolo, di andare a Gerusalemme. Proprio allora, quando sa che non vi è più possibilità di successo, provoca una dimostrazione festosa di «regalità» da parte della gente, Mc 11,1-10, mentre prima si era sottratto, Gv 6,15. Nel

---

[18] Cf. I volumi cit. a n. 16, ad anche J. GNILK, *Jesus von Nazaret*, cit. a n. 1, pp. 264-266.

[19] Per la storia della formazione e trasmissione del detto e del rapporto con Mt 12,39 e Lc 11,29, cf. R. PESCH, *Il vangelo di Marco*, cit. a n. 14, Vol. I, 1980, pp. 634-635.

[20] Cf. J. GNILKA, *Il Vangelo di Matteo*, cit. a n. 14, pp. 64-68. A. POLAG, *Fragmenta Q. Textheft zur Logienquelle*, Neukirchen-Vluyn, Neukirchener Verlag 1979, p. 66, n. 49, A. POLAG, *Die Christologie der Logienquelle* (WMANT, 45), Neukirchen-Vluyn, Neukinrchener Verlag 1977, pp. 87-88.

[21] Cf. P. BENOIT, *Jésus et le Serviteur de Dieu*, in J. DUPONT (ed.), *Jésus aux origines de la christologiey* (BETL 40) Gembloux, J. Duculot 1975, pp. 111-140. P. GRELOT, *Serviteur de YHWH*, in SDB fasc. 69, 1994, col. 1010.

tempo è poi lui stesso a suscitare il problema della filiazione del cristo, insinuando in modo esplicito una discendenza che non è quella dividica, Mc 12,35-37. Questi suoi comportamenti aggravano ancora più la sua situazione, ed allora egli, nella previsione della sua morte imminente, durante l'ultima cena con i suoi discepoli, dichiara il senso della sua uccisione come il dono della vittima sacrificale[22]. Durante il processo le sue risposte concernenti la sua persona saranno la ragione, dichiarata, della condanna a morte: il Cristo, il Figlio del Benedetto, cf. Mc 14,61-62, condannato a morte proprio da coloro che aspettavano il Cristo. Gesù di Nazaret, l'instauratore del regno di Dio, il Cristo, Figlio di Dio, crocifisso, che non discende dalla croce, cf. Mc 15,29-32, muore. Ma il primo giorno della nuova settimana è proclamato dal giovane misterioso il «buon annuncio», suggello del «buon annuncio», del «vangelo» di Gesù: «Gesù, il nazareno, che è stato crocifisso, è risorto. Non è più qui. Ecco il luogo dove lo avevano posto. Ma andate, dite ai suoi discepoli, specialmente a Pietro: vi precede in Galilea. Là lo vedrete, come vi ha detto», Mc 16,6-7. Il Vivente presente con i suoi discepoli.

Il vangelo del regno è questo Gesù presente. L'evangelizzazione è la continuità della vita di Gesù con i suoi discepoli; è la manifestazione di esperienza di Gesù, il Cristo Crocifisso e risorto, presente. Essa è la permanenza di questa presenza. Essa non è un sistema di verità che si presenti ben congegnato da dovere essere accettato. Evangelizzati sono «i poveri»: tutti gli uomini, sofferenti nel corpo e nello spirito, anelanti, in modi diversi e con gradi di coscienza diversi, ad un mutamento che appaia salvezza; ad essi viene reso presente Gesù, il Crocifisso, Figlio di Dio, salvatore, nel dono supremo di se stesso, per amore.

---

[22] X. LÉON-DUFOUR, *Jésus devant sa mort à la lumière des textes de l'institution eucharistique et des discours d'adieu*, in J. DUPONT (ed.) *Jésus aux origines*, cit. a n. 21, pp. 141-186. H. SCHÜRMANN, *Jesu ureigener Tod. Exegetische Besinnungen und Ausblick*, Freiburg i.B., Herder, 2 Aufl. 1976, R. PESCH, *Il Vangelo di Marco*, cit. a n. 14, pp. 524-555. J. GNILKA, *Jesus von Nazaret*, cit. a n. 1, pp. 280-290. R. PENNA, *I ritratti originali di Gesù il Cristo*, cit. a n. 16, pp. 153-166.

6. La nuova evangelizzazione dei vangeli sinottici

I discepoli del Risorto, per la missione da lui ricevuta, hanno annunciato «la buona notizia» di Gesù. Essa è l'annuncio della salvezza nel suo nome, cf. At 2,21, che deve essere testimoniata da loro «fino alle estremità della terra», At 1,8. Nei quattro vangeli, in cui è confluita la memoria e la predicazione apostolica, proprio perché sono il vangelo di salvezza, l'annuncio dell'unico vangelo si diversifica in rapporto alle situazioni delle popolazioni a cui è proclamato. Nei vangeli sinottici la novità dell'evangelizzazione nelle differenti situazioni si manifesta con particolare rilievo, per la circostanza della loro dipendenza da tradizioni in molta parte comuni.

6.1. *Matteo: il Dio della promessa e il suo popolo*

Matteo incomincia la sua narrazione con la genealogia di Gesù Cristo figlio di Davide, figlio di Abramo, Mt 1,1: Gesù è «Cristo», designazione che si colloca nell'ambito della attesa messianica di Israele, che però ora assume il valore di denominazione della persona ben individuata: Gesù Cristo. Egli è il «figlio» di Davide, il discendente erede delle promesse regali davidiche, e dunque «figlio» di Abramo, il padre del popolo della promessa. Gesù nasce in questa storia. È storia particolare di salvezza per l'iniziativa di Dio che si crea il suo popolo, in un progetto di salvezza universale. In questa storia di salvezza, azione sovrana salvatrice di Dio e storia e vita del popolo di Dio sono inscindibili[23]. E l'iniziativa di Dio ora si realizza nel concepimento di Gesù ἐκ πνεύμαματος ἁγίου, con l'imposizione del nome: Gesù, *IHWH salva*, che preannuncia la missione: «salverà il suo popolo dai suoi peccati». Nell'evento ha il compimento – πληρωθῇ – la parola del Signore, che per mezzo del Profeta annunciava la nascita verginale e il nome Emanuele: «Dio con noi», Mt 1,21.23. Questa nascita e la presenza di questo «nazareno» avveramento delle parole profetiche, Mt 2,23, è

---

[23] Cf. W. Trilling, *Das wahre Israel*. Studien zur Theologie des Matthäus-Evangeliums (StANT, Bd. X), München, Köser-Verlag, 3 Aufl. 1964.

il compimento di tutte le promesse e dei preannunci che avevano alimentato la fede e le attese del popolo; è la vita e la storia del popolo che ora è nuova nella continuità. Gesù, il galileo di Nazaret, si fa battezzare da Giovanni, perché così è bene che essi compiano tutta la giustizia, Mt 3,15. Egli vince le tentazioni ricorrendo sempre a una parola della Torah, Mt 4,11. Ritorna in Galilea, dando compimento alla profezia di salvezza proclamata da Isaia, Mt 4,12-15, e annuncia la venuta del regno, tanto attesa. L'evangelista narra subito la scelta di seguaci e descrive le tre attività caratteristiche del ministero di Gesù διδάσκων, κηρύσσων, θεραπεύων nel «popolo», Mt 4,23. Vi è un gran accorrere di gente anche da fuori dei confini della Galilea, per farsi guarire; ma incominciano anche ad esserci dei seguaci che provengono dai territori dell'Israele storico, Mt 4,25. E come Mosè, dopo la liberazione dall'Egitto, all'inizio della sua missione di guida del popolo, promulga la parola del Dio dell'alleanza, per la condotta fedele del popolo, l'evangelista riporta il primo grande «discorso» di Gesù. Ma egli non è il nuovo Mosè: egli, infatti, proclama le beatitudini del regno, e per autorità propria dà l'interpretazione della legge, esigendo comportamenti di fedeltà radicale, per la giustizia necessaria per entrare nel regno, che sopravanzi quella dell'osservanza della legge secondo l'insegnamento tradizionale degli scribi e farisei, Mt 5-7. L'attenzione di Mt per l'insegnamento di Gesù che istruisce il popolo di Dio del tempo della presenza del regno, appare dalle raccolte delle parole del Maestro. Poi tutta la azione di Gesù è la realizzazione della parola profetica a riguardo del servo di Dio che si sarebbe fatto carico di tutte le infermità, Mt 8,17. A lui si «commuovono le viscere» – ἐσπλαγχνίσθη – vedendo le folle «straziate ed abbattute come pecore senza pastore», Mt 9,36. Associa allora i dodici alla sua missione e li invia «alle pecore smarrite della casa di Israele», Mt 10,6, dando istruzioni per situazioni di missione, che sono già quelle dei discepoli, quando l'evanglista scrive. Ma il modo di operare di Gesù per Israele e il suo insegnamento non sono compresi, e proprio nelle città centro del suo ministero, Mt 11,16-24. Egli è osteggiato, anzi accusato di essere il capo dei demoni dalle guide spirituali del popolo, Mt 12,24. Egli si spiegherà; con le parabole indurrà a riflettere sulle caratteristiche della presenza del regno da essi atteso, perché si convertano e credano. Ai suoi dodici discepoli indirizzerà insegnamenti particolari, Mt 16,13-20; perché chi vuol essere suo discepolo sia pronto a seguirlo sulla via della abnegazione totale per lui, che, da giudice escatologico, renderà giustizia a tutti, Mt 16,21-28. I suoi discepoli costituiranno la sua ἐκκλησία, Mt 16,18; 18,17, per la quale egli imparte istruzioni, Mt 18,1-35. Egli, entrando a Gerusalemme, promuove una manifestazione, da parte di pellegrini giunti per la pasqua, che diventa una proclamazione messianica, Mt 21,1-9. Agisce contro il modo di esercizio del culto nel tempio, Mt 21,12-17. Contesta aspramente i responsabili del popolo, che, come i padri, sicuri della elezione di Dio, si servono della parola di Dio per costruirsi una loro giustizia di cui vantarsi, mentre stabiliscono una precettistica intollerabile, Mt 23,1-32. E nel caso che perseverino ad abusare della loro posizione nel popolo di Dio, non riconoscendo il momento della decisione per la sua presenza, egli li minaccia di punizione da parte del signore del regno, che, perciò, sarà affidato ad altri, che ne rendano il frutto. È una condanna che sovverte la loro concezione delle fedeltà alla legge e della vita e della storia del popolo di Dio: perciò decidono di ucciderlo, Mt 21,33-46. Nell'imminenza della sua fine Gesù parla della fine di quel mondo, proiettando lo sguardo verso la fine della storia, quando vi sarà il giudizio che avrà come criterio il comportamento verso i sofferenti e bisognosi, con cui il giudice si identifica. La sua cattura «deve» avvenire, perché si adempiano le Scritture, Mt 26,54. La sua condanna è sanzionata dal sinedrio perché «bestemmia» affermando di essere il cristo figlio di Dio, Mt 26,63-66. Pilato lo consegna per la crocifissione per l'insistenza di tutto il popolo, πᾶς ὁ λαός, che, sobillato dai maggiorenti, esclama: «il suo sangue su di noi e sui nostri», Mt 27,25. La sua morte è accompagnata da eventi «escatologici»: il velo del tempio si lacera, e vi sono risurrezioni e apparizioni di morti, Mt 27,51-53. Ma il giorno dopo il sabato appare vivo alle donne e poi ai discepoli, inviandoli, per il potere che egli ha in cielo e in terra, a battezzare e a fare discepoli, insegnando quanto egli ha comandato, e promette la sua presenza con loro fino alla fine del mondo, Mt 28,18-20.

L'evangelista, lo «scriba istruito sul regno di dei cieli è simile ad un uomo padre di famiglia che estrae dal suo tesoro cose vecchie e nuove», Mt 13,52. La sua comunità, legata alla tradizione giudaica, crede il nuovo di Gesù Cristo, Figlio di Dio, re di Israele, e, per il dramma del calvario, comprende in modo nuovo il vecchio, il passato di tutta la sua storia di popolo d'Israele, che nei suoi capi e rappresentanti ha rifiutato proprio il cristo a loro promesso ed inviato, e nello stesso tempo esperimenta la sovranità salvifica del suo Dio nella conversione dei pagani, con i quali già convive[24]. Mt nell'educare la sua comunità ad un approfondimento della sua fede e ad una piena fedeltà alle richieste di Gesù, annuncia il vangelo del regno mostrando che proprio in Gesù si è reso presente: la fedeltà alla parola di Dio nella Legge e nei profeti è ora la fede in Gesù il nazareno, che ha dato compimento alla Legge e ai profeti con la storia della sua vita e del suo insegnamento[25]. Il rifiuto ha la sua ragione nella persuasione orgogliosa dei farisei e dei capi, che ha impedito loro di saper vedere i segni della presenza di Dio in Gesù, non accettando di essere gli umili discepoli della Sapienza, cf. Mt 11,18-26. L'evangelista, mentre in questo modo proclama che la morte in croce non è la sconfessione divina di Gesù, – ed infatti Gesù risorge ed è ora sempre vivo con i suoi, – accentuando il comportamento negativo dei farisei, che pure erano considerati i pii giudei, mette in guardia la sua comuntà dal rischio sempre incombente di una pratica di vita che non è la giustizia richiesta da Gesù per il regno dei cieli. Il vangelo del regno presente in Gesù è annunciato dall'evangelista nella narrazione di Gesù vertice di convergenza dei differenti aspetti della speranza giudaica. Gesù è annunciato e rivelato dall'evangelista nell'ambito della storia del suo popolo. Questo sguardo su Gesù implica una visione di tutta la storia della salvezza per tutte le genti. La comprensione della storia del popolo di Israele e la lettura della S. Scrittura in seguito alla presenza di Gesù, salvatore di tutti proprio in quella storia e al vertice di

---

[24] Cf. G. BORNAKAMM, G. BARTH, H.J. HELD, *Überlieferung und Auslegung im Matthäusevangelium* (WMANT 1), Neukirchen, Neukirchener Verlag, 5 Aufl. 1968. E. SCHWEIZER, *Matthäus und seine Gemeinde*, Stuttgart, Verlag Katholisches Bidelwerk 1974. PH. ROLLAND, *Les premiers évangiles*. Un nouveau regard su le problème synoptique, Paris, Cerf., 1984, pp. 189-202. R. SCHNACKENBURG, *Jesus Cristus im spiegel der vier Evangelien* (Herders Theologischer Kommentar, Supplement-Band) Freiburg i.B., Herder 1993, pp. 90-115. R. PENNA, *I ritratti originali di Gesù il Cristo* Inizi e sviluppi della cristologia neotestamentaria. II. Gli sviluppi, Cinisello Balsamo, Edizioni S. Paolo 1999, pp. 346-362.

[25] J.P. MEIER, *Low and History in Matthew's Gospel* (Analecta Biblica 71) Roma, PIB 1976.

quella storia, rivelano in pienezza il valore della storia particolare di Israele per tutta l'umanità nelle differenti storie di ciascun popolo. Queste sono sempre peculiari ed irrepetibili, e gli eventi della storia d'Israele non possono essere paradigmi di comprensione e di valutazione mediante una operazione di semplice confronto. Ma la storia d'Israele, compiuta in Gesù salvatore di tutti, rivela l'azione incarnata di Dio nella vicenda del popolo scelto per una decisione universale di salvezza; essa è già la storia di salvezza di tutte le genti, e in essa si manifesta il rapporto continuo tra le molteplici manifestazioni della misericordia di Dio e le risposte dell'uomo peccatore. Ora la vicenda del popolo con Dio vive una svolta decisiva per il rapporto che si stabilisce con Gesù. Avvengono così nuove forme di rifiuto, ma soprattutto l'universalità della salvezza si manifesta nella dilatazione del popolo di Dio a tutte le genti; il vangelo di Gesù compitore della storia della salvezza è il vangelo del popolo di tutte le genti, salvate da Gesù. E proprio per il compimento di questo popolo di Dio di tutte le genti, raduna i suoi discepoli nella sua «chiesa». Per i discepoli, come membri del popolo di Dio della nuova alleanza, l'evangelo del regno di Dio in Gesù è anche la richiesta della giustizia conforme agli insegnamenti di Gesù. L'evangelista li propone con attenzione pastorale, preoccupato per le difficoltà che sorgono nella pratica, affinché non accada che dopo essere entrati al banchetto del regno, si sia trovati senza la veste del convito, cf. Mt 22,11-14. Mt poi sa che il vangelo, vissuto ed annunciato, procurerà persecuzioni, ma non si deve avere paura: mediante i discepoli sarà lo Spirito del Padre a prendere la parola in giudizio, e con loro, fino alla fine, vi è Gesù.

6.2. *Marco: l'evangelizzazione ai pagani*

Mc 1,1 scrive: «inizio del vangelo di Gesù Cristo», e la parola εὐαγγέλιον ricorre ancora in Mc 1,14-15; 8,35; 10,29; 13,10; 14,9 e nell'epigolo sommario 16,15; una frequenza caratteristica se considerata in confronto con l'uso degli altri sinottici: Mt 4,23; 9,35; 24,14; 26,13; in Lc ricorrono solo forme del verbo εὐαγγελίζομαι[26]. Sostantivo e verbo non vi sono in Gv. Mc è

---

[26] Per la valutazione sinottica di presenze ed assenze del sostantivo cf. W. MARXEN, *Der Evangelist Markus*. Studien zur Redaktionsgeschichte des Evange-

scritto in un mondo pagano[27], nel quale εὐαγγέλιον è usato nei contesti più diversi e con significati differenti[28]. Nella tradizione dell'Antico Testamento, sia ebraico che greco, per annunciare le azioni salvifiche di Dio si usano le forme verbali di *bśr* e di εὐαγγελίζομαι, ma i corrispondenti sostantivi non sono mai usati con significato religioso[29]. Mc esprime una specificità già dalla prima frase: «inizio del vangelo di Gesù Cristo». Il vangelo di Gesù è dunque una storia che inizia, che ha la preparazione profetica nel ministero di Giovanni il battista, il quale è pure la conclusione di tutta la storia dei preannunci profetici. Εὐαγγέλιον in Mc assume il valore attivo dell'azione, dell'evento della proclamazione. La storia inizia quando Gesù si reca in Galilea «annunciando il vangelo di Dio: Il tempo è compiuto, il regno di Dio è giunto, convertitevi e credete al vangelo» Mc 1,14-15: il vangelo di Dio è il suo annuncio della venuta del regno di Dio; è questo il «vangelo» che esige conversione e fede. Il vangelo di Gesù è dunque il vangelo di Dio ed è il suo ministero di evangelizzatore: vangelo ed evangelizzatore sono una storia unica. La relazione tra Gesù e il vangelo è affermata negli altri passi: Mc 8,35; 10,29; 13,9-11; 14,9. Sono tutti detti di Gesù «che riguardano il comportamento nei suoi confronti, anche oltre la circostanza della sua vita terrena. Il rapporto con lui si specifica dal comportamento nei confronti del vangelo, fino a dare la vita «per lui e per il vangelo». Il «vangelo» è la realtà della presenza di Gesù, anche dopo la sua morte....Il vangelo predicato in tutto il mondo è il vangelo come presenza di Gesù nell'annuncio che è fatto di lui proprio nella ripresentazione dell'annuncio fatto da Gesù, configurante tutto il suo ministero»[30].

---

liums, Göttingen, Vandenhoeck & Rupreche, 2. Aufl. 1959, pp. 80-81, 82. R. PESCH, *Il vangelo di Marco*, cit. a n. 14, pp. 178-179.

[27] Le indicazioni testuali e le attestazioni dell'antichità indicano una comunità cristiana in società pagana come situazione della composizione di Mc; cf. le introduzioni ai numerosi commentari di Mc. Cf. Ph. ROLLAND, *Les premiers évangiles*, cit. a n. 24, pp. 134-135. R. RIVA, *Il Vangelo di Marco: un annuncio di salvezza nel mondo pagano*, in *Studia Missionalia* 42 (1993) 17-40.

[28] Cf. G. FRIEDRICH, εὐαγγελίζομαι, εὐαγγλιον, κ.τ.λ., in ThWbNT II (1935) 721-725.

[29] Cf. O. SCHILLING, *bśr* in ThWbAT, II (1972-1973) 313-316.

[30] R. RIVA, *Il Vangelo di Marco*, cit. a n. 27, p. 30; per l'interpretazione dei testi, pp. 26-31.

E il suo ministero è la realtà della sua vita terrena di Figlio dell'uomo, Cristo crocifisso, Figlio del Padre.

Questo è appunto il «vangelo» di Mc: il «buon annuncio» della salvezza per la venuta del regno di Dio è l'evangelizzatore Gesù; la narrazione, la ripresentazione del vangelo che è Gesù, è la presenza permanente di Gesù evangelizzatore e salvatore. Tutta l'organizzazione narrativa e lo stile di Mc caratterizzano lo scritto come il vangelo-ripresentazione di Gesù.

Il vangelo-Gesù è il vangelo di Dio, che dà compimento al tempo dell'attesa del regno di Dio, al tempo della storia particolare della salvezza del popolo d'Israele: Dio, non un dio del mondo pagano; perciò ora si rivela anche il valore universale di quella storia particolare di preparazione. Il luogo del culto di Dio ora non è più riservato al popolo d'Israele, ma, come «è scritto» è «casa di preghiera per tutte le genti», Mc 11,17[31], e il vangelo sarà predicato a tutte le genti, Mc 13,10, e in tutto il mondo, Mc 14,9.

L'evangelista così esprime la ragione della sua stessa opera: nata fuori della Palestina e vangelo di Gesù Cristo figlio di Dio a Roma, il centro dell'organizzazione mondiale contemporanea.

Il vangelo-Gesù di Mc è sconcertante. La sua storia è preparata dall'annuncio profetico, Mc 1,7-8. La voce dal cielo lo proclama figlio diletto e lo Spirito divino rimane su di lui, Mc 1,10-11. Lo spirito immondo si sente minacciato dalla presenza di chi viene riconosciuto come il santo di Dio, e che lo scaccerà; e la gente è stupefatta constatando che al suo comando non possono sottrarsi i demoni e udendo il suo insegnamento nuovo proposto con autorità diversa da quella dei loro dottori, Mc 1,23-28. Guarisce ogni genere di infermità e nelle circostanze più diverse. Si comporta con una autonomia sorprendente a riguardo di pratiche della pietà giudaica e anche nel modo di osservare la stessa legge; e non perché si ritenga libero di violarla, ma perché pretende di interpretarla secondo il vero volere di Dio, Mc 2,13-3,5; 7,1-23. Si ritiene conoscitore dei se-

---

[31] Cf. G.C. BIGUZZI, «*Io distruggerò questo tempio*». *Il tempio e il giudaismo nel vangelo di Marco*, Roma, PUU, pp. 33-38. B.M.F. VAN IERSEL, *Leggere Marco*, Roma, Ed. Paoline 1989.

greti della misericordia di Dio nella sua azione con gli uomini e nell'attuazione del suo regno, Mc 2,1-12; 4,1-33. Si è scelto discepoli che lo riconoscono «cristo», Mc 8,27-30 e tre di essi, per sua iniziativa, faranno una esperienza eccezionale della realtà misteriosa della sua persona, oltre quanto essi possano di essa conoscere nella convivenza quotidiana, Mc 9,2-8; essi per lui hanno lasciato tutto, ed egli a chi già osserva i comandamenti afferma che gli manca ancora qualcosa e gli chiede di lasciare tutto per seguire lui, che garantisce il centuplo di qua e la vita eterna nel mondo venturo; però tutto questo non senza persecuzioni, Mc 10,17-30. Questa sorte non è altro che partecipazione alla sua. Infatti proprio l'eccezionalità del suo ministero suscita opposizione da parte dei maggiorenti politici e religiosi, e Mc li presenta già dall'inizio della sua narrazione decisi a metterlo a morte, Mc 3,6. È considerato un forsennato e perfino indemoniato, Mc 3,21-22. Anche i suoi discepoli non riescono a capire il suo comportamento, Mc 8,14-21. Quando poi egli preannuncia la sua morte, sia pure con la previsione della risurrezione, Pietro si ribella, e si sente rispondere che la sua protesta è tentazione e che egli non ha la «sapienza» di Dio, Mc 8,31-33. La loro incomprensione[32] è tale che essi non osano neppure interrogarlo, quando egli parla ancora della sua morte, Mc 9,30-32. E finirà come egli aveva predetto: condannato a morte per bestemmia per le sue affermazioni riguardanti la sua persona, Mc 14,62-64, e muore sul patibolo ignominioso della croce. Gesù il nazareno, suppliziato, sulla croce tra due malfattori, conclude la sua vita terrena, che, nonostante fatti straordinari, non fu, certo, la vita di una figura celeste e neanche come quella di uno degli eroi della credenze del mondo pagano. Ma al momento della sua morte «il velo del tempio si strappò dall'alto in basso. E il centurione, che gli stava dirimpetto, vedendo che così era spirato, disse: «Veramente questo uomo era figlio di Dio», Mc 15,38-39. Passato il Sabato nel

---

[32] In questa descrizione dell'esperienza dei discepoli si inserisce «il segreto messianico», presente nella tradizione evangelica, e rilevante in Mc. Cf. W. WREDE, *Das Messiasgeheimnis in den Evangelien. Zugleich ein Beitrag zum Verständnis des Marcusegnagliums*, Göttingen, Vandenhoeck & Ruprecht, 1901, 3 Aufl. 1963. R. SCHNACKENBURG, *Jesus Cristus*, cit. a n. 24, pp. 80-89.

sepolcro vuoto il giovane celeste annuncerà alle donne: «Gesù il nazareno è risorto», Mc 16,6; e il risorto dirà ai suoi discepoli: «Andate e annunciate il vangelo ad ogni creatura. Il credente e il battezzato sarà salvo, l'incredulo invece sarà condannato», Mc 1615-16[33].

Il vangelo-Gesù è il Nazareno, Cristo, Figlio di Dio, crocifisso, presente vivo per la risurrezione da morte. Il risorto salvatore presente è il Cristo crocifisso, che è stato rifiutato e ha accettato la croce, nell'abbandono figliale alla volontà del padre. Quando in quel morente si riconosce una presenza divina, nel Crocifisso si riconosce che l'onnipotenza divina opera in modo opposto a quello della sapienza umana della potenza; è proprio la «totalmente altra»; è il mistero divino che si rivela nella sua pienezza, a suggello di tutta quella vita di annuncio del vangelo del regno: il vangelo nella sua compiutezza è il Crocifisso. Al Crocifisso, che rifiuta di scendere dalla croce, ci si può accostare solo con la adesione personale della fede: al Crocifisso non ci si accosta se non per accettarlo come il dono totale di se stesso in una attrattiva di amore. E poiché l'onnipotenza divina si rende presente nella ignominia del Crocifisso, ogni pretesa di sapienza umana di salvezza è annullata. Appare la inantità, in ordine alla salvezza, di ogni atto religioso che per se stesso sia considerato garanzia della salvezza. Perciò stesso il Cristo Crocifisso è l'unico salvatore di tutti. Egli è «il buon annuncio», il vangelo-Gesù Cristo figlio di Dio», che Mc rende presente per il comando del Risorto; e nella presentazione dell'esperienza della difficoltà a credere dei discepoli è l'evangelista che educa la fede dei suoi lettori.

6.3. *Luca: la storia dell'evangelizzazione.*

Lc non usa mai il sostantivo εὐαγγέλιον, usa invece 10 volte il verbo εὐαγγελίζομαι (15 volte in At), che ricorre solo

---

[33] L'epilogo Mc 16,9-20 viene qui considerato per la sua appartenenza al vangelo canonico, a prescindere dalla questione della sua origine.

una volta in Mt 11,5, ispirato da Is 61,1, ed è assente da Mc. La scelta lessicale del verbo è l'espressione dichiarata che il fatto della situazione «buona notificata» è l'evento stesso della sua proclamazione. Di questa – «gli avvenimenti verificatisi tra noi» – Lc intende scrivere «con ordine», «dopo accurata indagine», «affinché il lettore conosca bene ciò di cui è stato catechizzato», e il suo scritto si colloca nella condizione storica determinata da scritti precedenti, Lc 1,1-4.

Inizia il suo racconto con l'indicazione temporale, che comporta anche l'indicazione locale; queste collocano la vicenda nelle sue circostanze storiche. La narrazione ordinata è il racconto dell'inizio della vita del personaggio, e non dalla nascita, bensì già dal concepimento. La narrazione delle due annunciazioni, di Giovanni e di Gesù, individua genitori e circostanze, che manifestano gli eventi storici come interventi divini, dal cui svolgimento appaiono la funzione della missione di Giovanni in rapporto alla persona e alla missione divina di Gesù, e la differenza di fede tra Zaccaria e la vergine Maria. Viene anche specificata la sorte dei due nascituri nella storia di Israele, Lc 1,5-38. La narrazione continua con la presentazione parallela degli eventi fino alla nascita, che si rivelano interventi divini in atto e manifestano la preminenza di Gesù e di Maria su Giovanni ed Elisabetta, Lc 1,39-2,21. E della nascita di Gesù si precisano circostanze temporali, in relazione con la storia dell'impero romano, e locali, in relazione con la storia di Israele, Lc 2,1-4. E un angelo del Signore annuncia – εὐαγγελίζομαι – ai pastori che «è nato oggi per voi un salvatore, che è Cristo signore nella città di Davide», Lc 2,11. Dopo la circoncisione, evento importante nella vita di un bambino ebreo è quello della sua presentazione al tempio «secondo la legge di Mosè»; Lc narra il fatto, che diventa la prima rivelazione pubblica di Gesù per il riconoscimento di Simeone, «mosso dallo Spirito» e per la divulgazione da parte di Anna «profetessa», Lc 2,22-38. Per un bambino di un villaggio della Galilea importante è una crescita sana e saggia assistito dalla grazia di Dio, appunto come Lc 2,39-40 narra. Dopo la circoncisione l'altro evento determinante nella vita di un ragazzo ebreo era il compimento del dodicesimo anno, quando veniva abituato ad essere partecipe nelle manifestazioni cultiche, a cui sarebbe stato obbligato dal compimento dell'anno successivo[34]. Secondo la consuetudine fanno anche i parenti di Gesù, quando egli ha dodici anni; egli allora, incominciando ad imparare ad essere responsabile per gli atti di fedeltà a Dio, rimane nel tempio, all'insaputa dei genitori, perché egli «si deve occupare delle cose del Padre» suo, Lc 2,14-50. Poi, torna a Nazaret, dove vive come ogni buon figlio sottomesso ai genitori, Lc 2,51-52. Gli eventi narrati da Lc sono quelli normali della vita di un ragazzo ebreo; proprio questi eventi «normali», dal concepimento alla crescita, si rivelano come gli interventi divini che costituiscono la fisionomia dei personaggi. Anche Mt 1-2 narra della vita di Gesù prima dell'inizio del suo ministero; gli eventi che egli narra sono tutti particolari non solo perché sono interventi divini rivelatori, come in Lc, ma anche perché non sono quelli normali di un bambino ebreo. Sul seguito della vita, fino all'inizio del ministero Lc, come anche Mt, non narra nulla; è la vita nascosta, di cui egli non dice nulla. Ma appunto quanto ha narrato finora mostra che quanto aveva da raccontare di normale particolare di quella vita, lo ha narrato. Il resto della vita di Gesù fino all'inizio del ministero è raccontato tutto in Lc 2,51-52: «Egli scese con loro a Nazaret, ed era loro sottomesso. Sua madre conservava tutte queste cose in cuor suo. E Gesù cresceva in sapienza, in età e grazia, davanti a Dio e davanti agli uomini». Lc non ha nulla da dire; come la madre di Gesù che conserva nel cuore «queste cose», quelle narrate. Il brevissimo «tempo narrativo», con la menzione di quanto è solo normale per un ragazzo e un uomo ebreo, è l'espressione del senso narrativo del luogo tempo della vita reale: l'eccezionale è allora proprio la normalità di vita secondo gli usi, che tutti conoscono, di questo Gesù, che è entrato nella storia di Israele con l'eccezionalità divina degli eventi normali della vita di un bambino.

È nell'anno decimoquinto del regno di Tiberio Cesare, Lc 3,1 che la storia di Gesù ha una svolta in connessione con il mi-

---

[34] Per gli obblighi e lo svolgimento dei pellegrinaggi a Gerusalemme, cf. J. JEREMIAS, *Jerusalem zur Zeit Jesu*. Eine Kulturgeschichtliche Untersuchung zur neutestamentlichen Zeitgeschicthe, Göttinge, Vandenthoeck & Ruprecht, 3, Aufl. 1969, pp. 91-102.

nistero profetico di Giovanni il battezzatore, a cui accorrono coloro che si gloriano di essere figli di Abramo, ma anche i pubblicani e i militari, e ad essi preannuncia la venuta escatologica di che avrebbe battezzato in Spirito Santo e fuoco Lc 3,2b-20. Da lui va anche Gesù per farsi battezzare e «mentre prega» lo Spirito Santo scende su di lui e la voce celeste lo proclama «Tu sei il Figlio mio diletto», Lc 3,21-22. Lc ora lo presenta mediante la genealogia ascendente che inserisce Gesù nella storia di tutta l'umanità dal suo principio in Adamo, Lc 3,23-38: alla introduzione del bambino mediante la «normalità eccezionale» degli eventi dell'infanzia, corrisponde la presentazione di chi è «il Figlio diletto» proclamato dalla voce celeste e su cui scende lo Spirito Santo come un uomo «di circa trent'anni» di cui si conosce la genealogia. Dopo le tentazioni vinte, l'inizio del ministero a Nazaret, nella sinagoga, di sabato, come è normale per un giudeo nazaretano. Egli legge ed interpreta il testo di Isaia riferendolo a se stesso, proclamandosi così il profeta escatologico della presenza dell'intervento salvifico di Dio. Dopo la normalità della vita a Nazaret è comprensibile l'ammirazione dei compaesani, e la loro indignazione per aver saputo di quanto ha già compiuto a Cafarnao, mentre non ha fatto nulla nel suo paese. Gesù interpreta la sua situazione come quella del profeta che proprio dai suoi è rifiutato, Lc 4,16-30[35].

Lc, fino a 9,50, narra il ministero itinerante «perché – Gesù afferma – è necessario per me evangelizzare il regno di Dio, infatti per questo sono stato mandato», Lc 4,43. Proclama la beatitudine dei poveri perché di essi è il regno di Dio, Lc 6,20, e annuncia il regno anche con le parabole, Lc 8,4-18; afferma più volte, in relazione alle sue azioni che il regno di Dio è venuto; con le sue opere di amore compassionevole, cf. Lc 7,13: ἐσπλαγχνίσθη, mostra come si debba amare e richiede l'amore dei nemici per esser figli del Padre misericordioso Lc 6,27-36; in questo ministero di evangelizzazione si inserisce anche il suo rapporto con i discepoli, che incominciano a riconoscerlo come il Cristo di Dio, Lc 9,20, e vengono essi pure in-

---

[35] Cf. Ph. ROLLAND, *Les premiers évangiles*, cit. a n. 24, pp. 181-188. R. SCHNACKENBURB, *Jesus Christus*, cit. a n. 24, pp. 152-205.

viati in missione, partecipi del suo annuncio e delle sue opere, Lc 9,1-10. Il racconto fino a Lc 9,50 «prolunga e verifica l'episodio di Nazaret: il riconoscimento di Gesù come Profeta, Inviato e Messia doveva avvenire ed è avvenuto, a gruppi separati; la sua fama ha addirittura superato le frontiere e nessuno è rimasto indifferente nei suoi confronti»[36].

A partire da Lc 9,51 la narrazione imprime al ministero di Gesù una direzione ben precisa: «Or avvenne che si compivano i giorni della sua assunzione, ed egli con decisione prese la direzione di Gerusalemme». Gli scribi e i farisei avevano incominciato presto a criticarlo per sue affermazioni «blasfeme», Lc 5,21 e per i suoi comportamenti circa la pratica della legge e l'osservanza delle norme tradizionali, arrivando ad una decisa opposizione Lc 5,27-6,11. E Gesù, subito dopo la confessione di Pietro, aveva annunciato ai discepoli la sua fine di morte e risurrezione, Lc 9,21-22; e durante la trasfigurazione Mosè ed Elia parlavano con lui del «suo esodo che egli avrebbe compiuto in Gerusalemme, Lc 9,31. Da ora il suo ministero continua a svolgersi nei vari luoghi e secondo le diverse circostanze, che capitano sul cammino, e nelle quali, tuttavia, egli è sempre il reggitore. Come prima peregrinava perché egli «deve» annunciare il regno di Dio, ora questo suo compito si svolge secondo un indirizzo preciso perché «è necessario – δεῖ – che io proceda oggi e domani e il giorno seguente, perché non è accettabile – οὐκ ἐνδέχεται – che un profeta perisca fuori Gerusalemme», Lc 13,33. E proprio all'inizio di questo cammino egli sceglie i settanta(due) discepoli che invia ad annunciare la venuta del regno di Dio, prevenendoli sul pericolo del rifiuto, che sarà motivo di condanna escatologica per le città incredule; e i discepoli tornano gioiosi del successo, Lc 10,1-21. Nel cammino verso Gerusalemme continua a guarire, ad insegnare e rivelare la misericordia del Padre, ammonendo farisei e scribi per la loro incomprensione, cf. L 15,1-32. Arriva a Gerusalemme quando i capi dei sacerdoti, gli scribi e i capi del popolo hanno deciso di toglierlo di mezzo, e aspettano solo l'occasione opportuna, perché il popolo pendeva dalle sue labbra, Lc 19,48. L'occasione propizia si

---

[36] J.N. ALETTI, *L'arte di raccontare Gesù Cristo*. La scrittura narrativa del vangelo di Luca, Brescia, Queriniana 1991, pp. 93-94.

offre, Gesù è condannato, sulla croce promette il paradiso al malfattore che lo riconosce innocente e muore riconosciuto «giusto» dal centurione. Il primo giorno del sabato i due uomini in veste splendente si rivolgono alle donne: «Perché cercate il vivente tra i morti? Non è qui, ma è risorto, Ricordatevi come vi parlò quando era ancora in Galilea affermando che è necessario che il figlio dell'uomo sia consegnato nelle mani dei peccatori, e sia crocifisso e il terzo giorno risorga», Lc 24,5-7. Gesù, apparendo sulla strada verso Emmaus e ai discepoli, dirà che era necessario che il Cristo patisse ed entrasse nella sua gloria, interpretando loro le Scritture, Lc 24,26-27. 43-46. «È necessario» secondo le Scritture: è il piano di Dio che si deve compiere; e il compimento, cioè la vita e il ministero di Gesù, mostra le modalità della realizzazione di quella necessità: non mediate interventi divini che ostacolino il corso normale della vita; bensì gli eventi e gli incontri normali della vita, che si svolge in piena libertà, sono le situazioni della presenza e della rivelazione di Dio che realizza il suo regno di salvezza. Gesù, la sua vita, è la novità dell'evangelizzazione del regno presente. La sua storia doveva essere così perché è l'avveramento delle promesse della storia di salvezza. Lc lo rivela nel modo stesso di scrivere la sua narrazione[37]. Gesù imprime alla storia una svolta definitiva: «Fino a Giovanni la legge e i profeti; da allora il regno di Dio è evangelizzato», Lc 16,16[38]. Gesù risorto, dopo aver spiegato la «necessità» della morte e risurrezione del Cristo secondo le scritture, aggiunge che è anche «scritto» che: «nel suo nome saranno predicati a tutte le genti la conversione e il perdono dei peccati. Voi sarete testimoni di tutto questo, cominciando da Gerusalemme. Ed ecco che io manderò su di voi la promessa del Padre. Orbene voi restate in città, finché non siate rivestiti di potenza dall'alto», Lc 24, 47-49. Gli Atti

---

[37] Cf. J.N. ALETTI, *L'arte di Raccontare Gesù Cristo*, cit. a n. 35; R. MEYNET, *Quelle est donc cette Parole? Lecture «rhétorique» de l'évangile de Luc (1-9 et 22-24)*, (Lectio divina 99) Voll. A-B, Paris, Cerf. 1979; ID., *Avez-vous lu Saint Luc? Guide pour la Rencontre*, Paris, Cerf 1990.

[38] Cf. H. CONZELMANN, *Die Mitte der Zeit,* Tübingen, J.C.B. Mohr (P. Siebeck) 1953. Bisogna tuttavia considerare che per Lc il tempo successivo a Gesù è il tempo della evangelizzazione, quindi della sua presenza, mentre quello prima di lui era quello della promessa e dell'attesa.

degli Apostoli sono la storia di questa testimonianza: la storia dell'evangelizzazione in atto nelle vicende dei differenti rapporti umani liberi, con consensi, opposizioni e persecuzioni, che fanno parte della realizzazione del piano divino di salvezza, che si compie. L'evangelizzazione come presenza continua della vita dell'evangelizzatore Gesù mediante la testimonianza e la storia dei discepoli di Gesù, ripieni dello stesso Spirito, per cui egli era stato concepito nel grembo della vergine, e che era sceso su di lui all'inizio del ministero, mentre il Padre lo proclamava suo Figlio diletto.

Gesù disse ai suoi discepoli: «Quando verrà il Paraclito che vi manderò dal Padre, lo Spirito di verità che procede dal Padre, egli mi darà testimonianza; e anche voi mi renderete testimonianza, perché siete con me fin dall'inizio», Gv 15,26, e ancora: «Quando verrà lo Spirito di Verità, egli vi guiderà in tutta la verità. Non parlerà infatti da se stesso, ma quanto sentirà dirà e vi annuncerà le cose venture. Egli mi glorificherà, perché prenderà da me e ve lo annuncerà», Gv 16,13-14. I vangeli sono testimonianza dei discepoli, illuminati sulla Verità, istruiti sulle cose venture nelle diverse circostanze, nelle quali il Vangelo, che è Gesù evangelizzatore, è reso presente nella novità perenne dell'evangelizzazione.

La bonne nouvelle du Père

JEAN GALOT

La bonne nouvelle que l'évangélisation s'efforce de répandre est l'heureux message de la venue du Christ en ce monde, de la lumière qu'il a répandue sur notre destinée, du salut que par son sacrifice rédempteur il a apporté à l'humanité. Dans sa première source, cette bonne nouvelle vient du Père, mais bien souvent l'évangélisation met trop peu en lumière le visage mystérieux de ce Père, qui, en demeurant invisible, n'attire pas suffisamment les regards. Le Père n'est pas assez présent dans l'oeuvre évangélisatrice; il inspire trop peu ceux qui évangélisent, ne possède pas assez leur coeur; sa véritable image s'imprime trop peu en ceux qui reçoivent la doctrine[1]. Il est donc utile de réfléchir plus spécialement à la place qui lui revient, qui devrait lui revenir, dans l'évangélisation.

Ne peut-on pas espérer, au seuil du nouveau millénaire, un nouvel élan qui ouvre plus largement la foi chrétienne et la vie chrétienne à l'amour souverain du Père? Un élan de découverte est nécessaire pour connaître dans son mystère ce Père que le Christ nous a révélé, cette personne divine qui ne s'était pas encore affirmée comme telle dans la religion juive et que Jésus, par son évangile, était chargé de nous faire connaître. Le dessein divin avait été de laisser au Fils incarné la mission de faire apparaître la face authentique du Père et d'offrir aux chrétiens la joie de la découvrir.

Certes, dans l'oeuvre du salut, le Père, tout en étant l'initiateur du mystère de l'Incarnation rédemptrice, a expressé-

---

[1] La place insuffisante occupée par le Père dans l'évangélisation est en relation avec le manque de développement de la théologie du Père: cf. J. GALOT, *Découvrir le Père. Esquisse d'une théologie du Père*, Louvain: Sintal 1985, 29-34.

ment mis en lumière le visage de son Fils. C'est lui qui l'a envoyé dans le monde et qui l'a fait concrètement connaître en lui donnant une nature humaine semblable à la nôtre. Il l'a voulu au centre du mouvement de foi et d'espérance qu'il voulait susciter dans l'humanité et a fait de lui la source immédiate de l'amour qui devait envahir l'univers. Mais c'est lui, le Père, qui doit être reconnu comme le premier auteur de toutes les merveilles que comporte l'action salvatrice qui a changé la face du monde. Tout l'évangile est l'expression de son suprême amour paternel[2].

Mon Père et votre Père

Significatif pour l'évangélisation est le premier message évangélique du Crist ressuscité. Marie-Madeleine, en s'entendant appeler par son nom, vient de reconnaître celui qu'elle cherchait. Elle voudrait le retenir mais est envoyée en mission: «Va trouver mes frères et dis-leur: je monte vers mon Père et votre Père...» (Jn 20,17). Les mots qui suivent: «vers mon Dieu et votre Dieu» paraissent une addition explicative, destinée à indiquer qu'il s'agit de Dieu le Père[3].

Par ce message, Jésus annonce l'événement de l'Ascension, en faisant comprendre à Marie-Madeleine que l'heure de ce départ n'est pas encore arrivée et qu'elle ne doit pas le retenir maintenant, parce qu'elle aura encore l'occasion de le revoir. En outre, il montre que lorsqu'il apparaît en ressuscité, ce n'est pas pour se laisser accaparer par les conditions de la vie terrestre ni par ceux qui voudraient retrouver la compagnie dont ils ont profité avant sa mort: il ne retourne pas sur terre; il vit désormais dans un état glorieux et prépare son retour définitif vers le Père.

---

[2] Selon la Lettre Apostolique *Tertio Millennio Adveniente*, le Jubilé doit être «un grand acte de louange du Père» (n. 49).
[3] Ailleurs, dans l'évangile de Jean, on ne trouve pas les expressions «mon Dieu» ni «votre Dieu» sur les lèvres de Jésus. Dans les textes évangéliques, la parole de dérélection comporte l'expression «mon Dieu», mais comme citation du psaume 22 (Mc 15, 34; Mt 27, 46).

La première parole du message concerne le Père. Elle confirme l'importance essentielle du Père dans la révélation que le Christ apporte à l'humanité. En apparaissant plein d'une nouvelle vie, Jésus manifeste son propre triomphe glorieux, mais de ce triomphe il veut d'abord faire un hymne au Père. Il indique par là ce qui doit être la préoccupation primordiale de toute évangélisation, la louange et la gratitude qui s'élèvent vers le Père pour la merveille accomplie dans l'oeuvre rédemptrice.

En disant: «mon Père et votre Père», il souligne l'effet le plus remarquable de cette oeuvre. Celui qu'il avait révélé comme son propre Père est désormais, à un titre nouveau, le Père de tous. Jésus veut partager sa vie divine filiale avec tous les hommes qu'il a sauvés. Ce qu'il a de plus précieux, son union de Fils avec le Père, il veut le communiquer à tous ceux pour lesquels il a offert son sacrifice; il élève ainsi, au plus haut niveau, leur condition de créatures.

Le sommet de la révélation qu'il avait adressée à ses disciples au cours de sa vie terrestre se trouvait dans le simple mot «Abba» qu'il prononçait comme invocation dans sa prière[4]. Ce mot constituait une nouveauté, en ce sens que jamais auparavant une telle invocation n'était apparue dans la prière juive. Locution araméenne, «abba» était l'appellation la plus familière que les enfants employaient pour s'adresser à leur père: «papa». Elle était tellement familière qu'elle semblait peu en accord avec la grandeur majestueuse du Dieu adoré dans la prière juive. Jésus, en l'employant, manifestait une certaine audace, celle d'un Fils qui vivait dans une totale intimité avec un Père qui était Dieu.

Lorsqu'il dit à Marie-Madeleine: «Je monte vers mon Père», il fait apparaître le triomphe de son intimité filiale avec

---

[4] Cf. J. JEREMIAS, *Abba; Studien zur neutestamentlichen Theologie und Geschichte*, Göttingen 1966; W. MARCHEL, *Abba, Père! La prière du Christ et des chrétiens*, Rome 1963; J. CARMIGNAC, *Recherches sur le «Notre Père»*, Paris 1969; S. SABUGAL, *Abba! ... La oración del Señor*, Madrid 1985; J. SCHLOSSER, *Le Dieu de Jésus. Etude exégétique*, Paris 1987; G. SCHELBERT, *Abba, Vater! Stand der Frage, Freiburger Zeitschrift fur Philosophie und Theologie*, 40 (1993) 259-281.

celui qu'il appelle «Abba»: cette intimité a triomphé de l'épreuve de la mort, et le triomphe va prendre une forme définitive dans l'événement de l'Ascension. C'est un triomphe d'autant plus éclatant que l'unique épisode où est rapportée dans les évangiles l'invocation «Abba» est la supplication angoissée de Gethsémani (Mc 14, 36). En ce moment dramatique, le recours au Père s'était exprimé en un cri déchirant. Après la résurrection, «mon Père» est prononcé dans la joie. C'est l'union au Père qui remporte la victoire.

Dans cette victoire, l'amour paternel du Père prend la plus large extension. «Mon Père» devient «votre Père». Celui qui demande à être reconnu et vénéré comme le Père de Jésus doit désormais être adoré et aimé comme le Père de tous ceux auxquels le Christ offre sa filiation divine. Le Père traite chacun d'eux comme son enfant, de telle sorte que chacun possède la dignité de fils du Père.

L'expression: «mon Père et votre Père» est bien choisie pour signifier à la fois unité et distinction de filiation. Jésus n'a pas dit «notre Père» pour unifier les deux paternités. Dans le cours de sa vie terrestre, il s'était servi de l'expression «notre Père», mais simplement comme invocation recommandée aux disciples pour leur prière à eux. La distinction entre «mon Père» et «votre Père» témoigne qu'une différence essentielle subsiste entre les deux paternités. Jésus est le Fils éternel du Père, qui possède la nature divine, tandis que les hommes n'accèdent à la filiation qu'en vertu d'une grâce qui leur est accordée.

La différence de nature ne doit pas, néanmoins, voiler la valeur du don. La merveille consiste dans l'élévation de l'être humain à un rapport filial avec le Père. La notion de filiation adoptive, habituellement utilisée pour définir ce rapport, ne suffit pas à en exprimer toute la qualité. L'adoption filiale a plutôt une portée juridique, tandis que la condition du chrétien se caractérise surtout par un état de vie filiale. Il s'agit d'une filiation participée, d'une filiation vitalement communiquée par le Christ.

Une telle filiation a pour conséquence, dans les relations du Christ avec ses disciples, l'instauration et le développement d'une véritable fraternité. Jésus y fait allusion en disant à Marie-Madeleine: «Va vers mes frères et dis-leur...». C'est la première fois qu'il parle des disciples comme ses frères; cette nouvelle appellation, attestée par l'évangile de Jean, est d'ailleurs confirmée par l'évangile de Matthieu (28,10). La nouvelle paternité attribuée au Père implique une nouvelle fraternité.

L'évangélisation reçoit ainsi, par les premières paroles du Christ ressuscité, une orientation fondamentale. Elle a pour premier objectif de faire connaître le Père de Jésus, qui se révèle désormais comme le Père de toute l'humanité rachetée. L'élan qui a porté le Christ, dans sa vie nouvelle, vers le Père, doit se communiquer à tous ceux qui sont appelés à partager sa vie filiale. C'est un élan qui cherche à faire entrer tous les hommes dans le mystère d'un Père plein d'amour, qui se veut infiniment proche de chacun de ceux en qui il reconnaît l'image de son Fils unique.

En fait, l'élan de l'évangélisation prolonge l'élan du Christ qui a vécu sa vie terrestre comme un chemin qui le conduisait vers le Père et qui a trouvé son aboutissement lorsqu'après sa mort il a pu rejoindre le Père en son triomphe glorieux. Evangéliser, c'est s'approprier ce regard du Christ pour orienter l'humanité vers le Père.

En outre, la première parole du Christ en vue de l'évangélisation fait apparaître le cadre de fraternité dans lequel le message doit être transmis. Evangéliser, c'est aller vers ceux qui sont appelés à être des frères dans un même amour filial pour le Père.

LUI QUI NOUS A BÉNIS DE TOUTE SORTE DE BÉNÉDICTIONS SPIRITUELLES

En suivant l'orientation donnée par Jésus au premier message évangélique, saint Paul se tourne vers le Père comme responsable suprême de toute l'oeuvre du salut: «Béni soit le Dieu et Père de notre Seigneur Jésus Christ, lui qui nous a bénis de toute sorte de bénédictions spirituelles, aux cieux, dans le Christ!» (Ep 11, 3). Le Père est à l'origine de tous les biens que nous avons reçus[5].

---

[5] Sur le Père dans l'hymne d'Ephésiens 1, 3-14, cf. J. GALOT, *Père qui es-tu?*, Versailles 1996, 45-58.

Dans le culte juif, Dieu était béni, loué, pour tous ses bienfaits. Dans l'hymne de la communauté primitive repris par Paul, ce n'est plus simplement vers Dieu que monte la louange ou la bénédiction, et ce n'est plus simplement lui qui est regardé comme l'auteur de toutes les bénédictions dont nous sommes comblés. C'est le Dieu qui est «Père de notre Seigneur Jésus Christ». C'est-à-dire que c'est la personne du Père, distincte de celle du Fils. Alors que dans la révélation de l'Ancien Testament, la paternité divine était simplement attribuée à un Dieu unique sans distinction d'une pluralité de personnes, le Christ avait révélé l'existence d'une personne divine qui a pour propriété caractéristique d'être Père, entièrement Père. On doit donc reconnaître un notable progrès dans la révélation de ce qu'il y a de plus fondamental dans la réalité mystérieuse de Dieu. Il ne s'agit plus d'une paternité attribuée globalement à Dieu, mais d'une personne divine qui existe comme Père.

Dans le mystère de Dieu, il y a quelqu'un qui est Père de toute éternité, quelqu'un qui éternellement a engendré un Fils. Il ne s'est révélé dans sa propre personne que lorsqu'il a envoyé son Fils dans le monde. En venant vivre parmi les hommes, le Fils a manifesté son identité filiale en se distinguant du Père qu'il appelait «Abba».

C'est ainsi que l'hymne est adressé «au Dieu et Père de notre Seigneur Jésus Christ». Alors que dans la religion juive Dieu était appelé Père en raison de son attitude paternelle envers le peuple et que la paternité divine désignait essentiellement un rapport avec les membres de la nation, la paternité qui se révèle dans l'évangile est avant tout une paternité à l'égard du Christ, destinée à s'étendre à l'égard de tous ceux qui sont appelés à vivre de la vie de Jésus. Le Père reporte sur toute l'humanité l'amour paternel qui le lie à son Fils unique.

Les bénédictions célestes sont donc les faveurs d'une bonté paternelle qui nous sont accordées dans le Christ. C'est en raison du Christ que l'amour du Père s'est complètement ouvert à nous. Mais c'est cet amour souverain qui a tout commandé dans l'oeuvre du salut.

L'hymne nous fait comprendre que bien avant la venue du Christ sur la terre, cet amour s'était déployé dans le ciel. Le Père «nous a élus dans le Christ, dès avant la création du monde, pour que nous soyons saints et immaculés devant son regard, dans l'amour; il nous a prédestinés à la filiation adoptive à son égard, par Jésus Christ, selon la disposition bienveillante de sa volonté à la louange de gloire de sa grâce, dont il nous a comblés en son Bien-Aimé» (Ep 1, 4-6).

A l'origine, il y a donc eu un acte d'amour du Père à l'égard de tous ceux qu'il prédestinait à être ses fils dans son Fils Jésus. Tous ont été «élus», c'est-à-dire aimés personnellement, et en totale gratuité, puisque cet amour s'est porté vers eux avant la création. Cette «élection» n'implique aucune discrimination; elle souligne simplement une attitude de faveur envers des personnes avant même leur existence, attitude qui a uniquement pour motif l'absolue générosité d'un amour paternel qui veut se donner des fils dans le Fils unique.

De ce qui s'est passé à l'origine, on peut formuler des conséquences importantes pour la vie actuelle de l'humanité. Si l'amour du Père, indépendamment de tout titre ou mérite de notre part, s'est porté sur chacun de nous avant la création du monde, cet amour ne peut manquer d'être présent à tout moment de notre existence et de nous guider dans l'accomplissement de notre authentique destinée, qui est une destinée essentiellement filiale. A travers toutes les difficultés que nous pouvons rencontrer, nous gardons la certitude de l'amour immuable du Père, qui nous vient de l'éternité et s'attache à tous nos pas. Cet amour, que nous n'avons nullement mérité, est devenu inséparable de notre existence quotidienne. Il confère une dignité supérieure à toute personne, si pauvre et si humble soit-elle.

En se référant à la première origine de toute l'oeuvre du salut, l'hymne nous invite à regarder la création du monde comme animée par l'intention du Père qui, étant Père d'un Fils unique, a voulu devenir le Père d'innombrables fils. Lorsque le Père a créé l'univers, il avait déjà décidé cette nouvelle paternité et il désirait en assurer la réalisation. On peut donc affirmer que si le monde existe, c'est parce que le Père, dans son éternité, a désiré être notre Père à tous. Le but de la création est la formation de la famille du Père, c'est-à-dire de la communauté universelle des fils dans le Fils unique, communauté rassemblée dans l'amour du Père.

La prédestination que l'hymne met en lumière, et qui vient du choix éternel du Père, a un sens exclusivement positif et favorable, puisque c'est la prédestination de l'humanité à la filiation divine. Le concept de prédestination a parfois reçu, dans l'histoire doctrinale, un sens négatif, celui d'une prédestination de certains à la damnation. Ce sens est exclu par l'intention du Père qui est celle d'un amour qui s'étend à tous et veut offrir à tous la dignité et le bonheur de la filiation divine. La prédestination signifie la décision éternelle, antérieure au temps de l'univers, d'assigner aux hommes la plus haute destinée en leur faisant partager la filiation et la vie du Christ.

Selon le terme employé dans l'hymne, la volonté divine, celle du Père, est caractérisée par une «disposition bienveillante»[6]. Souvent le terme a été traduit comme «bon plaisir» de cette volonté. Mais s'il est vrai qu'il s'agit d'une volonté souveraine, absolument maîtresse d'elle-même, le terme comporte plus exactement le sens d'une attitude bienveillante. A l'origine s'affirme d'une manière toute gratuite la bienveillance du Père qui constitue la suprême garantie de notre présent et de notre avenir. Le regard du Père, qui trop souvent a été interprété comme un regard redoutable, est en fait un regard foncièrement bienveillant. La puissance qui est la sienne et qui est réellement sans limites, a suscité de nombreuses craintes; mais elle s'est déployée dans le sens d'une bienveillance qui écarte tous les obstacles dans l'accomplissement des desseins les plus favorables à l'épanouissement de la vie humaine.

Par cette bienveillance s'explique la richesse de la grâce qui nous a été accordée. L'hymne adressé au Père met l'accent sur l'abondance des «bénédictions spirituelles», plus particulièrement sur la profusion de grâce qui nous a comblés à la suite du sacrifice rédempteur: «Dans le Fils bien-aimé nous trouvons la rédemption par son sang, le pardon des transgressions, selon la richesse de sa grâce, qu'il nous a prodiguée, en toute sagesse et intelligence» (Ep 1, 7-8).

Le sacrifice du Christ a obtenu le pardon des transgressions, mais l'effet de l'oeuvre rédemptrice ne s'est pas limité à

---

[6] Le terme «eudokia» se trouve également dans l'hymne d'action de grâces de Jésus, en Lc 10, 21 et Mt 11, 26, avec le sens de «bienveillance». Cf. GALOT, *Découvrir le Père*, 142s.

ce pardon: la grâce, dans sa richesse, signifie plus que la simple rémission des fautes. On pourrait entendre le salut en un sens minimum, la libération de l'assujettissement au mal. La grâce apporte bien davantage: elle communique une nouvelle vie, la vie de ceux qui sont devenus dans le Christ fils du Père et qui jouissent de tous les bienfaits de cette filiation.

C'est pourquoi l'évangélisation a pour mission de répandre l'abondance de la grâce. Elle ne pourrait se contenter de vouloir procurer un minimum, la délivrance du joug du péché. Elle est chargée de faire bénéficier tous les hommes de la richesse de la vie spirituelle procurée par le Christ, telle qu'elle avait été prévue et voulue par le Père. Elle doit donc faire connaître et faire apprécier cette richesse. Elle doit être animée de l'enthousiasme avec lequel l'hymne de la lettre aux Ephésiens expose la restauration de l'univers comme objectif du plan souverain du Père.

Par-dessus tout, la mission évangélisatrice est destinée à mettre sans cesse en lumière la bienveillance du Père, bienveillance universelle qui se manifeste à l'égard de tous les hommes et qui s'étend à tous les aspects de la vie humaine. C'est une vérité qui souvent a quelque difficulté à entrer dans l'intelligence humaine et à influencer tous ses jugements. Seule la conviction de cette bienveillance peut donner un fondement solide à l'espérance et inspirer un regard optimiste sur le monde et les événements. C'est la bienveillance qui a été révélée par le Christ lorsqu'il tournait ses regards vers le Père et lorsqu'il invitait ses disciples à entrer dans le mystère de cette révélation. Seule la bienveillance du Père permet une juste interprétation de l'existence humaine et de sa valeur.

Bienveillance du Père dans le drame du péché

Une des propriétés caractéristiques de Jésus dans sa mission de prédication fut la bienveillance qu'il témoignait aux pécheurs. Cette bienveillance surprenait ceux qui avaient été éduqués dans la religion juive et qui, en voulant prendre le parti de Dieu, tendaient à condamner les pécheurs; cette condamnation se manifestait notamment par un refus d'avoir des contacts sociaux avec eux: les pécheurs étaient mis au ban de la société.

Hardiment Jésus réagissait contre cette exclusion: il n'hésitait pas à fréquenter les pécheurs, à leur offrir sa sympathie et son amitié. Il s'efforçait de les convertir; sa visite à Zachée, un chef des publicains, est l'exemple de la démarche entreprise auprès de quelqu'un qui était considéré comme un grand pécheur et qui a changé de conduite, séduit par la bienveillance du Maître.

Accusé d'être l'ami des publicains et des pécheurs, Jésus répond par des paraboles qui montrent la valeur de la miséricorde. La plus significative est la parabole du fils prodigue, qui mériterait d'être plutôt appelée parabole du père miséricordieux. Dans cette parabole se trouve le portrait le plus saisissant du Père: il y a là, dans cette représentation imagée, un sommet de la révélation.

La parabole débute par une description du péché. On observe que cette description situe le péché dans le cadre de relations d'un fils avec son père. Souvent, le péché a été souligné dans sa gravité comme offense de la créature au Créateur. Intentionnellement, Jésus veut montrer dans le péché une offense qui a un caractère filial: il s'agit d'un fils qui veut s'éloigner de son père. Il fait comprendre la blessure infligée au coeur du Père. Le jeune homme réclame à son père sa part de fortune afin de pouvoir le quitter et de dépenser l'argent comme il l'entend. C'est l'acte du pécheur qui, avec les biens reçus du Père, veut vivre loin de lui et se procurer tout ce qu'il désire. L'acte apparaît ainsi comme un outrage à l'amour paternel qui, dans sa générosité, ne veut priver le fils d'aucun des biens qui lui appartiennent. La gravité du péché se mesure à la grandeur de l'amour paternel qui se voit bafoué.

On pourrait se demander cependant, dans le cadre de la parabole, pourquoi le père acquiesce si facilement à la requête de son fils, tout en sachant qu'il commet une lourde erreur et se prépare à dépenser l'argent de la façon la plus insensée. La première réponse est dans les coutumes ou institutions, qui garantissent au fils sa part de fortune. Une seconde réponse, plus éclairante, vient de la manière d'agir du Père, qui dans son amour veut sauvegarder la liberté de son fils parce qu'il veut de sa part un libre attachement: il ne désire pas contraindre son fils à demeurer près de lui comme un esclave. Il laisse partir son enfant en espérant que plus tard il reviendra librement à lui.

Le Père ne refuse donc pas ni n'enlève la liberté à ceux qui veulent le quitter. Lorsqu'on pose la question: «Pourquoi y a-t-il tant de mal dans le monde?», la réponse ne peut être donnée que dans la considération de la liberté humaine. Le Père n'est pas responsable de ce mal; c'est la personne humaine, dans l'exercice de sa liberté, qui commet le péché. En créant des personnes douées de liberté, le Père a requis de leur part un amour plus spontané et plus profond. La liberté est conservée, en ceux qui s'égarent, afin de permettre une conversion à l'amour, et en ceux qui demeurent fidèles, pour donner plus de valeur à leur fidélité.

Dans la parabole, la dégradation de l'état de péché est évoquée d'une manière suggestive. Le jeune homme qui a abandonné son père pour mener une vie où il se promettait bien des plaisirs est vite déçu par l'expérience qu'il a tentée. Lorsqu'il a tout dépensé, il est réduit à la misère. Souffrant de la privation, il est contraint de «se mettre au service d'un des habitants de la contrée, qui l'envoya dans ses champs garder les cochons» (Lc 15, 15). Pour un juif, garder les cochons ne pouvait être que le plus dégradant de tous les métiers, puisque le porc était considéré comme un animal impur.

En outre, la déchéance personnelle s'exprime par une autre notation: «Il aurait bien voulu se remplir le ventre des caroubes que mangeaient les cochons, mais personne ne lui en donnait» (Lc 15, 16). Non seulement il était tourmenté par la faim, mais il ne désirait plus que l'aliment des porcs, et il se heurtait à l'impossibilité de s'en procurer: le monde du péché est un monde dur, égoïste, cruel pour ceux qui souffrent.

C'est un monde tout à fait à l'opposé du monde tel que l'a voulu le Père. La comparaison s'impose au fils prodigue qui a tout perdu et qui commence à comprendre qu'il n'y a de solution à sa misère actuelle que dans un retour chez le père: «Combien d'ouvriers de mon père ont du pain en abondance, et moi je suis ici à mourir de faim!». C'est le souvenir de la maison du père qui suscite la conversion. Le jeune homme décide de s'en retourner, avec des sentiments qui font contraste avec ceux de prétention orgueilleuse qui avaient marqué son départ: il veut demander à son père de l'accueillir comme un de ses ouvriers.

Il prépare avec soin ce qu'il dira dans la rencontre délicate avec son père, et tout d'abord l'aveu de la faute: «Père, j'ai péché contre le ciel et contre toi» (Lc 15, 18). Dans la perspective de la parabole, qui est celle de la religion juive, l'offense est faite au ciel, c'est-à-dire à Dieu, et également au père; dans la nouvelle perspective de la révélation, Dieu et le Père s'identifient, et il semble que Jésus ait voulu attirer l'attention sur l'aveu de la faute commise contre celui qui est le Père. C'est plus particulièrement au Père qu'il faut demander pardon.

Mais ce n'est pas l'attitude du jeune homme qui forme l'enseignement essentiel de la parabole; c'est plutôt l'attitude du père. Nous pouvons y reconnaître les traits distinctifs du pardon accordé par le Père céleste à ses fils repentants.

D'abord, l'empressement du Père à pardonner est remarquable. Le Père désire donner ce pardon bien plus que son fils ne désire le recevoir. Il n'attend pas que son fils vienne jusqu'à lui. Selon la parabole, le père a aperçu son fils lorsqu'il était encore loin; c'est donc qu'il l'attendait depuis longtemps avec un intense désir de le revoir. Et aussitôt qu'il le voit, il se précipite vers lui. Nous savons ainsi que le Père céleste nous attend toujours avec sa ferveur paternelle lorsque nous nous éloignons de lui. Il désire, bien plus que nous, nous accorder son pardon et nous réconcilier avec son amour.

Ensuite, la rencontre, qui aurait pu être orageuse si le Père avait voulu manifester des sentiments de colère à la suite de l'offense qui lui avait été faite, ne fait paraître de sa part qu'une grande compassion pour la misère de son fils.

Non seulement il n'y a aucun mouvement de recul ni de préoccupation de garder une certaine distance à l'égard de celui qui revient, mais le Père «courut se jeter à son cou et l'embrassa longuement». Il ne met aucune réserve dans l'affection qu'il témoigne à son fils. Il montre qu'il ne l'aime pas moins qu'auparavant et que la blessure qu'il a reçue dans l'offense n'a fait que rendre son amour plus ardent.

Le Père n'adresse aucun reproche à son fils. Il aurait pu lui faire la leçon, prendre l'attitude d'un juge qui souligne la gravité de la faute commise. Il s'abstient de tout retour sur le passé. D'après le récit de la parabole, il ne laisse même pas au fils la possibilité de dire tout ce qu'il a préparé pour la rencontre. Le Père montre qu'il désire oublier l'offense commise et que seule lui importe la relation d'amour qui s'est renouée avec son fils.

Loin d'accueillir son fils comme un ouvrier, il veut l'accueillir en fils. Il ordonne que lui soient rendus immédiatement tout ce qui manifestait sa dignité de fils: le plus beau vêtement, l'anneau au doigt et les chaussures aux pieds. C'est le signe de la volonté du Père que tout ce qui appartenait à l'état de péché soit définitivement effacé et qu'une nouvelle vie filiale puisse reprendre en plénitude.

Par là s'exprime la vérité que le pardon divin a une efficacité à laquelle ne peut prétendre le pardon humain: c'est un pardon qui transforme la personne, qui supprime son état de péché et l'élève à une nouvelle vie d'amitié avec le Christ et avec le Père. Le pardon humain implique seulement que la personne offensée renonce à toute vengeance et veuille se réconcilier avec l'auteur de l'offense; il ne peut par lui-même changer les dispositions de celui-ci. Lorsque le Père pardonne, il fait passer celui qui est pardonné de l'état de péché à l'état de grâce et lui communique un souffle nouveau de vie.

La générosité et la sincérité du pardon apparaissent encore plus vivement dans la joie avec laquelle le Père accueille son fils. Le pardon est accordé volontiers, et jugé digne d'être célébré par un banquet de fête. Le Père veut partager sa joie avec tous: «Amenez le veau gras, tuez-le, mangeons et festoyons, car mon fils que voilà était mort et il est revenu à la vie; il était perdu et il est retrouvé» (Lc 15, 23-24).

La révélation de cette joie apporte un complément à la révélation de la tristesse infligée au Père par le péché. Cette double révélation montre à quel point le Père est proche de ceux qu'il traite et aime comme ses fils. Certes, le Père possède une immutabilité divine qui appartient à sa nature éternelle et demeure au-dessus de toutes les variations qui interviennent dans ses relations avec les créatures. Cependant, dans le domaine de ces relations, son amour paternel se déploie librement et peut éprouver tristesse ou joie selon les dispositions et la conduite de chacun de ses enfants.

L'évangélisation ne peut manquer de présenter le Père dans sa proximité à l'égard de tous, dans la tristesse qu'il éprouve par les péchés commis dans le monde, dans la bonté et dans la joie de son pardon.

Bienveillance et sollicitude du Père pour nos besoins: la Providence

La bienveillance du Père à notre égard s'est avant tout manifestée dans les décisions prises concernant notre destinée, dans notre prédestination à la filiation divine, dans l'envoi du Christ comme notre Rédempteur. Comme elle s'étend à tous les domaines et aspects de notre existence, elle concerne nos besoins de tout genre. La sollicitude du Père qui pourvoit à ces besoins prend le nom de Providence[7].

Le mot «Providence» ne se rencontre pas dans les évangiles, mais il avait été employé dans le livre de la Sagesse pour signifier l'action divine qui assure à un vaisseau l'aboutissement au port: «Ce vaisseau, c'est la soif du gain qui l'a inventé, c'est la sagesse artisane qui l'a construit, mais c'est ta Providence, ô Père, qui le guide, toi qui as ouvert un chemin jusque dans la mer et sur les flots un sentier assuré, montrant que tu peux sauver de tout danger, même si l'on prend la mer sans aucune compétence» (14, 2-4). L'action de la Providence qui guide le vaisseau sur les flots rappelle le souvenir de l'action divine qui, lors de l'Exode, avait ouvert un chemin dans la mer pour assurer le salut du peuple (cf. Is 43, 16). C'est une action protectrice qui est plus spécialement attribuée au Père et qui fait penser à la vie humaine, mystérieusement conduite par lui en toute sécurité, au terme de son voyage.

Le terme «Providence» est d'origine grecque, utilisé notamment dans la philosophie stoïcienne. On comprend que Jésus ne s'en serve pas. Mais il en exprime l'idée avec force, plus spécialement dans des recommandations qu'il adresse à ses disciples. En effet, ceux qui l'accompagnent en ayant tout quitté pour le suivre peuvent se laisser gagner par certaines préoccupations concernant leurs besoins en nourriture et en vêtement. Ils ont fait confiance à Jésus pour une vie à son service, mais cette vie peut leur sembler une aventure qui manque de garan-

---

[7] Concernant la Providence cf. J. GALOT, *Notre Père qui est amour*, Saint-Maur 1998, 119-139 ; *Découvrir le Père*, 132-157.

tie. Peut-être le Maître a-t-il entendu les réflexions de certains disciples qui manifestaient leurs inquiétudes; mais même lorsqu'elles ne s'expriment pas, Jésus connaît suffisamment les siens pour savoir ce qui les agite et il veut leur procurer la garantie qu'ils désirent.

C'est une parole d'autorité et de révélation qu'il leur adresse: «Je vous dis». Il commence ainsi par en souligner la valeur, car il connaît l'importance que peut prendre ce problème dans l'existence de ses disciples et le trouble qu'il peut provoquer dans leur pensée et dans leur activité. «Ne vous inquiétez pas pour votre vie de ce que vous mangerez, ni pour votre corps de quoi vous le vêtirez» (Mt 6, 25). Toute inquiétude doit être bannie, premièrement au nom d'un motif de bon sens: «La vie n'est-elle pas plus que la nourriture et le corps plus que le vêtement?». Si le Père a donné la vie et le corps, n'assurera-t-il pas le don de tout ce qui est nécessaire à leur entretien? Tout repose donc sur la conviction de la bonté du Père, qui s'est engagé lui-même à procurer aux disciples leur subsistance en leur prodiguant à chaque instant le don de la vie.

Pour faire mieux comprendre la sollicitude toujours présente du Père, Jésus ajoute certaines constatations fort simples qui en confirment l'évidence: «Voyez les oiseaux du ciel: ils ne sèment ni ne moissonnent ni ne recueillent en des greniers, et votre Père céleste les nourrit! Ne valez-vous pas plus qu'eux?». Jésus livre ainsi son interprétation de ce qui se produit dans la nature; au lieu de se borner à dire que les oiseaux cherchent et trouvent leur nourriture, il affirme que c'est le Père céleste qui les nourrit, et dans cette action il reconnaît une garantie donnée aux hommes qu'eux aussi, et à bien plus forte raison, reçoivent du Père céleste leur nourriture. Il révèle l'action invisible de la Providence, partout présente dans l'existence humaine.

Il ajoute une remarque sur l'impuissance de l'être humain à se procurer à lui-même la vie: par ses inquiétudes il ne pourrait s'assurer le prolongement de son existence: «Qui d'entre vous peut, en s'en inquiétant, ajouter une seule coudée à la longueur de sa vie?». Personne ne peut donc prétendre assumer un rôle qui est réservé à la bonté du Père, et personne ne peut attendre, de ses propres inquiétudes, un effet bienfaisant.

Pour le vêtement, Jésus recourt à une autre constatation, non moins suggestive. «Et du vêtement, pourquoi vous inquiéter? Observez les lis des champs, comme ils poussent: ils ne peinent ni ne filent. Or je vous dis que Salomon lui-même, dans toute sa gloire, n'a pas été vêtu comme l'un d'eux. Que si Dieu revêt de la sorte l'herbe des champs, qui est aujourd'hui et demain sera jetée au four, ne fera-t-il pas bien plus pour vous, gens de peu de foi!».

Expressément, parmi les fleurs, Jésus choisit les «lis des champs», une fleur toute simple et fort commune, petite anémone de belle couleur pourpre. Cette couleur pouvait évoquer la pourpre du roi le plus glorieux d'Israël, et la comparaison était à l'avantage de la fleur; le grand Salomon était moins bien vêtu que la petite fleur, parce que celle-ci avait reçu du Père sa parure. Jésus nous invite par là à reconnaître dans les beautés de la nature l'oeuvre du Père. Ces beautés ne sont pas seulement celles de grands paysages mais également celles des fleurs les plus humbles et plus généralement de tout ce qui pourrait paraître fort ordinaire, fort commun. Il s'agit notamment de découvrir dans toutes les beautés naturelles le don que le Père adresse à ses fils pour décorer et réjouir leur existence.

Cependant, ce que le Christ veut surtout inculquer par l'allusion à la beauté des lis des champs, c'est la confiance en le vêtement donné par la Providence du Père. Si le Père prend tant de soin pour vêtir une fleur destinée à être bien vite jetée au four, et pour la vêtir mieux que Salomon, comment ne procurerait-il pas le vêtement à ceux qui à ses yeux ont une valeur beaucoup plus haute que n'importe quelle fleur?

Pour rejeter tout motif d'inquiétude, Jésus affirme la présence d'un Père qui est parfaitement au courant de nos besoins: «Votre Père céleste sait que vous avez besoin de tout cela» (Mt 6, 32). La confiance doit donc être absolue, puisque de la part du Père il ne peut y avoir aucune ignorance des besoins à satisfaire; il ne peut non plus y avoir aucune négligence dans l'aide apportée, étant donné que le Père met sa toute-puissance au service de ses fils. L'appellation «gens de peu de foi» montre que même de la part des disciples la foi en la Providence était encore trop faible.

Tous les chrétiens sont certes invités à développer en eux cette foi en la Providence; elle est encore plus nécessaire chez ceux qui vouent leur activité au royaume du Christ. Cette foi permet en effet un dévouement plus libre de toute préoccupation, une activité plus efficace: «Cherchez d'abord le royaume de Dieu et sa justice, et tout cela vous sera donné par surcroît». Ceux qui consacrent leurs forces à l'évangélisation sont assurés de recevoir du Père tout ce qui est nécessaire à leur entretien.

On s'est parfois demandé si la Providence intervient dans tous les détails de l'existence ou si elle en assure seulement les besoins les plus essentiels ou les aspects les plus importants. La réponse nous est clairement faite à ce sujet par une parole évangélique: «Même vos cheveux sont tous comptés!» (Mt 10, 30; Lc 12, 7). Il n'y a aucun cheveu qui ne tombe de notre tête sans la volonté du Père. Cette volonté régit donc notre existence dans les plus minimes détails; la chute d'un cheveu est l'exemple d'un détail sans importance. L'amour du Père pour nous est si vaste et si complet que rien ne lui échappe dans le déroulement de notre vie.

La foi nous fait discerner les signes de la Providence; plus particulièrement elle nous aide à découvrir, même dans les difficultés et les épreuves, les manifestations d'une bonté paternelle toujours présente. Le Père n'a pas épargné à son Fils unique les douleurs de la vie humaine, et il associe tous ses fils à la destinée du Christ, destinée essentiellement caractérisée par le passage de la souffrance à la joie. La Providence ne nous met pas à l'abri des épreuves, mais le Père nous y accompagne et en assure l'heureux aboutissement.

Le Père, garant de l'efficacité de la prière

En nous révélant la présence universelle du Père dans notre vie par la Providence, Jésus a également attiré notre attention sur le rôle du Père dans l'efficacité de la prière. Cette efficacité est affirmée de la façon la plus catégorique: «Demandez et l'on vous donnera; cherchez et vous trouverez; frappez et l'on vous ouvrira. Car quiconque demande reçoit; qui cherche trouve; et à qui frappe on ouvrira» (Mt 7, 7-8; Lc 11, 9-10). Les affirmations sont répétées, pour un accent plus fort sur leur valeur universelle. Elles sont surprenantes, car elles semblent aller à l'encontre de la distinction que font souvent ceux qui prient, entre prières exaucées et prières non exaucées. Le principe affirmé est que toutes les prières sont exaucées.

Ce principe se justifie par une considération sur l'amour du Père, qui ne peut manquer de répondre aux demandes de ses enfants. «Qui d'entre vous, quand son fils lui demande du pain, lui remettra une pierre? Ou, s'il lui demande un poisson, lui remettra-t-il un serpent? Si donc vous, même mauvais, sachez donner de bonnes choses à vos enfants, combien plus votre Père qui est dans les cieux donnera-t-il de bonnes choses à ceux qui l'en prient!» (Mt 7, 9-11).

On sent que Jésus réagit contre les reproches souvent adressés au Père: le Père céleste est souvent accusé d'une dureté qu'on ne trouve chez aucun père humain, si mauvais soit-il. Aucun en effet ne voudrait donner une pierre à son fils lorsqu'il demande du pain, profiter de la ressemblance entre certaine pierres avec le pain pour se décharger de la tâche du père de procurer du pain à ses enfants. Aucun ne voudrait non plus donner un serpent au lieu d'un poisson, même si les serpents que prenaient les pêcheurs dans le lac de Tibériade n'étaient pas venimeux. Encore moins, selon l'image rapportée par Luc, donner un scorpion – ou un crottin – au lieu d'un oeuf[8].

Le Père céleste ne peut donner que «de bonnes choses» à ceux qui lui adressent leur prière. La réponse à toutes les demandes est donc positive, et en ce sens toute prière est exaucée. Cependant donner de bonnes choses comporte nécessairement un choix ou une vérification. Il peut se faire que la chose demandée ne soit pas bonne, qu'elle soit inutile ou nocive, sans que celui qui la demande s'en rende compte. Dans ce cas, le Père ne peut l'accorder. Il répond à la demande en donnant quelque chose de meilleur, en accord avec le bon désir qui inspire la demande.

Selon la version de Luc, c'est l'Esprit Saint que le Père céleste donnera à ceux qui l'en prient (11, 13). Cet Esprit Saint ne

---

[8] L'image d'un scorpion donné à la place d'un oeuf signifierait une chose dangereuse, nocive, ce qui ne serait guère en harmonie avec les deux autres images, qui signifiaient une chose inutile, sans valeur, donnée au lieu de la chose demandée. Selon une hypothèse présentée par J. VARA (dans *Salmanticensis* 30 (1983) 225-229), le texte primitif aurait pu être non pas *skorpion* mais *koprion*, crottin.

peut être que bonne chose; la demande qui se porte sur lui ne peut manquer d'être satisfaite.

De la volonté du Père de répondre à toutes les demandes, le Christ n'a pas seulement souligné le principe et indiqué l'intention d'amour; il l'a manifestée par son propre comportement en répondant volontiers à toutes les requêtes qui lui étaient adressées.

Le Père, modèle de perfection dans l'amour

Dans le chemin d'amour qu'il a parcouru sur la terre, Jésus a déclaré suivre la voie que lui traçait le Père. Ainsi, lorsqu'il opérait des miracles le jour du sabbat, il répondait aux critiques en invoquant l'exemple du Père qui, même le jour du sabbat, continue son oeuvre créatrice et salvatrice: «Mon Père travaille toujours et moi aussi je travaille» (Jn 5, 17). Il corrigeait ainsi l'affirmation du repos de Dieu le septième jour, dans le récit de la création (Gn 2, 2-3), de manière à montrer davantage l'amour incessant du Père pour l'humanité.

Il énonçait sa ligne de conduite par une conformité totale avec le comportement du Père: «En vérité, en vérité je vous le dis, le Fils ne peut faire de lui-même rien qu'il ne voie faire au Père: ce que fait celui-ci, le Fils le fait pareillement» (Jn 5, 19). Entre le Père et le Fils il y avait l'union la plus intime fondée sur le même être divin, au point que Jésus pouvait dire: «Le Père et moi, nous sommes un» (Jn 10, 30). Cette unité d'être avait pour conséquence une parfaite harmonie dans l'action, avec une complète ressemblance dans la manière d'agir.

C'est aussi la raison pour laquelle Jésus a pu répondre à Philippe, qui désirait que le Père lui soit montré: «Qui m'a vu, a vu le Père» (Jn 14, 9). Le Fils incarné a montré le Père non seulement par son enseignement mais par toute sa conduite. Pour connaître le vrai visage du Père, il importe donc de le saisir à travers le visage du Christ.

La réflexion doctrinale ne l'a pas toujours fait suffisamment. Dans l'interprétation que beaucoup ont donnée du drame de la Passion, l'attitude du Père a été représentée en opposition avec celle du Fils. On n'avait pas assez compris que le Père a été le premier à s'engager dans le sacrifice et qu'il n'était pas seulement celui qui imposait l'épreuve à son Fils. Il a été, dans le mystère rédempteur, le premier à souffrir[9]. C'est par la voie douloureuse, où il envoyait son Fils au supplice, qu'il a manifesté à l'humanité le sommet de son amour. Le Père a été le premier modèle de l'amour rédempteur.

Ce modèle, Jésus l'a proposé à l'imitation de ses disciples, lorsqu'il leur a dit: «Vous, vous serez parfaits comme votre Père céleste est parfait» (Mt 5, 45)[10]. Il n'aurait pas été possible d'indiquer un modèle plus élevé, ni par conséquent une règle de conduite plus exigeante. Seul le Christ pouvait rendre ses disciples capables de s'engager dans la voie de cette imitation et de se fixer comme objectif à atteindre l'amour le plus parfait.

Selon l'évangile de Luc, le modèle que constitue le Père et qui est livré à notre imitation est plus précisément celui de l'amour miséricordieux: «Soyez miséricordieux comme votre Père est miséricordieux» (6, 36). Cet évangile présente le plus haut exemple de miséricorde du Père dans la parabole du fils prodigue.

Dans cette même orientation de miséricorde et d'indulgence se situe le précepte de l'amour envers les ennemis. Jésus engage dans l'énoncé de ce précepte toute son autorité: «Moi, je vous dis: aimez vos ennemis, priez pour vos persécuteurs, étant donné que vous êtes fils de votre Père des cieux, lui qui fait lever son soleil sur les méchants et sur les bons, et tomber sa pluie sur les justes et sur les pervers» (Mt 5, 45). Le Père n'opère aucune discrimination entre ceux qui reçoivent ses bienfaits: il donne soleil et pluie à tous, amis et ennemis. Son amour se porte donc avec une réelle bienveillance sur ceux qui le repoussent comme sur ceux qui adhèrent à lui. Tous sont invités à suivre la même voie d'un sincère amour pour les ennemis.

---

[9] Sur l'engagement du Père dans le sacrifice rédempteur et sur le mystère de la souffrance divine, cf. J. GALOT, *Dieu souffre-t-il?*, Paris 1976; *Notre Père qui est amour*, 85-112.

[10] La traduction «étant donné que» semble préférable à «afin que». La particule grecque *opôs* correspond à la particule araméenne *di* qui peut avoir un sens de causalité ou de finalité. Le contexte requiert ici la causalité: parce qu'ils sont fils du Père, les chrétiens doivent aimer leurs ennemis. Cf. C.A. FRANCO MARTÍNEZ, *Jesucristo, su persona y su obra, en la carta a los Hebreos. Lengua e cristología en Heb 2, 9-10; 5, 1-10; 4, 14 y 9, 27-28*, Madrid 1992, 131-143.

Dans cet amour est incluse la générosité du pardon, que le Père exige pour pouvoir faire goûter toute le joie de son pardon: «Si vous pardonnez aux autres leurs manquements, votre Père des cieux vous pardonnera aussi; mais si vous ne pardonnez pas aux hommes, votre Père non plus ne vous pardonnera pas vos manquements» (Mt 6, 14-15). Le pardon qui imite celui du Père doit être un pardon sans limites, «jusqu'à soixante-dix fois sept fois» (Mt 18-22)[11].

La perfection de l'amour du Père doit donc se refléter dans le visage et la conduite de tous ses fils. La véritable évangélisation est celle qui réussit à imprimer dans les coeurs humains le modèle d'amour du Père.

Culte nouveau et prière nouvelle

Dans le dialogue avec la Samaritaine, Jésus annonce l'instauration d'un nouveau culte. A la femme qui aurait voulu opposer comme barrière infranchissable la divergence entre le culte rendu à Jérusalem et l'adoration sur le mont Garizim il répond: «Crois-moi, femme, l'heure vient où ce n'est ni sur cette montagne ni à Jérusalem que vous adorerez le Père... L'heure vient, et c'est maintenant, où les vrais adorateurs adoreront le Père en esprit et en vérité, car ce sont là les adorateurs tels que les veut le Père» (Jn 4, 21.23).

Le nouveau culte consistera donc dans l'adoration du Père. Jésus ne parle pas seulement d'adoration, d'une adoration normalement adressée à Dieu, mais plus précisément d'une adoration adressée au Père. Ce Père, étant le Père de tous, fonde un culte qui dépasse les barrières nationales dans lesquelles s'enfermaient beaucoup de religions. Il offre une garantie suprême de l'universalité du culte: Père unique de l'humanité, il unit tous ceux qui lui adressent leurs hommages.

---

[11] L'expression est d'autant plus saisissante qu'elle avait été employée, au livre de la Genèse, pour signifier une vengeance illimitée (4, 24). Elle montre comment un Dieu auquel on attribuait la vengeance cède la place à un Père dont l'amour s'ouvre par le pardon le plus large.

Le culte qui fait converger vers lui la vénération et les prières n'est plus exclusivement lié à un sanctuaire national; c'est un culte «en esprit et en vérité», c'est-à-dire un culte de qualité essentiellement spirituelle, où s'exprime l'âme des hommes, et un culte qui consiste dans la vérité de la foi et de l'amour. Concrètement, pour la Samaritaine, c'est un culte qui réclame une profonde conversion, une nouvelle manière de vivre. Le don de l'«eau vive», c'est-à-dire de la vie de l'Esprit Saint, à la suite de la rencontre du Christ, permet d'assurer cette conversion, avec une nouvelle existence.

La vérité du culte rendu au Père se manifeste plus particulièrement dans une prière vraie et sincère: «Quand vous priez, n'imitez pas les hypocrites: ils aiment, pour faire leur prière, à se camper dans les synagogues et les carrefours, afin qu'on les voie. En vérité, je vous le dis, ils ont déjà leur récompense. Pour toi, quand tu pries, retire-toi dans ta chambre, ferme sur toi la porte, et prie ton Père, qui est là dans le secret; et ton Père, qui voit dans le secret, te le rendra» (Mt 6, 5-6). La présence secrète, invisible, du Père, assure donc la valeur de la prière.

La note caractéristique de la prière nouvelle consiste dans le fait qu'elle appelle le Père par son nom. Jésus avait été le premier à invoquer le Père sous le nom de «Abba». Il a désiré communiquer à ses disciples cette manière de prier. Nous connaissons les circonstances où il a été amené à donner cet enseignement. Un disciple qui avait d'abord appris avec Jean-Baptiste à prier avait eu l'occasion d'observer Jésus en prière, et il aurait désiré prier comme lui. Après que Jésus eut terminé sa prière, il lui demanda: «Seigneur, apprends-nous à prier, comme Jean l'a appris à ses disciples». La réponse vient: «Quand vous priez, dites: Père...» (Lc 11, 1-2) . C'est alors qu'il enseigne la prière que nous connaissons comme étant le «notre Père», selon le début rapporté par l'évangile de Matthieu (6, 9)[12].

---

[12] Pour l'analyse du contenu de la prière enseignée par Jésus, cf., outre les ouvrages de CARMIGNAC, *Recherches sur le «Notre Père»*, et de SABUGAL, *Abba! ... La oración del Señor*, J. GALOT, *Abba Père*, Louvain 1990, 23-60; *Notre Père qui est amour*, 141-205.

La recommandation initiale, sous la forme rapportée par Luc, doit être spécialement retenue: Jésus nous exhorte à dire, au début de notre prière: «Père»; il a employé le mot araméen «Abba». Il souhaitait partager avec ses disciples l'usage de cette invocation, «Abba», où s'exprimait toute sa ferveur filiale, en même temps que le révélation de sa filiation divine. Nous savons que l'exhortation a eu des échos dans la manière de prier de certains disciples, puisque deux fois dans ses lettres Paul fait allusion à une coutume de prononcer le mot «Abba» sous l'inspiration de l'Esprit Saint (Ga 4, 6; Rm 8, 15), coutume considérée comme attestation de filiation divine.

On peut souhaiter que l'invitation du Christ à commencer la prière par l'invocation «Père» soit de plus en plus suivie dans la pratique chrétienne. L'évangélisation comporte la mission d'apprendre à tous prier comme Jésus lui-même a prié: tous à doivent être exhortés à prononcer le nom du Père avec un amour qui ressemble à celui du Sauveur.

The Absoluteness of Jesus Christ and of Christianity
(in the perspective of the third millennium)

MARIASUSAI DHAVAMONY

INTRODUCTION

"Contemplating the mystery of the incarnation of the Son of God, the Church prepares to cross the threshold of the third millennium. Never more than at this time do we feel the need to make our own the Apolstle's hymn of praise and thanksgiving: "Blessed be the God and Father of our Lord Jesus Christ, who has blessed us in Christ with every spiritual blessing in the heavenly places, even as he chose us in him before the foundation of the world that we should be holy and blameless before him. He destined us in love to be his sons through Jesus Christ, according to the purpose of his will... For he has made known to us in all wisdom and insight the mystery of his will, according to his purpose which he set forth in Christ as a plan for the fulness of time, to unite all things in him, things in heaven and things on earth" (Eph. 1.3-5; 9-10).

These words clearly indicate that in Jesus Christ the history of salvation finds its culmination and ultimate meaning. In him, we have all received "grace upon grace" (Jn 1.16), having been reconciled with the Father. (Cf. Rom. 5.10; 2 Cor. 5.18).

The birth of Jesus at Bethlehem is not an event which can be consigned to the past. The whole of human history in fact stands in reference to him: our own time and the future of the world are illumined by his presence. He is "the living One" (Rev. 1.18), "who is, who was, and who is to come" (Rev. 1.4). Before him every knee must bend, in the heavens, on earth and under the earth, and every tongue proclaim that he is Lord (Cf. Phil. 2.10. In the encounter with Christ, every man discovers the mystery of his own life (GS 22).

Jesus is the genuine newness which surpasses all human expetations and such he remains for ever, from age to age. The incarnation of the Son of God and the salvation which he has accomplished by his death and resurrection are therefore the true criterion for evaluating all that happens in time and every effort to make life more human[1].

The significant message in the above citation is that the history of salvation finds its culmination and ultimate meaning in Jesus Christ. The redemptive incarnation is not an event of the past but the whole history of mankind is centred on it, being illumined by its presecnce. In the mystery of Christ is discovered the mystery of human life. Jesus remains the genuine newness for all times, fulfilling all human expectations; and therefore is the true criterion to evaluate the whole of history and of human progress. The person and work of Jesus Christ give the ultimate meaning and culmination to the history of salvation.

They constitute the genuine newness and the criterion to judge of the human history both secular and religious. This is just another way of bringing out the absolute character of Jesus Christ. In the same Document John Paul II indicates that the Jubilee can serve to advance mutual dialogue between Jews, Moslims and people of other religions; that the coming of the third millennium prompts the Christian community to lift its eyes of faith to embrace new horizons in proclaiming the Kingdom of God; to shed new light upon the missionary task of the Church in view of the demands of evanglization today. At the Second Vatican Council the Church became more deeply conscious both of the mystery which she herself is and of the apostolic mission entrusted to her by the Lord[2].

---

[1] JOHN PAUL II, Bull of Indiction of the Great Jubilee of the Year 2000. N. 1, *Catholic International*, Vol. 10 (1999), January, p. 15.
[2] Cf. N. 2 of the Bull of Indiction of the Great Jubilee of the year 2000.

1. Pluralism, relativism, dialogue

The problem of the absoluteness of Jesus Christ and of Christianity becomes significant because of the following reasons. We live in a period in which there is an acute awareness of religious, cultural, and social pluralism in the contemporary world. Religious pluralism is closely linked to cultural, social and political pluralism, for human life is not rigidly compartamentolized, there is interpenetration of religion, culture and society. Again, cultural and philosophical pluralism reflects different ways of thinking, judging and evaluating with regard to value systems of diverse peoples. Is there unity in diversity of cultures, religions and social systems. What is the Christian attitude to such a diversity of cultures, religions and social institutions? Cultural pluralism should not be confused with religious pluralism. Cultural pluralism is an attitude that welcomes different cultural ways of living and acting within a society as enrichment to human life. No culture by definition is inferior or superior to another. Christian faith enhances diversity in cultures. Though cultures are relative, total cultural relativism is problematic, since there are universal elements in different cultures. Besides, not all aspects of culture are morally or religiously acceptable. Sometimes cultural pluralism is used as an instrument to relativize faith commitments by raising doubts about universal norms.

A second phenomenon that is characteristic of the present-day society is relativism which is of various kinds: cultural, epistemological, religious, historical, and theological. Cultural relativism, when used in connection with religion considers each religion as an appropriate response to its cultural environment since it meets with the needs of each particular people. We do not understand here by cultural relativism cultural pluralism which is in itself legitimate. The problem arises when descriptive relativism of culture is identified with the normative relativism where right and wrong, good and bad, are determined by cultural norms. Epistemological relativism which concerns the nature and ground of knowledge denies that the absolute truth can be known. All religions contain different aspects of the truth and therefore are true for their adh-rents. Christian truth may be true for Christians but they should not assert that it is valid for all. Since no single religion has the monopoly of truth, relativism proposes the principle of complementarity in arriving at truth, for the sum total of particular truths has greater value and significance than one single truth. Truth is found in consensus or synthesis or even syncretism. Hence, exclusivity and uniqueness are considered intolerant and aggressive.

Relativism can denote a recognition of the fact that in all human thinking and in all human judgements there is of necessity an element of imperfection, which is less than absolute and final truth. As Prof. C.H. Dodd observes: Religious belief is, even more than scientific propositions, subject to relativity. The religious man like the man of science should be aware that the best statement that he can make to himself is nothing more than a very inadequate symbol of ultimate reality"[3]. Is relativism thus understood inconsistent with Christian faith? No Christian would wish to doubt the claim to the absolute and final quality of the historic revelation of God in Jesus Christ. Bishop William Temple maintained that "The whole significance of Christianity depends on its claim to be absolute and final"[4].

Nearly all great religions have made a claim to absolute finality.

Judaism makes such a claim on behalf of the Moseic Law: "God, the immutable, gave us an immutable Law. No other Law will be revealed by the Creator"[5].

Also Islam: "The Holy Q'uran claims that it came as a judge to decide the differences of the various religions, and as a perfect revelation of the Divine Will[6]. Hinduism makes also a similar claim: "The highest knowledge of ultimate truth and

---

[3] *The Authority of the Bible*, London, 1928, p. 20.
[4] *International Missionary Conference at Jerusalem Report*, 1928, Vol 1, p. 469.
[5] M. FRIEDLANDER, *A Textbook of the Jewish Religion*, London, 1896, pp. 45ff.
[6] MUHAMMAD ALI, *A Translation of the Holy Q'uran*, Lahore, 1928, p. xxviii.

reality was regarded as having been once for all declared in the Upanishads"[7]. Hence the problem arises on what ground can the absolute claim of Christianity for Jesus Christ be sustained?

Another type of religious relativism is held by the great religions in the sense that all religions are equally true and propose one universal religion for the whole of mankind. Mahatma Gandhi teaches: "The need of the moment is not one religion, but mutual respect and tolerance of the different religions... Any attempt to root out traditions, effects of heredity, etc., is not only bound to fail, but is a sacrilege. The soul of religions is one, but it is encased in a multitude of forms. The latter will persist to the end of time... Truth is the exclusive property of no single scripture[8]. "My position is that all the great religions are fundamentally equal"[9]. "I cannot ascribe exclusive divinity to Jesus. He is as divine as Krishna or Rama or Mahomed or Zoroaster"[10]. Buddhism also invites the Christian Church to abandon its exclusive claims and join in co-operation with other religions. "Whatever a man believes to be true, he will... naturally wish to share with his fellow-men[11].

Finally, historical realtivism holds that all historical events are relative. The study of history and the meeting of mankind have brought out the relativity and historical interconnections of all human institutions and undertakings; what was considered unique is met with parallels and what was absolute is tempered by historical dependece. Christianity is no exception to this rule. To what extent can Christians appreciate the indispensable role of the other religions in the history of salvation?

Lastly, we live in an age of dialogue which consists in reciprocal respect and esteem for human persons, their views and beliefs, their preferences and choices and calls for encoun-

---

[7] S.N. DAS GUPTA, *The History of Indian Philosophy*, Vol. 1, Cambridge, 1932, p. 41.
[8] M.K. GANDHI, *Christian Missions*, Ahmedabad, 1941, p. 34.
[9] Ibidem, p. 210.
[10] Ibidem, p. 170.
[11] *What is Buddhism?*, London, 1931, p. 181.

ters between different persons and communities to seek for solution to common problems, to discern and obtain what is true, just and good for the community. Dialogue is a Conciliar term (i.e., of the Second Vatican Council), which has been used in the Conciliar documents more than forty times. There is question of fraternal dialogue between Christians and Jews, of ecumenical dialogue, of dialogue with non-Christians, of loyal and prudent dialogue with all men in view of building one human society. We can indicate a typology of inter-religious dialogue as a hermeneutical key to interpret the role of Christ in the salvation of humanity.

a) According to some, an inter-religious dialogue should insist only on what is common in various religions and not on differences. Religious experience and expression in all religions have many common elements between Christ and other Saviour figures. We have to note at once that religions are radically similar and radically also dissimilar. The radical dissimilarity pertains also to the essence of each religion. Hence we have to consider both similar and dissimilar elements.

b) Again, for others, an inter-religious dialogue should pay attention to only what is positive in other religions and ignore or not mention what are deficiences in other religions. True, we have to take a positive and not a condemnatory attitude toward other religions. But we cannot ignore the negative aspects for a theological evaluation of other religions, though at the practical level we may be silent to favour dialogue and further encounters. For instance, we canot accept the erroneous way how other religions view Christ as universal Saviour. To help mutual understanding with regard to what is essential in one's religion involves also to pay attention to certain negative aspects of other religions, not so much in one's failure in the practice of one's faith (Christians also can be accused of this) but in what pertains to the essence of religion with regard to the doctrince and morality such as pantheism, God's immanence and transcendence, polygamy, etc.

c) Some say that an inter-religious dialogue should seek what is more universal in world religions and not what is specific to each of them. What is more universal unites all religions and what is specific divides religions. God is more universal than Christ; or liberation is more universal than belief in a personal God. What is Absolute is more universal than a Creator God. In this sense Christ is not universal because other religions do not believe in him. A personal God is not universal because some religions do not believe in a personal God. A Christian theology of religions cannot accept such a position because there is no universal theology of religions nor is there any universal faith without its own specific and singular element which belongs to the essence of each religion.

d) Finally, insistence, some hold, on the uniqueness, universality and absoluteness of one religion over the others is not only unfavourable to inter-religious dialogue but implies intolerance and pretension to superiority over others. The whole problem here depends on the unique revelation of God as an intervention, positive and specific, in the history of salvation.

In as far as the absoluteness of Christ belongs to the essence of Christian revelation, a Christian has to be authentic to his witnessing to it and in dialogue he cannot ignore or be silent about the uniqueness of his religion. It is on the authority of God's Word that he adheres to this absolute uniqueness of Christ and not on any human authority.

The term 'absolute' means something that is self-existent, distinct from others: it is rendered by the words: perfect in itself, complete, not merely relative or comparative, and unconditioned. It should not be confused with the generic notion of a group of similar properties in the abstract nor in the concrete with one of the many members of the same class or genus. It is something specific to itself or essential to it. An absolute is opposed to the relative. Necessarily when a predicate belongs to the essence of a subject, it is absolute. Both the terms 'absolute' and 'relative' are opposites; one implies the other. There can be various grades of being absolute. God is the supreme Absolute and creatures are said to be absolute in an analogical way by being participations of God. It is thus that the attribute of absoluteness can be predicated properly also of created realities in as far as they are consistent, self-existent and possess necessary and essential qualities and values that are not relative. If only God were to be absolute, then follows either monism or pantheism or pure relativism of contingent beings or of truths[12].

Finite beings would be then illusory manifestations of the Absolute or apparent manifestations of the supreme God in the pantheistic context. In the strictly creational context as in Christianity, the creatures are participations of the absoluteness of God. In the case of Christ, absoluteness is attributed to him because he is the divine personality. The attribute of absoluteness from the point of view of its content includes also universality. Christ's human nature by itself is not absolute; but as God-Man he is absolute (communicatio idiomatum). Even Christ's human nature is absolute in the participated sense. Since absoluteness and universality are mutually inclusive, Christ as universal Saviour is also absolute Saviour. Again, Christ's absoluteness is inclusive, not exclusive. He contains in himself the religio-moral values of the saviour figures of other religious traditions, and other saviour-mediators within Christianity itself such as priests and saints.

Further, Christ is unique because of his unique relationship to God. This points to Christ whose being as a man in history is due to the peculiar intervention of God. "The divinity of Jesus was the deed of God. The uniqueness of Jesus was the absolute uniqueness of what God did in him"[13]. The knowledge of Christ leads us from his Work to his Person (from functional christology to the ontological christology). What Jesus did was because of what he was, and the uniqueness of his relationship to the historian is dependent upon the uniqueness of Jesus' own relationship to God. This absolute uniqueness of Christ does not mean exclusive but inclusive. That is to say that we do not wish to attribute to Jesus Christ such a uniqueness as marks him off exclusively from other men or the saviours of other religious traditions.

Reality or ontological truth is certainly distinct from the logical truth or truth of our human knowledge of it, since we

---

[12] Cfr. systems of Eastern philosophy, e.g., Sankara, or of Western type such as that of Spinoza.

[13] JOHN KNOX, *The Death of Christ*, Abingdon Press, New York, 1958, p. 123.

do not know reality exhaustively or adequately in all its aspects. Only God knows the reality adequately and totally. But this does not mean that we can know it only relatively; i.e., in as far as we know reality even partially we know it absolutely. What we know, in as far as we know, and in the manner we know, is absolute in itself, i.e., objectively. Only in purely mathematical cases, presuppositions and prejudices need not influence the knower; but in other cases, certainly we are influenced by some subjective conditions; this does not mean that our knowledge in this case is subjective or relative. Presuppositions and prejudices can work both ways; to help us attain the objective truth or against it. There are various grades of truth such as scientific, empirical truths in human sciences as sociology, psychology, anthropology, history and phenomenology of religions. Philosophical and theological truths have their own criterion dependig on the value judgements they make from Christian revelation and faith. The absolute value of these truths depends on the scope and method of each science, empirical, philosophical or theological. The absoluteness of these truths does not depend on time or on being fragmentary. Our knoledge of God's mystery is partial and imperfect but in as far as we know it either from natural knowledge or from supernatural revelation it is perfect and necessary; this is what we mean by the way we know him is absolute; i.e. necessary and perfect. Thus the truth of our faith is absolute; i.e., is necessary and perfect, though there can be various grades of being perfect and necessary.

Applying what has been said so far to the person of Jesus Christ, we have to say that the human consciousness of Christ, being human and limited, participates in the absoluteness of God and thus communicates the divine truths to us in an absolute manner. Thus the absoluteness of our faith wich depends on Christ's revelation is immutable and unconditioned and necessary. Christians' perception of these revealed truths is conditioned by time and presuppositions and prejudices but what has been perceived remains true beyond time and human conditions. As I said before, not always presuppositions and prejudices are negative; they can positively help perceive the truths. God's truth which is one can be perceived and expressed in a plurality of particular views of truth; this does not entail that the truth itself as revealed is relative. However, presuppositions and prejudices should not be confused with truth and meaning.

We distinguish between absoluteness and absolutism. The latter can be understood as favouring fanaticism, fundamentalism, exclusivism, self-glorification and self-righteousness, and might lead to proselytism, intolerance, religious wars and conflicts; it may include absolutism of domination by oppression, repression or control of others. Such an understanding of absoluteness is far from what we mean by the absoluteness of Christ or of Christianity which is a question of reality and truth[14].

2. The absoluteness of Jesus Christ

1. *The claim to absoluteness during Jesus' ministry (Gospel Christology)*

We are not taking isolated biblical texts which explicitly argue for sustaining Jesus' absoluteness. For although they do have their significance in their context and powerfully portray the early Church's faith in Jesus and we shall treat them later on, we have to examine first the biblical evidence on the whole in order to study the nature of Jesus' personality and his work. There is a discernible continuity between the evaluation of Jesus during his ministry and the evaluation of him in the New Testament writings.

It would be difficult to find support among biblical scholars for the thesis that Jesus used of himself or accepted the "higher titles" of the later New Testament christology such as "Lord" in the full sence, Son of God or God. This does not imply that they deny that Jesus was Lord, Son of God, or God. They may mean that they regard such appellations as the result of later Christian reflection on the mystery of Christ.

With regard to the "lower titles" of christology such as Messiah, the Prophet, the Servant of God, the Son of Man,

---

[14] Cfr. the position of Reinhold Bernhardt with which we do not agree; see his *Christianity without Absolutes*, SCM Press Ltd, London, 1994, Introduction.

there are two kinds of christology: explicit and implicit. Those who hold explicit christology[15] admit that during his ministry Jesus referred to himself or accepted designations of these titles. On the other hand the advocates of the implicit christology hold that Jesus did not express his self-understanding in terms of titles or accept titles attributed to him by others[16]. Rather Jesus showed what he was by speaking with unique authority and acting with unique power. By his deeds and words he proclaimed that the eschatological reign of God was making itself present in such a way that a response to his ministry was a response to God. Yet this implicit claim to uniqueness was not formulated in titles which would reflect the traditional expectations of Judaism. Apart from the fact of explicit or implicit christology in the ministry of Jesus, the line of continuity to the early Church's evaluation of him in the New Testament seems more firmly established[17].

Jesus speaks of God as his Father (abba) and addresses him as Father. The idea of the fatherhood of God is found in many ancient religions in vaious ways. Many religious persons invoke God as Father. The fundamental basis for this is probably the apotheosis of the head of the family and the idea of the family as the image of a deity. The Stoics used the term Father to express the idea that participation in the same Logos makes men a single race and all men are brothers having a common Father Logos. This idea apperas in Paul's Speech on the Areopagus. "Yet in fact he is not far from any of us, since it is in him that we live, and move, and exist, as indeed some of

---

[15] Most of the Roman Catholic writers on christology in 1960's; and Protestant writers like O. Cullmann, C.H. Dodd, J. Jeremias, V. Taylor. For a Catholic view cfr. X. LEON-DUFOUR, *The Gospels and Jesus of History*, Doubleday, Garden City, 1970.

[16] Roman Catholic authors of 1970's; F. Hahn, R.H. Fuller, N. Perrin among Protestant scholars. See B. VAWTER. *This Man Jesus*, Doubleday, Garden City, 1973.

[17] See RAYMOND E. BROWN, *"Who Do Men Say That I Am?" - A survey of Modern Scholarship on Gospel Christology*, in his book; *Crises Facing the Church*, Paulist Press, New York, 1975, ch. 2; also his *Jesus God and Man*, The Bruce Publishing Company, Milwaukee, 1967.

your own writers have said: "We are all his children" (Acts 17,28)[18].

The title 'Son of God' is used in the New Testament neither in the sense of Old Testament Judaism nor in that of Hellenistic mythology. The strict monotheism of the Old Testament did not accept any mythological, polytheistic or pantheistic connotations of the term. The title refers exclusively to election, mission and the corresponding obedience and service, and not to descent or any natural connection. Thus Israel is called the son whom God called out of Egypt (Ex. 4.22; Hos. 11.1; Jer. 31.9). As the representative of Israel the King (Ps. 2.7; 89.27-28), and similarly the Messiah (2 Samuel 7.14) is described as the son of God. Also the pious people are called the sons of God (Ps. 73.15; Wis 5.5. Not physical descent but adoption is the exclusive criterion of meriting this title. Paganism refers to the sons of God in the biological sense such as men born of a divine father and human mother. In the Hellenistic period famous men were called sons of God. According to Stoic philosophy, all those who participate in the same Logos were called sons of God[19].

2. *The Logos in the Prologue of St John*[20]

John sees the whole history of Jesus in the light of eternity and begins his Gospel with the words: "In the beginning was the Word and the Word was with God and the Word was God". The pre-existence of the Son of God and his existence in a human, historic form through the Incarnation is the principal theme of the Prologue. It is significant that only in the Prologue of the Gospel is Christ called Logos. Other important words of the Prologue such as life, light, truth, glory are

---

[18] The quotation is from the Fenomena 5 of Aratus, a poet and astronomer of Cilician origin, 3rd cent. B.C. Cleanthes, the Stoic (3rd Cent) used almost identical language.
[19] See WALTER KASPER, *Jesus the Christ*, Burns and Oates London, 1977, p. 109.
[20] All the citations in the text are to John's Gospel, unless otherwise mentioned.

developed in the Gospel itself. It is remarkable that John uses the name of Logos to refer to Christ. Logos exists from all eternity. He is with God from all eternity. He is God. Through him all things came to be; no single thing was created without him. "(1.3) The Logos is distinguished from God because he is with God"; yet at the same time he is God. The Logos is distinguished from the Father as Person, but he possessed the same unique and indivisible divine nature.

All along history God has been uttering his word; but when the fulness of time was come, the Word became flesh and dwelt among us. And we saw his glory – glory as of the only begotten of the Father – full of grace and of truth". By Logos is meant the person of Jesus, of whose life and activity John was the witness (1.14).

The term Logos in Greek signifies not only the spoken word but also the interior word of the mind, the thought, the idea. Even the faculty of reasoning, the mind itself is designated by the term Logos. For the Greeks, there is harmony between the objective order of things and the subjective view of them. Man's reason discovers the order of the cosmos. Thus the Logos signifies the harmony and order of things in the universe to which corresponds the human Logos[21].

For Stoics, Logos is the dynamic reason or plan which forms and organizes the material world. Logos permeates every reality as mind or consciousness pervades body and is described as God, Providence, Nature, the soul of the universe (anima mundi). Particular things are microcosms of the whole, each of which contains within its unity an active and passive principle. The active principle is the Logos. The seminal Logoi are the seeds through the activity of which individual beings come into existence. These are contained within the supreme, universal Logos. The soul in man is an emanation from the divine Logos; pervading his body, it gives form, character and organization. The immanent Logos in man is his reason, while the expressed Logos is his reason made known by the faculty

---

[21] R.H. LIGHTFOOT, *St John's Gospel*, OUP, Oxford, 1960, pp. 49-56.

of speech. Through his reason man shares in the divinity. And thus the divinity is immanent in man. Religion is the development of one's own human nature. To obey God means to follow one's reason (Logos)[22].

Philo's theology is very important in this context for the simple reason that he, being a Jew from Alexandria (c. 30 B.C. - 45 A.D.), made a serious attempt to interpret Jewish theology in terms of Hellenistic philosophy. God is utterly transcendent, and transcends even virtue, knowledge and absolute goodness and beauty and the eternal forms of Plato. God is pure Being, absolutely One, and self-sufficient, described as "without quality". Hence God cannot be included in any of our logical categories of human thought because of his absolute transcendence. In that case how to conceive of his relation to the world? Philo solved the problem by positing intermediary powers; among these the supreme and most important is the Logos, 'the eldest and most akin to God' of things that exist. As an intermediary between God and the world, Logos Plays the role of God's agent in creation, and of the means by which the mind apprehends God. God first created Wisdom and then used her to create the world. He identified Logos with the Platonic world of forms or archetypes of which the sensible reality is a copy. He did not regard the world as self-existing but simply as expressing the mind of the One God. As there is in man rational thought in the mind and the thought uttered as a word, so the divine Logos is the ideas of God's mind and then projected into matter. When he speaks of "the first begotten Son", the personification is not real. Being immanent in the world, it is transcendent in God's mind. By contemplating Logos as Platonic world of Forms, we can know God. Logos is the image of God, the prototype of creation, a mediator between God and man, the high priest and intercessor for man before God[23].

---

[22] H.J. ROSE, *Religion in Greece and Rome*, Harpers Tor book, New York, 1959, pp. 116ff; 256ff.
[23] WILLIAM GROSSOUW, *Revelation and Redemption*, Geoffrey Chapman, London, 1958, pp. 68ff.

Evidently John is not dependent on these hellenistic speculations on the Logos. His Logos is an historic figure, the living person of Jesus who died and rose again, to whom John bore witness in personal encounter. Jesus is neither an immanent World - principle nor an idea. He was sent into the world by the Father to save the world. Philo's divine Logos is not a person but a mental construct to connect the unknown God and the world. Possibly John was thinking of the divine Wisdom of the Old Testament which was with Yahweh "before he made anything from the beginning" (Prov. 8.22), and which "is the brightness of eternal light, and the unspotted mirror of God's majesty, and the image of his goodness" (Wis. 7.26) Besides, John never used the word wisdom (sophia). John's use of Logos is more in the tradition of the Old Testament in which the divine Word plays an active and important role in the story of creation and God's intervention in the history of Israel; it is also often represented as a subsistent entity. In fact the Old Testament describes God's powerful word of creation (Gen. 1.1-2.4; Ps. 33.6; Is. 48.13) The word of God acomplishes his will in history (Is. 55.11; Ps. 33.9; Wis. 18.15 ff). The personified wisdom of God is prehistoric and was present at the creation of the world and participated therein (Pro. 8.22-30)[24].

From eternity onwards, Christ in his own substance was with God and was himself God, and therefore, since God is one, was in God's substance (Prologue 1.1.). In time the Logos was the agent of creation. He is the life-creating power (1.3f).

The Logos is the light of men. In him alone does man understand himslef and find his way (1.4). For John, God is the Light, and the Logos is the Light of men, and the Christian is in the Light. Christ is our divine light precisely because He is the revelation of the Fahter. In the prologue it is evident. "The Word was with God... in him was life, and the life was the light of men". (1.1-4) The plenitude of divine Life and Light has come forth from the bosom of the divinity (Jo. 1.2ff)

---

[24] K.H. SCHELKLE, *Theology of the New Testament*, Vol. 2, The Liturgical Press. Collegeville 1976, pp. 171ff.

and has appeared among us in the person of Jesus Christ. But the world knew him not", for from the very beginning the darkness has been opposed to the Light. (1.5ff) The darkness consists in not accepting the divine revelation. Just as the Light is the manifestation of the divine Truth, so the darkness is a futile attempt to remove the operation of the Light. The stage of this struggle is the spirit of man. The world did not receive Christ (1.5.). His own people rejected him (1.11). Men have loved the darkness rather than the Light (3.19). The chapter 9 which relates the account of the cure of the man born blind portrays the marvelous radiance of the eternal divine light in the person of Jesus Christ, its glow on the man who accepts this revelation in faith and the dullness of proud unbelief. The light of the eye that has been restored to the afflicted man is the symbol of the divine illunination which Jesus sheds on the heart of the man who believes[25].

In Christ was the life and the life was the light of men. (1.4) John says, "This is the testimony, that God has given us eternal life, and this life is in his Son". (1 Jo. 5.11) The essence of the message of salvation, according to John, is that Christ, the Son of God, is the source of life for mankind. The imperishable gift of Christian salvation is life. The incarnate Word is for mankind the unique and unfathomable fountain of life. Life means quickening power, moral light and spiritual illumination. The life that is in God was made known to us by the Son and this is the historic saving mission of Christ, the reason why he became man. (1.4; 10.10,28). The life in man is expressed by John like this: "Now this is everlasting life, that they may know thee, the only true God, and him whom thou has sent, Jesus Christ" (17.3) Salvation for man consists in being liberated from the wrath of God, in escaping judgement, perdition and death. (3.15; 16,36) Man attains this life by faith in Jesus Christ, by believing that he is the Son and the One sent by the Father, by hearing his word (5.24) and by following him (8.12)[26].

---

[25] WILLIAM GROSSOUW, *Revelation and Redemption*, op. cit., pp. 27ff.
[26] M.E. BOISMARD, *St John's Prologue*, Blackfriars Publication, London, 1957, ch. VI.

Again, it is John who says: "God is Love" (1 Jo. 4.7-8) God is the immeasurable and personal Goodness which first shares its being with the Logos, who is "with the Father", and then through the Logos, with the entire world. "For God so loved the world that he gave his only-begotten Son..." (3.16). If the essence of God is love, and if Christ is the supreme revelation of God, the incarnate God, then he must also be the supreme Revelation, the highest realization of God's love. Jesus is the incarnate love of God, especially in his death by which he has redeemed the world. Thus Jesus is tue mediator of divine love. This love is entirely focused upon the Son and through him it reaches men. (17.23ff; 14,21ff) Jesus's entire work of salvation is directed towards the one end: that the believers may share in that love which is the essence of God (17.26)[27].

The crowning statement of the whole Prologue is: So the Word became flesh; he came to dwell among us. That is to say, the Word became a real man. God completed his long process of revelation by enclosing his saving purpose in human flesh and blood. Augustine tells us that he found all he wanted in the Geek philosophers – Plato and the rest – except this, that the Word became flesh. As of old God's glory had filled the tabernacle, so now it has been manifested in the person of Christ. He is "God's presence and his very self" among men. John portrays the life and ministry of Jesus as "the incarnate glory", a progesssive unveling of the splendour of God reaching its climax in the cross. The manifested glory of the Word was the glory which the eternal Father shared with his only Son. Finally, John says that the glory is full of grace and truth. Grace is the immense goodness of God to us, the undeserving men. Truth, for John, means the eternal reality as revealed to men-either the reality itself or the revelation of it[28].

Finally, John says:

"Out of his fulness we have all received grace upon grace; for while the Law was given through Moses, grace and

---

[27] WILLIAM GROSSOUW, *Revelation and Redemption*, op. cit., pp. 41 ff.
[28] JOHN MARSH, *Saint John*, Penguin Books, Harmondsworth, 1968, pp. 71ff.

truth came through Jesus Christ. No one has ever seen God; but God's only Son he who is nearest to the Father's heart, he has made him known".

Out of Christ's fullness, we have received superabounding grace. (1.16-18) For the Law of the old Testament, though it was a real gift of God, was only a preparation at best for the Gospel. It set before men the divine command, God's moral demand upon men; but it could not do what Christ now does; namely, to give life. Nobody has ever had direct vision of God; but in Jesus, God's only Son, his Word has become transparent. He reveals God at work. Because Jesus is in the most intimate relation to the Father, he is able to make him known, to interpret him, to disclose his nature to men. The whole history of Jesus is the truth about God. It is the word "God" translated into human terms and spelt out in human words and acts. All that men want to know about the nature of the unseen God is theirs in Jesus Christ.

According to the Prologue of John's Gospel, Christ was and is the light and life for men. Light and darkness are the divine world and the world hostile to God. (1.4f) Light is the strength of life.. "The true light that enlightens every man come into the world (1.9). The expression 'true light' (as in 1 Jo 2.8) means that there are also false assertions about the light, either simply because men deceive themselves or perhaps it is said in a polemic way, because there are in fact false teachings (perhaps the Gnosis) about pretended light. Christ himself says, "I am the light of the world. Whoever follows me will not walk in the darkness, but will have the light of life". (8.12) Christ is the light and he gives light. In the revelation of Christ the world is illumined. It is in this revelation that man first comes to understand himself. "For this purpose have I come into the world: so that no one who believes in me will remain in the darkness". (12.46) Those who believe are themselves a light in the world and for the world. Believe in the light, so that you may become children of light" (12.36).

The Prologue of St John makes three affirmations. 1) "In the beginning was the Logos" (verse 1). This Logos is the one who became flesh (verse 15). The historical person of Jesus Christ existed already at the beginning. This is an ontic statement about the pre-existence of Jesus Christ. 2) "The Logos was with God" (verse 1) This 'being with God' is described as fellowship in glory (Jn 17.5), as unity in love (Jn 17.24), as being filled with the life of God (Jn 5.26), so that Father and Son have everything in common (Jn 17.10); "I and the Father are one", (Jn 10.39) This is a unity in duality, a personal communion. It is because of the pre-existent 'being with God' that the authority and dignity of the incarnate Logos are to be justified. Since he participates in the glory, love and life of the Father, he can impart glory, love and life to all human beings. On account of this, the Logos is the life and light of men (1.4 and 1.9). It is in him that the origin of all things is manifest as well as the origin and goal of human existence become manifest. Thus the ontic statement is also the salvation statement. 3) "And the Logos was God". (Verse 1) The Logos has the character of divinity. Though God and the Logos are distinct, both are united by the one divine nature. "The Logos was God (theos)" is not merely the designation of a function but an ontological statement, orientatd to a salvation statement. Jesus Christ in his nature and being is the Logos of God in person in whom the question of life, light and truth is definitively answered. The definitiveness, decisiveness, the absoluteness, the uniqueness and the universality of Jesus Christ are affirmed because he in his nature and being is the Logos of God in person[29]. The ontological statement without being oriented to the salvation statement would be mere speculation; the salvation statement without the ontological statement would be without force and groundless[30].

What is the relation between *Logos en arche* and *Logos en sarx*? The Prologue begins with a reference to the *Logos en arche*; though the term Logos is not used in the rest of the Gospel, the idea that in Jesus we see the divine Logos pervades everything. Very little of this Gospel is not concerned with, in one way or another, with the truth that the Word became flesh

---

[29] See WALTER KASPER, *Jesus the Christ*, Burns & Oates, London, 1976, pp. 169ff.
[30] Ibidem.

and lived among us, and we saw his glory. (1.14). So with life (3.16; 4.10f). Similarly, Jesus is the light of the world (8.12; 3.19f). Can we hold that salvation, mediated through Eternal Christ, the Word of God, may be bestoweed upon those who have not known of the historic person and message of Jesus, and also upon those who have not accepted it because they were not convinced of the necessity to believe in Christ? This conception of "the larger Christ" (*Logos en arche* without *Logos en sarx* has its own dangers. In order to retain its distinctive Christian quality, such a conception needs to be linked with an emphasis on the centrality and supremacy of the historic revelation of God in Jesus of Nazareth. St John teaches that the Logos of God operates beyond the historic person of Jesus from the beginning of creation (1.1-1). We have to distinguish betwen the total Word of God or self-expression of God and the historic revelation in Christ. J.M. Creed remarks: "Christian theology need *not* claim that the Christian religion contains within itself *all* truth, or even all truth that is of religious value. But if it loses the conviction that in Christ it has found the deepest truth of God, it has lost itself"[31]. Baron von Hügel notes, "The unincarnate God has a wider range, though a less deep message, than the incarnate God"[32]. B.H. Streeter observes: "Incarnation purports to be, not an *exhaustive*, nor an *exclusive* but rather a *distinctive* expression of God. It must mean an expression through human personality of the very being of God, – and of the most characteristic and central element in that being. It does not mean that everything in the Divine finds expression there; or that nothing in the Divine is expressed elsewhere[33]. It is possible for a Christian to hold firmly to the essential principle of the absoluteness of Jesus Christ, and at the same time to approach other religions with an open mind that has not rejected the possibility that they may have something to contribute to our knowledge of God, and may have been used by God as a real (even if subordinate) channel of divine revelation.

---

[31] *The Divinity of Christ*, Cambridge, 1938, p. 112.
[32] *Essays on the Philosophy of Religion*, London, 1921, p. 134.
[33] *Adventure*, London, 1927, p. 150.

In this context we have to avoid a confusion that creeps in the above distinction between the unincarnate Logos and the incarnate Logos.

Although the fourth Gospel speaks more clearly than the others of the uniqueness of Christ, it interprets him at the same time in the light of the most universal of all concepts that were prevalent in this period, the concept of Logos, the universal principle of the divine self-manifestation, thus freeing the interpretation of Jesus from a particularism through which he would become the property of a particular religious group. Universality does not mean an attribution of an abstract universal concept which is predicated of many individuals such as the concept of man to different human beings. Again, it does not mean properties or truths that are common to other religious personages and are found also in Jesus Christ. It means that Jesus Christ is the concrete universal; i.e., Jesus Christ is the concrete historical God-man who is the universal Saviour of all humankind, not in the exclusive sense but in the inclusive sense.

What John seeks to say by Logos is that the only proper perspective in which to see the history of Jesus is a divine one; hence he begins in God's eternity and that Jesus Christ is God's saving purpose for human beings in terms of a human life. Logos is God's creative and redeeming Purpose. By the Logos all things were made. It was manifestad in the world as life and light, the light open to every man born. In the person and work of Jesus the saving purpose of God was embodied. He is the dynamic and redemptive Word of God. He has made God's gracious mind and purpose, and that purpose is one of God's love in action for men's salvation, which is eternal life. This is the ultimate, final and absolute meaning of the Fact of Christ.

The whole relation bewteen the *Logos en arche* and the *Logos en sarx* has to be explained in the light of salvation history, universal and special.

The universal and special history of salvation

The Christian theology distinguishes between the universal or general history of salvation and the special history of salvation for various reasons. First of all, God's intervention in history has taken various forms of revealing his salvific plan for mankind. God has long spoken and has made himself known to men in various manners, both universally and individually through creation, man's conscience and human events, and in a special way through human mediators and finally through his incarnate Son, Jesus Christ. Secondly, God has wished to save all men and has given a real possibility of saving them through his grace. Thirdly, the centrality of Christ in the whole salvation history radiates in various ways human history. Fourthly, the special history of salvation does not make abrupt and arbitrary interventions without due preparation on the part of man. For God respects man's dignity and freedom. Fifthly, the God of creation and the God of salvation are one and the same. The universal history of salvation and the special history of salvation are distinct but not separate, for the special history of salvation has its roots in the general history of salvation and has grown out of it. The special history of salvation itself is meant for the whole mankind, for Jesus Christ is the universal saviour of the whole human race and is the concrete universal (*universale concretum*). The redemptive incarnation is the most decisive fact in salvation history. The mystery of the Church imitates and continues the mystery of Christ, for it is the universal sacrament of salvation.

First of all, we have to note that the distinction between the universal and special history of salvation does not imply that both run parallel to each other, as if God has willed two ways of salvation, one for other religions and the other for Christianity. Actually there is only one history of salvation with two distinct aspects or dimesions. The universal history of salvation is not abrogated by the special history of salvation but is included in it. Though the special history of salvation has an absolute character, it is inclusive of the other, because other religions' salvific values are assumed by it and destined to it. Because of his universal function in creation and in history, Christ is the universal mediator of salvation. He is the centre from which the dynamism of salvation spreads out in every direction. The Church as Christ's body must mediate salvation for the believers of other religions, even though it does not reach them either through signs or words.

The distinction between the universal and special history of salvation is profound and essential; this becomes clear when we analyse the idea of universal revelation and the revelation in Christ and entrusted to the Church. The universal revelation does not reveal the economy of the mystery of Christ hidden for ages in God (Eph. 3.9), though actually oriented to it. Besides, humanity flounders in ignorance in comparison with the Judeo-Christian revelation. (Acts 17.30). Still, the universal history of salvation includes a paternal illumination from God, aimed at producing in men a real knowledge of God, to show the grandeur of his works (Ecc 17.10) so that they may acknowledge him and thank him (Rom. 1.21); to show men the law of good and evil (Rom. 2.25) and to help them on the way of salvation (Rom. 2.15.6).

3. *The Cosmic Christ in Paul*

Paul has always in mind the historical Christ in his concrete reality as God made man (Ph. 2.5 f; Col. 1.15f). Christ is the Wisdom (1 Cor. 1.24,30), and the image (2. Cor. 4.4), by which and in which all things were created (Col. 1.15-17), and have been recreated (Rom. 8.29), because into his own person is gathered the fulness of the Godhead and of the universe (Col. 2.9f). In him God has devised the whole plan of salvation (Eph. 1.3f), and he, no less than the Father, is its accomplishment (Rom. 11.36).

This title 'Wisdom' (Sophia) goes back to the figure of Sophia as God's personified Wisdom in *Proverbs* 8.22-31. This passage is significant for the early Church's Christological thinking. It begins thus: The Lord created me when his purpose first unfolded, before the oldest of his works. Ages ago I was set up, at the first, before the beginning of the earth. When there were no depths I was brought forth... When he established the heavens, I was there... I was beside him, like a master workman; and I was daily his delight, rejoicing before him always. Here is the personified figure of divine Wisdom, God's aid in the work of creation. Such a figure of the Cosmic Christ explains when Paul says: "for us there is one God, the Father, from whom everything comes, for whom we exist, and one Lord, Jesus Christ, through whom everything exists, through whom we exist" (1 Cor. 8.6). The Lord, Jesus Christ, is the pre-existent Wisdom of God, the agent of creation. This personified Wisdom recurs in Col. 1.15-18, where Christ, the Son of God's love, is described as "the image of the invisible God, the first born of all creation". By using the figure of the divine Wisdom to express what the Fact of Christ meant for him, Paul shows not only his belief in Christ's pre-existence, but chiefly his conviction that the created universe bears the mark of the Saviour. By the category of the divine Wisdom Paul set forth the absolute significance of Christ in whom he had found unsearchable riches. Through him Paul had gained access to the unseen Father. Hence he believed that the fact of Christ was embedded in the constitution of creation itself, and that all history was moving on to Christ. Paul is referring to the eternal Son of God, who in the fulness of time became man as Jesus of Nazareth. In relation to the old creation Christ exercises the right of heritage which is his as the Fahter's first-begotten; in relation to the new creation he exercises a parallel privilege because of his priority in resurrection. With regard to providence it is interesting to note that Paul says that the Israelites in the wilderness "drank from the spiritual rock which followed them, and the rock was Chirst" (1 Cor. 10.4) In current Jewish thought the rock from which Israel drank in the wilderness was associated with Divine Wisdom (Cfr. Wisdom 11.1-4).

Christ can claim to be the head of everything in two ways: he is the head of creation of all that exists naturally (Col. 1.15-17); and he is the head of the new creation and of all that exists supernaturally through having been saved (Col. 1.18-20). Here it is dealt with the pre-existent Christ, considered only in so far as he was manifest in the unique historic person that is the Son of God made man. It is as the incarnate God that Jesus is the image of God; i.e., his human nature was the visible manifestation of God who is invisible. In Philippians 2.6-11, Paul deals with different stages of the mystery of Christ: divine pre-existence, kenosis in the incarnation, his further kenosis in death, his glorification, adoration by the cosmos, new title of Lord. We have to note here that it is dealt with solely the historical Christ in whose personality godhead and manhood are not divided; Paul nowhere divorces the humanity and divinity of Jesus though he does distinghish his various stages of existence[34].

When Paul testifies to the finality of Jesus Christ he bears witness to the several aspects of the work of Christ. 1) It is from Jesus Christ that all things proceed and receive their vocation. (All things were created through him and for him, Col. 1.16). 2) Jesus Christ is he in whom all things cohere and work together (Col. 1.17). 3). Jesus is he by whom all things are judged and brought to judgement. (Prologue of St John). 4) Jesus is he through whom all things fulfil their destiny (Eph. 1.10). 5). Jesus Christ is he unto whom all things go (Rom. 8.16-17). The finality of Christ conists in the finality of the Person and Work of him. The early Christian community bears witness to this finality as a mark of its life[35].

According to St Paul, the mystery of Christ: the hidden plan which God had in mind from the beginning (Eph. 1.9) was realized in Jesus Christ and which is now universally proclaimed through the Gospel, brings out the significance of the Christ-event. The Christ-event is seen in the full context of the history of salvation; it gives the key to understand all God's mighty works on behalf of man and of the world universally from the beginning to the end. This Christo-centric theological reflection forces us to interpret religious pluralism not in the exclusive but inclusive sense. The absoluteness of Jesus Christ is inclusive. We can call it Christocentric universality. We have to include Christ in the universal plan of salvation and to relate the special revelation in Christ to the general revelation in the world religions. Paul complimented the Athenians for being "very religious" (Acts 17.23). Paul found basic similarity between their religion and the message he had come to bring. (Acts 17.25-28) Paul points out the place of Christ in God's universal design. "God overlooked that sort of thing when

---

[34] See ALLAN D. GALLOWAY, *The Cosmic Christ*, Nisbext & Co, London, 1941, Ch IV; JEAN-FRANÇOIS BONNEFOY, *Christ and the Cosmos*, St Anthony Guild Press, Peterson, 1965, pp. 173-215 especially ch.3: *The Absolute and Universal Primacy of Christ*.

[35] See DOW KIRKPATRICK (ed.), *The finality of Christ*, Abingdon Press, Nashville, 1966, ch. 1.

men were ignorant, but now he is telling everyone everywhere that they must repent, because he had fixed a day when the whole world wil be judged, and judged in righteousness and he has appointed a man to be the judge. And God has publicly proved this by raising this man from the dead"[36].

4. *The witness of the early Church to the finality of Jesus Christ*

The witness of the early Church to the finality of Jesus Christ when it is understood is brought out very clearly in the context of the finality of the person and work of Jesus Christ.

"No one knows the Son save the Father; neither does anyone know the Father save the Son and he to whomsoever the Son wills to reveal him" (Mt 11.27; Lk 10.22) "No man comes to the Father but by me".

"(God our Saviour) wants everyone to be saved and reach full knowledge of the truth. For there is only one God, and there is only one mediator between God and mankind, himself a man, Christ Jesus, who sacrificed himself as a ransom for them all". (1 Tim.2.4-6) This text is of fundamental theological value in which it is affirmed that God wants the salvation of all men. Christ has redeemed all men and he in the actual economy of salvation is the unique mediator between God and men.

A true, saving knowledge of God is possible only where there is knowledge of and faith in Jesus Christ as a historic person. The human community is constituted by the finality of Jesus Christ. All things are not only from him, but unto him.

"For of all the names in the world given to men, this is the only one by which we can be saved" (Acts 4.12) In the Bible the 'name' is often a symbol of the person named. *Jesus* means "God saves" (Mt. 1.21). Other believers do not know the name of Jesus explicitly but implicitly, i.e., inwardly, by feeling the virtues and the power of it, and hence they will also be saved.

---

[36] See THOR HALL, *The Evolution of Christology*, Abingdon, Nashville, 1982, ch. 5.

Some authors begin with the universal Logos acting in revelation and redemption throughout the whole of history. Jesus of Nazareth is the particularly powerful and effective actualization of the saving activity of God through his creative Logos. They never suggest that Jesus is the only or unique mediation of that saving activity[37]. The claim to a "unique" saviourhood of Jesus has to be developed in the context of universal history and on the assumption that in some sense God's saving activity was at work in that history, even prior to the coming of Jesus. In this perspective arises the theological question: in what sense is the saving activity of Jesus distinctive and peculiar to him? How is Jesus normative, i.e., final in significance and authority, for an understandig of how God works savingly in the whole history? The biblical evidence shows that Jesus saw himself as acting in the name of God and that the crucial decision for or against God was to be decisively linked with their attitude towards his own person whether in acceptance or rejection. The decisive question for the New Testament is obedience to Jesus: "There is no other name under heaven whereby men must be saved". (Acts 4.12) For the early Church the decisive difference was Jesus' resurrection. Certainly the bearing of this *event* on the claim that Jesus is the Son of God or the Saviour or the Lord becomes obvious. The heart of the matter is that the Christian faith has claimed that in Jesus we meet not only a prophet or a messenger from God but that God is personally and savingly active in Jesus[38].

Finally, Some think that the biblical passages which claim for Christian faith absoluteness ought to be interpreted in the context of confessions of Jesus by his disciples and followers. They are not metaphysical assertions about divine facts but an existential expression of unconditioned commitment and obli-

---

[37] E.g. J.B. COBB, *Christ in a Pluralistic Age*, Westminster, Philadelphia, 1967.

[38] See RUSSELL F. ALDWINKLE, *Jesus - A Saviour or the Saviour?*, Religious Pluralism in Christian Perspective, Mercer University Press, Macon, 1982, ch. 3.

gation. They are not eternal truths of God, revealed by Christ about himself[39]. This is the reason why we have treated this problem of the absoluteness of Jesus Christ from the point of view of Jesus' own claims, as is evident in the Gospels. Even the passages from St Paul and St John are not only confessions of faith in Jesus Christ by devoted apostles; they are ontological statements based on reality.

5. *The absoluteness of Christ and of Christianity according to Karl Rahner*

Christian theology centres upon the unique significance of Christ as God incarnate and as the source of salvation of all human beings. The historical Jesus was God the Son, the Second Person of the divine Trinity, living a human life, and by his death on the cross he has atoned for human sin, so that by responding to him in faith and repentence we may be reconciled to God. The salvation won by Christ is available to all humankind; whenever it occurs it has been made possible only by his atoning death. The divine Logos which became personally incarnate as Jesus of Nazareth has also been at work within other religious traditions, inspiring other spiritual leaders and thus being actively present. This doctrine embodies an absolute claim for Christ and for the Christian way of salvation. Karl Rahner says that we must recognize the genuine humanity of Christ, which entails that "the 'human nature' of the Logos possesses a genuine, spontaneous, free, spiritual, active center, a human self-consciousness, which as creaturely faces the eternal Word in a genuinely human attitude of adoration, obedience, a most radical sense of creaturehood"[40]. For otherwise Christ "would be the God who is active among us in human form, and not the true man who can be our Mediator with respect to God in genuine human freedom"[41]. The

---

[39] See for example REINHOLD BERNHARDT, *Christianity without Absolutes*, SCM Press, London, 1994, pp. 53-60.
[40] *Current Problems in Christology* in: *Theological Investigations*, 2 ed. Darton, Longman and Todd, 1965, Vol. 1, p. 158.
[41] Ibidem., 1.160.

incarnation is seen not as the unique exception to God's normal relationship to humanity, but rather as the uniquely perfect instance of that relationship. "For christological considerations have led the way back to the more general doctrine of God's relation to the creature and allowed christology to appear as the clearly unique "specifically" distinct perfection of this relation[42]. Accordingly, the relation of created spiritual beings to God "reaches its absolute peak in the case of Christ"[43].

Thus the incarnation is not to be seen as a divine intervention which lies apart from God's creative work in human life, but as "the ontologically (not merely morally) unambiguous goal of the movement of creation as a whole in relation to which everything prior is merely a preparation of the scene[44]. Thus the incarnation is seen as the supreme instance of the operation of divine grace. For is not grace "the unfolding within human nature of the union of the human with the Logos... therefore and *arising thence*, something which can also be had in those who are not the existence of the Logos in time and history but who do belong to his necessary environment?"[45]. Hence Rahner says:

> "Suppose someone says: Jesus is the man whose life is one of absolutely unique self-surrender to God". He may very well have stated the truth about the very depths of what Christ really is, *provided* that he has understood (a) that this self-abandonment presupposes a communication of God to the man; (b) that an absolute self-surrender implies an absolute self-communication of God to the man; one which makes what is produced by it into the reality of the producer himself: and (c) that such an existential statement does not signify something "mental", a fiction, but is in the most radical way a statement about being"[46].

---

[42] Ibidem, 1.163.
[43] Ibidem, 1.164.
[44] Ibidem, 1.165.
[45] Ibidem, 1.199-200.
[46] Ibidem, 1.182.

Hence human nature is essentially endowed with the possibility of self-transcendence, and the incarnation of God is therefore the unique, supreme case of the total actualization of human reality[47]. The incarnation is unique and absolute. This uniqueness and absoluteness are necessitated by the divine personality of Christ. Although Jesus was genuinely human yet this man is God[48]. Thus Rahner holds the absolute claim of Jesus Christ and of Christianity in his theology of religions and regards devout and godly people of other religions as anonymous Christians.

According to Rahner uniqueness of Christ is central to Christian absoluteness.

Some followers of Rahner do not interpret the role of Christ in the salvation of humankind on an historical plane. Rather it is based on an ontological model that restores the Patristic idea of the Logos asarkos. This logos has replaced the Word in biblical history in defining the relation between God and the world, between his salvation and other religions. The basic intention is to integrate the world religions into the divine plan of salvation. This type of universalism would be acceptable only if it were clearly projected as a function of the Gospel and its history of promise, rather than as a synergism of the two ways of salvation in Christianity and other religions. For instance, William B. Frazier makes conclusions from the new trends in Catholic theology: the missionary aim of the Chruch is not to bring men the gift of salvation[49]. The grace of Christ always precedes the Christian Mission. The world and not the Church is the focal point of God's saving action. The purpose of the Christian Mission is to help Muslims be better Muslims, Hindus better Hindus, Buddhists better Buddhists, and not to change their loyalties from one faith to another.

Karl Rahner treats the problem of Christianity as being an "Absolute Religion". No other religion claims to be *the*

---

[47] Ibidem, 4.110.
[48] Ibidem, 1.173.
[49] See his *Guidelines for a New Theology of Mission*, in: *Mission Trends*, n. 1, ed. Gerald H. Anderson and Thomas F. Stransky, Erdmans, 1974, p. 29, Grand Rapids.

religion and the absolutely unique and only valid revelation of the one living God. Christianity claims to be the absolute religion destined for all men and women, which cannot accept any other having equal rights beside it. This thesis is basic for the Christian theological understanding of the other religions. "Christ, the absolute Word of God, has come in the flesh and reconciled, that means united the world to God through his death and resurrection, not only theoretically but in reality[50]. Ever since, Christ and his permanent historical presence in the world which we call the Church are *the* religion which binds man to God. It should however be noted that Christianity has a historical beginning in Christ; but this means only that this absolute religion too must come to men historically, confronting and claiming them as their letitimate religion". Christianity is meant to be the absolute and therefore unique religion of all humankind. Other religions contain not only elements of a natural knowledge of God mixed with depravation caused by original sin and human elements, but also supernatural elements of grace. They can therefore be acknowledged to be legitimate religions even though in different gradations[51].

Further, Rahner explains how Jesus is God's definitive promise of himself in history. Christians confidently live the history of Christian faith that "in Jesus and his word, his fate and his triumph in death God's irrevocable promise of himself to human history has taken on historically concrete form as history that actually reaches its goal in God".

"But when we say "God" and "Jesus" in this sense: "God" as the mystery as the most real and sublime over every reality of the world, the mystery that as ultimate ground, as innermost dynamism and as final goal gives itself to its world in immediacy; "Jesus" as God's promise of himself to the world and its history, a self-promise that is definitive, irrevocable, and establish itself by the power of God himself then,

---

[50] KARL RAHNER, *Is Christianity an "Absolute Religion"?* in: *Grace in Freedom*, Herder and Herder, New York, 1969, p. 82.
[51] Ibidem, p. 83.

actually we have already stated the core content of Christianity[52]. Again Rahner further makes this point more precise: "Only in Jesus Christ did the divine and the human reach an absolute and indissoluble unity; only in the self-revelation of Jesus is this unity also historically present; only now is this saving history clearly and permanently distinguished from all profane history; and everything, such as the Church, the sacraments and the Scriptures, which follows from this Christ-event and which participates in its own way in this unsurpassable finality of the Christ-event, participates also in its distinction from profane history. Here in Christ and in the church, saving history reaches its clearest and absolutely permanent distinction from profane history and becomes really an unequivocally distinct manifestation within the history of the world, thus bringing the general salvation-history to self-realization and to its historical reality in word and social structures within the history of the world"[53].

6. *The absoluteness of Christ and of Christianity according to Yves Congar*

Yves Congar affronts the problem of absoluteness of Christianity with the following questions. Do not all religions claim to originate in a revelation? Have they not many features in common? Are they not all good, if they are faithfully practised[54]. He answers by stating that the Christian faith's essential affirmation about Christianity is that it is *absolute*. If religion consists in a certain relation of man with God, then the relation of man with God established *in* and *by* Jesus Christ is perfect absolutely. It is not merely perfect as *things are*; there could not be any more perfect relationship, or even one that could be properly compared to it. If Jesus Christ is God and

---

[52] See KARL RAHNER, *Christianity's Absolute Claim*, Theological Investigations, Vol. XXI, Daryon, Longman and Todd, London, 1988, p. 177.

[53] KARL RAHNER, *World History and Salvation History*, in *The Christian and the World*, Danisianum, P. J. Kennedy and Sons, New York, 1965, pp. 60ff.

[54] Cfr. his *The Wide World My Parish*, Salvation and its Problems, Helicon Press, Baltimore, 1961, p. 27.

man, if humankind and the living God are united in his person, then it follows clearly that no religious relationship can equal that, or equal that which it brings about in us through faith. Jesus Christ is *the* religious relationship, he *is* religion. No other religion is comparable to the one instituted or constituted by him. All others can have value only through him. This is what we mean by the absoluteness of Christianity which could be either exclusive or inclusive with regard to other religions; i.e., either it can reject any value in them or recognize in some way a value in them. The Catholic tradition holds that Christianity is inclusive. St. Paul speaks of *the mystery of Christ* (Cfr. the Captivity Epistles, Ephesians and Colossians). The One Mystery of God, revealed and realized in Christ, comprises the whole of creation which finds its effective meaning only in Christ. All is for him and he is for all.

Pius XII in his Radio Message to the Congress in Ernakulam in 1952 says: "Make sure that people see that everything true and good in other religions finds its deepest meaning and perfect complement in Christ". "Again, in the context of "the preparation for the Gospel", the idea of a certain presence of the Word in other religions is ascertained. This presence is explained as captive that has to be freed from by the Gospel; a debased and misrepresented presence that has to be purified by Christ. In fact, everything that is insufficient, false or idolatrous in other religions in a way has got to die, so that they may be in their good elements taken over by Jesus Christ and in him brought back to the father. (Cfr. Evangelii Precones). Here the essential thing is the dogmatic assertion of a certain relation of other religions to the absolute of Christianity, and in the end a restorableness of them to it. Something analogous must be said of the Church herself[55].

In systematic theology the kingship of Christ is explicitly attributed to his humanity, as one of the consequences of the capital grace (gratia capitis) called forth by the grace of union. In the Christ of the incarnation there is a passage from "theology" to "economy", as the "economy" has its founda-

---

[55] Y. CONGAR, *The Wide World My Parish*, op. cit., pp. 29ff.

tion in "theology". The economy of the Kingship of Christ can be expressed in the following statements.l). The Lordship of Christ is total and absolute; 2) its full effective exercise is eschatological; 3) its "economic" exercise (the earthly administration of redemption) includes a duality of domains, the Church and the world, a struggle (the resistance of the Powers and of the flesh), and in Christ himself, a priestly mode of suffering servant[56]. The Lordship of Christ is total and absolute, as to its extent and to its domain. Christ's domain is both double and unique, absolutely universal. The New Testament links the Lordship of Christ sometimes to his position as Son of God (the hypostatic union) and sometimes to the incarnation and the Pasch, which embraces indissolubly the obedience of the Cross, the resurrection and ascension. But the Lordship of Christ is also connected with the divine filiation of the Son of man. The Lordship of Christ can be participated but in its proper dignity incommunicable[57].

7. *Religious personality of Jesus*

We take the term 'personality' not in the metaphysical sense of an intellectual being subsisting in itself and distinct from others, which is the formal constitutive of a person; such a personality in Jesus is not something created. The human nature of Jesus does not subsist in itself but exists only in the subject which is the eternal person of the Son of God. We use the term in the psychological sense to designate the sum total of the human dispositions, intellectual and voluntary, natural or supernatural which one has towards the scale of values. Such a personality is religious in as far as it refers to the religious values, God-man relationships. The Good News Jesus revealed does not refers to his religious personality directly because it is something of doctrine rather than a kind of dispositions. But it refers to it indirectly in as far as it pertains to the supernatural human wisdom of Jesus about religious things and the riches of his heart.

---

[56] See Y. CONGAR, *Jesus Christ*, Herder and Herder, 1966, pp. 172ff.
[57] Ibidem, pp. 273ff.

The Good News of Jesus was the Gospel of the Kingdom of God which Jesus preached; i.e., the Kingdom of God the Father and of Christ, the Son of God. Thus the Good News of the Kingdom contains the mandate which is of filial religion towards the Father and of cultivating this religion under the supreme reign of Christ. Phenomenological perfection of religion means the state of religion which, considered under the light of religious phenomena, attains the species of perfect religion; i.e., appears to have the structure of perfect religion. The religion which in its integrity is of the species of perfect religion is distinct from the religion which contains this species only in its fundamental notes. The Christian religion exhibits in itself the integral perfection of this religion.

Such a religion means profound and exacting love of God, mutual relationship of familiarity, love, trust, obedience, with the hope of the final Kingdom of God (Cfr. paternity of God in Old and New Testament). It includes universal love of men because of God the Father and also faith with the confession of the proper insufficiency.

Jesus completed his Message of filial religion with the christological Message. Jesus, man living among men, is also the Son of God by the singular reason which puts him above the sphere of creatures before his Father. Hence Jesus is the revealer of the Father, instaurator of the Kingdom of God in which men become true sons of God under the reign of him, the unique Son. Jesus instaurated the Kingdom not as national king but as the son of man. As such he sometimes comes in glory, but also as Son of man - signifies men - is united with his brethren, men, assuming the function of their representative, of sinful men before the Father, and their Saviour.

Man's encounter with God has completely become irrevocable in the man Christ. God who becomes man, Christ, becomes a personal encounter with God. His being a person and his dialogue with man have become a concrete reality. The absoluteness of the personality of Christ is the foundation of the absoluteness of Christianity. Man's encounter with God as a person manifests itself in its definitive concreteness and reality in Christ. Christ is the sign not only of the encounter between God and human being but of the intimate union between God and the human being. "There are no more distinctions between Jew and Greek, slave and free, male and female, but all of you are one Christ Jesus. Merely by belonging to Christ you are the posterity of Abraham, the heirs he was promised". (Gal.3.28-29) The Reconciliation of the Jews and the pagans is more forcefully brought out by St. Paul as follows: "But now in Christ Jesus, you that used to be so far apart from us have been brought very close, by the blood of Christ. For he is the peace between us, and has made the two into one and broken down the barrier which used to keep them apart, actually destroying in his own person the hostility caused by the rules and decrees of the Law. This was to create one single New Man in himself out of the two of them and by restoring peace through the cross, to unite them both in a single Body and reconcile them with God. In his own person he killed the hostility. Later he came to bring the good news of peace, peace to you who were far away and peace to those who were near at hand. Through him both of us have in the one Spirit our way to come to the Father". (Eph.2.13-22) Paul gives a description of the pagans in general; they had no Christ; i.e., they had no Messiah; they were without hope; i.e., hope of a Messiah, which was hitherto confined to Israel; they were without God; i.e., they had many gods but not the one true God (1 Cor. 8.5ff). The crucifixion of Christ brought together Jews and pagans and reconciled both with the Father.

The New Man is the prototype of the new humanity that God recreated (2 Cor. 5.17) in the person of Christ, the second Adam (1. Cor. 15.45) after killing the sinfully corrupt race of the first Adam in the crucifixion. Christ is unique because in him the boundaries between any one group and the rest of human race all disappear. The absoluteness of Christ from the viewpoint of its content is a universality based on Israel's universality which worships the God of the universe.

8. *The exact signification of the absoluteness of Christianity*

We cannot speak of the absoluteness of Christianity in whatever characterizes Christianity. By Christianity we understand the Christian revelation at the interior of the present history, not of the eschatological revelation which includes the actual history of salvation as preparation of the future perfect salvation. We think of the present history as established in Christians as the way of salvation, differentiated from other religions. The first precision of the absoluteness of Christianity is that in the perspective of the eschatological revelation of God, we deal with the preparatory revelation; i.e., preparation means "not yet accomplished", "not yet perfect", "not yet absolute". Our knowledge of it is partial, our prophecy is partial, when the perfection comes, that which is partial ceases". (1 Cor.13.9ff).

The second precision of the absoluteness of Christianity is that all our knowledge is produced in reflected image and similitude. "Now we regard as in a mirror, in a confused fashion, but then it will be face to face". (Cor.13.12). Theologically it means that our knowledge is only analogical. Christ himself has recounted the mystery of the Kingdom of God in parables. (Mk 4.33ff.) The Son of God has spoken to man as man; he has translated the divine mysteries into human language; he has conceived them under the form which has given us a veritable comprehension of them but which makes more to grasp the truth than to comprehend entirely what is found behind it. We can say that it is here a humanization of the mysteries of God; but without counting that it is the only form under which it is possibile to speak about it, this does not present the danger of misunderstanding in as far as one remains conscious of the analogy. More dangerous is the tentative of theology to seize things in concepts, for then a conceptual thought gains easily the terrain which loses its clarity of discourse by similitudes and it falls finally in a game of concepts. Certainly, theology cannot pass over concepts but in order to avoid the dangers of a thought purely conceptual, it ought to come back without ceasing to the ways of speaking of the Lord. The divine mystery for us is without form because inexpressible; the conceptual thought signifies an isolating thought which can go astray easily from the living reality.

The third precision of the absoluteness of Christianity is found in the notion of "historical evolution". Surely, Christianity is realized all pure in Christ, such that all the ulterior developments ought to take their norm and their legitimation in him. Speaking of a pure realization of Christianity in Jesus Christ we admit that all other realization is necessarily limited without being false for that. Christianity is never linked to a cultural form, determined though it can and ought to penetrate in all cultures. But all penetration is a particular conformation and not a universal representation or universally valuable of Christianity. Catholicity is not uniformity. Qualitative and quantitative Catholicity signify that it is a question of progress which still remains to realize. Cfr also the progress of the evolution of dogma. All true values at the interior of cultures and religions belong to the Church as the plenitude of Christ. Hence Christianity is not absolute under all aspects.

The fourth precision is that we cannot consider this pretension simply in the formal orthodoxy, but see it in relation with love, the essential commandment. Christianity is not only doctrine but the way of salvation; not every one who says Lord, Lord is saved but who does the will of God. (Mt 7.21ff; 1 Cor. 13). The Church has to be open and remain so to the Kingdom of God in plenitude and perfection. The claim of Christianity for absoluteness finds its justification in the fact that it is the definitive divulgation of God in the Son who does not announce only the way of salvation but he is himself the way and is without ceassing glorified in the witness of the Holy Spirit: here the truth and love are become one[58].

Christianity is a particular religion in as far as it is historical, and contains God's intervention in history. Hence, it is absolute by God's positive will because it represents God's unique intervention in Jesus Christ at a particular stage of history. Christianity is the concrete universal. Absoluteness of Christianity does not imply that it alone possesses all truths; that it involves totalitarian levelling and inexorable imposition; that it denies values that are inherent in other religions by reason of creation and of the universal economy of salvation. The absoluteness of Christianity signifies an awareness that God intervened in a decisive and irreversible manner in the Church at the service of mankind and that gift made to the Church is true and meaningful for all men. The absolute character of Christianity is derived from that of Jesus

---

[58] MAURUS HEINRICHS, *Théologie Catholique et pensée asiatique*, Casterman, Tournai, 1965, pp. 85-89.

Christ, its founder, who continues his salvific activity by his Spirit in the Church. Now, with respect to the claim to the absolute truth in Christianity, we have to note that this is entirely dependent on the claim which Jesus Christ made for himself: "I am the light of the World". (Jn 8.12) The claim that Jesus made is that he and he alone can savingly irradiate the dark mystery of men's existence and give their life meaning, purpose an destiny. Christ is the fullness of Truth; but this does not mean that the Church has exhausted the mystery of Christ; the Church is at the service of Christ who is the absolute truth, for he is God incarnate. The Church has to grow in the perception and actualization of the mystery of Christ in its life and teaching. It has to learn from the Teacher, the Holy Spirit whom Christ promised as the revealer of truth. Besides, the Church has to learn in and through dialogue from other religions where Christ and his Spirit are present and active. "The Catholic Church rejects nothing that is true and holy in these religions. She regards with sincere reverence those ways of conduct and of life, those precepts and teachings, which though differing in many respects from the ones she holds and sets forth, nonetheless often reflect a ray of that truth wich enlightens all men". (NA 2)

8. *The hermeneutics of testimony according to Paul Ricoeur*

What is the kind of philosophy that is implied in the problem of the absolute, which seeks to join an *experience* of the absolute to the *idea* of the absolute, which finds neither in example nor in symbol the depth of this esperience, that is proper in this problem of testimony. We have to develop a hermeneutics of the absolute and of testimony. A testimony should be applied to words, works, actions, and to lives which attest to an intention, an idea at the heart of experience and history which nonetheless transcend experience and history. The philosophical problem of testimony concerns the absolute testimony of the absolute. The question is proper only if the absolute makes sense for consciousness, beyond the critique of the ontological argument and proofs of the existence of God; if reflection is able to elevate self-consciousness to an original affirmation which is truly an absolute affirmation of the absolute. This original affirmation for the reflexive philosophy is not an experience. It is the act which accomplishes the negation of the limitations which affect individual destiny. It is divestment by which reflection is brought to the encounter with contingent signs that the absolute in its generosity allows to appear of itself. Absolute testimony in concrete singularity gives a caution to the truth without which its authority remains in suspense. Testimony, singular each time, confers the sanction of reality on ideas, ideals, and modes of being that the symbol depicts and discovers for us only as our most personal possibilities. What right does one have to invest a moment of history with an absolute character? How can we conjoin the interiority of primary affirmation and the exteriority of acts and of existences that are said to give testimony of the absolute? A hermeneutics of testimony tries to solve this problem[59].

In the case of biblical witnessing, the problem arises as to whether we have the right to invest a moment of history with an absolute character. There appears to be an unbridgeable chasm between the interiority of original affirmation and the extriority of acts and of existence which would claim to give testimony of the absolute. What is it to interpret testimony? It is a twofold act, an act of consiousness of itself and an act of historical understanding based on the signs that the absolute gives of itself. The signs of the absolute's self-disclosure are at the same time signs in which consciousness recognizes itself. It is the convergence of these two paths that has to be explained. The hermenutics of testimony arises in the confluence of two exegeses; the exegesis of historic testimony of the absolute and the exegesis of the self in the criteriology of the divine. The concept of testimony as given in the biblical exegesis is hermeneutical in a double sense. It gives something to be interpreted (the content of interpretation) and the interpretation itself. In testimony there is an immediacy of the absolute without which there would be nothing to interpret. The self-manifestation of

---

[59] See PAUL RICOEUR, *The Hermeneutics of Testimony*, in: *Essays on Biblical Interpretation*, Fortress Press, Philadelphia, 1980, pp. 119ff.

the absolute here and now indicates that there is no infinite regress of reflection. The absolute manifests its presence and this constitutes an experience of the absolute. It is only about this that testimony testifies. As testimony gives something to be interpreted, it demands to be interpreted.

Testimony has to be interpreted because of the dialectic of meaning and event that traverses it. The fusion between the confessional pole and the narrative pole of testimony has a notable hermeneutical significance in that the testimony cannot be interpreted from without as a violence which would be done to it. In testimony narration and confession are joined to each other without distance. The Gospel witnesses confess the significance of Christ directly on the Jesus-event: "You are the Christ". There is no separation between the Jesus of history and the Christ of faith. The fusion of meaning and event signifies also a tension; the event is both apparent and hidden; hidden to the extent that it is apparent. The appearances of the living Christ are also the empty tomb. Every relation between a sign and an object can be explained by means of a sign which plays the role of interpretant with regard to their relation. We can apply this to testimony and to the relation of confession to narration and point out that the manifestation of the absolute in persons and acts is indefinitely mediated by means of available meanings borrowed from previous scripture. Thus the primitive Church continued to interpret the "testimony of Christ" from Hebrew and Greek tradition (Titles of Jesus: Son of Man, Messiah or Christ, Judge, King, Logos). Thus it is possible to mediate the relation of meaning and event by another meaning which plays the role of interpretation with regard to their very relation. Interpretation is not external to testimony but implied by its initial dialectical structure.

Testimony evokes a critical activity in its being interpreted. It is necessary to choose between a true and false witness. Taken in this second sense, testimony, the hermeneutic structure of testimony consists in that testimony concerning things seen only reaches judgement by means of things said. *Fides ex auditu*. The works and signs that the revealer "gives" are so many bits of evidence and means of proof in the grand trial of the absolute. Only a trial can decide between Yahweh and the "idols of nothing".

Finally, testimony gives something to be interpreted by the dialectic of witness and of testimony. The witness testifies about something or someone which goes beyond him. Thus testimony proceeds from the *Other*. But the involvement of the witness is his testimony. The testimony of Christ is his works, his suffering; and the testimony of the disciple is analogously his suffering. There is a hermeneutic circle here: the circle of Manifestation ad Suffering.

On the path of original affirmation towards testimony, original affirmation changes into a criteriology of the divine. There is no unitary intuition nor absolute knowledge in which consciousuness would grasp both consciousness of the absolute and consciousness of itself. The moment of awareness can only be broken up and dispersed in the predicates of the divine. These predicates are not qualities of a being in itself but they are the multiple expressions of a Pure Act which can only be spoken of by being predicated with these qualities. Proceeding from the reflexive pole, the original affirmation develops a reflexive type of interpretation, called a criteriology of the divine by means of which consciousness makes itself judge of the divine and consequently chooses its God or gods. In the perspective of the criteriology of the divine original affirmation is led to encounter the crisis of idols that testimony calls forth.

"The hermeneutics of testimony is aboslute-relative; it is twice absolute and twice relative. It is absolute as original affirmation in search of a sign, absolute as the manifestation in the sign. It is relative as the criteriology of the divine for philosophic consciousness, relative as the trial of idols for historical consciousness"[60]. The act of a self-consciousness which divests itself and tries to understand itself, the act of testifying by which the absolute is revealed in its signs and its works: there is reciprocity between these two acts. The promotion of consciousness and the recognition of the absolute in its signs are reciprocal. "The essential idea is to demonstrate an established

---

[60] P. RICOEUR, *The hermeneutics of testimony*, in: *Essays on biblical Interpretation*, p. 151, Fortress Press, Philadelphia, 1980.

correspondence between historical affirmation of the absolute and the degrees by which a consciousness proceeds to raise itself and transform itself for an original affirmation"[61].

Conclusion

The centrality of Christ

Christianity stands or falls with the person and work of Jesus Christ who is the revelation of God in history, in whom and through whom we can find the meaning and purpose of life. Christian faith is that Jesus Christ is Lord of all who reveals to us the nature of our heavenly Father. It affirms that "there is salvation in no one else, for there is no other name under heaven given among men by which we must be saved". (Acts 4.12). We derive this truth from God's revelation of himself in Jesus Christ who is the true and living way. The central tenet of the Christian faith is that Jesus Christ is the one and universal Mediator between God and man. Christ is the Event by which all other events are judged. He is the watershed of time, the focus of meaning in history.

The universality of Christ

The absoluteness of Christianity's claim for Jesus Christ is at the same time inclusive or universal. "God loved the world so much that he gave his only son, so that everyone who believes in him may not be lost but may have eternal life" (Jn 3.16). The Christian Gospel has a universal view. "There are no more distinctions between Jew and Greek, slave and free, male and female, but all of you are one in Christ Jesus". (Gal. 3.28) Christians believe that in Jesus Christ God has come to redeem all people to gather together from every kindred and tongue and nation those who accept him as Lord.

---

[61] Ibidem.

The absoluteness of Jesus Christ and of Christianity

Christ is seen as the central mystery of Christianity. Faith in Jesus determines all the rest: redemption, trinity, grace and the Church. Jesus Christ is the paradigmatic event of the divine-human union. Christianity insists on the absolute distinction between humanity and divinity, the absolute reality of both, the absolute divine identity of Jesus Christ, and the absolute incarnation of the Eternal Word once for all in a single historical personage. The distinctive core of Christianity is the belief in Jesus Christ, eternal Son of God incarnate. This belief about Jesus entails an understanding of God as a Triunity, the divinization of the human race, and a special mission for Christians as the Church. This does not mean that the Christian understanding is in opposition to that of others. In varying degrees, Christian belief is in accord with that of other believers and goes beyond that of others. Through Jesus Christ and in the Holy Spirit divine life is offered to all mankind. Jesus' redemption affects every human being, whether one knows it or not. All human salvation is inextricably linked with the mystery of Christ. As the Second Vatican Council says: "All this (the Mystery of Christian salvation) holds true not for Christians only but also for all men of good will in whose hearts grace is active invisibly. For since Christ died for all, and since all men are in fact called for the one and the same destiny, which is divine, we must hold that the Holy Spirit offers to all the possibilty of being made partners, in a way known to God, in the paschal mystery". (GS. n. 22; cfr also LG 14-16) All somehow share in the Easter mystery of Christ. All are involved in one and the same salvation. All have received the Holy Spirit poured out in the world; the Holy Spirit is active wherever good is being achieved. Wherever the Spirit is active the human salvation is being furthered. Reality and the understanding of reality are not the same thing. There are various degrees of awareness of one and the same reality that all live: some understand reality only to the extent that they pursue honest and right living; others worship God acknowledging God as creator and helper; Christians know and understand what God has accomplished through Jesus Christ and the Holy Spirit. It is one thing to be in love; it is another to acknowledge and avow that love. The reality itself, the love, remains the same reality. But once acknowledged and avowed, it takes on a new degree of perfection[62]. It does not follow that Christians are necessarily better people than others. Christians are not always faithful to their faith, and live accordingly.

Some (e.g., K.P. Aleaz) propose a pluralistic inclusivism as a viable alternative for an Indian Christian theology of religions. "Pluralistic inclusivism is an attempt to make Christian faith pluralistically inclusive, i.e., the very content of the revelation of God in Jesus is to become truly pluralistic by other faiths contributing to it as per the requirement of different places and times and it is through such pluralistic understanding of the Gospel that its true inclusivism is to shine forth. Here pluralism transforms itself to focus on its centre which is God as God in the universally conceived Jesus and inclusivism transforms itself to bear witness to the fulfilment of the Christian understanding of Christ in the universally conceived Jesus. Here the two axions of the "universal salvific will of God" and "salvation comes through God in Christ alone" lose their separateness in the one axiom "universal salvation comes through God in the universally conceived Jesus"[63]. There is real inclusivism only when people of other faiths will contribute to the very understanding of Christ in and through whom God gives salvation. The Christian understanding of Christ has to get its fulfilment through contributions from people of other faiths rather than it fulfils other faiths[64]. The problem here is that other faiths have different mutually exclusive and often contradictory understanding of Christ which are not reconcilable from the Christian point of view, as attested by the Bible and Tradition.

Not withstanding the irreconcilable elements that are found among different religions (i.e., dissimilarities), we do

---

[62] Cfr. B. LONERGAN, *Method in Theology*, Herder Herder, New, York, 1972, pp. 112-3.

[63] K.P. ALEAZ, *Religious Pluralism and Christian Witness: A Biblical-theological analysis*, in: *Bangalore Theological Forum*, XXI (1989, n. 4 and XXII (1990), n. 1.

[64] Ibidem, p. 62. See also the same author's article: *Pluralistic Inclusivism. A viable Indian Theology of Religions*, in: *Asia Journal of Theology*, 12 (1998), n. 2, pp. 206-88).

find positive elements of truth, goodness and sanctity among them which can contribute to the enrichment of Christian experience and of the understanding of the mystery of Christ in a more profound way. This aspect is often considered in terms of complementarity between Christianity and other religions. In other words, in order to avoid exclusivism and pluralism, we propose complementary inclusivism that safeguards both the absoluteness of Jesus Christ and of Christianity and the admittedly valid religious and moral riches of other religions in our dialogical understanding and communion with other religions.

The vertical complementarity

Jacques-Albert Cuttat speaks of a verical complementarity between the monotheistic traditions of the West and the metaphysical (immanentist) traditions of the East which is of help to explain the complentarity between Christianity and other religions.

"The fact that these two spiritual 'dimensions' of mankind are the only authentic ones rules out the posssibily of synthetizing them into a third, which would be their common denominator. Moreover, the fact that both are authentic prevents us from reducing either one to the other. Fnally, their mere apposition would contradict the transcendent unity of God as well as the immanent unity of human nature. This unity requires that we look upon the two dimensions in question as being fundamentally complementary and, therefore, that one be subordinate to the other. In simple logic, we are thus led to consider which of these two viewpoints is capable of including the other without absorbing or mutilating it. The problem is to join them in a complementarism which would not be merely horizontal, like that of the sexes - this would bring us back to syncretism, but rather vertical, like that of nature and grace. This requirement arises because our dilemma is in the spiritual realm, and because there dwells in every man an image of God ordered to his likeness, a supernatural vocation"[65].

---

[65] See his *The Encounter of Religions*, Desclee Company, New York, 1960, pp. 29f.

Thus Christianity is capable of being enriched by the values of other religions without mutilating them, and even carry them to their maximum of development. In the plenitude of the divine revelation and of its divine revealed truth and in the reception of its catholicity Christianity includes infinitely more than it excludes, and receives, by elevating them even in quality, the religious values of other believers. Christ assumes and elevates the spiritual riches of other religions to draw away from their 'solitude' and to include them in a communion in which the human self, all incorporated in Christ, hears the Father saying to him: "You are my well-beleved son and I have engendered you today. One such vision of other religions throws much light not only on the positive values of other religions but also on Christianiy itself in its work of evangelization and on the fundamental Christian attitude in interreligious dialogue. Thus a Christian can say: "The more I deepen my faith the more I can understand from within the faith of others".

As in God every perfection of being is found in a supereminent manner, so also in Christ is found the plenitude of grace and supernatural efficay, by which he not only can effect every work of grace but also can lead others to grace. "It was the good pleasure of the Father that in him (Christ) should all the fulness dwell". (Col. 1.16) St Paul speaks of what God has done for all men through Christ: "and through him to reconcile all things unto himself" (Col. 1.20), and "in him ye are made full". The fulness of grace is in Christ and it is by him that this fulness is made available for all men. The whole fulness of the Godhead was in Christ alone and no other manifestation was necessary or even possible. (Col. 2.9-10).

The Church, according to Paul, is said to be "the fulness of him that filleth all in all". (Eph. 1.23) Christ fills the whole universe; "in him all things hold together". (Col. 1.17) Christ fills especially the Church and makes it a living whole through which he realizes his purposes and thus the Church is his body. Christ not only fills the Church but also is filled up or completed by the Church, for without the Church Christ would not be complete. The Church continuing the work of Christ and extending his efficacious presence in time and space is the pleroma of Christ. She is the pleroma of Christ not only because she undergoes the influence of Christ's grace fully but also because she completes him by building up his mystical body. Just as the soul cannot exercise its functions fully without the help of its body, so does also Christ by his own free choice need the Church to carry out his redemptive design[66].

Christianity cannot evade encounter with other religions; while in dialogue with them, it must realize its basic, distinctive feature which flows from its being the Church as the Body of Christ as it brings out its absolute uniqueness which is inclusive of the religious and moral values of other religions. This inclusiveness is not just an appropriation of others' values without recognizing their own authenticity but an enrichment of Christianity itself by these values as of others. It is in this sense that we can speak of the Asian, African Church as fully Christian and authentically Asian or African. Thus we see that the criticism made against inclusiveness as spiritual colonialism or illegitimate appropriation of others' property, or the spirit of superiority over others is not theologically valid. It really brings out the catholicity and universality of the Church which is both universal and paritcular or concrete universal, similar to Jesus Christ as the concrete universal Saviour of mankind. Christian theology of religions can be called vertical inclusivism or concrete universal inclusivism which calls for an expression which is fully Christian and authentically diverse or particular to safeguard the unity in diversity of the Christian faith and life.

Select Bibliography

Russel F. Aldwinkle, *Jesus - A Saviour or the Saviour?*, Religious Pluralism in Christian Perspective, Mercer Univ. Press. Macon, 1982, ch. 3.

Angelo Amato, *Jesus Christ, centre de l'histoire du salut et de la vie de l'Eglise*, in: *Tertio Millennio Adveniente, Commentaire théologique et pastorale*, Mame, Paris, 1996, ch. 4.

Reinholdt Bernardt, *Christianity Without Absolutes*, SCM Press, London, 1994.

Werner Bieder, *Christ the Sacrament for the World*, in: *Theologische Zeitschrift* 19 (1963), pp. 241-249.

Jean-François Bonnefoy, *Christ and the Cosmos*, St Anthony Guild Press, Paterson, ch. 3: The Absolute and Universal Primacy of Christ, 1965.

---

[66] St Thomas Aquinas, *De Veritate*, 29.4, ad. 3m.

A.C. Bouquet, *Revelation and the Divine Logos*, in: Gerald H. Anderson, *The Theology of the Christian Mission*, McGraw-Hill, New York, 1961, pp. 183-98.

A.C. Bouquet, *The Doctrine of the Logos*, in: *The Christian Faith and non-christian religions*, London, 1958, ch. VI.

Raymond E. Brown, *"Who do men say that I am?"* - A survey of Modern Scholarship on Gospel Christology, in: Crises Facing the Church, ch. 2, Paulist Press, New York, 1975.

Raymond E. Brown, *Jesus God and Man*, The Bruce Publishing Co., Milwakee, 1967.

P. Th. Camelot, *Le Christ, Sacrement de Dieu*, in: *L'Homme devant Dieu*, Mélanges Offerts au Henri de Lubac, Vol. 1, Aubier, Paris, 1963, pp. 355-365.

Sarah Coakley, *Christ Without Absolutes*, A Study of the Christology of E. Troeltsch, Oxford University Press, London, 1988.

Yves M. Congar, *The Wide World My Parish*, Helicon Press, Baltimore, 1961.

Yves M. Congar, *Jesus Christ*, Herder and Herder, New York, 1966.

Yves M. Congar, *Christ in the Economy of Salvation and in our Dogmatic Tracts*, in: Concilium, 1966, Vol. 1, n. 2.

Richard Cote, *Some Pretensions to the Absolute in the History of Christian Missions*, in: Concilium. 1980, n. 135, pp. 14-22.

Mariasusai Dhavamony, *Christian Theology of Religions*, Studien zur Interkulturellen Geschichte des Christentums, n. 108, Peter Lang, Bern, 1998, ch. 5-7.

Dow Kirkpatrick, *The Finality of Christ*, Abingdon Press, Nashville, 1966, ch. 1.

Jost Eckert, *The Gospel for Israel and the Nations: The Problem of the Absoluteness of Christianity in the New Testament*, in: Concilium, 1980, n. 135, pp. 35-45.

Jacques Dupuis, *Jesus Christ at the Encounter of World Religions*, Orbis Books, Maryknoll, 1991.

Jacques Dupuis, *Toward a Christian Theology of Religious Pluralism*, Orbis Books, Maryknoll, 1997.

Denis Edwards, *Jesus and the Cosmos*, Paulist Press, New York, 1991, ch. 5 The Relationship between Jesus and the Evolving Cosmos.

M.A. Feuillet, *Etudes sur la christologie paulinienne*, Institut Chatolique de Paris, 1972.

Jean de Fraine, *Adam and Christ as corporate personalities*, in: *Theology Digest*, X(1962), n. 2, pp. 99-102.

Reginald H. Fuller and Pheme Perkins, *Who is This Christ?*, Fortress Press, Philadelphia, 1983.

Allen D. Galloway, *The Cosmic Christ*, Nisbet & Co., London, 1941, Ch. 4.

Jean Galot, *Qui dites-vous que Je suis?*, Parole et Silence, Socomed, Au seuil du troisième millénaire, Saint Maur, 1996.

Aloys Grillmeier, *The Figure of Christ in Catholic Theology Today*, in: *Theology Today, Renewal in Dogma*, Vol. 1, The Bruce Publishing Co. Milwaukee, 1964, pp.66-109.

Romano Guardini, *The Humanity of Christ*, Pantheon, New York, 1964, ch. 5, The Absolute Otherness of Christ.

Thor Hall, *The Evolution of Christology*, Abingdon Press, Nashville, 1982, ch. 5.

Gabriel Hebert, *Christ of Faith and the Jesus of History*, SCM Press, London, 1962.

A.E. HARVEY (ed.), *God Incarnate. Story and Belief*, SPCK, London, 1981.
JOHN HICK, *Religious Pluralism and Absolute Claims*, in: *Religious Pluralism*, Leroy S. Rouner (ed.), University of Notre Dame Press, Notre Dame, 1984.
L.D. HURST and N.T. WRIGHT (ed.), *The Glory of Christ in the New Testament*, Clarendon Press, Oxford, 1987, Ch. 14: *The Historical Jesus and the Theology of the New Testament*, by Robert Morgan.
WALTER KASPER, *Absoluteness of Christianity*, in: *Sacramentum Mundi*, Burns and Oates, London, 1968.
PAUL KNITTER, *Christianity as Religion: True and Absolute?* A Roman Catholic Perspective, in: *Concilium*, 1980, n. 135, pp. 12-21.
JOHN MACQUARRIE, *Truth in Christology*, in: *God incarnate: Story and Belief*, ed. 1994, Grand Rapid, A.E. Harvey, SPCK, London, 1981, pp. 24-33.
JEAN NABERT, *Le temoignage absolu du divin a Dieu*, in: *Le Désir de Dieu*, Aubier-Montaigne, Paris, 1966, pp. 265ff.
JEAN NABERT, *L'ermeneutique de l'absolu*, ibidem, pp. 314ff.
JEAN NABERT, *L'absolu et le divin*, ibidem, pp. 176ff.
HAROLD A. NETLAND, *Dissonant Voices*. Religious Pluralism and the Question of Truth, Leicestér, Apolles, 1991, ch. 7.
LESSLIE NEWBIGIN, *Religious Pluralism and the Uniqueness of Jesus Christ*, in: *International Bulletin of Missionary Research*, Vol. 13 (1989), pp. 50ff.
BRUCE J. NICHOLLS (ed.), *The Unique Christ in our Pluralist World*, Baker Book House, 1994, Grand Rapid.
JAMES PETER, *Finding the Historical Jesus*, Collins, London, 1965.
SWEE-HWA-QUEK, *Adam and Christ according to Paul*, in: *Pauline Studies*, ed. Donald A. Hagner and Murray J. Harris, Wm B. Eerdmans, Grand Rapid, Michigan, 1980, pp. 67-79.
KARL RAHNER, *Is Christianity an "Absolute Religion"?*, in: *Grace in Freedom*, Herder and Herder, New York, 1969.
KARL RAHNER, *Christianity's Absolute Claim*, in: *Theological Investigations*, Vol. XXI, Darton, Longman and Dotty, London, 1988.
KARL RAHNER, *World History and Salvation History*, in: *The Christian and the World*, Canisianum, P. J. Kenedy é Sons, New York, 1965.
KARL RAHNER, *The One Christ and the Universality of Salvation, Theological Investigations*, Vol. XVI, Darton, Longman and Todd, London, 1979, ch. 13.
KARL RAHNER, *What do I mean when I say: Jesus is God?*, in: *Karl Rahner in Dialogue, Conversations and Interviews*, 1969-82, Crossroad, New York, 1986, n. 11.
KARL RAHNER, *Christianity on the threshold of the third millennium*, Ibidem, pp. 268ff.
KARL RAHNER, *Christianity and World Religions* (The original title: Is Christianity an Absolute Religion?), in: *The Content of Faith*, Crossroad, New York, 1992.
JOSEPH RATZINGER, *Das Problem der Absolutheit des Christlichen Heilsweges*, in: *Kirche in der ausser-christlichen Welt*, Verlag Friedrich Pustet, Regensburg, 1967.
CHARLES E. REAGAN and DAVID STEWARD (ed.), *The Philosophy of Paul Ricoeur*, An Antology of his work, Beacon Press, Boston, 1978.
LUCIEN RICHARD, *Some Recent Developments on the Question of Christology and World Religions*, in: *Eglise et Théologie*, 8(1977), pp. 209-44.

HELMUT RIEDLINGER, *How Universal is Christ's Kingship. A Bibliographical Study*, in: *Concilium*, 1966, n. 2, pp. 56-66.

PAUL RICOEUR, *The Hermeneutics of Testimony*, in: *Essays on Biblical Interpretation*, Fortress Press, Philadelphia, 1980.

PAUL RICOEUR, *Interpretation Theory: Discourse and the Surplus of Meaning*, The Texas Christian University Press, Fort Worth, 1976.

PAUL RICOEUR, *Les incidences théologiques des recherches actuelles concernant le langage*, Institut d'Etudes oecuneniques, Paris, 1988.

PAUL RICOEUR, *The Reality of the Historical Past*, Marquette University Press, Milwaukee, 1984.

PAUL RICOEUR, *L'attestazione tra fenomenologia e teologia*, Edizioni Biblioteca dell'immagine, 1993.

PAUL RICOEUR, *Essays on Biblical Interpretation*, Fortress Press, Philadelphia, 1980.

OLIVIER ROUSSEAU, *The Idea of the Kingship of Christ*, in *Concilium*, 1966, n. 2, pp. 67-67-73.

SCHILLEBEECKX E., *Christ the Sacrament of the encounter with God*, Sheed and Ward, New York, 1963.

RUDOLF SCHNACKENBURG, *Christologie des Neuen Testamentes*, in: J. Feiner-Löhrer (Mgb.), *Mysterium Salutis*, III/1, Einsiedeln, 1970.

ROBIN SCROGGS, *The Last Adam*, Basil Blackwell, 1966.

GEORGE EDGAR SHANKEL, *God and Man in History*, Southern Publishing Association, Nashville, Tennessee, 1967, ch. XIV, Christ, the Axis of History.

CALVIN E. SHENK, *Who do you say that I am?* Christianity encounters other Religions, Herald Press, Scottdale, 1997.

GERARD S. SLOYAN, *Jesus, Redeemer and Divine Word*, Michael Glazier, Wilmington, 1989.

M.M. THOMAS, *The Absoluteness of Jesus Christ and Christ-centred Syncretism*, in: *Ecumenical Review*, 37(1985), n. 4, pp. 387-397.

MARK THOMSEN, *The Finality of Jesus Crucified and the Global Mission of the Church*, in: *Word and World*, Vol. IX(1989), n. 3, pp. 17-21.

ERNST TROELTSCH, *The Absoluteness of Christianity and the History of Religions*, SCM Press, London, 1972.

G. ERNEST WRIGHT, *God Who Acts*, SCM Press, 1960.

The Holy Spirit, the Principal Agent of Evangelization

EARL MULLER

INTRODUCTION

Paul VI in his apostolic exhortation, *Evangelii Nuntiandi*, asserted in 1975 that "the Holy Spirit is the principal agent of evangelization"[1]. John Paul II reiterated this in his 1990 encyclical, *Redemptoris Missio*[2]. The purpose of this article is to explore some of the ramifications of this affirmation.

Evangelization, in its empirical form, is the proclamation of the gospel of Jesus Christ to individuals and communities that have not yet been touched by that gospel. It is in this regard distinct from catechetics which is directed toward the fuller instruction of those already convinced of the truth of the gospel. It is also distinct from that ongoing instruction of the community which is highly paraenetic in focus, offering reinforcement and encouragement for a faith already accepted and more or less assimilated[3].

---

[1] *EN* 75. The following abbreviations will be used in the notes: *AG* - *Ad Gentes Divinitus*; *CL* - *Christifideles Laici*; *DV* - *Dominum et Vivificantem*; *EA* - *Ecclesia in America*; *EN* - *Evangelii Nuntiandi*; *GS* - *Gaudium et Spes*; *LG* - *Lumen Gentium*; *PO* *Presbyterorum Ordinis*; *RM* - *Redemptoris Missio*; *TM* - *Tertio Millennio Adveniente*. The Third Synod on Evangelization held in Rome in 1974 will be referred to simply as Synod 1974. The Synod produced declarations, questions and Paul VI's opening and closing addresses. Unidentified numbers refer to the declarations.

[2] *RM* 21. This is not to deny that Jesus Christ himself is the principal agent, ibid., 36. Cf. also 9 - Christ carries out his mission through the Church principally in terms of endowing his Church with his Spirit. Cf. also *TM* 45.

[3] Cf. *AG* 6.

This descriptive account is misleading because it gives the impression that evangelization is one activity among several that the Church undertakes. The same pontiffs have made it clear that this is not the case. Paul VI wrote that "evangelizing is in fact the grace and vocation proper to the Church, her deepest identity. She exists in order to evangelize"[4]. John Paul II recalled the Second Vatican Council's emphasis on the missionary nature of the Church at the very beginning of his encyclical.

They ground the ecclesial missionary vocation within the dynamic of the Trinitarian missions themselves: "The Church on earth is by its very nature missionary since, according to the plan of the Father, it has its origin in the mission of the Son and the Holy Spirit. This plan flows from 'fountain-like love', the love of God the Father"[5]. The character of these missions establish the parameters for the Spirit's role in the evangelistic efforts of the Church and must, accordingly, be considered in some detail. There are three pivotal moments in which the Spirit enters into the mission of Jesus: his conception, his baptism by John, his death and resurrection. These will be considered in turn with special attention paid to the import they have for the mission of the Church. This extended treatment will provide the foundation for the final two sections which attempt to synthesize what magisterial documents have had to say on the role of the Spirit in evangelization in general and in the new evangelization in particular.

The New Creation in Christ

The mystery of the Incarnation is deeply paradoxical. Considered from the side of humanity it is simply impossible. But with God all things are possible except the truly contradictory. It is within his power to make actual that for which

---

[4] *EN* 14. John Paul II took over this theme in his Opening Address to the Puebla conference of Latin American bishops in 1979 (hereafter, Puebla), I.7.
[5] *AG* 2; *RM* 1.

there is no prior potency, to make a preexisting reality be something for which it had had no potency. God is the Creator: he makes all things from nothing, he takes material creation and makes it to be rational, he takes that rational creation and makes it to be himself. In each case there is no prior potency for the actuality that God makes to be.

"How can this be since I do not know man?" One might argue that parthenogenesis, however unlikely, is nonetheless within the possibilities inherent in the biological basis of human reality. Christians see a miracle worked by God here. This is of lesser importance in comparison to the revelatory character of the event. Throughout the patristic tradition, and already in the New Testament, the virginal conception was seen as a sign of a yet greater reality:

> Wherefore also the Lord Himself gave us a sign, ... which man did not ask for, because he never expected that a virgin could conceive, or that it was possible that one remaining a virgin could bring forth a son, and that what was thus born should be "God with us"[6].

The reference is to Is. 7:14, a prophecy taken to refer to Jesus who is in reality "God with us". The real impossibility of this conception lies not in Mary remaining a virgin in her conceiving of Jesus but in her being the mother of God. If a virginal conception can somehow be understood to lie within the intrinsic intelligibility of a rational-biological species, it lies completely outside of that intelligibility that a human mother should generate a child who is by nature God. Mary nonetheless generated God. "How can this be?" "The Holy Spirit will come upon you". F.X. Durrwell has been attentive to these themes: the Spirit "makes Mary *capable* of being the mother of a child, the Son of God"[7]. He sets as his starting point the

---

[6] IRENAEUS, *Adversus Haeresis* III.xix.3.
[7] *Holy Spirit of God: An Essay in Biblical Theology*, trans. Sr. Benedict Davies, O.S.U. (London: Geoffrey Chapman, 1986), p. 9. "Pour une christologie selon l'Esprit Saint", *Nouvelle Revue Theologique* 114 (1992): 653-77; abstracted in *Theology Digest* 40 (1993): 221-27. Occasionally my translations coincide with those of this abstract.

death and resurrection of Jesus holding that "the action of the Holy Spirit is fully manifested" and the "divine sonship of Jesus is revealed in its fullness" at this time[8]. From this starting point and the image of the power of the Spirit who "*is the omnipotence of God*" he proceeds to tie together all the various aspects of the new creation:

> Whenever, then, God is active, when he creates, intervenes in history, enters through the incarnation into creation, raises Christ from the dead, establishes a covenant between himself and a people, even when, in his trinitarian action, he begets an eternal Son, it is in the Spirit that all this is brought about, for the Spirit is the power and action of God[9].

The pervasive character of the Spirit's action in different mysteries of the faith deserves further reflection but before this can be done Durrwell's confused presentation of the eternal begetting of the Son needs to be clarified since the relevant issues have important implications for understanding the relation between the universal Spirit in the world and the historical figure of Jesus Christ and the Church which proclaims him. Durrwell is serious in his affirmation of the Spirit's involvement in the eternal begetting of the Son: "in the mystery of the Father who engenders, of the Son engendered, the Spirit is the divine power of engenderment". He makes an explicit reference to Augustine's love triad as a parallel example[10].

There is no appropriate parallel here. Love and the power of engenderment have significantly different ontological structures. Love, even self-love, requires a prior existing object that is in some way present to the mind in knowledge: "there is no love where nothing is being loved.... But what does loving itself mean but wanting to be available to itself in order to enjoy itself... Now the mind cannot love itself unless it also knows itself"[11]. The same is not true of the power of engen-

---

[8] Ibid., pp. 6-7.
[9] Ibid., p. 10.
[10] "Pour une christologie", p. 661.
[11] *De Trinitate* IX.ii.2-iii.3.

derment. That power can exist even in the absence of a child. Furthermore, there can be no child apart from an ontologically prior power to engender. To claim that the Spirit is the eternal Father's power of engendering is to claim that the Spirit proceeds from the Father prior to the Son. But the faith of the Church, at least in the West, is that the Holy Spirit "proceeds from the Father and the Son".

The East itself would have problems with Durrwell's claim, even if it might be sympathetic with his 'Spirituque', since the power to engender is proper only to the Father; it is the *proprium* that distinguishes him from the Son and the Spirit. Omnipotence is the characteristic of all three Persons, not simply of the Spirit. Omnipotence takes the form in part of engendering in the Father because he is the Father. The same omnipotence takes a different proper form in the Son and the Spirit.

This does not resolve all of the difficulty. There is in the West the conviction that we can know the inner life of God from the way the Persons relate to one another in the economy and Durrwell builds his case from the economy[12]: "The child will bear this name [Son of God] because he is born under the action of the Spirit"[13]; "God begets the Son solely in the Spirit, and this Son in the world is the Christ"[14]; "But the Spirit is the one *through whom* this is effected, this coming out, this begetting of the Son in the world. It is *through him* that Jesus is born Son of God... The Spirit is like the divine womb from which Jesus is born Son of God in the world"[15]. The Spirit is temporally present in the economy before Christ, if not in the Incarnation then in the inspiration of the prophets and the sanctification of the just. Why does this temporal priority not reveal something about the eternal processions?

---

[12] Pour une christologie, p. 661: "the paschal mystery is the door open onto the eternal mystery of God".
[13] "Pour une christologie", p. 659.
[14] *Holy Spirit*, p. 7.
[15] *Holy Spirit*, p. 35.

The Incarnation is a work *ad extra* by God - the Father, Son, and Spirit acting together inseparably. But in so acting the Persons of the Trinity do not act in the same way. After noting the inseparable activity of the Trinity in creation Thomas wrote that "nevertheless the divine Persons, according to the nature of their procession, have a causality respecting the creation of things"[16]. This is true also of the Incarnation. Thus, the Father brings about the Incarnation by sending the Son and the Spirit, the Son brings about the Incarnation by being the term of the assumption of human flesh, the Spirit brings about the Incarnation by making that flesh apt for union with the Son[17].

All of this happens simultaneously in a single divine act but according to processional priority. Thus, the mission from the Father has absolute priority. Less clear is the priority between the making of flesh apt for union with the Son which is the work of the Spirit and the assumption to himself of that flesh which is the work of the Son. Does God need, in a distinct act, to make flesh apt for union before that union can take place? Does God need a prior potency before he can act? It is precisely Christ's assumption of human flesh that releases the Spirit onto that flesh making it to be apt in that union. It is a new act of creation, for which there was no prior potency.

The final question is how this united action on the part of God appears in the economy. Is it able to be temporally extended? This is important in a consideration of the fundamental unity of the Paschal mysteries: the Last Supper, Christ's passion and death, the Resurrection, and so forth. If God's unitary action cannot be extended in time then the relation between the Last Supper (and, implicitly, any Eucharist) and Christ's death on the cross can only be intentional, a remembrance (whether proleptic or after the fact), and not a representation. The converse question is whether temporally diverse events can be a single divine act. Several issues turn on this question: the salvation of the just before the time of Christ; the Marian

---

[16] *ST* I.45.6.corp.
[17] Cf. STIII.iii.4.corp. These statements are illustrative rather than exhaustive.

graces (her Immaculate Conception, the overshadowing of the Spirit of her in the Incarnation); the universal presence of the Spirit in the world. This last is the most general case; the first two are important particular instances.

The Church has from the beginning known of dilemma presented by the just in the Old Testament. If, through their justice, they obtained salvation (and no one would deny that Abraham at least was a just man since Scripture was explicit on the point[18]) then there is salvation apart from Christ or the just of the Old Testament did not obtain salvation. It resolved the problem by holding these individuals in limbo where they awaited Christ's victorious descent into hell to lead them into heaven. This does not fully address the problem, however, since the justice of these individuals is itself a grace which implies possession of the justifying Spirit of God. If they possessed that Spirit, then they possessed eternal life since that Spirit is the Giver of Life.

The doctrine of the Immaculate Conception presents similar difficulties since Christ's salvific death would seem to be unnecessary for a putatively sinless Mary. The Catholic response is that Mary's grace is nonetheless derived from Christ's redemptive merit: "Consequently, through the power of the Holy Spirit, in the order of grace, which is a participation in the divine nature, *Mary receives life from him to whom she herself*, in the order of earthly generation, *gave life* as a mother"[19]. This is possible because her Son is her Creator. What is also in view, though not explicitly stated here, is the communication of idioms whereby things proper to the divine nature are also said of the human by virtue of the hypostatic union. God, in the person of Jesus, died. The power of *that* death transcends space and time.

This same principle addresses as well the question of the relation of the Spirit universally present in the world to Christ though this topic will be taken up in more detail later. What is determinative with respect to the ability of the economy to

---

[18] Gen. 15:6.
[19] *Redemptoris Mater* 9.

reveal the inner life of God to us is the relationships between the persons of the Trinity revealed in that economy. If the Spirit enters the world by virtue of the salvific actions of Christ then the temporal priority of the Spirit proves to be of little significance.

As noted above, the descent of the Spirit upon Mary in the conception of Christ is not an isolated mystery. The same creative power occurs in several crucial contexts that need to be examined since each involves the mission activity of the Creator-Spirit. These generally cause theological difficulties precisely because of their paradoxical character. The Thomistic discussion will be followed for the sake of brevity.

Thomas raised the issue of the difference between sacred doctrine and philosophy at the beginning of his great *Summa*. The objection was made that another mode of knowledge is not needed since philosophy already purports to study all of being, including God. But there are some things that natural reason cannot know and yet which are necessary for salvation. They must be revealed. But revelation cannot be received simply through an external proclamation; the mind of the hearer must be made receptive to and acceptant of the proclamation since, naturally, no such knowledge is possible apart from grace. This latter is the work of the Spirit.

Humans have a final end for humans which exceeds the potency of their nature. In the fourth article of the twelfth question Thomas argues that we cannot see the essence of God, the beatific vision, with our natural powers. The next article insists on the necessity of a special created light or "supernatural disposition" which prepares the created intellect for the vision of that which exceeds its nature. God is Pure Act and himself acts as the form of the intellect in this vision. What then is this "disposition"? It can only be the correlate to act, which is potency. There is no natural potency to see God in any creature; that potency must itself be created and given. As such, it is a potency appropriate only to God himself but belongs to the creature as a gift. This gift of glorification is the proper activity of the Spirit within the individual.

An awkwardness has long been felt over Thomas's doctrine of transubstantiation. A severe philosophical problem is created by his contention that the "accidents continue in this sacrament without a subject"[20] because accidents exist only as an *esse ad*, only as inhering in a subject. They have no rationality, at least in an Aristotelian framework, outside of that correlation. What is involved here is an abandonment of the Aristotelian framework, even while using some of its conceptual equipment, in the face of the demands of the faith. Accidents here are something other than an *esse ad*.

One may well wish to avoid attributing to these nonetheless existing accidents substantial reality. It would be hard to avoid distinguishing this from an impanationist position where the Eucharistic elements continue to exist as bread and wine even as the Lord begins to be present "in the bread" and wine. The alternative would be to invent some mediating term that allows to the accident the substantial grounding that it needs to continue to be an accident, an *esse ad*, without erecting some substance parallel to the substance of the body and blood of the Lord. One possibility would be to see the Lord's substance itself as providing the substantial base for the perduring accidents but Thomas rejects this possibility: "the substance of the human body cannot in any way be affected by such accidents; nor is it possible for Christ's glorious and impassible body to be altered so as to receive these qualities". Accidents must be part of the intrinsic intelligibility of the substance in which they inhere and the accidents of bread and wine are not part of the intrinsic intelligibility of the human body. The Eucharistic accidents can corrupt, the Lord's glorified body cannot.

Thomas speaks of a miracle which holds accidents in existence without a proper substance. This, as noted above, is philosophically irrational. Still, his recourse to a miraculous explanation points to the paradoxical character of the Eucharistic mystery. The bread and wine offered by the Church have no potency to be the body and blood of Christ. An act of creation, making them "apt" for such an actualization, is clearly needed. At that point in the liturgy we have the prayer for the

---

[20] *ST* III.77.1.corp.

descent of the Spirit upon the gifts: "Let your Spirit come upon these gifts to make them holy, so that they may become for us the body and blood of our Lord, Jesus Christ"[21]. The Spirit, as such, does not make the elements to be the body and blood of the Lord - the priest, acting *in persona Cristi*, does this (which is to say, it is Jesus himself who makes them to be his body and blood). What is the Spirit's role? He makes the gifts "holy". What this means is not really spelled out in the liturgy but it clearly means, at a minimum, that they are made apt for the consecratory transformation. The parallel with Mary's conception of Jesus is clear. It is Jesus' assuming of flesh in Mary's womb that actually makes her mother of God. Her overshadowing by the Spirit makes her apt, or "in potency", for this. In the Eucharistic transformation we have an instance of God's creative activity, Trinitarian in structure, where the consistent role of the Spirit is to make the object of the transformation apt or in potency to actualization as a new and higher reality.

Much of the preceding analysis holds also for grace, particularly for sanctifying grace. Under traditional Thomistic analysis it is difficult to avoid reducing grace to an accident superadded to human nature which does not contain the potency for it as part of its intrinsic intelligibility – grace is supernatural, not natural. This conundrum has led many to try to describe grace in terms of personalist or existentialist categories rather than in terms of the essentialist categories of matter-form, substance-accident. For present purposes it suffices to note that we again have a situation where the human individual has no prior potency for that grace. It is created with the gift itself of grace. This transformation, making the individual apt to receive uncreated grace into his heart, which is to say, the indwelling Trinity, is accomplished by the action of the Spirit.

A special application of this is the preparation by the Spirit of the individual who hears the proclamation of the gospel

---

[21] Second Eucharistic Prayer. The Third and Fourth make the same point in other words. So too does the First Eucharistic Prayer though it is a bit vaguer.

making him apt for or receptive to the Word. "It is the Spirit who opens people's hearts so that they can believe in Christ and 'confess him'"[22]. It would seem to follow also that this particular grace is unavailable apart from the actualizing proclamation of the Church.

Athenasius once wrote that "to dispense and convey the Holy Spirit at pleasure, is a thing peculiar to the Divine Power, and it is an impossible thing for any made or created being to do so"[23]. The scribes, not incorrectly, asked, "Who can forgive sins except God alone?" Who alone but Christ can turn simple bread and wine into his body and blood? Yet the Church, through its sacramental ministry, does all these things and more. They were possible to Christ, not by virtue of his humanity, but by virtue of the hypostatic union. There is no prior potency in any other human person or community to do these things. But the Holy Spirit overshadowed the early disciples. That Spirit was the first gift of Jesus to his Church, the fruit of his sacrificial death and resurrection, a gift which, in the actuation of the nuptial covenant between Christ and his Church, makes that covenant to be possible, makes the Church holy, which is to say, apt to receive her Lord.

If there are clear parallels between the dissemination of ideas by the disciples of some great philosopher and the proclamation of the gospel by the disciples of Jesus, there is a decisive difference in the power of the disciples to impart his Spirit. The power to dispense the Spirit freely is the defining mark of the Church: "For where the Church is, there is the Spirit of God; and where the Spirit of God is, there is the Church, and every kind of grace"[24]. Hands are laid upon the sacramental ministers of the Church in the ancient symbol of the imparting of the Spirit enabling them to act with Christ's power. What had not been possible before becomes actual.

Even if one presumes that the salvific transformation that takes place through the power of the Spirit – grace, union with

---

[22] RM46.
[23] *Contra Arianos* II.18.
[24] IRENAEUS, *Adv. Haer.* III.xxiv.1. Cf. DV3-4, 14, 22-23, 25, 63.

God, the beatific vision – is possible outside the formal confines of the Church, and this has been clearly and repeatedly taught by the magisterium throughout most of this century, it remains true that such graces are inseparable from the sacraments entrusted to the Church. The story of Cornelius in Acts 10 is a case in point. While the grace of the Spirit was imparted to Cornelius as a response to the apostolic kerygma it was outside the context expected by Peter. He found the conclusion inescapable – Baptism and the laying on of hands, which was the normal context for receiving the Spirit, could not be denied to them. The grace received and the sacramental sign dispensing that grace were inseparable.

It follows that where the Church discerns that the Spirit of God has been active in an individual or a community, Baptism and the proclamation of the gospel that is inseparable from that sacramental action cannot (or rather should not) be withheld from them. Discernment of the activity of the Spirit in the lives of adherents of other religions in the world becomes an added compelling reason for the Church to proclaim the gospel to them. They have a right to know what God is doing in their lives and what the source of the grace that they experience is[25].

The question of the inseparability of the grace of salvation from the proclamation of the gospel and of both from Baptism is grounded in the inseparability of the grace of salvation from Christ or, more profoundly, the inseparability of the Spirit in the world, who makes salvation possible to all, from Christ. This in turn is grounded in the uniqueness of Christ and its corollary, the uniqueness of the Church. A full discussion of these issues is not possible here though two brief comments are perhaps in order.

First, the rationale for multiple incarnations of God could only be to multiply the opportunities for humans to come into contact with the divine and to enter into that union which is salvific. This, however, is not required for salvation to be avail-

---

[25] *RM* 46.

able to everyone if there is a universal access to the Spirit who effects saving union with God in the lives of individuals. Multiple incarnations could only obscure this fact. On the other hand the transformation of the disciples into the Church, into that supernatural reality in which the Spirit is freely accessible, underscores the role of the Spirit in the transformation of the world. The Church herself provides the access to the Spirit that would be the putative purpose of multiple incarnations.

It follows as a corollary to this that the Church must be the sign in the world of this universal access to the Spirit, that the Church must act on this foundational aspect of her identity. To be the Church, the Church must reach out to everyone throughout the world with this offer of the Spirit. To do otherwise would be to reject her raison d'etre, it would deny that there was any significant transformation in the disciples as a result of the missions of the Son and the Spirit. For this reason the Church must ineluctably be missionary.

The Baptizer in the Holy Spirit

It will be argued in what follows that, if the Incarnation provides the pattern for the new creation in all of its facets, the baptism of Jesus, and more particularly, the descent of the Holy Spirit upon him at that time, provides the pattern for evangelization. The power of the Spirit overshadowing Mary and the human flesh she provided made them to be in potency to the Incarnation of the eternal Son. With the actualization of what had been impossible comes the potency; with the Incarnation of the Son comes the Spirit who transforms humanity. At this moment Jesus, the God-man, the giver of the Holy Spirit, is constituted. The Spirit descending on Jesus after his baptism drives him into the desert, inaugurating his public mission. This does not, as such, constitute who Jesus is except in a functional sense.

Jean Zizioulas has described two styles of Pneumatology with corresponding Christologies and ecclesiologies. In the first style, which he sees to be a more Western approach, the "Spirit is given to the Church as a force which renders us capable of accomplishing the work of the mission" of proclaiming the gospel to the world. The Spirit appears "as a manifestation of the coming of the Spirit into history". The Spirit is given by Christ, whom he glorifies, as his agent in the accomplishment of his mission. The Spirit is preeminently the Spirit of Christ and is seen to depend on Christ. "Christology ... becomes the source of Pneumatology"; it is "a Pneumatology conditioned by Christology". The corresponding ecclesiology will be dominated by the notion of mission, "the Church is the people of God in *dispersion*"[26]. The second style of Pneumatology is more eschatological. If "the Spirit is given by the risen Christ in the first type of Pneumatology, in the second the Spirit leads to the resurrection of Christ". "Pneumatology is the source of Christology"; we have "a Christology conditioned by Pneumatology". The Church is not understood as a people dispersed on mission but as gathered together into a community, as will be the case in the eschaton[27].

Zizioulas points to those Gospel texts which speak of Jesus promising or giving the Spirit as well as those in which the Spirit is active in guiding and empowering the missionary expansion of the Church as grounding the first style of Pneumatology. He points to those texts which speak of Jesus being raised in the power of the Spirit (e.g. Rom. 1:4) or which speak of his identity (his baptism by John, his nativity) as indicative of the second style. The most primitive form of Christology is the baptism story in Mark where "the Christ event is constituted by his baptism, which is to say: in and by the Spirit".

Both Zizioulas and Durrwell closely parallel the moment of the Incarnation with other Christological mysteries and effectively reverse the priority of the processions of the Son and the Spirit. Zizioulas characterizes the second type of Pneumatology as one in which "there is, so to say, *no Christ* until the Spirit is at work, not only as *a forerunner* announcing his coming, but also as the one who *constitutes his very identity as*

---

[26] "Implications ecclesiologique de deux types de pneumatologie", in *Communio Sanctorum: Melanges offerts à Jean-Jacques von Allmen* (Genève: Éditions Labor et Fides), p. 141. The translations and paraphrases are mine.
[27] Ibid., p. 142.

Christ, either at his baptism (Mark) or at his very biological conception (Matthew and Luke)"[28]. The key moment is the baptism of Jesus, in which Jesus is anointed or constituted by the Spirit. More than a functional understanding of Jesus as the Christ is in view given this understanding of Jesus' conception. Durrwell, on the other hand, identifies the constitutive event with the death and resurrection of Christ: "The enthroning of Jesus as 'the Son of God in power' is realized in the Holy Spirit: it is the effect of 'the resurrection of the dead', which we know (Rom. 8:11) is due to the Holy Spirit"[29]. Acts 13:33 cites Ps. 2:7 ("You are my son; this day I have begotten you"), and Durrwell uses this, and other texts to justify seeing in the Paschal mysteries the perfection of his Sonship: "When, at Easter, God invests Christ with the fullness of the Spirit, he awakens to life without end, in an eternal birth (cf. Acts 13:33). By begetting his Son in the outpouring of the Spirit, God calls into being what does not exist"[30].

It is certainly true that there are common elements between these various narratives: the presence of the Spirit and the announcement of the Sonship of Jesus are only two of several. It is also true, as Zizioulas insists, that there are two ecclesiological moments which could roughly be described as missionary-dispersive and communitarian-eschatological though they are both, rather than just the latter, centered on the Eucharist which at once gathers the community together to send it out into the world. Durrwell, for his part, is surely correct in naming the Paschal mysteries as central in both Christology and Pneumatology.

Still, some of the differences between these passages are passed over too quickly. In the conception of Jesus we read that it is Mary whom the Spirit overshadows, not Jesus. In the baptism story, it is Jesus on whom the Spirit descends. The over-identification of these two (or more) moments encourages the view that it is the Spirit who constitutes Christ: for

---

[28] *Being as Communion*, pp. 127-28.
[29] "Pour une christologie", pp. 657-58.
[30] *Holy Spirit*, p. 18. Cf. also "Pour une christologie", p. 659.

Zizioulas, according to the pattern of the baptism; for Durrwell, according to the pattern of the Paschal mysteries.

It is not problematic to say that Jesus is constituted the Christ by the Spirit but what does it mean to say that he is constituted Son of God? Are we to understand that, at least in the economy, the Spirit has a certain priority to the Son? Certainly this is Zizioulas's intent; he is explicit on the point and on what lies behind his interest in affirming the economic priority of the Spirit – the Filioque. He makes his own the critique of Eastern theologians of the Western insistence on reading the economy into the inner life of God[31]. He, like many Orthodox, is content if "the question of priority can remain a 'theologoumenon'"[32]. Obviously if he can point to a 'Spirituque' in the economy his case is not weakened.

This has corresponding implications for evangelization. Under Zizioulas's conception the Spirit present in the world prior to the coming of Christ (in the flesh or in evangelistic proclamation) prepares hearts receptive to that coming, indeed, orients all of history to Christ, but does not, as such, derive from the Christ-event. The Spirit in the world is fundamentally independent of Christ; it is Christ who is dependent on, constituted by that Spirit. There is, although Zizioulas would not want to conclude to this, the possibility of means of salvation other than those provided by Christ since salvation is, in the last analysis, possession of the life-giving Spirit who is available apart from Christ and who, at least in the eschaton, will lead to Christ. It is not surprising that this view supports comparatively little missionary impetus.

The alternative is to insist that the Spirit present everywhere and at all times is himself the gift of Christ, given in the context of his saving death and resurrection. There is no salvation, there is no Spirit apart from the name of Jesus (Acts 4:12). Even if by the mercy of God one is given possession of that Spirit apart from the sacramental economy of the Church, the root cause of that grace is the reality which the sacraments sign

---

[31] "Implications", p. 149.
[32] *Being as Communion*, p. 129.

forth and make present, Christ's saving actions. The inner reality worked by the Spirit calls for its normative and freely accessible expression. This is what Peter recognized in the house of Cornelius.

Whatever else is happening at the baptism of Jesus, he is not being constituted who he is; it is not, as such, an event of the new creation. If Jesus, prior to the descent of the Spirit on him after his baptism, was not already the Son of God, was not already capable of all miracles, was not already filled with that Spirit from whom he is eternally inseparable, then he is not God. Jesus did not receive the Spirit for the first time at that moment. He did not receive a power for which he had no prior potency. If God was incarnate than the man Jesus was "capable" of all things from the first moment of his human existence.

And yet, the baptism does mark a transition. Prior to that event Jesus worked no miracles, at least any that were public knowledge. The scandal felt by his neighbors at his words and actions make this clear – "They said: 'Where did he get all this? ... How is it that such miraculous deeds are accomplished by his hands?'" (Mk. 6:2-3). These things were possible to Jesus because of who he was but were actualized in his life only after the baptism and the Spirit was the agent of that actualization[33]. From that moment Jesus was humanly impelled by the Spirit – "the Spirit cast him out into the desert" (Mk. 1:12). It is a violent image. The word Mark uses, ἐκβάλλει, is the same one he uses to describe exorcisms. When he returns from the desert Jesus begins proclaiming the gospel of God, he gathers disciples to aid him in this mission (Mk. 1:14-17), he leaves to preach in ever-widening circles (Mk. 1:38-39). The baptism of

---

[33] Cf. YVES CONGAR, *I Believe in the Holy Spirit*, vol. 3: *The River of Life Flows in the East and in the West*, trans. David Smith (New York: The Seabury Press, 1983), p. 167. Congar, p. 166, maintains, against Thomas who held that the Baptism represented "simply a manifestation for *others* of a reality that is already there" that the baptism represents a qualitative moment in God's "communication of himself to and in Jesus Christ". He does not explain how this is not adoptionistic. To speak of an "actualization of a reality already there" avoids this difficulty without losing the notion of a qualitative moment.

Jesus thus marks the historical beginning of the evangelization of the world. In this sense it is not inappropriate to say that he is constituted as the Christ by the Spirit, where this is understood in functional rather than ontological terms.

There are two further things to note. The baptism of Jesus by John is distinct from the event of the descent on him by the Holy Spirit. George Montague rightly observes that "Mark is careful to note that it is not at the moment of the baptism by John, but rather after Jesus' coming up from the water that the Spirit is manifested (a sequence Matthew and Luke will reinforce)"[34]. Luke has the Spirit descending after the baptism while Jesus was praying. He also has Jesus later rejoicing in the Spirit (Lk. 10:21) which may indicate multiple infusions even if the one at the baptism remains pivotal. These themes will be important in assessing a similar distinction between Christian Baptism and the reception of the Holy Spirit in what follows[35].

The Gospels are not consistent in their witness to the reception of the Spirit by the disciples though they all presume it in one way or another. John (20:21-23) has it taking place on the evening of the Resurrection. There is a mandate to go forth as Jesus had gone forth from the Father. Jesus then gives them the Spirit with the revelation that they now have a power that transcends human potentiality and is properly a divine power – they can forgive sins (or not). Clearly we have an instance here of a new creation[36].

The mandate for evangelization is given here but, in point of fact, no discernible (or successful) evangelistic activity follows upon it. In the appendix we are informed that a number of disciples returned to Galilee. There, the only activity they engage in, so far as we are told, is fishing. The story is highly

---

[34] KILIAN MCDONNELL and GEORGE T. MONTAGUE, *Christian Initiation and Baptism in the Holy Spirit: Evidence from the First Eight Centuries* (Collegeville, Minnesota: The Liturgical Press/A Michael Glazier Book, 1991), p. 7.

[35] Ibid. p. 24. Montague also queries whether this could not have been "a Lukan retrojection of the procedure for Christian baptism – water rite followed by prayer for the outpouring of the Holy Spirit".

[36] MONTAGUE, *Christian Initiation*, p. 58.

symbolic. These "fishers of men" have had no success although they toiled through the night. When light returns and Jesus' call hovers over the waters (cf. Gen. 1:2-3) they suddenly are enormously successful (Jn. 21: 1-6). What is in view is the effectiveness of the apostolic mission[37]. Thus there are two distinct moments – the substantive transformation of the disciples into "forgivers of sin" and the subsequent actualization of their new power through the guidance of Christ, presumably exercised through the Spirit.

In point of fact this was not the first time that Jesus bestowed the Spirit. All of the Gospels are somewhat consistent in narratively tying the baptism in the Holy Spirit with Christ's death on the cross. Mark's Gospel, in the more probable shorter ending, does not even have resurrection appearances. The only possible fulfillment to the Baptist's prophecy that the one to follow him would "baptize you in the Holy Spirit" (Mk. 1:8) is Mk. 15:37-39 where Jesus "uttering a loud cry, breathed his last (ἐξπνευσεν, literally, 'spirited' out)". Mark is emphatic on this point, repeating that it was Jesus' "spiriting out" which convinced the centurion that he truly was the Son of God. Matthew and Luke did not miss the significance of the Markan scene and make the point more explicitly: "Once again Jesus cried out in a loud voice, and then gave up his spirit" (Mt. 27:50 – ἀφῆκεν τὸ πνεῦμα); "Father, into your hands I commend my spirit" (Lk. 23:46 – παρατίθεμαι τὸ πνεῦμά μου). John has Jesus delivering over his Spirit (Jn. 19:30 – παρδωκεν τὸ πνεῦμα). We will come back to this scene in the next section on the Paschal mysteries.

Luke-Acts provides us with the greatest variety of stories. The initial gift of the Spirit is at the moment of Christ's conception which is accompanied by the descent of the Spirit on Mary. It is an event of new creation as described above. Mary immediately goes out, however, and proclaims to Elizabeth what God has done for her. The result of this "kerygmatic" journey is that John and Elizabeth themselves are filled with

---

[37] RAYMOND BROWN, S.S., *The Gospel according to John XIII-XXI*, The Anchor Bible 29A (Garden City, New York: Doubleday, 1970), p. 1097.

the Spirit. Narratively Luke links the Annunciation with the descent of the Spirit on the disciples on Pentecost. Mary is told by the angel that "The Holy Spirit will come upon you and the power of the Most High will overshadow you (Lk. 1:35 – πνεῦμα ἅγιον ἐπελεύσεται ἐπὶ σὲ καὶ δύναμις ὑψίστου ἐπισκιάσει σοι). The disciples at the end of the Gospel are told by Jesus, "See, I send down upon you the promise of my Father. Remain here in the city until you are clothed with power from on high" (Lk. 24:49 – ἐγω ἀποστέλλω τὴν ἐπαγ-γελίαν τοῦ πατρός μου ἐφ᾽ ὑμᾶς . . . ἕως οὗ ἐνδύσησθε ἐξ ὕψους δύναμιν). This is repeated at the beginning of Acts and the promise of the Father, this power from on high, is identified with the baptism with the Holy Spirit. At this point the command to evangelize is given – "You will receive power (δύναμιν) when the Holy Spirit comes down on you; then you are to be my witnesses in Jerusalem, throughout Judea and Samaria, yes, even to the ends of the earth".

After the Ascension the disciples wait. We are told that they were constantly at prayer (Acts 1:14), perhaps, as Montague suggests, in conscious imitation of the prayer of Jesus after his baptism (Lk. 3:21). In what did that prayer consist? Acts 2:42 indicates that the members of the community "devoted themselves to the apostles, instruction and the communal life, to the breaking of bread and the prayers". We are further told that "they went to the temple area together every day, while in their homes they broke bread" (v. 46). If "bold proclamation" characterized them after Pentecost one might presuppose the absence of such in the period prior to Pentecost though there is early concern expressed for witnessing to Jesus' resurrection (Acts 1:22).

On the day of Pentecost "there came a noise like a strong, driving wind which was heard all through the house where they were seated.... All were filled with the Holy Spirit. They began to express themselves in foreign tongues and make bold proclamation as the Spirit prompted them" (Acts 2:2-4). "Devout Jews of every nation under heaven ... heard the sound, and assembled in a large crowd" (Acts 2:5-6). Two distinct scenes have been conflated by Luke, presumably to underscore the fundamental identity of the two experiences – one taking place indoors, another, later event taking place out-of-doors in an area capable of holding large crowds, presumably the temple area.

This suggests that the initial evangelistic descent of the Spirit on the disciples was in the context of the "breaking of the bread" or other prayer conducted "in the house". There is no way to determine historically the precise sequence of events. Theologically we can say that the descent of the Spirit substantively transforming the disciples and rendering them capable of doing what Jesus did at the Last Supper, had to have taken place first. Absent that transformation their act of breaking bread would have been a memorial of a past event and nothing more. When would this have taken place? It could have been done at the Last Supper itself (which has traditionally been taken to be an "ordination" of the Twelve) though this is not strictly required. The decisive event could have been in conjunction with an appearance of the Lord as in John's account. It could also have taken place the first time the disciples "attempted" to remember the Lord in the breaking of the bread, transforming an attempt into the reality. At any event, there is some likelihood that the disciples were celebrating the Eucharist prior to Pentecost and that it was in that context that the evangelizing power of the Spirit descended on them.

Luke narrates other instances of the descent of the Spirit, not simply in individual cases but also on the community as a whole (Acts 4:31). The amassed evidence makes it clear that there was not a single event where the Spirit descended on the disciples but several interconnected infusions which in some instances had different purposes. Some were for transformation, others were for actualizing a potentiality already present.

The first and subsequent generations of converts were initiated in a three-stage process described in Acts 2:37-38 as reformation of life, Baptism in the name of Jesus for the forgiveness of sin, and reception of the Holy Spirit. The distinct stages are not always explicitly mentioned but are nonetheless consistently presumed. Three verses later only the number who were baptized is indicated. In the story of the Ethiopian eunuch we are told only that he was baptized. One can perhaps surmise that he had also received the Spirit since he went away rejoicing though nothing explicit is said (Acts 8:38-39). The baptism of Saul likewise does not distinguish between

Baptism and the reception of the Spirit. Ananias comes to him at the Lord's command that Saul may recover his sight "and be filled with the Holy Spirit". The narrative speaks only of Saul's healing and his Baptism (Acts 9:17-18)[38]. The Spirit is not even mentioned in the stories of Lydia (Acts 16:14-15), of the jailer (Acts 16:30-34), or of Crispus (Acts 18:8).

Still Acts otherwise makes the distinctions between repentance, Baptism in the name of Jesus, and reception of the Spirit. The second narrative in which Baptism is explicitly mentioned is in chapter eight. Philip has baptized a number of people in Samaria. Peter and John came to them "and prayed that they might receive the Holy Spirit. It had not as yet come down upon any of them since they had only been baptized in the name of the Lord Jesus" (Acts 8:12-17). The conversion of Cornelius is the exception that proves the rule. Precisely because the Spirit descended on that household in a manifest form, Peter concludes that Baptism with water in the name of Jesus could not be denied them. The two events are inseparable yet also clearly distinct.

Acts 19:1-7 distinguishes between the baptism of John and Baptism in the name of Jesus. The former "was a baptism of repentance" whereas the latter, as we saw earlier, is "for the forgiveness of sin". Forgiveness is a gift of God now freely accessible through Christ and Baptism in his name. In a separate action Paul lays hands on these former disciples of John and the Spirit descends on them[39]. Christian Baptism, though

---

[38] MONTAGUE, *Christian Initiation*, p. 37, interprets Ananias's laying on of hands (prior to Paul's baptism) as a prayer for the bestowal of the Spirit. It could, however, simply be a prayer for healing, the only effect mentioned as the immediate result of the action.

[39] J.D.G. DUNN, *Baptism in the Holy Spirit* (Naperville, Illinois: Allenson, 1970), p. 228, is wrong when he writes that Christian Baptism "is not a channel of grace, and neither the gift of the Spirit nor any of the spiritual blessings which he brings may be inferred from or ascribed to it". Forgiveness of sins is a spiritual blessing and is clearly attributed to water Baptism in the New Testament. What is less clear, precisely because water Baptism and the prayer for the reception of the Spirit are often so closely linked, is that this forgiveness of sins already presupposes a bestowal of the Spirit. The prayer for the Holy Spirit is a prayer for a second infusion for a different purpose than forgiveness of sins. Acts indicates that it is for "bold proclamation". However, see Montague, *Christian Initiation*, pp. 31-35, who resists seeing a second infusion of the Spirit in these texts.

it is patterned on John's, acquires its efficacy because of Jesus[40]. His immersion blesses the waters so that a baptism of repentance is transformed into something it could not have been before, a Baptism of forgiveness. In this sense Jesus' baptism was an event of new creation constituting, not who Jesus is, but what Baptism is.

The locus classicus for the sacrament of Confirmation has long been Acts 8:14-17[41]. Hans Conzelmann, in his Acts commentary, argues that all the text presupposes is "an intimate connection between baptism and the Spirit". Peter and John's action was the legitimation of the Samaritan church by the Jerusalem community; it was, in effect, only a juridical action. The scene is not an historical recollection, it is "an ad hoc construction" with an ecclesial-political purpose[42]. This is to reject the clear sense of the text. "They received the Holy Spirit" is more than a juridical sanction. There is a clear expectation that Christian initiation normally concludes to a reception of the Spirit and the observation that this did not take place. This expectation grounds the conclusion that there is an "intimate connection" between Baptism and reception of the Holy Spirit but the terms of that connection are not made explicit.

Baptism is not equated with reception of the Spirit in this narrative. If it were, one would have to presuppose that something was defective in Philip's baptismal activity but, apart from the notice that they had not yet received the Spirit, there is no such indication. Indeed, signs and great miracles were performed by him, he continued baptizing people. And yet, the Holy Spirit "had not fallen on any of them". Are we to conclude that the prayer of Peter and John, in Luke's view, was so much more potent than that of Philip who worked signs

---

[40] MONTAGUE, *Christinan Initiation*, p. 57, is correct in distancing the action of the disciples in Jn. 3:22, 4:2 from Christian Baptism. "The Spirit had not yet been given". Still, their actions were clearly done with the approval of Jesus and provided a pattern for what they would do later.

[41] HERBERT VORGLIMLER *Sacramental Theology*, trans. Linda M. Maloney (Collegeville, Minnesota: The Liturgical Press, 1992), p. 123.

[42] *Acts of the Apostles: A Commentary on the Acts of the Apostles*, trans. James Limburg, et al., Hermeneia (Philadelphia: Fortress Press, 1987), p. 65.

and miracles? The text, as a narrative, makes sense only if baptizing, which is what Philip was doing, is seen as a distinct action from praying for the Holy Spirit, even if this latter is understood as an essential complement of the former. Arguing that the prayer for the Spirit has an "intimate connection" with Baptism in no way tells against seeing here a primitive form of the sacrament of Confirmation.

Another objection comes from Calvin who, following Chrysostom, held that "the Samaritans, who had only been baptized, had truly received the Spirit of forgiveness though not yet the Spirit of the signs". This, however, corresponds exactly to the distinction between Baptism for the forgiveness of sins and the prayer for the Holy Spirit for "bold proclamation". Heribert Schutzeichel has noted that many Catholic theologians now agree that these texts deal with the "Spirit of charisms" as if this told against seeing a reference to a primitive form of Confirmation[43]. It was on this basis that Congar concluded that one cannot "discover" in these texts a reference to the sacrament[44]. Confirmation, understood as the sacrament of evangelization, is a prayer for signs, a prayer for charisms, as well as a prayer for fortitude and the strengthening of the graces of Baptism.

If Christ's reception of the Spirit after his baptism marked the beginning of the evangelization of the world, then Pentecost marked the insertion of the Church into that mission and the sacrament of Confirmation marks the comparable sacramental insertion of each Christian. This is an actualization of the potentialities of their ontological status as children of God effected in Baptism just as Jesus' anointing by the Spirit actualized the Christological mission which was always a potential of the hypostatic union. Through the initiation sacraments, then, Christians share in Christ's role as prophet, priest, and king[45].

---

[43] The references are found in Heribert Schützeichel, "Calvins Kritik an der Firmung", *Zeichen des Glaubens: Studien zu Taufe und Firmung. Balthasar Fischer zum 60. Geburtstag* (Zürich: Benziger, 1972), p. 128, n. 26. Congar incorrectly refers to E.J. Lengeling's article which appears later in the same volume.

[44] *The River of Life*, p. 220.

[45] Cf. CONGAR, *The River of Life*, p. 219; CL 51.

The Paschal Mysteries, the Love of God Poured Out

Jesus breathed forth his Spirit on the cross. In this God's love for the world was demonstrated – that he gave his only-begotten Son (Jn. 3:16). It was an act that was at once for Israel, for the Church, and for the world.

Jesus' response to the Syro-Phoenician woman is revealing: "My mission is only to the lost sheep of the house of Israel" (Mt. 15:24). The issue was God's fidelity to his covenants with Israel: "you are a people sacred to the Lord, your God... because the Lord loved you and because of his fidelity to the oath he had sworn to your fathers" (Deut. 7:6-8). This love for Israel frequently took the form of nuptial imagery, particularly in the prophets. Hosea affirmed God's benevolent intention notwithstanding Israel's infidelity: "I will espouse you to me forever; I will espouse you in right and in justice, in love and in mercy; I will espouse you in fidelity, and you shall know the Lord" (Hos. 2:16, 21-22). A similar theme is found in Isaiah: "For he who has become your husband is your Maker . . . My love shall never leave you nor my covenant of peace be shaken" (Is. 54:5, 10). Ezekiel likewise reaffirms God's nuptial covenant with Jerusalem: "Yet I will remember the covenant I made with you when you were a girl, and I will set up an everlasting covenant with you" (Ez. 16:60). The Syro-Phoenician woman was granted her request precisely because she accepted this special relationship with Israel and defined herself in terms of it.

Christ also died for the Church. At the Last Supper he told the disciples gathered with him that his body was "for you" (Lk. 22:19, I Cor. 11:24), that his blood would "be shed for you" (Lk. 22:20). During his lifetime he replicated the key moments of Israel's history: he passed through the water with his disciples (Mk. 6:45-51; Mt. 14:23-33; Jn. 6:16-21)[46]; he pro-

---

[46] Mark intends an allusion to the events of the Exodus (Ex. 12:37-14:31) through specific parallels – the time, vocabulary, the setting – including the divine affirmation, "I am".

vided bread in the wilderness (Mk. 6:32-44; Mt. 14:13-21; Lk. 9:10b-17; Jn. 6:1-15); he arranged the community in the pattern of the divisions of Israel (Mk. 6:40; cf. Ex. 18:25; Deut. 1:15); the Twelve will sit on thrones judging the tribes (Mt. 19:28; Lk. 22:30). Jesus' followers were the true Israel, their mother was the heavenly Jerusalem (Gal. 4:21-31, 6:16). Membership in Israel was determined by kinship relations; the true kin of Jesus are those who do the will of God (Mk. 3:35; Mt. 12:50; Lk. 8:21). The descent from Abraham that is relevant for the covenant promises are those who believe as Abraham believed (Gal. 3:7).

Jesus also picked up the nuptial imagery of the prophets and applied it to himself. He is the Bridegroom in whose presence the "children of the bridal chamber" cannot fast (Mk. 2:19), for whom the ten virgins wait (Mt. 25:1), for whom the king gave a wedding banquet (Mt. 22:2). As he lived so he died. John insists that blood and water flowed out from the side of the pierced Christ, an image which reminded the patristic Church of the sleeping Adam from whose side Eve was fashioned.

God's promise to Israel opens up to the world. He made a solemn oath to Abraham: "I swear by myself, declares the Lord that ... in your descendants all the nations of the earth shall find blessing" (Gen. 22:16, 18). Isaiah proclaimed that all nations would stream toward the mountain of the Lord's house (Is. 2:2) and that even the foreigner who wished to join himself to the Lord would be included in God's people – "For my house shall be called a house of prayer for all peoples" (Is. 56:3-7). It follows that if Jesus, in calling people to himself and structuring them in the pattern of Israel, brought into existence the true Israel, then that community was to be the focal point for the fulfillment of God's promise to Abraham to bless all nations in him. This is certainly Paul's understanding of the matter (Gal. 3:6-14) but a similar view is expressed in Acts 2:14-21 though it takes the rest of the book for Luke to work out the implications of the opening citation of Joel. On that first Pentecost the nations came to Jerusalem but it has remained the abiding responsibility of those who are the descendants of Abraham in faith to be that light which blesses the nations.

God showered gifts on his beloved. In Hos. 2:17 vineyards are promised and "the valley of Achor as a door of hope". In Is. 54:1 Jerusalem is promised numerous children and in v. 11, ornamentation with precious stones. Yahweh bathes and anoints the young Jerusalem with oil, clothes her in fine garments and jewelry, sets a "crown of boasting" on her head in Ez. 16:6-12. In other contexts it is the divine spirit, synonymous with life, that is promised to a redeemed or reconstituted Israel, a theme quite common in Isaiah and Ezekiel but also touched on in Zech. 4:6, Hag. 2:5 and particularly Joel 3:1 (LXX 2:28-29) where the perspective shifts to the whole world[47]. In this latter case the world is blessed because of the faithful remnant on Mount Zion. By stressing as they do Jesus' breathing out at his death, the Gospels highlight this fundamental gift of Christ to his Church and through the Church to the world.

Empirically, spatio-temporal events exercise only a future-directed causality. Jesus' death provides an example that motivates future generations, for instance, as does Socrates' and the range of that influence is determined by the extent reached by the explicit proclamation of these events. As purely natural events they cannot exercise a backward causality, nor can their effect outstrip the mechanisms of diffusion. But this is not the only appropriate perspective under which Jesus' death can be considered. Jesus, who has the relation to all of space and time that God has, died and rose from the dead. The effect of this cannot be limited to an empirically determined chain. By an eternal decision the Son has been conditioned by his human life, by his death, by his resurrection. Wherever Jesus is present he is present as having been incarnated, having lived, died, as having been raised from the dead, and as pouring forth his Spirit into the world.

---

[47] Is. 4:4, 32:15, 42:1, 44:3, 48:16, 59:21, 61:1; Ez. 11:19, 18:31, 36:26-27, 37:9-10, 14, 39:29., Is. 32:15 (ἕως ἂν ἐπέλθῃ ἐφ᾽ ὑμᾶς πνεῦμα ἀφ᾽ ὑψηλοῦ) may find an echo in Lk. 1:35 (Πνεῦμα ἅγιον ἐπελεύσεται ἐπὶ σὲ καὶ δύναμις ὑψίστου ἐπισκιάσει σοι·).

This much the communication of idioms demands. Everywhere and at every time that the Spirit enters the world he does so through the action of the Son of God who gave his life for the salvation of the world. There is a double, not a single causality which links the universal Spirit and Jesus Christ. That Spirit bears witness everywhere to Christ in the hearts of those receptive to God's Word; that universally accessible Spirit is present because of what Christ has accomplished.

There is a further implication relevant to our present purpose in this line of thought. What Christ has accomplished is "for you", which is to say, for the Church. Jesus is present everywhere not simply as the eternal Son who was incarnated, lived, died, rose, and gave the Spirit; he is present as the one who poured out his life for the Church. All grace is relational because the Giver of Grace is himself subsistent relationality, he is constituted by eternal Trinitarian relations but also by freely chosen economic ones. The grace we receive as individuals is never ours alone; it is a grace received in the context of Christ's death, a context determined by the divine-human community brought into existence by that death.

The Church in principle, therefore, cannot be separated from the grace made available to everyone wherever or whenever they may live. They have that grace because at the fullness of time the Spirit overshadowed Mary and the Word became incarnate, because the Spirit overshadowed the bridal Church, sealing the nuptial covenant enacted by Christ. The "preexistence" of the Church that this implies is virtual; it is nonetheless real because that Jesus whose subsistent relationality entails the Church is himself real. Every grace that exists in the world, then, is properly a grace mediated by the Church as the recipient of the promise made to Abraham that all the nations would be blessed. In proclaiming the gospel to the world the Church lays claim to what is hers – "For where the Church is, there is the Spirit of God; and where the Spirit of God is, there is the Church, and every kind of grace". To hold back in proclaiming the gospel the Church would have to deny who she is and what Christ has done for her.

The Holy Spirit as the Principal Agent of Evangelization

The Son was sent by the Father to give the Spirit. The "fountain-like love" of the Father has extended to include us. The purpose of Christ's coming is sometimes variously described in terms of salvation, or grace, or eternal life but at root all of these are given in the fundamental gift of the Holy Spirit who is the Lord, the Giver of life. We are recreated, made capable of a divine life impossible to us apart from the transformation of humanity accomplished in the Incarnation and under the power of the Holy Spirit who testifies in our hearts to our adoption by God. The Spirit "alone stirs up the new creation, the new humanity of which evangelization is to be the result, with that unity in variety which evangelization wishes to achieve within the Christian community"[48]. The entire economy of salvation is thus summed up in this expansive Trinitarian dynamic.

This Gift, however, is not simply a passive possession which recreates us as children of God but is the very power of God stirring up within us the recognition of our need for redemption and the acceptance of the Good News of salvation that is proclaimed to us. The first part of this dynamic involves the uncovering of the mystery of iniquity and our involvement in and subjection to sin. The Spirit who "searches the depths of God" searches our depths as well and through our conscience brings to our consciousness the reality of our own sinfulness, the sinfulness of our social contexts and cultures, the sinfulness of the entire human race from the beginning. The Spirit convicts "the world concerning sin and righteousness and judgment"[49].

The Spirit's action is not simply an exposition of the sinfulness of the world but it is a revelation of the relationship of sin to the cross of Christ. Sin has intervened between the first and the second beginnings and consequently "there is no send-

---

[48] *EN* 75.
[49] Jn. 16:8. DV27-48.Cf.36.

ing of the Holy Spirit... without the Cross and the Resurrection"[50]. The Spirit gives witness to Christ and the first witness concerns "the sin which is the rejection of Christ even to his condemnation to death"[51]. This "convincing" is not limited to that one particular sin but uncovers "the evil of sin, of every sin" and "*demonstrates its relationship with the Cross of Christ*"[52]. But in the same act the Spirit reveals the reverse side of this relationship of every sin to the cross because "through the *mysterium pietatis* love can reveal itself in the history of man as stronger than sin", that *sin is conquered through the sacrifice of the Lamb of God*[53]. The Spirit is given to the disciples, in John's account, "*for the remission of sins*"[54]. The proclamation of Christ's death and resurrection in the evangelistic activity of the Church, therefore, is invariably tied to a call to conversion from sin, a call which was ingredient in Christ's own missionary proclamation[55]. In this "the Holy Spirit remains the transcendent principal agent of the accomplishment of this work in the human spirit and in the history of the world"[56].

Further, the Spirit draws us into the dynamic of love that is the continuance of the mission of Christ. He is the love of God poured out into our hearts, not only God's love for us but God's love in us loving the neighbor even to the ends of the earth. This divine Love impels us, as he impelled the first disciples and Jesus himself, to make "bold proclamation" announcing the coming of the Kingdom in the person of Christ[57]. This same Love was Christ's first gift to his Bride, his Church. This "love of Christ impels" the Church to proclaim that "since one died for all, all died" (II Cor. 5:14).

---

[50] DV13,24.
[51] DV30.
[52] DV32.
[53] DV39.
[54] DV40.
[55] RM46-47.
[56] DV31,42.
[57] Ibid.; cf. also *LG 17,* cited in DV2: "For the Church is driven by the Holy Spirit to do her part for the full realization of the plan of God, who has constituted Christ as the source of salvation for the whole world".

There is a natural correspondence between the activity of the Spirit within the hearers making them receptive to the word of the gospel and the activity of the same Spirit in the missionaries impelling them to proclaim the gospel. In this way the work of the Spirit within the heart of the world comes to concrete expression in the explicit witness to Christ of the Church. This correspondence has a double grounding. The Spirit active in the hearer is already a gift from Christ, a participation in his gift to the Church whereby the nations are blessed through her[58]. The Spirit also draws hearers to Christ, gathering them into the Eucharistic community united in Christ[59]. "Evangelization – over and above the preaching of a message – consists in the implantation of the Church, which does not exist without the driving force which is the sacramental life culminating in the Eucharist"[60].

Many gifts have been given to the Church through the one Spirit for the sake of the world[61]. The fundamental missionary gift is apostleship which is given to those who are called to the episcopacy. Christ's mandate to preach the gospel to the ends of the earth falls most directly on the successors of the apostles[62]. Clergy, both priests and deacons, insofar as they participate in Orders, share in this charge to preach the gospel[63]. There are, in addition, individuals and communities especially called to missionary work and endowed with appropriate talents and charisms[64]. The responsibility is not theirs alone, however, but belongs to the whole Church by virtue of the common gift of the Spirit for "bold proclamation" sacramentalized in Confirmation[65]. This is accom-

---

[58] Cf. *RM 9*.
[59] *RM 29*.
[60] *EN 28*.
[61] *LG 4, 7; DV 25; CL 20-21, 45, 64*.
[62] *LG 23-24; AG 1; RM 63; TM 45*.
[63] *LG 28; PO 2*; cf. also Paul VI's opening address to the Synod of Bishops in 1974.
[64] *AG 23; RM 69*.
[65] *AG 4*. Cf. also *Synod 1974 5. EN 70-73*. John Paul II calls to mind the boldness or *parrhesia* described in Acts in *RM 45* and the universal responsibility for mission in ibid. *71*. Baptism as establishing our fundamental dignity is often named – *EN 75, RM 77, CL 51*. Cf. also *EA 66. Cristifideles Laici* treats these topics in detail.

plished in the first instance by the example of a holy, love-filled life as well as by the sharing of their faith in whatever situation they find themselves[66]. The Spirit works in them for their sanctification and provides the courage to bear witness to their faith. All are called to offer prayer for the salvation of the world but certain individuals and communities have been given special gifts of prayer for this purpose[67]. Others are called to provide support as catechists or to help in a variety of ways with gifts of administration and the provision of resources for the support of missionary work[68]. Others have been given extraordinary charisms for the good of the Church and the furtherance of its mission[69]. There are, in short, a great variety of gifts given by the Spirit to the Church for the sake of evangelization.

A complete account of a spirituality of evangelization is not possible here but a few points are worth making, especially as they relate to the role of the Spirit. In the last analysis "one cannot give to others what one does not possess"[70]. The fundamentum is that the Church, "as a community totally involved in evangelization, must conform to Christ who explained his own mission" in terms of his anointing by the Spirit to "announce glad tidings to the poor, to give prisoners their freedom, the blind their sight, to set the oppressed free" (Lk. 4:18)[71]. Individuals, in accord with their state, make an offering of themselves, "with the encouragement and help of the Holy Spirit" in the pattern of Christ who humbled himself and was obedient to the Father's call even to the point of death[72]. The kingdom is spread throughout the world "following the narrow way of the cross" in which God's self-sacrificing love

---

[66] *AG* 11, 21, 36; *Synod 1974* 9. Evangelization begins in the family. "The family is the school of love, of knowledge of God, of respect for life and human dignity". Cf. John Paul II, Puebla, IV.a.; *CL* 14, 62.
[67] *AG* 18, 40; *RM* 78.
[68] *AG* 17, 41; *RM* 73-74.
[69] *CL* 24.
[70] Paul VI, "Closing Address", *Synod 1974* in the seventh consensus point.
[71] *Synod 1974* 12; *RM* 88; *EA* 67.
[72] *AG* 24.

is manifest in their own unfeigned love which has been poured into their hearts through the Holy Spirit[73]. Along with the embrace of the cross the Spirit inspires in the Church and in individual missionaries a lively hope and sustains them unbowed by discouragement in difficult situations[74].

The Spirit is the fire which fuses us together into a oneness in Christ. He is the seal of our union with Christ and is the supreme source of unity drawing all Christians together and ultimately all of humanity[75]. The kingdom proclaimed by Christ "is one of communion among all human beings – with one another and with God"[76]. "The ultimate purpose of mission is to enable people to share in the communion which exists between the Father and Son". Thus "the Spirit leads the company of believers to 'form a community,' to be the Church"[77]. The Spirit continues to lead the Church to establish communities and found particular churches[78]. It is precisely because the Church is a reality "whose innermost life is unity in love" that the world will know and believe[79]. For this reason a missionary spirituality will always be a communitarian spirituality where one, under the guidance of the Spirit and in union with the successors to the apostles, constantly seeks to work in harmony with others so that all the gifts of the Spirit serve the common good, the common mission[80].

One does not remain untouched by the Spirit who impels one to mission and fellowship. The same Spirit works an ongoing transformation and renewal of mind and heart in which the life of virtue flourishes[81]. Indeed, "the call to mission derives, of its nature, from the call to holiness"[82]. Such a life of love

---

[73] *AG* 1, 5; Rom. 5:5.
[74] *CL* 7. Cf. *EN* 28; *RM* 35.
[75] *Synod* 1974 2 and the preface of Paul VI's closing address; *DV* 2; *RM* 89; *CL* 18-19; *EA* 33.
[76] *RM* 15.
[77] *RM* 26; *CL* 32.
[78] *RM* 20.
[79] *RM* 23; *CL* 41.
[80] *TM* 47; *CL* 21.
[81] *Synod* 1974 6; *CL* 16.
[82] *RM* 90; *CL* 17. Cf. *LG* 39-42 and *EA* 30 on the universal call to holiness.

requires "intimate union with God, through assiduous prayer, meditation of the word of God, contemplation, all strengthened and sustained by frequent participation in the sacraments"[83]. Conversely, one's own faith is strengthened when it is given to others[84]. The end result of this transformation is an ever greater docility to the action of the Spirit, an ever greater conformity to Christ[85]. This leads to the gifts of fortitude and discernment, the courage to give bold proclamation and the guidance of the Spirit in one's actions[86].

This power of discernment and the cognate gifts of wisdom and understanding touch on every facet of the evangelistic task. Natural aptitudes are essential as well as solid programs of instruction, but natural talents and natural means by themselves are not sufficient for the spread of the gospel. They must be infused and transformed by the power of God's Spirit[87]. Likewise, wisdom and discernment is needed in adapting the gospel message to particular contexts[88]. Societies and cultures, enmeshed as they are in the common sinful human condition, must be converted and transformed, every bit as much as individuals. This transformation which preserves all that is true and good and noble is done "in the Spirit" who recreates all things[89]. "Between evangelization and human advancement ... there are in fact profound links". The love of God that is proclaimed by the Church demands the preservation of human dignity through the promotion of peace and justice. This too is the work of God's Spirit[90]. Finally, the Spirit guides individuals and the Church in the discernment of the "signs of the times"[91]. The Spirit who searches even the depths of God is found also at the heart of the historical process. Proper docility

---

[83] *Synod* 1974 7; cf. also *AG* 36, *EN* 28; *TM* 59.
[84] *RM* 2.
[85] *EN* 75.
[86] RM 87.
[87] *EN* 75. Cf. also *AG* 23, 29.
[88] Cf., for instance, *DV* 26.
[89] *AG 13; DV* 59; *CL* 44; *EA* 70; cf. also the first consensus point in Paul VI's closing address to *Synod* 1974 and John Paul II, Puebla, III.5.
[90] *EN* 31. Cf. Puebla III.2.
[91] *GS* 11.

to the Spirit leaves one free to take advantage of providential opportunities (I Cor. 16:9, II Cor. 2:12, Col. 4:3) and even extraordinary charisms[92].

The Spirit and the New Evangelization

In papal documents since Vatican II a distinction has been made between evangelization *ad gentes* and what has been called re-evangelization or the new evangelization. The former activity is directed toward those who have never before heard, or heard effectively, the proclamation of Christ. The latter designation covers a variety of situations whose common denominator is that the gospel has been previously proclaimed and in some sense accepted but no longer has the effect in the lives of individuals and societies that one might otherwise expect[93]. The general lines of the Spirit's role in evangelization would hold for both of these types. Clearly, though, the latter presents special problems because the normal means of communicating the faith in an otherwise Christian context have in some measure failed.

A survey of some of the reasons for this phenomenon highlights the impossibility of pursuing a single strategy in response. Eastern Europe and China have been under the domination of Marxist ideology since the end of the Second World War, Russia since the First.

Dialectical materialism can only look upon all religion as an "idealistic illusion" that is to be discouraged[94]. The possibilities for religious instruction varied greatly in the Communist bloc countries from almost complete suppression in states such as Albania to the relatively high degree of freedom experienced by the Church in Poland. Although this situation has been ameliorated in Europe there are still many countries, Communist and otherwise, in which religious liberty is sharply curtailed.

---

[92] *GS* 11; *Synod 1974* 6, 13. These too must be discerned. Cf. *CL* 24.
[93] *RM* 32-34.
[94] *DV* 56.

In the West the rise of a secularist and materialistic culture combined with the dissolution of traditional societal ties to family and community have led many to a vague uninformed religiosity if not to a practical or even systematic atheism. Rapid changes have only exasperated this situation[95]. In other areas of the world past alignment of the Church with oppressive govemments have led to widespread disenchantment with the Church. This was as true in the overthrow of the *ancien regime* as with more recent developments in Latin and South America[96]. In yet other contexts a history of neglect or large ratios between priests and laity or the movements of peoples which have prevented adequate pastoral care have led either to lax practice or to an increased vulnerability of the faithful to others preaching a different gospel or message than that proclaimed by the Church[97]. There has been a diminished sense of sin in this century, despite abundant evidence that sin has not disappeared from the world, which has undermined the felt need for redemption[98]. The arms race, "death dealing poverty", terrorism, abortion, genocide mark this century with "ever darker 'signs of death'"[99]. Modern humanity, in spite of its achievements, "seems to have lost its sense of ultimate realities and of existence itself"[100].

If these negative signs of the time underscore the present need for re-evangelizing activity, not only toward "the nations" who have not yet heard the Good News, but also toward traditionally Christian areas, it is also true that there are many positive signs of God's present activity. Within the world at large Paul VI pointed to a nostalgia for evangelical values and a thirst for authenticity which serve as stepping stones to the Christian message[101]. John Paul II, noting these

---

[95] *GS* 19-20; *EN* 55-56; *CL* 4, 34.
[96] It is also possible to neglect pastoral care for the leading sectors of society. *EA* 67.
[97] *AG* 1; *Synod 1974* 8-9; *EN* 1, 52-56; *RM* 2-3, 32, 35-37; *CL* 34; *EA* 5-6.
[98] *DV* 47.
[99] *DV* 57.
[100] *RM* 2.
[101] *EN* 55, 76.

same "signs of the times", but buoyed also by "the collapse of oppressive ideologies and political systems", sees "the dawning of a new missionary age" because God has opened "the horizons of a humanity more fully prepared for the sowing of the Gospel"[102].

The point of the Jubilee, then, is less the marking of a millennial milestone as it is a recognition of what God is currently doing in the world and in the Church. The millennium is a convenient focal point for these processes[103]. They will bear fruit, however, only to the extent that the Holy Spirit inspires the preparatory phase[104]. "If Christians are docile to the action of the Holy Spirit" then there will be a *"new springtime of Christian life* which will be revealed by the Great Jubilee"[105]. The signs are already visible[106]. Preparation for the millennium, then, *"is aimed at an increased sensitivity to all that the Spirit is saying to the Church and to the Churches,* as well as to individuals through charisms meant to serve the whole community"[107].

Foremost among the signs that are already visible, in John Paul II's view, was the Second Vatican Council, *"a providential event, whereby the Church began the more immediate preparation* for the Jubilee of the Second Millennium"[108]. The openness of the Council to the world "was an evangelical response" to the events of the Twentieth Century which demonstrate the need of the world for purification and conversion. The Council's purpose was "to make the Church of the twentieth century ever better fitted for proclaiming the Gospel to the people of the twentieth century"[109]. The Council was as much a pneumatological as it was an ecclesiological one: "In a certain sense, the Council has made the Spirit newly 'present' in our difficult age"[110].

---

[102] *RM* 3, 92. Cf. also *CL* 4-5.
[103] *EA* 66.
[104] *DV* 51-54; *TM* 44.
[105] *TM* 18.
[106] *RM* 86.
[107] *TM* 23, 45.
[108] *TM* 18, 36.
[109] *EN* 2.
[110] *DV* 26.

But precisely because the Council opened itself so widely to the world spiritual discernment has been necessary for the implementation of the Council's work. John Paul II saw the various Assemblies of the Synod of Bishops held in the years after the Council as providing this "testing and bringing together of the salvific fruits of the Spirit bestowed in the Council"[111]. Indeed, this was the sense expressed in the first two declarations of the Third Synod on evangelization itself and echoed in Paul VI's seventh point of consensus in his closing comments:

> There has been placed clearly in evidence the action of the Holy Spirit in the work of evangelization, for it is he, "the soul of the church", who is the infuser of grace and charity... the bishops have sought to listen, together with "Mary, his mother" (Acts 1:14), and gathered about Peter, as in a new Cenacle, to the voice and impulse of the Holy Spirit. And, in the certainty that in the carrying out of their task of teaching they are authoritatively assisted by the Spirit, they have placed themselves 'under the shadow of his wings'... in order to reflect and decide[112].

The Synod further expressed the confidence that "more deeply rooted in the perennial actuality of Pentecost, the church will know new times of evangelization"[113]. The preparation of the Church for this renewed missionary effort leading up to the Jubilee was the purpose behind the series of continental synods held in the past few years in Rome[114]. Convinced that the Spirit has been particularly active in this regard the pope has called for a commitment of "all of the Church's energies to a new evangelization and to the mission *ad gentes*"[115]. This preparation has been the "hermeneutical key" to John Paul II's own pontificate. He has been indefatigable in his

---

[111] Ibid.
[112] Cf. *LG* 7; *EN* 75; *DV* n. 96; *CL* 20, 24 for the Spirit as "the soul of the Church".
[113] *Synod* 1974 13.
[114] *TM* 21.
[115] *RM* 3, 86.

travels around the world bringing the message of the gospel. It is also clear that these efforts have borne abundant fruit on several levels. First, it has given a higher profile to the Christian message in many contexts where that message would not have otherwise received such notice. This is as true of highly secularized contexts as well as non-Christian ones. Second, his journeys have often been in conjunction with other efforts of renewal in the Church or have been the spark which initiated new efforts in this regard. They have as well been the occasion of grace, leading many to return to the Church[116]. Evidences of the Spirit's activity in the present context are not limited to magisterial initiatives. "The Holy Spirit arouses a missionary spirit in the Church in many ways, and indeed often anticipates the work of those whose task it is to guide the life of the Church"[117]. This is certainly true in the case of various religious missionary institutes whose founding charisms have often been unplanned. Mother Teresa's call to serve the poor of Calcutta and the subsequent founding of the Missionaries of Charity is one of the more recent examples.

But there have been, as well, many lay movements that have emerged in the Church in the latter decades of this millennium which have proved important to the missionary effort of the Church in general and more particularly to the new evangelization[118]. John Paul II has observed that "the commitment of the laity to the work of evangelization is changing ecclesial life"[119]. It was not by accident that he called the various representatives of lay movements and ecclesial communities to meet in Rome for a series of meetings concluding on the vigil of Pentecost. The groups represented included members of Focolare, l'Arche, the Neocatechumenate Way, Communion and Liberation, the Catholic Charismatic Renewal, Crusillo, and many others. Speaking to them he gave thanks

---

[116] Cf., for instance, *St. Louis Post-Dispatch,* Sunday, Mar. 21, 1999, 3C. The Spirit clearly used that visit as an important moment of re-evangelization for the archdiocese.
[117] *AG* 29.
[118] *AG* 40. Cf. 4, 23; *CL* 2, 34, 56.
[119] *RM* 2.

for this "springtime of the Church" that they represented. He described them as "the first tangible proof of the outpouring of the Spirit" in this latter part of the millennium[120]. Paul VI earlier, even while warning of the danger of proceeding apart from the hierarchy, had noted "with satisfaction the hope furnished by small communities and the reminder they give of the work of the Holy Spirit"[121]. Such groups are particularly important for the new evangelization because their members, as lay, permeate society. Through their daily contacts they reach countless individuals that official missionaries cannot[122]. Young people have consistently been singled out in this regard[123]. Lay zeal, then, is a concrete sign of the activity of the Spirit who impels all to proclaim Christ's love for everyone[124]. Those groups whose express purpose is not missionary will nonetheless have an evangelistic effect[125].

Correlated with the more evangelistic effect of these groups, and the driving force for them, is the renewal of prayer. Indeed, some of the lay movements have this as their explicit focus. Their contribution is a "revival of prayer among the faithful, who have been helped to gain a clearer idea of the Holy Spirit as he who inspires in hearts a profound yearning for holiness"[126]. Paul VI described this as "a privileged moment of the Spirit" because "everywhere people are trying to know him better ... to place themselves under his inspiration". This has a direct connection with the evangelizing mission of the Church since it is there that the Spirit is most active. He echoed the exhortation of the Bishops' Synod of 1974 that the role of the Spirit's action in evangelization be

---

[120] *Catholic* WorldNews (CWNews.com), June 1, 1998. JOHN PAUL II, Homily for Pentecost, 1998 (vatican.va), *CL* 64.
[121] *Synod* 1974, "Closing Address". He was referring to communautes de base. They are discussed in more detail in EN 58. John Paul II echoed Paul VI's sentiment in *RM* 51.
[122] *AG* 15; *RM* 71-72; *EA* 44; *CL* 15, 28.
[123] *Synod* 1974 5; JOHN PAUL II, Puebla IV.c.; *TM* 58; *CL* 2, 46.
[124] *CL* 2.
[125] An evangelistic intent is one of the criteria for the "ecclesiality" of such a group. Cf. *CL* 30.
[126] *DV* 65.

studied in more detail and that all "pray without ceasing to the Holy Spirit with faith and fervor and let themselves prudently be guided by him as the decisive inspirer of their plans, their initiatives and their evangelizing activity"[127]. The gifts and charisms which the Spirit gives in response to such prayer is to be received with gratitude by the individual and by the entire Church. "They are in fact a singularly rich source of grace for the vitality of the apostolate and for the holiness of the whole Body of Christ"[128].

Cardinal Eugenio Araujo de Sales of Rio de Janeiro recently announced a program of new evangelization as part of preparations for the Jubilee in his archdiocese. It is intended as a comprehensive effort involving "not only pastors and parish structures, but Catholic lay people and any Catholic organization, movement, or group". The plan calls for "missionaries", primarily young people, to visit some one hundred thousand homes, stores, and offices inviting people to return to the Church. A second phase would involve specific encouragement to return to the sacraments[129]. It is clear that if the new evangelization is to be effective such efforts on the part of the whole community will be necessary [130]. It is also clear that the effectiveness of such efforts will also depend on the extent in which the love that has been poured out into our hearts through the Holy Spirit is manifested forth. The Spirit and the Bride say to the Lord Jesus, particularly in this time leading up to the third Millennium after Christ, "Come!"[131]. They repeat the same message, through the actions of such missionaries, to each and every person.

---

[127] *EN* 75.
[128] *CL* 24.
[129] *Catholic World News* (CWNews.com), March 18, 1999.
[130] *CL* 64; EA 36, 44.
[131] *DV* 66.

John Paul II
and the New Evangelization*

AVERY DULLES, S.J.

John Paul II first mentioned the "new evangelization" in a speech at Port-au-Prince, Haiti, on May 9, 1983. The fifth centenary of the first evangelization of the Americas (1492-1992), he declared, should mark the beginning a new era of evangelization, "new in ardor, methods, and expression". This proposal, often repeated in papal utterances since 1983, gives rise to the questions I shall address in this paper: What is distinctive to the new evangelization? What is John Paul II's contribution toward it? And how is it related to the coming jubilee of the year 2000?

I

Evangelization itself is nothing new. The term is biblical, and goes back to the Old Testament. In the Greek Bible, the verb "evangelize" (*euaggelizesthai*) means to proclaim good news. In the Septuagint the term occurs in the historical books, in the Psalms, and most prominently in Deutero-Isaiah. This last work has a famous description of the herald who runs ahead of the people on their return from Babylon to Jerusalem, proclaiming that Yahweh is triumphing over all his enemies and establishing his kingdom (Is 52:7).

---

* This article is based on a lecture given at Our Lady of the Lake Seminary, Mundelein, Illinois, October 21, 1998.

In the New Testament the verb *euaggelizesthai* frequently appears in Luke, Acts, and the Pauline corpus. Jesus is anointed to proclaim the Kingdom of God and evangelize the poor (Lk 4:18 and 7:22). After the Ascension the apostles have the task of "preaching *(euaggelizomenoi)* Jesus Christ" (Acts 5:42). Quoting the previously mentioned passage in Deutero-Isaiah, Paul in Romans 10:15 exclaims: "How beautiful are the feet of those who bring [the] good news!" Paul is driven by a sense of his own call to be the apostle to the Gentiles (Rom 15:20; 2 Cor 10:16; Gal 1:16; 2:7). Conscious of standing under a divine constraint, he exclaims, "Woe to me if I do not evangelize!" (1 Cor 9:16).

In the New Testament, therefore, the verb "evangelize" means to proclaim with authority and power the good news of salvation in Jesus Christ. The evangelist is one sent by Christ and endowed with a corresponding charism from the Holy Spirit. The preached word comes from God and arouses saving faith in those who believe it.

The Catholic Church has been involved in evangelization throughout its long history. In the early Middle Ages monks such as Boniface in the West and Cyril in the East, with a veritable army of collaborators and followers, successfully evangelized almost the whole of Europe, founding monasteries, cathedrals, churches, schools, and hospitals. After the great voyages of discovery in the fifteenth century, Catholic missionaries fanned out to spread the faith to North and South America, Africa, and Asia. Although missionary activity declined in the eighteenth century, the Catholic revival of the nineteenth century witnessed the foundation of many missionary orders and congregations, which still continue their labors. But, as John Paul II notes in his great missionary encyclical, *Redemptoris missio,* the years since Vatican II have been plagued by doubts and ambiguities concerning evangelization and missionary activity.

The crisis of evangelization has its roots in the Counter-Reformation, when the terms "gospel" and "evangelical" were taken over by Protestants and became suspect to Catholic ears. Catholics put the accent not so much on announcement as on teaching, not so much on the message of salvation as on the moral law, the Church, and the sacraments. Their missionary activity was therefore less evangelical and more ecclesiastical.

In the modern period, moreover, the Catholic Church became preoccupied with the problems of schism and heresy. Great pains were taken to protect the faithful against modern errors. The Church as a whole turned in upon itself; it became more preoccupied with the instruction and pastoral care of its own faithful than with reaching out to new audiences. Missionary activity still went on, but it was seen as the preserve of apostolic religious orders and societies rather than a concern of the Church as a whole.

The terminology of evangelization re-entered Catholic literature toward the middle of the present century, thanks in part to the influence of Protestant thinkers such as Karl Barth. From the 1930s through the 1950s, Catholic religious educators promoted a new style of kergymatic theology, in which evangelization was taken to mean a confident proclamation of the basic message of God's offer of salvation through Jesus Christ. The kerygmatic sermons of Peter and Paul, as found in the Book of Acts, were studied as models for revitalizing the faith in dechristianized sections of Europe.

The future Pope John XXIII was exposed to the new kerygmatic theology during his years as nuncio to France, where he seems to have picked up many of his ideas for the Second Vatican Council. In the apostolic constitution *Humanae salutis* (1961), officially convoking the Council, he expressed his hope that the Council would "bring the modern world into contact with the vivifying and perennial energies of the gospel"[1]. He called on the Council to demonstrate that the Church, "always living and always young, which feels the rhythm of the times and which in every century beautifies herself with new splendor, radiates new light, achieves new conquests...."[2]. In his opening speech at the Council John XXIII expressed the hope that the Church would be able to draw all men and women of good will to herself not by threats and condemnations but by beneficence and gentle persuasion[3].

---

[1] John XXIII, Apostolic Constitution "Humanae salutis", *The Documents of Vatican II*, ed. WALTER M. ABBOTT (New York: America Press, 1966), 703.
[2] Ibid., 706.
[3] John XXIII, Opening Speech at the Council, Ibid., 710-19, esp. 716.

Following these directives, Vatican II did in fact make evangelization one of its central themes. In the very first sentence of its Constitution on the Church it affirmed that Christ had sent the Church to preach the gospel to every creature (LG 1; cf. Mk 16:15). Since the Church is missionary by its very nature, said the Council, the task of evangelization is incumbent on every Christian (LG 16-17; cf. AG 23, 35). The bishops, in union with the pope, are charged with leading the process (LG 23; CD 6; AG 29, 30). Priests are to stir up zeal for evangelization (PO 4; AG 39), and all the laity are expected to cooperate in this effort, especially in the environments of their work and family life (LG 35; AA 2, 3, 6; AG 41).

The commentaries on Vatican II published in the first decade after the Council (1965-1975) generally overlooked the centrality of evangelization. They focused attention on collegiality, ecumenism, dialogue, and social teaching. But Paul VI, who had played a major part in shaping the agenda of the Council even before his election to the papacy, corrected this oversight. In 1975, on the tenth anniversary of the close of Vatican II, he published his great apostolic exhortation *Evangelii nuntiandi*. The objectives of the Second Vatican Council, he there stated, could be definitively summed up under a single heading: "to make the Church of the twentieth century ever better fitted for proclaiming the gospel to the people of the twentieth century" (EN 2). In this document Paul VI expressed his hope of giving a "fresh forward impulse" and launching what he called "a new period of evangelization" (ibid.)[4].

Cardinal Wojtyla was an eager participant in the Synod of Bishops of 1974, which prepared materials for Paul VI's apostolic exhortation. As pope he has sought to carry out the programs of Vatican II and Paul VI, the sources from which he draws the principal elements of his program of evangelization.

---

[4] Paul VI did not actually use the term "new evangelization", but it had already been used in 1968 by the Latin American bishops at Medellín in their "Message to the Peoples of Latin America". See General Conference of the Latin American Bishops, *The Church in the Present-Day Transformation of Latin America in the Light of the Council. II. Conclusions* (Bogatá, Colombia: General Secretariat of CELAM, 1970), 41.

In his many speeches, encyclicals, and other documents he has given further clarity and precision to what is involved. Evangelization, he asserts, is "the primary service which the Church can render to every individual and to all humanity in the modern world" (RM 2). He has, in fact, made himself the principal evangelizer of our day. "The Lord and Master of history", he said in 1990, "has wished my pontificate to be that of a pilgrim pope, walking down the roads of the world, bringing to all peoples the message of salvation"[5].

II

With the help of this background it may be possible to summarize under ten headings some defining traits of the new evangelization. In each case the new trend was introduced by Vatican II and further clarified by Paul VI and John Paul II. The present pope did not invent the "new evangelization", but he has promoted it in enormously effective ways.

1. **Centrality of Christ**. Vatican II, with its program of *ressourcement*, sought to speak in biblical language and to focus on Christ, the light of the world, whose radiance sustains the Church. It recognized a "hierarchy of truths", in which the Lordship of Christ the Son of God stands at the highest level (UR 11).

Paul VI spoke often of the centrality of Jesus Christ. "There can be no true evangelization", he wrote, "if the name, the teaching, the life, the promises, the kingdom and the mystery of Jesus of Nazareth the Son of God, are not proclaimed" (EN 22; cf. 27). After quoting Paul VI to this effect, John Paul II states that all missionary proclamation must have its center in Christ (RMis 44). On another occasion he declares:

> The new evangelization begins with the clear and emphatic proclamation of the gospel, which is directed to

---

[5] John Paul II, Arrival Speech in Mexico City, May 6, 1990; ORE 7 May 1990, pp. 1 and 12. (The abbreviation ORE in these footnotes stands for *L'Osservatore Romano*, English weekly edition).

each and every person. Therefore it is necessary to awaken again in believers a full relationship with Christ, mankind's only Savior. Only from a personal relationship with Jesus can an effective evangelization develop[6].

If this aspect of evangelization were put into practice, the Catholic Church might keep pace with Protestant Evangelicals in its missionary expansion. There would be no occasion for Catholics to leave their Church and join fundamentalist or Pentecostal communities on the ground that that Catholicism gave them no sense of being personally related to the Lord.

2. Ecumenism. The new evangelization, unlike most of the Catholic preaching since the Reformation, is ecumenical. In line with Vatican II, the recent popes have called attention to the authentic elements of faith in other Christian communities. They are seriously committed to promoting the unity of all Christians in accordance with the high-priestly prayer of Jesus (John 17:20-25).

Vatican II in its Decree on Ecumenism called upon all Christians to bear witness to their common hope (UR 12) without falling into false conciliatory approaches (UR 11). It noted that the lack of unity among Christians seriously damages the witness of the Church (UR 1). Paul VI and John Paul II have frequently repeated this important observation. Paul VI called upon all Christians to give greater common witness to Christ before the world when they engage in missionary proclamation (EN 77).

John Paul II asks how it is possible to proclaim the gospel of reconciliation without at the same time being concerned for reconciliation among Christians (UUS 98). The very name of Christ, which is the focus of evangelization, should draw Christians together. The spread of what the present pope calls "para-Christian sects" makes it more urgent than ever, in his estimation, for different churches and ecclesial communities to bear harmonious witness to Christ (RMis 50). But he insists that the existing differences must be honestly faced. "The obligation to respect the truth is absolute" (UUS 79).

---

[6] Ad Limina visit of Bishops of Southern Germany, December 4, 1992; ORE 23/30 December 1992, pp. 5-6, at 5.

3. **Interreligious Dialogue.** The necessary relationship of evangelization to interreligious dialogue has been strongly emphasized in the past two generations. Some missionaries are suspicious of dialogue because it seems to undermine evangelization, and conversely, some proponents of dialogue feel that their efforts are impeded by any intent to evangelize. Yet Vatican II, while strongly urging the missionary imperative, encouraged dialogue and collaboration with followers of other religions (AG 41; NA 2).

Paul VI and John Paul II find no conflict between authentic dialogue and proclamation. Having emphasized the need for mutual respect and dialogue in his encyclical *Ecclesiam suam* (ES 81, 112), Paul VI in *Evangelii nuntiandi* warned that esteem for other religions should not lead us to refrain from proclaiming Jesus Christ (EN 53; cf. ES 82).

John Paul II makes similar points. The assurance of possessing universally valid truths is not an obstacle but a help to sincere and authentic dialogue (F&R 92). An honest dialogue requires the parties to trust one another and to speak frankly about their differences. Because Christians who engage in dialogue must declare their own faith, dialogue includes proclamation as an integral part. Proclamation itself must be carried on in a spirit of dialogue, with respect for the conscience of the other party and a ready willingness to learn (RMis 55-57).

4. **Religious Freedom.** In centuries past, moral and physical force were sometimes used to induce people to accept the true faith. The new evangelization, by contrast, presupposes full acceptance of Vatican II's Declaration on Religious Freedom, which taught that people should be encouraged to follow their free and responsible judgment, without external pressure (DH 1). Paul VI in *Evangelii nuntiandi* taught that the Church should propose the truth of the gospel without seeking to impose anything on the consciences of the hearers (EN 80). Echoing this thought, John Paul II declares: "The Church proposes; she imposes nothing" (RMis 39). Recognizing that the assent of faith must by its very nature be free, the Church avoids offensive proselytization. It proclaims the gospel in a way that honors the sanctuary of every human conscience (RMis 8, 39). The acceptance of Christ, far from diminishing

freedom, fulfills it, according to the saying of Jesus, "The truth shall make you free" (Jn 8:32).

5. **Continuing Process.** Evangelization has often been restrictively understood as though it meant only the first proposal of the gospel to people who had not as yet heard it. Vatican II used the noun *evangelizatio* only rarely (e.g. CD 6; AA 6; AG 38) and then chiefly as a synonym for the initial "proclamation of the gospel" ("nuntium *evangelicum*", AG 10). But it sometimes used the term in a broader sense that would seem to include interaction between the gospel and the local culture (GS 44).

Paul VI in *Evangelii nuntiandi* spelled out a very comprehensive conception of evangelization, including the ministry of preaching and sacraments and indeed the whole process by which human life is penetrated and transformed by the gospel (EN 14; 17-18). Pastoral care of the faithful, therefore, is a matter of continuing evangelization. The Church itself, he explained, is in constant need of being evangelized (EN 15).

John Paul II, building on these insights, distinguishes three phases of evangelization. "First evangelization", in his terminology, is missionary proclamation in regions where Christ is still unknown or where the Church has not yet taken root. The second phase, continuing evangelization, consists in the pastoral care of Christians who are seeking to put their lives more fully under influence of the gospel. Finally, the process includes the re-evangelization of those who have fallen away or allowed their faith to grow cold (RMis 33). The viability of communities of faith is put to the test in situations of hedonistic consumerism or grinding poverty. In these situations re-evangelization will involve an overcoming of the separation between the gospel and daily life in family, work, and society (CL 34).

6. **Social Teaching.** In past centuries it became customary to draw a sharp line of demarcation between the spiritual realm, which was that of the Church and eternal life, and the temporal realm, which belonged to the State and worldly institutions. In this framework evangelization was seen as speaking to people's inner life with a view to their eternal salvation. The Church, to be sure, was deeply engaged in corporal works of mercy, including charity toward the sick and the poor, but

these charitable activities were distinguished from evangelization.

In the present century it has become increasingly clear that authentic conversion includes a commitment to the common good. The 1971 Synod of Bishops made the famous statement: "Action on behalf of justice and participation in the transformation of the world fully appear to us as a constitutive dimension of the preaching of the gospel or, in other words, of the Church's mission for the redemption of the human race and its liberation from every oppressive situation" (JW 6). The Church has a responsibility, said the Synod, to witness before the world that the gospel message contains clear imperatives to work for peace and justice in society (JW 36).

Paul VI took up the socioeconomic aspects of evangelization in an important section of *Evangelii nuntiandi*. He affirmed the importance of denouncing oppressive and dehumanizing structures as antithetical to the gospel itself. But he also warned against the temptation to reduce the Church's mission to that of a purely temporal project. Priority, he said, must always be given to the religious finality of evangelization and to the interior conversion that is required for salvation (EN 32-35). No social structures can assure a truly human culture, he said, unless the rulers and the people have undergone a conversion of mind and heart (EN 36).

John Paul II frequently returns to the same theme. His position is substantially that of Paul VI. "Authentic human development", he writes, "must be rooted in an ever deeper evangelization" (RMis 58). At the Puebla Conference of the Latin American bishops in 1979 he said: "If the Church makes herself present in the defense of or in the advancement of man, she does so in line with her mission, which although it is religious and not social or political, cannot fail to consider man in the entirety of his being"[7].

A social system in which some are lured into ruthless competition for wealth and luxury, while others are driven into

---

[7] John Paul II, Address to General Assembly of Latin American Bishops at Puebla, III, 2; *Origins* 8 (February 8, 1979): 529-38, at 536.

abject poverty, is contrary to the vision of society held forth by the gospel. Evangelization must therefore include determined efforts to build a civilization of peace, solidarity, and love. Total or integral evangelization will inevitably "penetrate deeply into social and cultural reality, including the economic and political order"[8]. The pope sees his program of human rights as a vital component of the new evangelization.

7. **Evangelization of Cultures.** In the past evangelization has generally been understood rather narrowly as consisting in the direct proclamation of the gospel. Without neglecting the importance of personal conversion, the new evangelization takes cognizance of the general cultural setting. As Paul VI explained in an important section of *Evangelii nuntiandi*, evangelization is often impeded by an unwholesome split between faith and culture. Cultures themselves need to be "regenerated by an encounter with the gospel" (EN 20).

John Paul II speaks frequently of the evangelization of cultures and of the necessary dialogue between faith and cultures. While cultures serve the gospel by supplying the necessary means of expression and communication, cultures themselves can be interiorly purified, elevated, and transformed by openness to Christian faith and values. As the pope explains in *Centesimus annus*, evangelization "plays a role in the culture of various nations, sustaining culture in its progress toward truth and assisting in the work of its purification and enrichment" (CA 50). Where the prevailing culture remains closed and hostile, faith cannot fully express itself, nor can the culture achieve its full potential. To overcome these difficulties the Church must seek methods of proposing the gospel that are effective in the existing culture. Without dilution or distortion, the Christian message has to be integrated as far as possible into the "new culture" created by modern technology (RMis 37c). In his latest encyclical on "Faith and Reason" the pope calls for greater attention to philosophy as a service to the new evangelization. The word of God, he asserts, gives access to

---

[8] Ad Limina visit of Puerto Rico bishops, October 27, 1988; ORE 5 December 1988, pp. 7 and 14, at 14.

new dimensions of the true, the good, and the beautiful (F&R 103).

8. **New Media.** Still another characteristic of the new evangelization, mentioned by John Paul II in his Port-au-Prince speech, is its employment of new methods and expressions. Vatican II had already spoken of the need to use the new instruments of social communication in preaching the good news of redemption (IM 3). Paul VI in his apostolic constitution noted that since our age is deeply influenced by the mass media, evangelization must make use of these channels. "The Church would feel guilty before the Lord if she did not utilize these powerful means that human skill is daily rendering more perfect" (EN 45). But he added that public proclamation cannot take the place of person-to-person contact, which remains indispensable for touching and transforming consciences (EN 46).

Here again, John Paul II follows in the footsteps of his predecessor. "The evangelization of modern culture", he says, "depends to a great extent on the influence of the media" (RMis 37c). Elsewhere he writes: "The world of mass communications represents a new frontier for the mission of the Church because it is undergoing a rapid and innovative development and has an extensive worldwide influence on the formation of mentality and customs" (CL 44).

St. Paul saw the necessity of proclaiming the gospel at the cultural center of the ancient world-the Areopagus of Athens. In a similar way, the pope contends, the world of the mass media constitutes a new Areopagus, which the Church must not neglect. It is insufficient, he says, simply to use new techniques of dissemination; the message itself must be integrated into the new styles of thought and expression, the "psychology" of the new cultural sectors (RMis 37c). Radio, television, and computer technology must not be allowed to dictate the message but must be prudently employed to open new avenues of access to the gospel.

The Catholic Church, with its rich patrimony of art, architecture, music, and ritual is in some ways extraordinarily well suited to the electronic media. John Paul II has effectively used these media in televised liturgies, but he recognizes that esthetic delight does not amount to personal conversion.

Because faith and holiness are always essential, he writes, the true missionary is the saint (RMis 90).

9. **Involvement of All Christians.** As noted earlier in this paper, evangelization has often been seen in the past as the special concern of apostolic associations of priests and members of missionary orders. While recognizing the unique role played by religious communities, the Second Vatican Council insisted that the whole Church is missionary, and that "the work of evangelization is a basic duty of the People of God" (AG 35). The laity, incorporated in Christ by baptism, confirmation, and the Eucharist, are in duty bound to cooperate in the expansion and growth of Christ's Body (AG 36; cf. LG 16-17).

Ten years after the Council, Paul VI pointed out that "it is the whole Church that receives the mission to evangelize" (EN 15). Toward the end of *Evangelii nuntiandi*, he distinguished among the respective responsibilities of the pope, the bishops, priests, religious, and laity (EN 66-73).

John Paul II makes similar distinctions. Bishops, he says, "are the pillars on which rest the work and the responsibility of evangelization, which has as its purpose the building up of the Body of Christ"[9]. Priests, he holds, are by vocation "responsible for awakening the missionary consciousness of the faithful"[10]. Members of religious orders and congregations can play a special role because of their total gift of self through the vows of chastity, poverty, and obedience, which dramatically attest to the values of the kingdom of God (RMis 69; cf. VC 87-92).

In his apostolic exhortation on the laity, the pope calls attention to the duty of lay Christians to make their daily conduct a shining and convincing testimony to the gospel (CL 34, 51). It is their special responsibility, he says, to demonstrate how Christian faith constitutes the only fully valid response to

---

[9] John Paul II, "Address to Italian Bishops' Conference", May 18, 1989; ORE 5 June 1989, pp. 7 and 16, at 16.

[10] John Paul II, "Message for World Mission Day", October 21, 1990; ORE 11 June 1990, p. 9.

the problems and hopes that life presents to every person and society (CL 34).

In his apostolic exhortation on the family, John Paul II includes a section on the family as an evangelizing community in which the members evangelize one another as well as other families. Parents, he says, are the first evangelizers of their children (FC 51-54).

10. **Primacy of the Holy Spirit.** From some earlier presentations of evangelization and missionary activity one might get the impression that, while the Holy Spirit inspired the apostles, apostolic activity in subsequent generations depends of merely human initiative. The new evangelization, avoiding any such crypto-Pelagianism, explicitly calls attention to the continuing role of the Spirit.

Vatican II, in its Decree on the Church's Missionary Activity, pointed out that the Holy Spirit unceasingly accompanies and directs the Church in its salvific labors (AG 4). Paul VI carried this theme forward in *Evangelii nuntiandi*. "The Holy Spirit", he wrote, "is the principal agent of evangelization: it is he who impels each individual to proclaim the gospel, and it is he who in the depths of consciences causes the word of salvation to be accepted and understood" (EN 75).

John Paul II in *Redemptoris missio* has an entire chapter bearing the title "The Holy Spirit: The Principal Agent of Mission". Without recourse to the Spirit, he writes, we cannot have the wisdom, enthusiasm, courage, and convincing power that enables us to pass on our experience of Jesus and the hope that motivates us (RMis 24). And in another context he writes: "Missionary dynamism is not born of the will of those who decide to become propagators of their faith. It is born of the Spirit, who moves the Church to expand, and it progresses through faith in God's love"[11]. The new evangelization, as both these popes understand it, relies less on human plans and projections than on the unforeseeable initiatives of the Holy Spirit.

---

[11] John Paul II, Address of February 12, 1988 to Italian Bishops on Liturgical Course, ORE 14 March 1988, p. 5.

III

John Paul II, at the beginning of his pontificate, pointed out that with the approach of the year 2000 the Church was already in the season of a new Advent, a time to render thanks for past favors and to ask God's blessing on the years to come. Since the Marian Year of 1987, and especially since 1990, he has linked the great Jubilee with the new evangelization. These Advent years, he says, should be the occasion of an examination of conscience regarding the extent to which the Church of the past millennium has been faithful to her mission. As the Church enters the third millennium of her existence, he asks, can she give a good account of her fidelity to her mandate?

In discerning the signs of the present time, the pope expresses his conviction that evangelization is more urgent than ever, for the number of people who do not know Christ has practically doubled since the close of Vatican II (RMis 3). Seeking to escape from the dehumanizing pressures of technology and consumerism and from the barren agnosticism of the prevalent philosophies, many are hungering for richer spiritual nourishment. New opportunities for evangelization are offered by the rapidity of travel and by instant communications. Certain gospel values, such as those of human dignity and freedom, have become part of the universal patrimony of all peoples. The year 1989 witnessed the collapse of some oppressive regimes that were blocking the spread of the gospel. As the present millennium draws to a close the pope feels authorized to declare:

> God is opening before the Church the horizons of a new humanity more fully prepared for the sowing of the gospel. I sense that the moment has come to commit all the Church's energies to a new evangelization and to the mission *ad gentes*. No believer in Christ, no institution of the Church can avoid this supreme duty: to proclaim Christ to all peoples (RMis 3).

The task of evangelization under current conditions is awesomely complex. It is no easy matter to spread the gospel in ways that respect the freedom and dignity of every conscience. Nor is it easy to direct our evangelizing efforts to the many cultures, religious traditions, and political and social structures that make up the world of our day. The correct balance between proclamation and dialogue is difficult to maintain. Each of the new worlds of science and technology, mass media and popular culture, is an Areopagus awaiting the arrival of a new St. Paul.

No individual can hope to accomplish more than a tiny fragment of the total task. The whole Catholic Church, notwithstanding its membership of about a billion persons, often appears as a little flock, riddled with internal dissension and surrounded by immense armies of hostility, indifference, and doubt. Our courage could easily fail unless we recalled the circumstances in which the Church received its original mandate. How could the first disciples, few, poor, and unlearned as they were, hope to preach the gospel to every creature and make disciples of all nations? Conscious that the Lord was with them, they overcame imprisonment, exile, and martyrdom in carrying the message of Christ to the ends of the known world. Even with lesser sacrifices than theirs, we may be privileged to reap a harvest that we did not sow, and to bring an abundant catch of fish into the nets that we have lowered at the Lord's command. Our obedience and trust in the Lord may make it possible for the prediction of Pope John Paul II to be fulfilled: "As the third millennium of the redemption draws near, God is preparing a great springtime for Christianity, and we can already see its first signs" (RMis 86).

Abbreviations

Documents of Vatican II

AA – *Apostolicam actuositatem* - Decree on the Apostolate of the Laity
AG – *Ad gentes* - Decree on the Church's Missionary Activity
CD – *Christus Dominus* - Decree on the Pastoral Office of Bishops in the Church
DH – *Dignitatis humanae* - Declaration on Religious Freedom
GS – *Gaudium et spes* - Pastoral Constitution on the Church in the Modern World
IM – *Inter mirifica* - Decree on the Means of Social Communication
LG – *Lumen gentium* - Dogmatic Constitution on the Church
NA – *Nostra aetate* - Declaration on the Relationship of the Church to Non-Christian Religions
PO – *Presbyterorum ordinis* - Decree on Ministry and Life of Priests
UR – *Unitatis redintegratio* - Decree on Ecumenism

OTHER

CA   – *Centesimus annus* (1991) - John Paul II, Encyclical to commemorate the centenary of Leo XIII's *Rerum novarum*
CL   – *Christifideles laici* (1988) - John Paul II, Apostolic Exhortation on the Laity
EN   – *Evangelii nuntiandi* (1975) - Paul VI, Apostolic Exhortation on Evangelization in the Modern World
ES   – *Ecclesiam suam* (1964) - Paul VI, Encyclical on "The Paths of the Church"
FC   – *Familiaris consortio* (1981) - John Paul II, Apostolic Exhortation on the Christian Family
F&R   – *Fides et ratio* (1998) - John Paul II, Encyclical on Faith and Reason
JW   – *Justice in the World* (1971) - Document of the Synod of Bishops
RM   – *Redemptoris mater* (1987) - John Paul II, Encyclical on Mary
RMis – *Redemptoris missio* (1990) - John Paul II, Encyclical on the Church's Missionary Activity
UUT   – *Ut unum sint* (1995) - John Paul II, Encyclical on Ecumenism
VC   – *Vita consecrata* (1995) - John Paul II, Apostolic Exhortation on the Religious Life

Nueva Evangelización y espiritualidad misionera (en el inicio del tercer milenio)

JUAN ESQUERDA-BIFET

La «Nueva Evangelización», en su aspecto más importante, se concreta en el «nuevo fervor de los apóstoles», que equivale al espíritu o «espiritualidad misionera». Sólo a partir de esta espiritualidad será posible encontrar los «nuevos métodos» y «nuevas expresiones», que reclama la «Nueva Evangelización»[1].

---

[1] Como es sabido, la expresión «nueva evangelización» ya se encuentra en el documento de Puebla (n. 366). Con las tres aplicaciones indicadas («nuevos métodos, nuevas expresiones, nuevo fervor»), la expresión fue usada por Juan Pablo II, por primera vez, en Puerto Príncipe, Haití, el día 9 de marzo de 1983 (Insegnamenti VI, 1983, 698), y luego en Santo Domingo, los días 11 y 12 de octubre de 1984 (Insegnamenti VII/2, 1984, 885-897). El Papa ha hecho frecuentes llamamientos en esta perspectiva, matizándolos según las situaciones geográficas y los contenidos de los documentos: RMi 2-3, 30, 33, 59, 72-73, 83, 85-86; CA 5; VS 107; EA 63; FR 103. El documento de Santo Domingo dedica al tema el capítulo primero de la segunda parte (nn. 23-30), señalando su significado dinámico, el sujeto (toda la comunidad eclesial), la finalidad, los destinatarios, el contenido, el nuevo ardor, los nuevos métodos y las nuevas expresiones. Ver también «Ecclesia in America» nn. 6, 66-74. Recojo alguna bibliografía en: *Renovación eclesial y espiritualidad misionera para una nueva evangelización*: Seminarium 31 (1991) n. 1, 135-147. Ver tanmbién: CELAM, *Nueva evangelizción, génesis y líneas de un proyecto misionero* (Bogotá 1990); (Conferencia Episcopal Española) *Impulsar una nueva evangelización* (Madrid 1991); P. GIGLIONI, *Perché una «nuova» evangelizzazione*: Euntes Docete 43 (1990) 5-36; J. LOPEZ GAY, *Il rapporto tra la «nuova evangelizzazione» e la missione «ad gentes» secondo l'enciclica «Redemptoris Missio»*: Seminarium (1991) n. 1, 91-105; B. MONDIN, *Nuova evangelizzazione dei paesi d'antica cristianità*, en: *Cristo, Chiesa, Missione* (Roma, Pont. Univ. Urbaniana, 1992) 187-214; A. SALVATIERRA, *Retos y factores de la Nueva Evangelización*: Lumen 40 (1991) 234-295.

El inicio del tercer milenio pone de relieve las nuevas situaciones geográficas, sociológicas y culturales (cfr. RMi 3738), así como los nuevos «signos de esperanza» (TMA 46) y las nuevas gracias, que indican el «amanecer» de «una nueva época misionera» (RMi 92). Todo ello reclama unas actitudes nuevas por parte de los evangelizadores, que se concretan en la espiritualidad misionera[2].

El problema que queda por estudiar es el de las líneas actuales de la espiritualidad misionera, en relación con la nueva evangelización y en vistas a la evangelización en el tercer milenio del cristianismo. Las nuevas situaciones y las nuevas gracias abren nuevas posibilidades de evangelización, mientras, al mismo tiempo, indican unas nuevas exigencias, que se traducen en espiritualidad misionera. No se trata sólo de una reflexión teológica sobre el tema, sino de discernir esas exigencias y señalar las actitudes que debe asumir el evangelizador.

Los documentos magisteriales postconciliares del Vaticano II indican una dinámica nueva, más existencial o experiencial, que intentamos resumir en el apartado n. 3. En realidad, la misión, bajo la fuerza del Espíritu Santo, se concreta en «transmitir a los demás la propia experiencia de Jesús» (RMi 24). Según parece, el desafío mayor de toda la historia de la evangelización, hasta el presente, es el encuentro entre experiencias de Dios: por parte del cristianismo y de las otras religiones. La respuesta a ese desafío deberá ser por parte de «testigos de la experiencia de Dios» (RMi 91; cfr. EN 76).

Si, por una parte, «al encontrar a Cristo, todo hombre descubre el misterio de su propia vida» (Bula «Incarnationis Mysterium», n. 1), por otra parte, «nuestra poca fe ha hecho caer en la indiferencia y alejado a muchos de un encuentro auténtico con Cristo» (ibídem, n. 11)[3]. De ahí deriva una urgen-

---

[2] El tema de la «espiritualidad misionera» ha entrado ya ampliamente en los estudios misionológicos. La expresión se encuentra en AG 29; los contenidos son los aportados por AG 2325, pero, de modo especial, por EN 75-82 y RMi 87-92. Hacemos una síntesis del tema en el primer apartado del presente estudio, para indicar las pistas hacia la nueva evangelización en el inicio del tercer milenio.

[3] La llamada al «encuentro con Cristo» parece ser una idea central de los documentos de Juan Pablo II, a partir de su primera encíclica «Redemptor hominis». Ver una síntesis de esta llamada a la experiencia de encuentro con Cristo, especial

cia mayor de renovación eclesial (Iglesia misterio, comunión y misión), en la línea de la espiritualidad misionera.

1. La espiritualidad misionera se abre camino en la misionología

Los temas de «espiritualidad» y de «misión» han encontrado su lugar respectivo en la teología (Teología de la espiritualidad y Misionología). La «espiritualidad» indica una «vida» o «camino» según el «Espíritu» (cfr. Gal 5,25; Rom 8,4.9). «Se llama espiritual quien obra según el Espíritu»[4]. La «misión» puede estudiarse en su naturaleza (teología dogmática), en su metodología (teología pastoral) y en su vivencia (teología espiritual o espiritualidad).

La espiritualidad misionera indica, pues, el «espíritu» con que se vive la misión, o también una vida según el Espíritu Santo que es la fuerza de la misión. «La actividad misionera exige, ante todo, espiritualidad específica», que se delinea como «plena docilidad al Espíritu» (RMi 87) y «comunión íntima con Cristo» RMi 88)[5].

Hoy la «espiritualidad misionera» ya tiene carta de ciudadanía, respecto a la terminología (cfr. AG 29; RMi 87) y a los contenidos. Éstos han quedado resumidos especialmente en AG 23-25, EN 75-82 y RMi 87-92: fidelidad al Espíritu Santo, intimidad con Cristo (o experiencia de Cristo), vocación misionera, virtudes del misionero, oración y contemplación, fidelidad y amor de Iglesia, la figura materna de María. El punto de

---

mente en los apartados nn. 2-3 del presente estudio (con referencias a la encíclica «Fides et ratio»). La exhortación postsinodal sobre América, «Ecclesia in America» (EAm), tiene esta misma perspectiva: El encuentro con Jesucristo vivo en el hoy de América (cap. I-II). «El encuentro con el Señor produce una profunda transformación de quienes no se cierran a Él. El primer impulso que surge de esta transformación es comunicar a los demás la riqueza adquirida en la experiencia de este encuentro» (EAm 68).

[4] San Basilio Magno, *De Spiritu Sancto*, cap. 26, n. 61: PG 32. 179.

[5] La misión de Cristo se realiza en plena docilidad al Espíritu: Lc 4,1.14.18; 10,21; Hech 10,38. Es la misma misión que Cristo comunica a los suyos bajo la acción del Espíritu: Jn 20,21-23; cfr. Hech 20,22.

referencia es la figura del Buen Pastor y su imitación por parte de las diversas figuras misioneras de la historia, según las diversas líneas de la «vida apostólica» (seguimiento radical de Cristo, vida comunitaria y disponibilidad misionera)[6].

Esta espiritualidad es una función de la misma teología, en cuanto que toda reflexión teológica debe tender simultáneamente a la fundamentación dogmática, a la aplicación pastoral y a la vivencia espiritual. Cada uno de los temas o contenidos, que hemos anotado en el párrafo anterior, puede desarrollarse según diversas dimensiones: trinitaria, cristológica, pneumatológica, eclesiológica, histórica, antropológica, etc.

Pero, más allá de los conceptos (por válidos que sean), la espiritualidad misionera debe dejar traslucir el misterio de Dios Amor manifestado en Cristo, que llama a la contemplación de la Palabra, al seguimiento evangélico, a la vida de comunión eclesial y a la disponibilidad misionera. Todavía cabe distinguir, en la profundización de los conceptos, si se trata de la espiritualidad misionera de todo cristiano, del apóstol en general o del misionero en particular (vocación misionera específica, carisma misionero peculiar, etc.).

He querido sintetizar brevemente el significado y los contenidos de la espiritualidad misionera, tal como hoy van entrando pacíficamente en los estudios misionológicos, para intentar dar un salto de calidad, que nos sitúa ante la urgencia de esa misma espiritualidad misionera, en vistas a la nueva evange-

---

[6] Resumo los contenidos y la bibliografía especializada en: *Teologia della evangelizzazione, Spiritualita missionaria* (Pontificia Università Urbaniana 1992). Ver también: L.A. CASTRO, *Espiritualidad misionera* (Bogotá, Paulinas, 1993); M. COLLINS REILLY, *Spirituality for mission* (New York, Orbis Books, 1978); J. DAO DINH DUC, *Spiritualità missionaria*, in: *Cristo, Chiesa, Missione* (Roma, Urbaniana Univ. Press, 1992) 381-397; J. ESQUERDA BIFET, *Espiritualidad misionera (Madrid*, BAC, 1982); Idem, *La espiritualidad misionera*, en: *La misionología hoy* (Buenos Aires, Ed. Guadalupe, 1988) 566-588; Idem, *Teología de la evangelización* (Madrid, BAC, 1995) cap. X-XI; S. GALILEA, *Espiritualidad de la evangelización, según las bienaventuranzas* (Bogotá, CLAR, 1980); J. MONCHAMIN, *Théologie et spiritualité missionnaires* (Paris, Beauchesne, 1985); K. MÜLLER, *Pour une spiritualité missionnaire, repenser la mission* (Paris, Desclée, 1965); Y. RAGUIN, *Espíritu, hombre, mundo* (Madrid, Narcea, 1976); K. WOJTYLA, *La evangelización y el hombre interior*: Scripta Theologica 11 (1979) 39-57; F. ZALBA, *Espiritualidad misionera*: Rev. Telógica Limense 18 (1984) 371-382.

lización (como nuevo fervor de los apóstoles) y en el inicio de un tercer milenio del cristianismo.

En efecto, el problema más urgente de la evangelización actual es el encuentro entre las diversas experiencias religiosas, como auténtica experiencia del mismo Dios que ha ido sembrando las «semillas del Verbo» en todas las culturas y religiones. Se podría decir, pues, que la espiritualidad misionera se concreta hoy especialmente en el testimonio de la experiencia de Dios (traducida en anuncio, servicios de caridad, etc.), por parte del apóstol (cfr. EN 76, RMi 91), como fidelidad a la acción actual del Espíritu Santo en la Iglesia y en el mundo, para que las semillas del Verbo lleguen a «su madurez en Cristo» (RMi 28). Es lo que intento analizar en los apartados siguientes.

2. Situaciones nuevas que piden la experiencia contemplativa del apóstol (contenidos de la encíclica «Fides et ratio»)

Probablemente la inmediatez del problema impide ver su perspectiva e importancia. La sociedad actual (¿postmoderna?), cansada de ideologías e inclinada hacia lo útil y constatable, no deja de buscar la trascendencia: «Paradójicamente, el mundo, que, a pesar de los innumerables signos de rechazo de Dios, lo busca, sin embargo, por caminos insospechados y siente dolorosamente su necesidad, el mundo exige a los evangelizadores que le hablen de un Dios a quien ellos mismo conocen y tratan familiarmente, como si estuvieran viendo al Invisible» (EN 76).

A pesar de la ambigüedad del fenómeno religioso actual, hay que constatar que «se busca la dimensión espiritual de la vida como antídoto a la deshumanización» (RMi 38). Mientras tanto, las religiones buscan el contacto con el cristianismo para preguntar sobre su peculiar experiencia de Dios. De ahí que pueda afirmarse que «el futuro de la misión depende en gran parte de la contemplación» (RMi 91)[7].

---

[7] Estudio el tema y presento bibliografía actual, en: *Huellas del Verbo encarnado en las diversas experiencias de Dios. A propósito del Jubileo del año 2.000*: Bur-

El tema de las «semillas del Verbo» (y «preparación evangélica»), que ya ha sido objeto de diversos estudios actuales, se presenta hoy como momento de llegada a su «madurez en Cristo». Si hay que admitir «la presencia y la actividad del Espíritu... en las culturas y las religiones», no es menos cierto que «Es también el Espíritu quien esparce las semillas de la Palabra presentes en los ritos y culturas, y los prepara para su madurez en Cristo» (RMi 28)[8].

Habrá que profundizar en la experiencia de Cristo, por parte del apóstol, en el sentido de adoptar «actitudes interiores» (EN 75), es decir, convicciones, motivaciones, decisiones, que se traduzcan en encuentro o relación personal con Cristo, seguimiento, comunión eclesial y misión. Más allá de un análisis teológico, filosófico o psicológico del tema de la experiencia, habrá que partir de la realidad revelada expresada por San Juan: «Hemos visto su gloria» (Jn 1,14); «lo que hemos visto con nuestros ojos, lo que contemplamos y tocaron nuestras manos acerca de la Palabra de vida... Lo que hemos visto y oído, os lo anunciamos» (1Jn 1,1.3).

Por esto, se puede afirmar que «el misionero, si no es contemplativo, no puede anunciar a Cristo de modo creíble» (RMi 91). En este sentido, el desafío actual del encuentro entre las diversas experiencias de Dios en las religiones, se convierte en el mayor desafío que ha tenido la historia de la evangelización. Pero ello es un signo de esperanza.

---

gense 36 (1995) 333-359. La aplicación a cada una de las religiones, en: *Hemos visto su estrella. Teología de la experiencia de Dios en las religiones* (Madrid, BAC, 1996). Ver también: AA.VV., *La preghiera, bibbia, teologia, esperienze storiche* (Roma, Città Nuova, 1988); AA.VV., *Prayer-Priere:* Studia Missionalia 24 (1975); M. DHAVAMONY, *Teología de las religiones (Madrid,* San Pablo, 1998); L. GARDET, O. LACOMBE, *L' expérience du Soi. Étude de mystique comparée* (Paris, Desclée B., 1981); W. JOHNSTON, *El ojo interior del amor, Misticismo y religión* (Madrid, Paulinas, 1987); Idem, *Teología mística, la ciencia del amor* (Barcelona, Herder, 1997).

[8] Resumo los contenidos y recojo bibliografía actual, en: *Orme del Verbo Incarnato nelle diverse esperienze di Dio. In occasione del Giubileo dell'anno 2000,* «Euntes Docete» 49 (1996) 47-61. La expresión «semillas del Verbo» es de San JUSTINO, *Apologia* I, 6,3; 10,1-3; 13,2-3; I, 46,1-4; II, 8: PG 6, 457-458. Cfr. AG 3,11; LG 18; EN 53,80; RMi 29; VS 94. Sobre la «preparación evangélica, cfr. LG 16; AG 3, citando a EUSEBIO DE CESAREA, *Preparatio evangelica* I,1: PG 21,28 a-b.

El deseo y la búsqueda de Dios, hoy, por parte de la sociedad en general y, de modo especial, por parte de las religiones, pone en evidencia que «en lo más profundo del corazón del hombre está el deseo y la nostalgia de Dios» (enc. «Fides et Ratio», FR n. 24). «El hombre busca un absoluto que sea capaz de dar respuesta y sentido a toda su búsqueda» (ibídem, 27). Es «búsqueda de verdad y búsqueda de una persona de quien fiarse» (ibídem, 33). Por esto, el apóstol debe saber anunciar con franqueza que «en Jesucristo, que es la Verdad, la fe reconoce la llamada última dirigida a la humanidad, para que pueda llevar a cabo lo que experimenta como deseo y nostalgia» (ibídem).

Se necesita mucha audacia y coherencia (nacidas de un encuentro personal con Cristo), para poder anunciar al mundo de hoy esta experiencia de fe, que es siempre fruto del Espíritu Santo (cfr. RMi 24). Cualquier destello de verdad, que Dios ya ha sembrado en el corazón humano, se dirige necesariamente hacia la verdad completa, que Dios nos ha manifestado por su revelación en Cristo. Sin la experiencia verdadera de encuentro con Cristo, el apóstol caería en un de esos dos extremos igualmente erróneos: pensar que todas las religiones ya son la verdad plena (sin Jesucristo) o querer imponer la propia fe sin respetar la hora de Dios (la acción de la gracia).

La búsqueda de Dios, que anida en todo corazón humano y que conduce al encuentro definitivo con Cristo, es un cuestionamiento para la persona del apóstol. La verdad completa se encuentra sólo en Cristo. A la luz de esta convicción y en la línea de la paciencia milenaria de Dios, «es posible superar las divisiones y recorrer juntos el camino hacia la verdad completa, siguiendo los senderos que sólo conoce el Espíritu del Señor resucitado» (FR 92).

El camino de la reflexión humana, inherente a toda cultura y religión, no se opone a la revelación sobrenatural. Por esto, el anuncio de la fe cristiana (aunque sea con términos filosóficos y teológicos de otra cultura) «ha estimulado ciertamente la razón a permanecer abierta a la novedad radical que comporta la revelación de Dios» (FR 101). Por este mismo anuncio, «el hombre contemporáneo llegará así a reconocer que será tanto más hombre cuanto, entregándose al Evangelio, más se abra Cristo» (FR 102).

Pero este anuncio misionero comporta, por parte del apóstol, una convicción y una vida coherente, de suerte que se vea en él la experiencia de haber encontrado a Cristo. Entonces aparecerá que «la revelación cristiana es la verdadera estrella que orienta al hombre... es la última posibilidad que Dios ofrece para encontrar en plenitud el proyecto originario de amor iniciado en la creación» (FR 15). Un testimonio de las bienaventuranzas, por una caridad heroica, se hace transparencia del misterio de la muerte y resurrección de Cristo y, consecuentemente, «rompe los esquemas habituales de reflexión» para abrirse a la fe (cfr. FR 23). Toda cultura «tiene en sí misma la posibilidad de acoger la revelación divina» (FR 71), pero necesita la gracia y el testimonio cristiano, «que sabe acoger cada cultura, favoreciendo el progreso de lo que en ella hay de implícito, hacia su plena explicitación en la verdad» (ibídem)[9].

La actitud de espiritualidad misionera equivale a detectar con respeto, tanto las «semillas del Verbo», presentes en toda cultura y religión, como la plenitud que sólo se encuentra en Cristo, el Verbo encarnado. «La Iglesia sabe que los tesoros de la sabiduría y de la ciencia» «están ocultos en Cristo (Col 2,3)» (FR 51). Y también cree que «la promesa de Dios en Cristo llega a ser, ahora, una oferta universal... como patrimonio del que cada uno puede libremente participar» (FR 70). Aunque hay semillas de verdad y de bien en todas las culturas y religiones, como dones de Dios concedidos a todos los pueblos, «el anuncio o kerigma llama a la conversión, proponiendo la verdad de Cristo que culmina en su Misterio pascual. En efecto, sólo en Cristo es posible conocer la plenitud de la verdad que nos salva

---

[9] La actitud de «bienaventuranzas» es una línea básica de la espiritualidad misionera: «El misionero es el hombre de las Bienaventuranzas... Viviendo las Bienaventuranzas el misionero experimenta y demuestra concretamente que el Reino de Dios ya ha venido y que él lo ha acogido. La característica de toda vida misionera auténtica es la alegría interior, que viene de la fe. En un mundo angustiado y oprimido por tantos problemas, que tiende al pesimismo, el anunciador de la Buena Nueva ha de ser un hombre que ha encontrado en Cristo la verdadera esperanza» (RMi 91). La misión es anuncio y testimonio de las bienaventuranzas, porque «en su profundidad original son una especie de autorretrato de Cristo y, precisamente por esto, son invitaciones a su seguimiento y a la comunión de vida con él» (VS 16).

(cfr. Hech 4,12; 1Tim 2,4-6)» (FR 99). Cristo es la «única respuesta a los problemas del hombre» (FR 104).

Los caminos o vías que conducen a la verdad son muchos y variados. La única meta final y el «Camino» verdaderamente salvífico es sólo Jesucristo. Por esto, «cualquiera de estas vías puede seguirse, con tal de que conduzca a la meta final, es decir, a la revelación de Jesucristo» (FR 38). Cualquier reflexión humana, filosófica y teológica, debe estar abierta al infinito del misterio de Dios Amor en Cristo. Por esto, «la Verdad, que es Cristo, se impone como autoridad universal que dirige, estimula y hace crecer (cfr. Ef 4,15) tanto la teología como la filosofía» (FR 92).

La espiritualidad misionera ayudará a adoptar una actitud equilibrada, para descubrir los valores auténticos de toda cultura (como valores universales y preparación evangélica), purificarlos cuando sea necesario, abrirlos a la plenitud en Cristo y compartir con todos los pueblos y culturas esos dones y gracias recibidas del mismo Dios (cfr. FR 71-72). Este proceso de inculturación será auténtico si se convierte en misión universal. La misión de insertar el evangelio en una cultura hace posible que el mismo proceso de inculturación se convierta en proceso de misión a todos los pueblos[10].

---

[10] Siendo tan abundante la bibliografía sobre la inculturación, me limito a señalar los documentos magisteriales en que se habla de tema: LG 13,17; GS 44; AG 3,10-11,22; EN 20,53,63; RH 12; SA (enc. Slavorum Apostoli); RMi 52-54; CA 24,50,51; PDV 55; CEC 1204-1206; VC 79-80; EA 62. El lector encontrará abundante bibliografía en: AA.VV., *Inculturazione, concetti, problemi, orientamenti* (Roma, Centrum Ignatianum Spiritualitatis 1979); AA.VV., *Fede e culture e il problema dell'inculturazione con esemplificazioni moderne*, en: *Portare Cristo all'uomo* (Roma, Pont. Univ. Urbaniana 1985) I; M. DHAVAMONY, *Christian Theology of inculturation* (Roma, Pont. Univ. Gregoriana, 1997); (Documento de la Comisión Teológica Internacional) Fede e inculturazione: La Civiltà Cattolica 140 (1989) 158-177; P. GIGLIONI, *Inculturazione, teoria e prassi* (Lib.Edit.Vaticana 1999); B. MONDIN, *Principi generali sull'inculturazione della Chiesa e dell'Evangelo:* Euntes Docete 46 (1993) 227-256; P. POUPARD, *Théologie de l'évangélisation des cultures:* Esprit et Vie 96 (1986) 353-362; A.A. ROEST CROLLIUS, *Missione e inculturazione. Incarnare l'Evangelo nelle culture dei popoli*, en: *Cristo, Chiesa, Missione* (Roma, Urbaniana University Press 1992) 293-305; J. SARAIVA, *Missione e cultura* (Roma, Pont. Univ. Urbaniana, 1986).

El problema misionero más urgente de la evangelización actual es el de la espiritualidad misionera del apóstol: ¿Qué actitud debe asumir el apóstol ante la realidad de gracia existente en culturas y religiones, a partir del hecho de que «el Verbo Encarnado es el cumplimiento del anhelo presente en todas las religiones de la humanidad» (TMA 6)? Se trata de saber reconocer gozosamente esta realidad, discernirla a la luz del Espíritu Santo y encontrar los caminos evangélicos para que se realice el encuentro explícito con Cristo.

Este desafío forma parte de los «signos de esperanza» de nuestra época (TMA 46). Las nuevas situaciones geográficas, sociológicas y culturales (cfr. RMi 37-38) urgen a reconocer que «la Iglesia tiene un inmenso patrimonio espiritual para ofrecer a la humanidad: en Cristo, que se proclama «el Camino, la Verdad y la Vida» (Jn 14,6). Es la vida cristiana para el encuentro con Dios, para la oración, la ascesis, el descubrimiento del sentido de la vida. También éste es un areópago que hay que evangelizar» (RMi 38).

3. La dinámica experiencial de los documentos magisteriales postconciliares

El paso que intento dar, en el presente estudio sobre la espiritualidad misionera, consiste en presentar la urgencia de esta espiritualidad como «experiencia» de Dios, para responder a los desafíos de la nueva etapa de evangelización (que he resumido en el apartado anterior). Pero este paso (que describiré en el apartado n. 4) necesita una aportación previa y que ofrezca garantía, es decir, la dimensión experiencial y vivencial de los documentos magisteriales en relación con la misión (que resumo en el presente apartado).

No resulta fácil, en la reflexión teológica, aceptar términos psicológicos, como es el caso de la «experiencia». Pero es un hecho de la revelación cristiana constatado por Juan: «Hemos visto su gloria» (Jn 1,14), «lo que hemos visto y oído, os lo anunciamos» (1Jn 1,1.3). La realidad existe (es decir, la «experiencia» de haber encontrado a Cristo); la naturaleza de la misma queda siempre para el estudio teológico, que deberá tener en cuenta los dos factores básicos: la gracia y la naturaleza humana. Para nuestro caso, nos basta, por el momento, con constatar esta realidad en los documentos magisteriales actuales, referentes a la evangelización[11].

En la exhortación apostólica «Evangelii nuntiandi», Pablo VI indicó esta línea experiencial para poder responder a los desafíos de la sociedad actual: «El mundo exige a los evangelizadores que le hablen de un Dios a quien ellos mismo conocen y tratan familiarmente, como si estuvieran viendo al Invisible» (EN 76). En esta misma perspectiva experiencial, Juan Pablo II, en la encíclica «Redemptoris Missio», presenta la misión como comunicación de una «experiencia»: «La venida del Espíritu Santo los convierte (a los Apóstoles) en testigos o profetas (Hech 1,8; 2, 17-18), infundiéndoles una serena audacia que les impulsa a transmitir a los demás su experiencia de Jesús y la esperanza que los anima» (RMi 24).

La misma «espiritualidad misionera», cuyos contenidos quedan descritos en RMi cap. VIII, tiene esta línea experiencial por parte del apóstol: «Precisamente porque es enviado, el misionero experimenta la presencia consoladora de Cristo, que lo acompaña en todo momento de su vida. «No tengas miedo... porque yo estoy contigo» (Hech 18, 9-10). Cristo lo espera en el corazón de cada hombre» (RMi 88).

El resultado de esta perspectiva existencial de la espiritualidad misionera se concreta en esta afirmación: «El misionero es un testigo de la experiencia de Dios y debe poder decir, como los Apóstoles: «Lo que contemplamos... acerca de la Palabra de vida..., os lo anunciamos» (1Jn 1,1-3) (RMi 91). Por

---

[11] Ver algunos estudios actuales sobre la experiencia: A. CASTIÑEIRA, *La experiencia de Dios* en la *postmodernidad* (Madrid, PPC 1992); J. ESQUERDA BIFET, *Valor evangelizador y desafíos actuales de la «experiencia» religiosa:* Euntes Docete 43 (1990) 37-56 (con bibliografía); IDEM, *La experiencia cristiana de Dios, más allá de las culturas, de las religiones y de las técnicas contemplativas*, en: *Portare Cristo al mondo* (Roma, Pont. Univ. Urbaniana 1985) I, 351-368; IDEM, *Experiencia «religiosa» y experiencia cristiana de Dios:* Athéisme et Dialogue (Pont. Consilium pro Dialogo cum non credentibus) 23/4 (1988) 370-387; IDEM, *Contemplación cristiana y experiencias místicas no cristianas*, en: *Evangelizzazione e culture* (Roma, Pont. Univ. Urbaniana 1976) I, 407-420; J. MOUROUX, *L'expérience chrétienne. Introduction a une théologie* (Paris, Aubier-Montagne, 1952); H. SMITH, *La experiencia de Dios* (Santander, Sal Terrae 1975).

esto, «nota esencial de la espiritualidad misionera es la comunión íntima con Cristo» (RMi 88).

La realidad de fe, a la que hace referencia esta experiencia misionera, es la presencia de Cristo resucitado en la vida del apóstol (cfr. Mt 28,20) y la unión del mismo Cristo con cada ser humano redimido: «El Hijo de Dios con su encarnación se ha unido, en cierto modo, con todo hombre» (GS 22; cfr. Jn 1,14).

En realidad, todo ser humano experimenta la voz de Dios en el fondo de su corazón: «Porque el hombre tiene una ley escrita por Dios en su corazón, en cuya obediencia consiste la dignidad humana y por la cual será juzgado personalmente. La conciencia es el núcleo más secreto y el sagrario del hombre, en el que éste se siente a solas con Dios, cuya voz resuena en el recinto más íntimo de aquélla» (GS 16). El misterio del hombre se descifra, a la luz del misterio de Cristo, escuchando la voz de Dios en el propio corazón: «Por su interioridad (el hombre) es, en efecto, superior al universo entero; a esta profunda interioridad retorna cuando entra dentro de su corazón, donde Dios le aguarda, escrutador de los corazones, y donde él personalmente, bajo la mirada de Dios, decide su propio destino» (GS 14).

Todo ello reclama, por parte del creyente y, de modo especial, por parte del evangelizador, una fe más vivencial, que no se reduzca a la afirmación de unos conceptos (cuya validez no se pone en duda): «Urge recuperar y presentar una vez más el verdadero rostro de la fe cristiana, que no es simplemente un conjunto de proposiciones que se han de acoger y ratificar con la mente, sino un conocimiento de Cristo vivido personalmente, una memoria viva de sus mandamientos, una verdad que se ha de hacer vida... La fe es una decisión que afecta a toda la existencia; es encuentro, diálogo, comunión de amor y de vida del creyente con Jesucristo, Camino, Verdad y Vida (cfr. Jn 14,6). Implica un acto de confianza y abandono en Cristo, y nos ayuda a vivir como él vivió (cfr. Gal 2,20), o sea, en el mayor amor a Dios y a los hermanos» (VS 88)[12].

---

[12] Las exigencias de la moral cristiana sólo se aceptarán en la medida en que el creyente tenga esta adhesión personal a Cristo. De ahí que la moral cristiana sea básicamente actitud relacional comprometida: «Seguir a Cristo es el fundamento esencial

La «mirada contemplativa» del apóstol (cfr. EV 83) le ayudará a «ver» a Cristo donde, humanamente hablando, parece que no está (cfr. Jn 20,8). Esa mirada de fe vivencial sabrá respetar los valores culturales y religiosos (como «semillas del Verbo»), mientras, al mismo tiempo, sabrá purificarlos y llevarlos a «su madurez en Cristo» (cfr. RMi 28). Una señal de autenticidad será la capacidad de no absolutizar ninguna cultura (ni reflexión filosófico-teológica, por válida que sea). De este modo, la inculturación del evangelio, en unas determinadas coordenadas, se convertirá en una nueva plataforma para evangelizar a todas las culturas y a todos los pueblos.

La terminología existencial o experiencial tiene, pues, carta de ciudadanía en el campo misionológico, gracias también a los documentos magisteriales. Será difícil, es verdad, precisar los términos y evitar excesos de más o de menos. Pero la evangelización será siempre, si es auténtica, un «amor apasionado por Jesucristo» (VC 109), que lleva necesariamente al «anuncio apasionado de Jesucristo» (VC 75). Se pasa necesariamente de la contemplación a la misión: «Alimentando en la oración una profunda comunión de sentimientos con El (cfr. Fil 2,5-11), de modo que toda su vida esté impregnada de espíritu apostólico y toda su acción apostólica esté sostenida por la contemplación» (VC 9).

La «pasión» del «anuncio» no es fundamentalismo, sino «conocimiento amoroso», convicción profunda, motivación clara y entrega generosa, dentro de los planes salvíficos de Dios en la historia humana, que dejan entrever su paciencia milenaria... Esta «pasión» se puede concretar en esta afirmación clave referente al tercer milenio: «En el 2000 deberá resonar con fuerza renovada la proclamación de la verdad: «Ecce natus est nobis Salvator mundi» (TMA 38). En efecto, «del conocimiento amoroso de Cristo es de donde brota el deseo de anunciarlo, de evangelizar, y de llevar a otros al sí de la fe en Jesucristo. Y al mismo tiempo se hace sentir la necesidad de conocer siempre mejor esta fe» (CEC 429).

---

y original de la moral cristiana... No se trata aquí solamente de escuchar una enseñanza y de cumplir un mandamiento, sino de algo mucho más radical: adherirse a la persona misma de Jesús, compartir su vida y su destino, participar de su obediencia libre y amorosa a la voluntad del Padre» (VS 19).

La espiritualidad misionera se concreta en actitud relacional con Cristo, puesto que él es el punto de referencia para «comprender y vivir la misión» (RMi 88). En realidad, no es más que la puesta en práctica de las directrices paulinas sobre la sintonía con «los sentimientos de Cristo» (Fil 2,5): «El estudio y la actividad pastoral se apoyan en una fuente interior, que la formación deberá custodiar y valorizar: se trata de la comunión cada vez más profunda con la caridad pastoral de Jesús... un modo de estar en comunión con los mismos sentimientos y actitudes de Cristo, buen Pastor» (PDV 57).

Esta «relación» con Cristo se traduce en «una comunión de vida y de amor cada vez más rica, y una participación cada vez más amplia y radical de los sentimientos y actitudes de Jesucristo» (PDV 72). Toda la formación del apóstol consiste en «un itinerario de progresiva asimilación de los sentimientos de Cristo hacia el Padre» (VC 65).

La espiritualidad misionera es, pues, «fe vivida», de la que María es modelo perfecto (cfr. TMA 43). Por esto, «la misión, además de provenir del mandato formal del Señor, deriva de la exigencia profunda de la vida de Dios en nosotros» (RMi 11). Sin esta perspectiva «espiritual» (que es fidelidad al Espíritu Santo), las teorías sobre la misión surgen sin control, según las preferencias intelectuales de quien las elabora. Una actitud de fe sabrá encontrar teorías válidas y estimulantes, basadas en que la misión «dimana del amor fontal o caridad del Padre» (AG 2) y tiene un objetivo final: «Así, por fin, se cumple verdaderamente el designio del Creador, al hacer al hombre a su imagen y semejanza, cuando todos los que participan de la naturaleza humana, regenerados en Cristo por el Espíritu Santo, contemplando unánimes la gloria de Dios, puedan decir: «Padre nuestro» (AG 7).

Si la misión tiende al encuentro con Cristo, ello reclama, por parte del evangelizador, la propia experiencia de encuentro con el Señor (cfr. RMi 88, citado más arriba). Entonces, «al encontrar a Cristo, todo hombre descubre el misterio de su propia vida» (Bula «Incarnationis Mysterium», n. 1)[13].

---

[13] La exhortación postsinodal «Ecclesia in America» (EAm) ofrece este significado vivencial de la misión: «No se trata sólo de enseñar lo que hemos conocido, sino también, como la mujer samaritana, de hacer que los demás encuentren personalmente

La reflexión filosófica y teológica, así como los esquemas metodológicos de pastoral, son necesarios; pero deben dejar traslucir el «más allá» que es el misterio de Cristo y que «supera toda ciencia» (Ef 3,19). Toda búsqueda humana, si es auténtica, tiende a llegar, guiada por la gracia, al encuentro y «a la revelación de Jesucristo» (FR 38). «La Verdad, que es Cristo, se impone como autoridad universal que dirige, estimula y hace crecer (cfr. Ef 4,15) tanto la teología como la filosofía» (FR 92)[14].

4. Inicio del tercer milenio: Hacia una nueva etapa de la evangelización por medio de la espiritualidad misionera

A primera vista, puede parecer pretensión exagerada el querer acaparar la atención sobre la espiritualidad misionera; pero, como hemos indicado en el apartado n. 1, se trata de la vivencia de la misión, sin olvidar sus contenidos y desafíos teológicos y pastorales. La espiritualidad no es espiritualismo, sino vivencia (bajo la acción del Espíritu) del ser y del obrar.

---

a Jesús: «Venid a ver» (Jn 4, 29)... La Iglesia, que vive de la presencia permanente y misteriosa de su Señor resucitado, tiene como centro de su misión «llevar a todos los hombres al encuentro con Jesucristo»... En efecto, encontrar a Cristo vivo es aceptar su amor primero, optar por Él, adherir libremente a su persona y proyecto, que es el anuncio y la realización del Reino de Dios» (EAm 68).

[14] El enfoque de toda la encíclica «Fides et Ratio» (FR) es predominantemente de *encuentro con Cristo*. Sin este enfoque relacional, los comentarios resultan unilaterales y pueden producir una reacción contraria al objetivo de la encíclica. Toda cultura y toda religión queda abierta, salvo obstáculos, a la revelación de Dios por medio de su Hijo. Los comentarios que el mismo Santo Padre está realizando en sus discursos (desde finales de 1998 e inicio de 1999) subrayan la línea básica: todas las culturas y religiones están buscando el rostro de Dios Padre, que finalmente se ha revelado como Dios Amor por medio de Jesucristo. La defensa de la razón, por parte de la encíclica, no privilegia ningún sistema fisolófico concreto (ni de oriente ni de occidente)l sino que los valora todos en esa prespectiva de apertura a la trascendencia de Dios Amor, revelado por Jesucristo. La razón ya «puede alcanzar el bien sumo y la verdad suprema en la persona del Verbo encarnado» (FR 41). Son interesantes también los contenidos de esta encíclica sobre la «inculturación», que hemos resumido más arriba, en este mismo apartado n. 3. Es importante observar, en los documentos de Juan Pablo II, a partir de la primera encíclica («Redemptor hominis», 1979), esa línea de fuerte llamada al encuentro con Cristo. Lo hemos visto también en el apartado n. 2 (con referencia a la enciclica «Fides et ratio»).

La llamada a la misión, en estos momentos de inicio de un tercer milenio, tiene esta perspectiva de llamada a la santidad, que es elemento esencial de la espiritualidad misionera: «Nunca como hoy la Iglesia ha tenido la oportunidad de hacer llegar el Evangelio, con el testimonio y la palabra, a todos los hombres y a todos los pueblos. Veo amanecer una nueva época misionera, que llegará a ser un dia radiante y rica en frutos, sin todos los cristianos y, en particular, los misioneros y las jóvenes Iglesias responden con generosidad y santidad a las solicitudes y deseos de nuestro tiempo» (RMi 92).

En realidad, ésa fue también la llamada del concilio en el decreto «Ad Gentes»: «Puesto que toda la Iglesia es misionera y la obra de la evangelización es deber fundamental del Pueblo de Dios, el Santo Concilio invita a todos a una profunda renovación interior a fin de que, teniendo viva conciencia de la propia responsabilidad en la difusión del Evangelio, acepten su cometido en la obra misional entre los gentiles» (AG 35).

El inicio de un tercer milenio se encuadra en la perspectiva de la revelación sobre el Verbo encarnado. Es el gran evento: «Al llegar la plenitud de los tiempos, envió Dios a su Hijo, nacido de mujer» (Gal 4,4). Es, pues, normal que se urja a anunciar esta revelación divina a todas las gentes, sin ambigüedades: «En el 2000 deberá resonar con fuerza renovada la proclamación de la verdad: Ecce natus est nobis Salvator mundi» (TMA 38).

Nos encontramos ante el significado salvífico del tiempo (que no necesita que sea exacto cronológicamente en cuanto a las fechas concretas que se quieren celebrar). Efectivamente, «en Jesucristo, el tiempo llega a ser una dimensión de Dios» (TMA 10). Es decir, si desde la Encarnación, «el Hijo de Dios... se ha unido, en cierto modo, con todo hombre» (GS 22), ello significa que la historia de cada pueblo (cultura y religión) tiene las huellas o «semillas» del Verbo, que esperan un encuentro de madurez o plenitud (cfr. Jn 1,14; RMi 28)[15].

---

[15] El «Instrumentum Laboris» para el Sínodo de Asia, en el n. 33, resume los valores positivos de las religiones como signos de la acción del Espíritu Santo: centralidad de la voluntad de Dios (Islam), práctica de la meditación, orientación de la propia voluntad y espíritu de no violencia (Hinduismo), desprendimiento y compasión

Con esta perspectiva de experiencia de encuentro con Cristo, el apóstol capta, por sintonía de fe, que «el Verbo Encarnado es, pues, el cumplimiento del anhelo presente en todas las religiones de la humanidad: este cumplimiento es obra de Dios y va más allá de toda expectativa humana» (TMA 6). Solamente una actitud contemplativa, a modo de «un conocimiento de Cristo vivido personalmente» (VS 88), será capaz de aceptar gozosamente y de descubrir las enormes potencialidades misioneras de estas afirmaciones: «En El (Cristo) el Padre ha dicho la palabra definitiva sobre el hombre y sobre la historia» (TMA 5).

El paso a un tercer milenio pone más en evidencia que «la encarnación del Hijo de Dios y la salvación que Él ha realizado con su muerte y resurrección son, pues, el verdadero criterio para juzgar la realidad temporal y todo proyecto encaminado a hacer la vida del hombre cada vez más humana» (Bula «Incarnationis Mysterium» 1).

Para que «al encontrar a Cristo, todo hombre descubra el misterio de su propia vida» (Bula IM 1), se necesita que el apóstol sea testigo experiencial de este mismo encuentro, según los contenidos que hemos explicado sobre la espiritualidad misionera (cfr. nn. 1-3 del presente estudio). El objetivo de la evangelización, en linea paulina, es el de «formar a Cristo» en los demás (Gal 4,19). Es el objetivo que «deriva de la exigencia profunda de la vida de Dios en nosotros» (RMi 11), también al estilo de San Pablo: «Cristo quien vive en mi... vivo en la fe del Hijo de Dios que me amó y se entregó a sí mismo por mi» (Gal 2,20).

El testimonio de las «bienaventuranzas», que ya hemos resumido más arriba (apartado n. 2), se concreta en la disponibilidad «martirial». El martirio, tan frecuente en nuestros dias, es una nota constante de la misión. «Un signo perenne, pero

---

(Budismo), piedad filial y humanismo (Confucionismo), sencillez y humildad (Taoismo), reverencia y respeto por la naturaleza (Religiones Tradicionales). Mientras hay que preservar la singularidad de cada religión, habrá que anunciar con audacia que «la singularidad del cristianismo se encuentra en su creencia en un Dios personal y en un Salvador personal, histórico, Jesucristo» (W. JOHNSTON, *Teología mística, la ciencia del amor,* Barcelona, Herder, 1997, p. 185).

hoy particularmente significativo, de la verdad del amor cristiano es la memoria de los mártires. Que no se olvide su testimonio. Ellos son los que han anunciado el Evangelio dando su vida por amor. El mártir, sobre todo en nuestros días, es signo de ese amor más grande que compendia cualquier otro valor... El creyente que haya tomado seriamente en consideración la vocación cristiana, en la cual el martirio es una posibilidad anunciada ya por la Revelación, no puede excluir esta perspectiva en su propio horizonte existencial. Los dos mil años transcurridos desde el nacimiento de Cristo se caracterizan por el constante testimonio de los mártires» (Bula IM 13)[16].

La espiritualidad misionera del apóstol es una experiencia de la propia pobreza, en la que se han encontrado las huellas de Cristo (por el don de la fe). De esta experiencia humilde y agradecida nace la misión sin fundamentalismos ni reduccionismos. El encuentro con Cristo no es una conquista de la razón, sino una gracia que reclama la propia colaboración. «¡La fe se fortalece dándola!» (RMi 2)

Con esta actitud experiencial, se aprende a discernir y apreciar todas las «semillas del Verbo», escondidas bajo los signos pobres de cualquier cultura y situación humana, apreciando cualquier valor cultural (que es siempre de interés universal), sin hacerlo exclusivo y sin absolutizarlo por encima de la revelación. Cualquier valor humano es un don de Dios que lleva al encuentro con Cristo. Con esta audacia, Juan Pablo II formula un deseo para el tercer milenio: «De-

---

[16] Es frecuente a alusión al martirio en los documentos magisteriales del concilio y del postconcilio: LG 42; AG 24; DeV 60; EN 76; RMi 42: CEC 2473-2474; VS 89, 92-93; UUS 84; TMA 37; FR 32; Bolla IM 13. El texto de FR 32 presenta la fuerza del martirio por el «encuentro con Cristo». Ver algunos estudios sobre martirio y misión: AA.VV., *La Iglesia martirial interpela nuestra animación misionera* (Burgos, 1989); U. Von BALTHASAR, *Sólo el amor es digno de fe* (Salamanca, Sigueme, 1988); J. ESQUERDA BIFET, *La fuerza de la debilidad* (Madrid, BAC, 1993) cap. VI; R. FISICHELA, *Il martirio come testimonianza: contributi per una riflessione sulla definizione di martire*, en: *Portare Cristo al mondo* (Roma, Pont. Univ. Urbaniana, 1985) II, 747-767; P. MOLINARI, S. SPINSANTI, *Mártir*, en: *Nuevo Diccionario de Espiritualidad* (Madrid, Paulinas, 1991) 1175-1189; T. NIETO, *Raíces bíblicas de la misión y del martirio*: Misiones Extranjeras n. 127 (1992) 5-15.

seo expresar firmemente la convicción de que el hombre es capaz de llegar a una visión unitaria y orgánica del saber. Este es uno de los cometidos que el pensamiento cristiano deberá afrontar a lo largo del próximo milenio de la era cristiana» (FR 85)[17].

Conclusión:
La renovación de la Iglesia
por la espiritualidad misionera

Es un hecho fácilmente constatable el de la llamada a una renovación eclesial por la línea de la espiritualidad y santificación. El decreto «Ad Gentes» ha dejado constancia de esta llamada urgente en vistas a la misión: «El Santo Concilio invita a todos a una profunda renovación interior» (AG 35)[18].

La espiritualidad misionera (sin ser exclusiva ni excluyente) será la nota dominante de la nueva evangelización en el inicio del tercer milenio. Efectivamente, «la santidad de vida permite a cada cristiano ser fecundo en la misión de la Iglesia» (RMi 77). Por esto, «la llamada a la misión deriva, de por sí, de la llamada a la santidad. Cada misionero lo es auténticamente si se esfuerza en el camino de la santidad. La santidad es un presupuesto fundamental y una condición insustituible para reali-

---

[17] El hecho de que la revelación cristiana se haya inculturado ya relativamente en los ambientes greco-latinos, no debe producir el resentimiento de otras culturas donde el cristianismo sólo ha iniciado un proceso de inculturación. Al mismo tiempo, hay que mirar al futuro con la disponibilidad de aceptar gozosamente la aportación de otras culturas, para la mejor comprensión del mensaje cristiano (cfr. FR 71-72).

[18] Ver otras llamadas parecidas en los mismos textos conciliares: SC 1, 43; Po 12; oT 1; pc 2-4; UR 6-7. Me remito a los estudios citados en la nota 1 del presente trabajo, sobre la nueva evangelización; he resumido los contenidos y bibliografía más actualizada en: *Il rinnovamento ecclesiale per una pastorale missionaria*, en: *Chiesa locale e inculturazione nella missione* (Roma, Pont. Univ. Urbaniana, 1987) 47-75; *Renovación evangélica de la Iglesia, camino de comunión y misión*, en: AA.VV., *Ecclesia tertii millenni advenientis* (Casale Montferrato, Piemme, 1997), 391-410.

zar la misión salvífica de la Iglesia. La vocación universal a la santidad está estrechamente unida a la vocación universal a la misión... La espiritualidad misionera de la Iglesia es un camino hacia la santidad. El renovado impulso hacia la misión ad gentes exige misioneros santos... Es necesario suscitar un nuevo anhelo de santidad entre los misioneros y en toda la comunidad cristiana» (RMi 90).

Estas afirmaciones pueden sonar a tópico, por el hecho de repetirse con frecuencia; pero, en el presente estudio, hemos centrado la atención sobre la experiencia de Dios Amor (revelado en Cristo) por parte del apóstol, en vistas a poder presentar el mensaje cristiano a quienes ya tienen una verdadera experiencia del mismo Dios, pero todavía no hay llegado al encuentro explícito con Cristo. No estaría bien confundir la «espiritualidad misionera» con cualquier tipo de enfoque o de estilo de la misión. La «espiritualidad» es una «vida según el Espíritu», que pide a la Iglesia una fidelidad mayor para hacerse transparencia del mensaje evangélico. Se trata de un compromiso de «santificación y renovación para que la señal de Cristo resplandezca con mayores claridades sobre el rostro de la Iglesia» (LG 15).

Si la espiritualidad misionera es una fidelidad al Espíritu Santo en el campo de la misión, los campos actuales del diálogo interreligioso, de la inculturación y de la nueva evangelización, constituyen un nuevo modo de «escuchar la voz del Espíritu» (Apoc 2,7). «Hoy la Iglesia debe afrontar otros desafíos, proyectándose hacia nuevas fronteras, tanto en la primera misión ad gentes, como en la nueva evangelización de pueblos que han recibido ya el anuncio de Cristo. Hoy se pide a todos los cristianos, a las Iglesia particulares y a la Iglesia universal la misma valentía que movió a los misioneros del pasado y la misma disponibilidad para escuchar la voz del Espíritu» (RMi 30).

Acertar en el camino de la nueva evangelización con ocasión de iniciar un tercer milenio, supone, también por parte del apóstol, un actitud de propia «conversión». Esta actitud cristiana de conversión equivale a la apertura generosa hacia los nuevos planes salvíficos de Dios en Cristo. «Es necesaria una radical conversión de la mentalidad para hacerse misioneros, y esto vale tanto para las personas, como para las comunidades... Sólo haciéndose misionera la comunidad cristiana podrá superar las divisiones y tensiones internas y recobrar su unidad y su vigor de fe» (RMi 49)[19].

El encuentro del cristianismo con los creyentes de otras religiones comporta, por parte del cristiano, una actitud de permanente conversión: «Cada convertido es un don hecho a la Iglesia y comporta una grave responsabilidad para ella... porque, especialmente si es adulto, lleva consigo como una energía nueva, el entusiasmo de la fe, el deseo de encontrar en la Iglesia el Evangelio vivido. Sería una desilusión para él, si después de ingresar en la comunidad eclesial encontrase en la misma una vida que carece de fervor y sin signos de renovación. No podemos predicar la conversión, si no nos convertimos nosotros mismos cada día» (RMi 47).

La *espiritualidad misionera para una nueva evangelización en el inicio del tercer milenio* del cristianismo, es un campo de educación y formación de la comunidad eclesial para colaborar a que las «semillas del Verbo» realicen el encuentro con las huellas explícitas del Verbo. Se podrían señalar tres líneas de actuación: 1a) tomar conciencia de este momento de nuevas gracias para el campo de la evangelización («kairós»); 2a) responder con el testimonio de una vida más contemplativa y evangélica (bienaventuranzas y consejos evangélicos); 3a) disponerse para una preparación cultural y teológica que responda a los desafíos y a las necesidades del diálogo interreligioso y de la inculturación.

La Iglesia se inspira en la figura de María, «trono de la sabiduría», quien, «engendrando la Verdad y conservándola en su corazón, la ha compartido con toda la humanidad para siempre» (FR 108). Así se presenta como Iglesia misterio (signo de Cristo), que es fraternidad y comunión misionera[20].

---

[19] En el campo ecuménico el tema es de permanente actualidad: «El auténtico ecumenismo no se da sin la conversión interior» (UR 7). M. ZOVKIC, *Conversio et renovatio Ecclesiae tamquam conditio et sequela evangelizationis*: Bogoslacka Smotra 45 (1975) 221-234.

[20] La figura de María es programática para la Iglesia en el inicio del tercer milenio, según las pautas de «Tertio Millenio Adveniente»: «modelo de fe vivida» (TMA 43), «dócil a la voz del Espíritu» (TMA 48), «modelo perfecto de amor» (TMA 54). La exhortación «Ecclesia in America» recuerda: «María Santísima de Guadalupe es invocada como Patrona de toda América y Estrella de la primera y de la nueva evangelización» (EAm 11).

Interreligious Dialogue in the Third Millennium

Francis Card. Arinze

Interreligious dialogue, understood in the full sense of the whole range of relations between believers in various religions, is a dimension of life which is assuming greater and greater proportions in the world of our time. We are at the threshold of the Third Millennium. Here are four reasons that argue for the urgency of interreligious dialogue and four arguments that seem to me to make this apostolate eminently purposeful at this point in history. I shared these reflections with a Conference on Religion and the Media in June 1998 and I think they may interest a wider public.

1. Religious Plurality

There is not only one religion in the world. There are in fact quite a number. Catholics number about 18% of the total world population. Orthodox Christians, other Oriental Rite Christians, Anglicans, Protestants and all other Christians make 15%. Therefore all Christians together form about one third of humanity.

Muslims number 17%, Hindus 13% and Buddhists 7%. But there are many other religions besides. There are Jews, followers of Traditional Religions, Sikhs, Baha'i, Jainists, Zoroastrians and Shintoists and others[1].

These religions are the ways of life of a greater part of humanity. They are the living expressions of the souls of vast

---

[1] Cf. D. Barrett: *World Christian Encyclopedia*, Nairobi, 1982, pp. 782-785.

groups of people. They carry with them the echo of thousands of years of searching for God. They possess an impressive patrimony of deeply religious texts and contribute in transmitting the proven wisdom of diverse cultures and peoples. They have taught generations of people how to live, how to pray and how to face the fundamental questions that torment human earthly existence[2].

These religions are to be taken seriously. Believers in one religion should not ignore the fact that there are believers in other religions who are living with them in the same town, state or country, or who are their partners or interlocutors in international business, political, cultural, educational, religious or other contacts. To accept and respect other people who have a different religion must include an effort to understand their religion and openness to collaboration with them. In short, interreligious dialogue is postulated by the fact of religious plurality in our world.

2. A World thirsting for Unity and Collaboration

We live in a world which is thirsting for contacts, encounters, understanding, harmony, unity and collaboration. Peoples, nations and states want to meet, to listen to one another, to share and to see what they can do together, especially to heal possible wounds and build a more stable and enduring peace. In our days there are more cultural exchanges than perhaps at any other period in human history.

Isolationism is being frowned upon more and more. What people have in common is being recognized increasingly as more important than what divides them.

There are some factors which tend to make the world look more and more like a global village. The increasing facility of modern communications has made an important contribution. The jet, the television, the fax, the internet and electronic mail are significant elements. International travel, for

---

[2] Cf. Paul VI: *Evangelii Nuntiandi*, 53.

business or tourism, for pilgrimages or for educational purposes, for political or for economic reasons, has reached an all-time high. The sciences of anthropology, ethnology and religions have made tremendous progress. There is a growing awareness among peoples that we need each other and that we should build up a more harmonious community worldwide.

The religions cannot afford to be absent from this world on the move. The followers of the various religions are called to meet one another, to try to understand one another better, and to ask themselves what they can do together as believers to make this world a better place to live in.

3. Tackling together some major challenges and problems

There are some major problems and challenges in the world which require for their solution the cooperation of all believers. Foremost among them are questions related to justice and peace. There are people who are discriminated against because of their race, religion, language, social status or sex. There are actual situations of conflict and war which can trace their causes to diverse historical or other reasons. To precipitate injustice or war, a few people are enough. To promote justice and peace the collaboration of all is required. Problems of justice and peace do not respect religious frontiers.

Moreover, there are situations of refusal to practise solidarity between rich and poor on the national or international levels, and refusal of the rich to accept that ownership of property, even if justly acquired, entails social responsibilities because of the universal destination of earthly goods.

There are acts of discrimination and injustice against women and children which sometimes descend to the level of condemning them to prostitution for the benefit of their masters. There are street children who live at the margins of society because of harsh economic and social structures or the failure of their families.

Nor should we forget the modern scourges of AIDS and drug abuse which cause great physical and moral suffering and in some cases reduce people to a type of slavery.

Believers in the various religions cannot remain unconcerned in front of such major challenges and problems. They are convinced that the highest ideals of their religions oblige them to join hands to find lasting solutions. Moreover, none of these situations can be changed without a certain conversion of hearts. And religion offers the most powerful and the deepest motives to initiate such a change of heart, a conversion. Interreligious cooperation in such matters goes beyond being merely desirable and becomes a necessity.

4. The Spectre of Violence

A harsh reality in the present-day world which interreligious cooperation is urgently called upon to counteract and help to remove is the spectre of violence. This takes many forms.

There is tension which sometimes escalates into open violence, because of ethnic or racial causes, or due to unhealed historical memories.

There is violence which is generated by economic frustration, unemployment, poverty and marginalization of some groups of people in the community.

Sometimes violence breaks out because of political factors which some interested people exploit for their own purposes.

A more pernicious type of violence is that which can be traced to religious sensitivities, rightly or wrongly interpreted. Genuine religion in itself is not the cause of violence, because every religion worthy of the name teaches the Golden Rule: "Do unto others as you would that they do unto you". But when religion is brought in to motivate people to engage in violent acts, the results can be disastrous indeed, because for religious reasons some people will not hesitate to lay down their lives.

Violence in the world has taken such forms as intertribal conflicts, civil wars, terrorist attacks, acts of religious fanaticism, and so-called ethnic cleansing. These can lead to wholesale massacres and even to genocide. Nor should one forget the violence against women and children and even against the unborn by way of abortion.

The followers of the various religions are called upon to join hands to promote acceptance and confession of guilt, repentance, forgiveness, reconciliation, love and unity. True religion teaches that forgiveness is no sign of weakness. God is the God of life and not of death. He is the God of peace and not of war; the God of reconciliation, and love and not of tension and hatred. It is a contradiction of true religion to promote violence, war or killing in the name of God.

Violence in the name of religion needs particular disapproval and condemnation. Religious leaders have the serious duty not only to conscientize their co-religionists against the use of violence as a means of propagating or defending one's religion, but also to make joint declarations when such abuses have taken place.

It is good to note that voices are being raised in condemnation. When a bomb was exploded at the World Trade Centre in New York, the President of the Catholic Bishops' Conference of the U.S. and the President of the American Muslim Council made a joint statement deploring this act. At the last meeting of the liaison committee of the Pontifical Council for Interreligious Dialogue with representatives of International Islamic Organizations, condemnation was expressed of violence in Algeria, and in particular of the kidnapping and assassination of the seven monks. Such joint declarations need to be multiplied, so that people see that their religious leaders stand together at such crucial times.

Hoping, therefore, that we have convinced ourselves that interreligious dialogue is really urgent in our times, we may now consider four aims or purposes that make this engagement eminently desirable.

5. Mutual Enrichment

Interreligious dialogue can help each participant to grow in his or her own faith when one encounters another of a different religious persuasion and confronts one's faith with that of the other. Truth is often better reached, further studied, deepened, appreciated, understood and lived when met by other views. Also such encounter can purify and deepen one's own faith.

Apart from a positive value for individuals in dialogue, there is also mutual enrichment between religions in dialogue. In interreligious dialogue, Christianity can contribute to other religions elevation, inspiration and universality. Christianity has helped some religions to shed some of their unworthy beliefs or practices. It has helped Buddhists show more interest in social work and in initiatives towards human promotion. Buddhists and Muslims can see in Christianity a religion which gives women a higher status than theirs. Christianity also brings a sense of universality. In some majority Buddhist or Islamic countries there is the danger of identifying the country's culture with Buddhism or Islam. Christians, and especially Catholics, bring to dialogue a universalism which is second to none: in doctrine, race, culture, administrative machinery, language and worship. Indeed, Christianity is really saying: God is our Father, and we are all brothers and sisters. Let us hold hands together. Let us work together, build our nation together, move forward together.

When they meet in dialogue, Christianity also receives contributions from other religions. These religions bring with them the cultural settings in which they exist. They bring with them languages, philosophical categories, ritual expressions and local styles proper to their peoples. They enrich Christianity with these gifts. The Church is happy to receive these gifts of the various peoples and cultures, and she moves on to purify, consolidate and elevate them. The Second Vatican Council said that the Church fosters and takes to herself "in so far as they are good, the ability, resources, and customs of each people. Taking them to herself, she purifies, strengthens, and ennobles them. The Church in this is mindful that she must harvest with the King to whom the nations were given for an inheritance and into whose city they bring gifts and presents"[3]. The Church is not tied down to any culture and is not identified with any. She is at home in all cultures and with all cultures.

---

[3] Vatican II : *Lumen Gentium*, n. 13.

6. Openness to the action of the Holy Spirit

Interreligious dialogue helps the believer to be more and more open to the action of the Holy Spirit. The Church believes that the Holy Spirit works also outside the boundaries of the Church[4]. The Second Vatican Council exhorts Catholics prudently and lovingly, through dialogue and collaboration with the followers of other religions, and in witness of Christian faith and life, to acknowledge, preserve and promote the spiritual and moral goods found among these other believers, as well as the values in their society and culture. Then they will learn "what treasures a bountiful God has distributed among the nations of the earth"[5].

By interreligious dialogue the Church puts herself as an instrument into the hands of divine providence and in God's working out of His own mystery of salvation. In such a dialogue the Church discovers the working of God in the other religions, elements of truth and grace, seeds of the Word, seeds of contemplation, elements which are true and good, precious things both religious and human, ways of truth which illuminates all mankind, and preparation for the Gospel, as the Second Vatican Council says in various documents[6].

Interreligious dialogue, therefore, enables Christians to appreciate better that such dialogue is demanded by the deep respect for all that is good, true, beautiful and holy, which the Holy Spirit, Who blows where He wills, has brought about in the souls of other people of good will. It manifests the dignity and requirements of genuine dialogue between believers and shows that such dialogue is no mere academic debate, but is a normal part of the evangelizing mission of the Church whenever Christians are in contact with other believers.

The other religions can also challenge Christians to examine more deeply their own identity and the authenticity of their witness to Jesus Christ, the one Lord and Saviour of all.

---

[4] Cf. *Redemptor Hominis*, 6.
[5] Vatican II: *Ad Gentes*, 11; cf. also *Nostra Aetate*, 2.
[6] Cf. *Ad Gentes*, nn. 9, 11, 15, 18; *Optatam Totius*, 16; *Gaudium et Spes*, 92; *Nostra Aetate*, 2; *Lumen Gentium*, 16.

7. Dialogue and Proclamation

Interreligious dialogue, properly understood and faithfully carried out, helps to show how complementary this element is to proclamation and how the Catholic Church is committed to both.

Proclamation of Jesus Christ as the one Lord and Saviour for all humanity is the high point, the apex of evangelization. Jesus sent His Church with a clear mandate: "Go, therefore, make disciples of all nations; baptize them in the name of the Father and of the Son and of the Holy Spirit, and teach them to observe all the commands I gave you" (Mt 28: 19-20). Saints Peter and John bravely announced to the Sanhedrin: "We cannot promise to stop proclaiming what we have seen and heard" (Acts 4: 20). And St Paul is aware of the consequences of neglecting proclamation: Woe to me if I preach not the Gospel" (I Cor 9: 16). The mystery of Christ, says St Paul, "must be broadcast to pagans everywhere, to bring them to the obedience of faith" (Rm 16: 26).

The Second Vatican Council while showing respect to other religions, states unequivocally in the same document that the Church "proclaims and must ever proclaim Christ "the way, the truth and the life" (Jn 14: 16), in Whom men find the fulness of religious life, and in Whom God has reconciled all things to Himself"[7]. Recognizing that other believers are also included in God's plan of salvation, but that they do not have all the abundant benefits which are available to full members of the Church, the Council says that "the Church painstakingly fosters her missionary work"[8].

Pope Paul VI regards proclamation as the apex of evangelization. "Evangelization", he says, "will always contain – as its foundation, centre and at the same time summit of its dynamism – a clear proclamation that in Jesus Christ, the Son of God made man, Who died and rose from the dead, salvation is offered to all men"[9]. "Proclamation is the permanent priority

---

[7] *Nostra Aetate*, 2.
[8] *Lumen Gentium*, 16.
[9] *Evangelii Nuntiandi*, 27.

of mission"[10], declares Pope John Paul II. "To proclaim the name of Jesus and to invite people to become His disciples in the Church is a sacred and major duty which the Church cannot neglect"[11].

Proclamation and dialogue, though not on the same level, are both elements of the Church's evangelizing mission. They complement each other. Dialogue promotes better knowledge and communication between the participants. If the preacher of the Gospel is good at dialogue he will have learned how better to present Christ and Christianity to people from other religions and cultures. The necessity of the Church being at home among all peoples and cultures is being stressed more and more in our days. Dialogue promotes this.

Interreligious dialogue encourages friendly relations between believers in differing religions. It helps to knock down, or at least to reduce, prejudices, exclusiveness and intolerance. All this is also in favour of proclamation.

Interreligious dialogue need not cause syncretism or religious relativism. Every participant in dialogue retains his religious identity. He should sincerely witness to his faith among the other believers.

Speaking to the Plenary Assembly of the Pontifical Council for Interreligious Dialogue on 28 April 1987, Pope John Paul II said: "Your Assembly must thus reaffirm the commitment of the Catholic Church both to dialogue and to the proclamation of the Gospel. There can be no question of choosing one and ignoring or rejecting the other. Even in situations where the proclamation of our faith is difficult, we must have the courage to speak of God who is the foundation of that faith, the reason for our hope, and the source of our love. It is also true that in those circumstances in which the proclamation of the Gospel bears much fruit we must not forget that dialogue with others is a Christian work desired by God. Moreover, the proclamation of the Gospel has to take due notice of the religious and cultural background of those to whom it is addressed"[12].

---

[10] *Redemptoris Missio*, 44.
[11] *Dialogue and Proclamation*, 76.
[12] In *Insegnamenti di Giovanni Paolo II*, X, I, 1987, p. 1450.

8. Paving the Way to Inculturation

The Catholic Church sets great value on the fact that the Gospel is meant for all peoples and cultures, can and should be at home among them all, but is not identified with any one of them. When the Congregation for the Evangelization of Peoples sent its first missionaries to Eastern Asia, it gave them the famous Instruction of 1659 to tell them to respect all customs that are good and that are not incompatible with the Gospel. It insisted that they bring with them to the peoples of Asia the Gospel of Jesus Christ and not the cultures of Italy, Spain or France[13].

Aware that neither all missionaries nor all theologians have paid due attention to this principle, and with the help of modern means of information and communication, the Church in our times lays greater stress on the necessity of inculturation than perhaps in any century hitherto.

The Church considers that for our redemption the Son of God took on human nature and was born in one particular culture. Following this pattern, Jesus Christ must be preached such a way that the Good News takes root in the life-situation of the hearers of the Word. Inculturation is this incarnation of the Gospel in cultures. The Special Assembly of the Synod of Bishops for Africa insisted very much on this dimension of evangelization[14].

Interreligious dialogue produces as one of its beautiful fruits the facilitation of inculturation. For how could one hope to bring the Gospel to the people of Thailand in such a way that the Good News of Jesus Christ takes deep root in Thai culture, unless one not only knows about Buddhism and Thai culture but also meets those who live it? Can the faith be at home among the people of Ghana, or Zaire or Nigeria unless one takes African religion seriously?

The Traditional Religions merit special mention in this context. They are to be found in varying forms among Afri-

---

[13] Cf. *Collectanea SCPF* no. 135, p. 42.
[14] Cf. *Ecclesia in Africa*, 60; *Message of African Synod*, 14-19.

cans, some Asian tribes, the Australian aborigines and the Amerindians. These religions are generally marked by belief in God or a Supreme Spirit, in non-human spirits good and bad, and in ancestors. These beliefs then flow into worship. The traditional religions are often friendly to Christianity and can be regarded as a providential preparation of peoples for the Gospel. The Pontifical Council for Interreligious Dialogue has sent a letter to all Bishops who have such religions in their areas to urge for committed pastoral attention to these religions and the cultures they influence, with a view to better and deeper inculturation of the Gospel Message. Considering especially that many adherents of these traditional religions are becoming Christians, interreligious dialogue and inculturation can be seen to work hand in hand.

Conclusion

As we get set to step into the Third Millennium, the followers of the various religions have no choice but to come closer to one another, to listen one another, to try to understand one another better, and to strive to collaborate more for a better world. They have no choice but to promote dialogue or interreligious relations.

The Catholic Church, under the leadership of Pope John Paul II, is organizing a four-day meeting of the religions of the world in October 1999 for reflection on these matters.

These are epochs of great moment in human history. And which believer would not like to be an active participant in promoting interreligious relations in this world on the move? May the Holy Spirit inspire, guide and vivify all such efforts.

Théologie des religions non-Chrétiennes et l'Islam

A. Dupré La Tour

La présentation de la théologie, ou plutôt des théologies, des religions non-chrétiennes qui m'a été demandée voudrait conduire à envisager une reflexion téologique sur l'Islam lui-même.

En abordant ce sujet, je voudrais avouer la difficulté à laquelle nous allons nous heurter. En liant ensemble les théologies des religions non-chrétiennes et une reflexion théologique sur l'Islam, il semble que nous allons situer cette réflexion dans le cadre général des religions et considérer l'Islam comme une religion parmi tant d'autres. Or en prenant ce chemin, ne risquons-nous pas de mépriser ou de sous-estimer ce qui fait la spécificité de la religion musulmane? Car il est important de garder una honnêteté sincère et une véritable humilité en abordant une reflexion chrétienne sur une religion que nous côtoyons chaque jour et dont bien souvent nous ne connaissons que des caricatures.

En effet, ce qui frappe de prime abord chez les théologiens qui ont envisagé une telle réflexion, c'est que rares sont ceux qui abordent l'Islam sans passion, dans un sens ou dans un autre: ou bien c'est une condamnation sans appel, ou bien, parmi certains théologiens occidentaux, c'est une volonté secrète de voir dans l'Islam ce que les chrétiens n'ont pas su reconnaître dans leur propre Révélation. Dans cette ambiguïté fondamentale, il est difficile de discerner la libération du coeur à laquelle Jésus nous a invités, et vers laquelle l'Esprit de Jésus nous conduit.

C'est donc vers une libération de tout préjugé que nous sommes appelés à marcher en abordant notre sujet. Nous avons d'abord à écouter les autres, l'autre, et non à raisonner à partir d'une attitude déjà établie. C'est que, en abordant ce sujet, nous abordons un peu le mystère même de Dieu. Le théologien est d'abord un croyant qui se meut à tâtons dans le mystère du plan de Dieu. Or ce plan nous dépasse infiniment. L'existence et la persistance des religions non-chrétiennes, et particuliérement de l'Islam, participe de ce mystère. C'est à cet esprit d'écoute humble de la Parole de Dieu, que je voudrais vous inviter dans cet essai de réflexion théologique.

Et si nous commençons à parcourir les différents courants théologiques contemporains sur les religions non-chrétiennes, ce sera surtout pour situer ensuite quelques balbutiemens sur une attitude théologique chrétienne spécifique face à l'Islam.

I. La réflexion théologique contemporaine sur les religions non-chrétiennes

Dès l'abord, il convient de distinguer clairement la réflexion théologique à l'égard des religions non-chrétiennes, ce qui est notre propos, et cette réflexion lorsqu'elle envisage les croyants de ces religions. Qu'un croyant non-chrétien puisse être sauvé en suivant avec sincérité la voix de sa conscience, cela est évident dans l'état actuel de l'enseignement chrétien. Qu'il nous suffise de rappeler l'enseignement de Vatican II: «Ceux qui, sans qu'il y ait de leur faute, ignorent l'Evangile du Christ et son Eglise, mais cherchent pourtant Dieu d'un coeur sincè re et s'efforcent, sous l'influence de sa grâce, d'agir de façon à accomplir sa volonté, telle que leur conscience la leur révèle et la leur dicte, coux-là peuvent arriver au salut éternel»[1].

En d'autres termes, celui qui cherche Dieu et écoute l'appel que Dieu lui fait entendre à travers la voix de sa conscience et y répond dans la sincérité de son coeur, avec le secours de la grâce sans laquelle il ne peut rien, celui-là est déjà en communion avec le Dieu Vivant. Or le Dieu vivant fait entendre son appel dans le secret, en utilisant tous les chemins concrets qui s'offrent à son action et par lesquels il peut rejoindre la voix de

---

[1] «Lumen Gentium» n° 16.

la conscience ou encore par lesquels l'homme le cherche, ou en utilisant le langage par lequel il peut se faire comprendre.

Ainsi les croyants des religions non-chrétiennes peuvent entendre cet appel et y répondre, à travers le chemin que leur offrent ces religions, dans la mesure où ces religions peuvent nourrir cette recherche.

C'est ici que se situe notre question: dans quelle mesure les religions non-chrétiennes peuvent-elles nourrir cette recherche et la favoriser? C'est à cette question que répondent les différents essais de «théologie des religions non-chrétiennes».

Que voulons-nous dire par «théologie des religions non-chrétiennes»? Pour nous, cette expression définit une vision chrétienne de ces religions, ou encore la manière dont ces religions se situent dans le dessein créateur et salvifique de Dieu. Les différents courants théologiques que nous allons d'abord envisager, s'efforcent donc de rendre compte positivement de la place de ces religions dans le plan de Dieu, autant que nous pouvons le faire. Cependant on peut discerner trois lignes générales d'interprétation.

Le premier courant prend comme point de référence *le christianisme* comme seule expression de la Révélation, de la Révélation que l'on appelle surnaturelle en la distinguant de la révélation naturelle qu'est la Création, à laquelle fait allusion la Lettre aux Romains[2]. La Création manifeste le Dieu créateur dont elle est le reflet, comme les oeuvres manifestent leur auteur. C'est cette connaissance naturelle de Dieu qui a inspiré les religions non-chrétiennes, leurs doctrines, leur culte et leur rite. Par contre, la Révélation surnaturelle ou historique manifeste une *histoire privilégiée* de Dieu avec son peuple qui culmine dans la Révélation de Dieu en Jésus-Christ, d'un Dieu qui fait alliance avec l'humanité pour la sauver. Cette connaissance particulière du Dieu Amour qui fait alliance avec l'humanité, inspire la religion chrétienne qui en est l'expression privilégiée et unique dans son dogme et sa doctrine, dans son culte et dans ses rites.

A vrai dire, entre religions non-chrétiennes et christianisme, il n'y a pas d'équivalence possible. «Les religions sont un

---

[2] Rom. 1,

geste de l'homme vers Dieu, la Révélation chrétienne est le témoignage d'un geste de Dieu vers l'homme (auquel celui-ci répond par la foi)... Les religions sont des créations du génie humain: elles attestent la valeur de hautes personnalités religieuses, Bouddha, Zoroastre, Orphée», écrit le P. Jean Daniélou par exemple, qui continue: «Elles ont les déficiences de ce qui est humain. La Révélation chrétienne est oeuvre de Dieu seul. L'homme n'a rien à s'y attribuer, elle ne lui appartient pas. Elle est pure grâce (pure initiative de Dieu). Elle est, par là même, infaillible, vraie en un sens qui ne vaut que de Dieu»[3]. Ainsi les religions non-chrétiennes ne peuvent, par elles-mêmes, apporter le salut puisqu'elles viennent de l'homme; seul le christianisme qui s'enracine dans la Révélation peut apporter le salut, puisqu'il s'attache à répondre à cette initiative divine de l'envoi par le Père du seul Sauveur, Jésus-Christ.

Cependant, parce qu'elles sont l'expression de l'attente humaine du salut et qu'elles peuvent rencontrer le Dieu créateur du monde, elles contiennent de réelles valeurs qui devront être respectées, assumées par le christianisme, purifiées et transfigurées. On peut voir en elles des précurseurs, des pédagogues qui préparent l'humanité à recevoir la Révélation de l'Evangile, un peu comme les Pères de l'Eglise ancienne considéraient la philosophie platonicienne, par exemple: la philosophie était considérée comme la voie préparant les païens à recevoir la Révélation, comme les prophètes de l'Ancien Testament y préparaient le peuple hébreu[4].

De plus, les religions non-chrétiennes offrent à la Révélation chrétienne et à la foi de l'Eglise tout un langage religieux humain qui sera assumé dans le christianisme et qui lui permettra de s'exprimer, même s'il doit le transposer au niveau du mystère de Dieu qui se révéle, et prendre ainsi une signification nouvelle plus haute.

Ainsi, selon ce courant d'interprétation, les religions non-chrétiennes n'ont qu'une valeur humaine et sont distinguées de la Révélation chrétienne et ne peuvent apporter par elles-mêmes aux hommes le salut.

---

[3] *Axes* octobre 1979 – mars 1980, p. 73.
[4] CLÉMENT D'ALEXANDRIE, *Stromates* VI, 5.

Le *second courant* que nous allons envisager maintenant, dépasse le dualisme précédent entre révélation naturelle et Révélation surnaturelle et historique et prend résolument une orientation universelle *christocentrique*. Dans chaque homme, Dieu a imprimé son image qui constitue fondamentalement la vocation humaine. En ce sens, chaque homme a été créé pour connaître Dieu et ainsi pour trouver en lui son accomplissement et son salut. Le P. de Lubac appelle cette orientation fondamentale de l'Homme «le désir naturel du surnaturel»[5], le P. Karl Rahner l'appelle «l'existential surnaturel»[6]. A cette orientation innée en l'homme, correspond dans l'histoire la figure du Christ qui appelle à lui tous les hommes et qui les récapitule tous en lui. Ainsi le Christ révèle l'homme à lui-même, tout en lui révélant le Dieu pour qui il a été fait et créé.

Les différentes religions du monde, mise à part la Révélation judéo-chrétienne, sont donc des expressions humaines de cette orientation originelle et déjà surnaturelle de la nature humaine et donc de ce rapport primordial de tout homme au Christ. Et c'est à partir du Christ qui en est le terme, qu'on peut découvrir dans ces religions comme des balbutiements, des approches inconscientes de la Vérité de Dieu dont le Christ est la plénitude. On peut se rappeler ce mot de St. Augustin dans ses Confessions: «Tu nous a faits pour Toi, Seigneur, et notre coeur est sans repos jusqu'à ce qu'il repose en Toi»[7]. Les religions non-chrétiennes ne doivent pas être considérées en elles-mêmes, mais en fonction du terme que toutes, incosciemment ou non, visent et qui ne peut être que le Christ. Et c'est donc à partir de la Vérité plénière du Christ que l'on peut déceler et discerner les traits de lumière que cache ou révèle toute religion et que l'on peut voir en elles une «préparation évangélique» selon le mot d'Eusèbe de Césarée repris par Vatican II[8].

---

[5] Cf H. DE LUBAC, *Le mystére du surnaturel*, coll. Théologie 64, Paris Aubier 1965.
[6] Cf KARL RAHNER, *Traité fondamental de la foi*, Paris le Centurion 1983, p. 150 ss. De même K. RAHNER, *Mission et Grâce*, Tome I p. 156, Paris Mame 1962.
[7] *Confessions* Livre XIII, IX, 10.
[8] «Lumen Gentium» n° 16.

Par elles-mêmes, ces religions ne peuvent apporter le salut, mais elles portent en elles d'une façon incomplète et souvent faussée, cette orientation vers le salut que le Christ seul vient apporter et révéler.

Faudrait-il dire alors, puisque le Christ est la Vérité totale de Dieu, que l'Eglise ne doit accueillir dans les religions non-chrétiennes que ce qui se trouve déjà en elle. Sans doute le Christ contient en lui toutes les Vérités partielles des autres religions. Mais l'Eglise, créature humaine, est nécessairement limitée par l'appartenance de ses membres à telle ou telle culture. C'est pourquoi l'Eglise, – et non le Christ, – aura à renoncer parfois à ses propres catégories pour accueillir l'autre tel qu'il est. Une certaine suffisance dogmatique, «une certaine disposition inconsciente de triomphalisme et de récupération»[9] sont des obstacles à la compréhension totale des autres. Mais acceptées dans leur différence culturelle, les religions peuvent être une source d'enrichissement pour les chrétiens.

Le Christ, – et non l'Eglise directement, – demeure donc le point de référence de ce courant. Il est le *point de convergence* de toutes ces approches humaines où s'inscrit cette orientation fondamentale du coeur humain. On retrouve, dans ce courant de pensée théologique, la doctrine d'un certain nombre de Pères de l'Eglise ancienne, en particulier Justin ou Clément d'Alexandrie.

Un troisième courant que nous voudrions présenter maintenant, – ou nous pardonnera ici de faire un choix, – a le mérite de ne pas être seulement le fruit d'un travail de théologiens de métier, mais de s'enraciner dans une *expérience concrète* et vécue dans un milieu pluri-religieux. Comme l'écrit Jacques-Albert Cuttat dans «La rencontre des religions» livre remarqué lors de sa parution en 1957: «De toutes les données de la conscience, la donnée religieuse est celle qui se prête le moins à être abordée «de l'extérieur». Ce qui est vrai de l'amour simplement humain, à savoir que sa vraie nature nous échappe à mesure que nous la considérons en spectateur, est in-

---

[9] YVES CONGAR, «Les religions non-bibliques sont-elles des mediations de salut» in Yearbook/Annales 1972-1973, Tantur/Jérusalem, p. 94.

comparablement plus vrai encore de l'essence de toute religion: que cette essence soit révélation divine, vision inspirée ou tradition primordiale, elle est toujours vécue comme une réalité d'origine non-humaine, donc supra-rationnelle, irréductible à un jugement discursif, comme radicalement inobjectivable et, partant, accessible seulement «de l'intérieur»[10].

Or dans cette expérience concrète de la coexistence de religions différentes, basée aussi sur une amitié profonde entre les croyants de ces religions, se construit une sorte de reconnaissance de l'autre en tant qu'autre, une acceptation de la différence. Au-delà de la différence des doctrines qui doit demeurer, naît un respect réciproque de l'option religieuse, qui permet de discerner dans l'autre un mystère caché et inconnu, une Parole de Dieu différente qui interpelle dans son «étrangeté».

A partir de cette expérience, naît pour le chrétien la conviction qu'il existe dans les religions non-chrétiennes une présence divine, encore non reconnue. Pour le chrétien, le Christ demeure le sommet de la Révélation de Dieu et en Lui tout a été dit.

Cependant certains théologiens iront même jusqu'à dire que l'Absolu de Dieu manifesté en Jesus-Christ, n'est pas épuisé par le phénomène chrétien ou même que Dieu, dont les voies sont mystérieuses et diverses, peut dépasser l'événement à la fois particulier et universel qu'est l'événement christique[11].

Sans aller jusque là et tout en maintenant la place centrale et irremplaçable du Christe dans la vision chrétienne de l'Univers, d'autres théologiens en appellent à *la présence universelle de l'Esprit-Saint dans le monde*. Cette présence de l'Esprit, au travail dans tout l'Univers, peut être discernée à travers «ses inépuisables modes de présence qui devraient nous tenir en éveil et nous faire suivre des voies toujours renouvelées pour le retrouver»[12]. L'Esprit-Saint, mystérieux et difficile à cerner, «est

---

[10] JACQUES-ALBERT CUTTAT, *La rencontre des religions*, Paris Aubier 1957, pp. 11-12.
[11] PAUL KNITTER, *La théologie catholique des religions à la croisée des chemins*, in «Concilium» n° 203, 1986, pp. 133-135.
[12] ANDRÉ SCRIMA, *Le Christ et les religions non-chrétiennes*. Inédit 1985.

finalement le Vivant, au coeur du Dieu Vivant, le grand Englobant de l'intérieur et de l'extérieur de la création toute entière» qui à la fois inspire et continue l'oeuvre du Christ et qui ramène tout au Christ. Sur la route qui mène à l'Avènement dernier du Christ où se manifestera sa Plénitude, l'Esprit a marqué et marque de son empreinte toute quête de Dieu, toute nomination du Divin (sans exclure le discernement au nom de ce même Esprit). Reconnaître sa présence sera toujours à poursuivre. Mgr Georges Khodre écrit dans la même ligne: «L'Esprit opère par ses énergies selon son économie propre et l'on peut, dans cette perspective, considérer les religions non-chrétiennes comme les lieux de l'inspiration de son oeuvre»[13].

II. Une vision Chrétienne de l'Islam?

Il nous reste à envisager maintenant u*ne vision chrétienne* de l'Islam, vision qui puisse être introduite dans la théologie chrétienne. Arrivés à ce stade, nous abordons la question qui nous intéresse tous dans ce Proche-Orient, et cependant nous éprouvons une certaine inquiétude à l'aborder, parce qu'elle nous concerne directement, et qu'elle fait partie de notre histoire. Pouvons-nous atteindre une attitude objective à son égard, alors que notre sensibilité profonde y est tellement engagée, surtout après 13 ans de guerre. Toute approche religieuse de ce genre doit assumer les ambiguïtés multiples des situations historiques[14]. Et pourtant, parce que les chrétiens d'Orient ont une histoire commune, une langue commune et pour beaucoup une culture commune avec l'Islam, peut-être sont-ils plus à même de le comprendre et de l'accueillir dans leur vision chrétienne En abordant donc notre question, nous avons d'abord à purifier notre regard.

---

[13] Mgr. Georges Khodre, *Le christianisme dans un monde pluraliste. L'Economie du Saint Esprit*, in «Irénikon» 44 (1971), pp. 191-202.
[14] Mgr Henri Teissier, *L'épreuve du dialogue islamo-chrétien* in «Etudes, août-septembre 1982, pp. 244-246.

Beaucoup de théologiens récents, parmi les théologiens de métier, qui appartiennent au monde occidental se sont essayés à une réflexion de ce genre.

Les uns se sont arrêtés aux négations du dogme chrétien contenues dans la tradition musulmane: refus de reconnaître dans le message du Christ le dernier mot, le mot suprême, de Dieu aux hommes, refus de reconnaître dans Jésus le Fils de Dieu, Dieu même, refus du mystère de sa Croix, méconnaissance du monothéisme chrétien et de la Trinité. Dans ce contexte, l'Isam serait à rejeter d'une vision chrétienne.

D'autres, au contraire, ont voulu souligner les ressemblances entre l'Islam et le Christianisme; l'Islam reconnaît son origine en Abraham, le père des croyants, il reconnaît en Jésus un prophète qui a apporté un message divin et qui reviendra à la fin des temps juger tous les hommes, il vénère la mère de Jésus et reconnaît sa conception virginale, il a recueilli l'héritage d'un christianisme judéo-chrétien à travers sans doute la secte des ébionites, et à travers les apocryphes. Et surtout, par son monothéisme strict, – «Il n'y a de dieu que Dieu», – l'Islam a su maintenir la transcendance absolue de Dieu. Dans cette ligne d'intrerprétation, certains n'hésitent pas à voir dans la religion musulmane une voie de salut.

A vrai dire, cette interprétation théologique de l'Islam peut se réclamer, du moins dans son orientation fondamentale, de Vatican II: «*Le dessein de salut*, – le mystère de salut caché depuis des siècles, – enveloppe également ceux qui reconnaissent le Créateur, en tout premier lieu les musulmans qui professent avoir la foi d'Abraham, adorent *avec nous* le Dieu unique, miséricordieux, futur juge des hommes au dernier jour»[15]. Et dans la Déclaration sur les relations de l'Eglise avec les religions non-chrétiennes: «*L'Eglise regarde avec estime* les Musulmans qui adorent le Dieu un, vivant et subsistant, miséricordieux et tout-puissant, créateur du ciel et de la terre, qui a parlé aux hommes. Ils cherchent à se soumettre de toute leur âme aux décrets de Dieu, même s'ils sont cachés, comme s'est soumis à Dieu Abraham, auquel la foi musulmane se réfère vo-

---

[15] «Lumen Gentium» n° 16.

lontiers. Bien qu'ils ne reconnaissent pas Jésus comme Dieu, ils le vénèrent comme prophète; ils honorent sa Mère virginale, Marie, et parfois même l'invoquent avec piété. De plus ils attendent le jour du jugement, où Dieu rétribuera tous les hommes ressuscités. Aussi ont-ils en estime la vie morale et rendent-ils un culte à Dieu, surtout par la prière, l'aumône ou le jeûne»[16].

Ainsi le dessein de salut enveloppe les musulmans à cause même de leur foi dont on souligne les points communs avec la foi chrétienne.

A vrai dire, la méthode d'analyse et de discernement employée dans ces textes s'adapte-t-elle à la vision que nous avons inconsciemment en nous? Cette méthode consiste à glaner dans la doctrine de l'Islam les affirmations dans lesquelles le christianisme se reconnaît, et à y voir ainsi les «semences du Verbe»[17] ou les traces de la Révélation chrétienne. Ainsi le regard ne quitte pas comme point de référence le christianisme. Cependant cette méthode s'apparente à l'apologétique chrétienne des premiers siècles, telle celle de Justin de Rome. Nous ne contesterons donc pas sa valeur. Mais à travers ces traces, ces traits communs, atteignons-nous réellement le coeur même de la foi de l'Islam ? Est-ce à ce niveau que nous pouvons y découvrir les traces vivantes et créatrices de l'Esprit de Dieu, dans lequel nous avons reconnu, à la suite du troisième courant étudié, le dynamisme même de l'économie divine du salut.

Arrivé à ce point de notre réflexion, nous devons bien avouer que nous en sommes encore à des balbutiements et qu'il est encore trop tôt pour avancer sur un terrain encore inconnu. Malgré tout, nous pouvons nous inspirer du discours que Jean-Paul II adressait à la jeunesse musulmane du Maroc dans le grand stade de Casablanca le 19 août 1985; «Les voies de Dieu ne sont pas toujours nos voies. Elles transcendent nos actions, toujours incomplètes, et les intentions de notre coeur, toujours imparfaites. Dieu ne peut jamais être utilisé à nos fins, car il est au-delà de tout»[18]. Ce qu'il y a de sûr pour nous, c'est

---

[16] «Nostra Aetate» n° 3.
[17] Vatican II, «Ad Gentes» n° 15.
[18] *Documentation Catholique* n° 1903, 6 octobre 1985, p. 943.

que, si les conflits entre les religions engendrent normalement une incompréhension totale de l'autre, une *recherche commune de la Vérité du Dieu Vivant* nous rapproche et nous fait reconnaître dans l'autre, encore étranger à nous, un compagnon dans cette grande aventure humaine, un compagnon dont nous sentons le coeur battre à l'unisson du nôtre.

Il s'agit d'abord de reconnaître en l'autre cette présence de l'Esprit, partout active dans l'Univers, qui utilise des chemins différents et qui pourtant peut être discernée. Car si tout homme est appelé à participer à la Rédemption dans le Christ, mort «pour la multitude», «il est permis de penser qu'en tout homme le fond de l'âme est capable, en certaines circonstances privilégiées, d'éprouver quelque chose de la présence divine, même si la raison n'a pas d'abord joué son rôle, même si elle ne sait pas reconnaître la réalité qui vient de se faire sentir»[19].

A partir de cette foi en la présence de Dieu en tout homme, et de son activité, salvatrice, il est possible de dépasser la «religion», c'est-à-dire «le protectionnisme des institutions religieuses», pour atteindre, au-delà de toute expression religieuse teintée de cultures dédeterminées, le noyau spirituel présent en tout homme de bonne volonté où se cache la présence du Dieu Vivant. C'est à ce niveau que l'on peut reconnaître dans l'autre, une expérience authentique de Dieu que déjà nous pouvons reconnaître comme nôtre. Car «les hommes de bonne volonté ne recherchent pas une idole faite à l'image d'une culture limitée ou d'une religion particulière, mais ils recherchent le Dieu Vivant qui se reflète de mille manière dans les cultures qui, dans leur ensemble, contribuent à éclairer la route de l'humanité vers sa réalisation finale totale»[20].

Expérience indéniable, dont on ne peut refuser l'authenticité, arriverons-nous à l'expliciter dans des termes où les uns et les autres se reconnaissent, donc dans un langage qui ne se référerait plus à des catégories chrétiennes traditionnelles, in-

---

[19] H. DE LUBAC, préface de «La Mystique et les mystiques», Desclée de Brouwer, 1965, pp. 37-38.
[20] Emilio Galindo Aguilar, «Foi en avant. Les problèmes de fond du dialogue islamo-chrétiens» dans «Se Comprendre» 20 octobre 1988 pp. 2-3.

compréhensibles pour l'autre, mais qui saurait se plier à l'apophatisme dont l'Eglise d'Orient reconnaît le seul langage adapté au Dieu Vivant?[21].

Car en définitive l'Islam avec lequel nous vivons, demeure pour nous un grand Mystère dont nous saisissons à la fois la grandeur au-delà d'une pratique parfois déviée en laquelle ses croyants eux-mêmes ne se reconnaissent pas, et la différence avec nous. De toute façon, nous ne pouvons en faire abstraction parce qu'il s'impose à nous par sa présence même dans notre monde, et parce qu'il se présente à nous comme un «signe des temps»[22] que le Concile, et donc l'Eglise nous demande de prendre en considération comme un appel de Dieu.

C'est que, ce Mystère que l'Islam représente pour nous, nous appelle à un dépassement de nos propres convictions à une remise en question de nos attitudes politico-religieuses spontanées et sentimentales, sans que nous arrivions encore à le pénétrer. Mais il nous appelle aussi à comprendre que notre théologie n'est pas un donné définitif, mais une recherche continuelle, une marche constante, toujours en avant, dont l'élan pour avancer ne vient pas de nous, mais d'Ailleurs.

Non, le musulman n'est pas un étranger por nous, et nous sentons entre lui et nous, à une profondeur de rapports et d'échanges, une sorte de «complicité» que nous avons encore à expliciter, et dont l'explicitation nous aiderait à prendre conscience de notre identité propre.

Une expérience personnelle

Ces lignes sont un témoignage, un écho de l'expérience que j'ai faite dans mes rapports avec des musulmans dans le cadre de l'Institut d'Etudes Islamo-Chrétiennes depuis 1977, date de sa fondation, jusqu'à maintenant. Témoignage, mais aussi réflexion sur le problème du salut des musulmans: comment un chrétien peut-il considérer un musulman? En fait, c'est à travers des contacts très intimes et dans une amitié très

---

[21] Cf Mgr Georges Khodre, art. cit. p. 201.
[22] Vatican II, «Gaudium et Spes» n° 11.

profonde avec un musulman cultivé et convaincu que j'ai été amené à réfléchir et à concevoir comment cet ami pouvait participer au dessein salvifique de Dieu.

Je reste convaincu depuis le début qu'il n'y a qu'un seul Sauveur des hommes, Jésus-Christ «Il n'y a qu'un seul Nom par qui nous puissions être sauvés, c'est le Nom de Jésus (Actes 4, 12)». Le Verbe de Dieu en devenant homme, a assumé en lui tout le genre humain. Il a donc assumé tous les hommes quels qu'ils soient. L'Ancien Testament avait préparé sa venue, mais la doctrine des Apôtres telle qu'elle nous été transmise par les Evangiles et le Nouveau Testament est claire. Il n'y a pas d'autre sauveur que Jésus, Fils de Dieu et Fils de Marie qui a souffert sous Ponce Pilate, a été crucifié, est mort et est ressuscité.

Comment peut-on parvenir à ce salut? Ici l'Evangile de Marc est clair: «Allez par le monde entier, proclamez la Bonne Nouvelle à toute la création. Celui qui croira et sera baptisé, sera sauvé. Celui qui ne croira pas, sera condamné» (Mc 16, 15-16). C'est sur ces mots de Jésus que se termine cet évangile. On ne peut participer au salut que par le baptême.

Par ailleurs, les Evangiles rapportent plusieurs traits qui semblent contredire cette affirmation. Le Christ a souligné et donné en exemple la foi du Centurion romain païen: «Jamais je n'ai trouvé une telle foi en Israël» (Mt 8, 19), la foi de la Syrophénicienne (Marc 7, 24-30). Le centurion Corneille dans les Actes des Apôtres reçoit l'onction de l'Esprit-Saint avant d'être baptisé (Actes 10, 44). On peut donc être sauvé sans avoir reçu le baptême et même sans participer à la foi de l'Eglise.

Ce qu'il y a de sûr, c'est que «Dieu veut que tous les hommes soient sauvés et parviennent à la connaissance de la Vérité» (1 Tim. 2, 4) car «nous avons mis notre espérance dans le Dieu vivant, le Sauveur de tous les hommes, des croyants surtout» (Tim 4, 10). Dieu veut sauver tous les Hommes, et cette volonté veut être efficace et aucun homme n'est exclu de cette volonté de salut.

Dans le même sens, nous savons que Dieu n'est pas lié par les sacrements: il ne serait pas lié par l'exigence du baptême. Nous savons aussi que l'adage de Tertullien «Hors de l'Eglise, pas de salut» ne doit pas être compris en un sens restrictif. Oui, Dieu veut sauver tous les hommes.

Plusieurs theologieus ont tenté de découvrir les différents chemins que Dieu pouvait emprunter pour atteindre tous les hommes, même les non-chrétiens. On nous a présenté aussi la position de certains Pères de l'Eglise, en particulier celle de saint Justin, découvrant dans certains courants religieux des «semences du Verbe». En fait comment discerner ces «semences du Verbe»?

Il me semble que nous les découvrons dans une recherche commune de Dieu. La recherche de Dieu me semble essentielle pour que nous nous retrouvions, croyants de différentes religions, sur un même registre. «Tu ne me chercherais pas si tu ne m'avais déjà trouvé». Nous nous retrouvons ainsi frères au-delà de toutes nos divergences, au delà de toutes les différences de doctrine.

J'ai pensé souvent que dans ce domaine nous pourrions faire appel aux modes que St Ignace nous propose dans les Exercices Spirituels à propos de l'élection. Mais est-ce la bonne orientation? Faut-il analyser et réfléchir comme le font les théologiens de métier qui ont été évoqués? Mais n'en reste-t-on pas à un point de vue purement intellectuel? Les relations que j'ai pu avoir avec des musulmans sont sans doute à base intellectuelle, mais, en fait, dépassent largement ce domaine. Suffit-il de reconnaître la loyauté de son interlocuteur? Mais que signifie la loyauté? On peut être dans l'erreur tout en étant loyal avec soi-même et cette attitude est pire, car elle peut aboutir à un fanatisme qui se ferme réellement à la Vérité. Enfin pourquoi ne pas rappeler le discours eschatologique de St Matthieu (Mt 25, 31-46): «Ce que nous avez fait au plus petit d'entre les miens, c'est à moi que vous l'avez fait», même si vous l'avez ignoré. Mais toutes ces différentes pistes de recherche ne correspondaient pas à mon expérience.

J'en revenais toujours à la même piste dans laquelle je me retrouvais en paix. Ce musulman est vraiment mon frère, parce que je retrouve en lui cette même hantise de Dieu, d'un Dieu jamais atteint, mais d'un Dieu dont je suis, comme lui, à la recherche dans une obscurité que je n'arrive pas à nommer. Oui, je le retrouve comme mon frère, parce que nous ne considérons pas nos fois respectives comme un terme, comme une Vérité que nous possédons, mais parce que nous y soupçonnons une Personne vers laquelle nous tendons, que nous cherchons à rencontrer sans arriver à la saisir. C'est à ce niveau que nous avons pu nous rencontrer dans une même recherche du Dieu vivant. Pour moi, ce fut une expérience qui s'est renouvelée presque continuellement.

Je cite un exemple. Mon ami musulman et moi, nous avons proposé pendant trois ans un cours sur la prière: lui présentait la prière en Islam et moi la prière en christianisme. Ainsi parallèlement nous exposions nos deux conceptions sans chercher le moins du monde à faire des comparaisons, mais en gardant la plus grande fidélité possible à notre point de vue. Puis un beau jour, il m'a posé la question suivante: «Que comptez-vous faire pendant vos vacances?» Et j'ai répondu tout simplement: «Je vais sans doute prêcher une retraite et faire moi-même ma retraite». Comme il ne comprenait pas ce que je voulais dire, j'essayais de lui expliquer en quoi consistait une retraite: le silence pour écouter dans le coeur la Parole de Dieu, et ainsi pour prier. Ce fut pour lui une découverte: «Nous ne connaissons pas en Islam des organisations de ce genre. Nous aurions besoin de nous inspirer de votre exmple». C'est sa soif de Dieu qui s'exprimait ainsi.

C'est donc dans les relations de travail, dans la droiture d'une amitié partagée, que nous nous sommes retrouvés, à une profondeur que nous ne pouvions soupçonner dès le début. Car tout d'abord, c'est la différence qui nous était apparue: chrétien et musulman, nous devons reconnaître la différence. Je n'ai jamais pu accepter l'attitude de P. Lelong. Le Christ que nous adorons et en qui nous croyons n'est pas le Christ du Coran. La Révélation que nous recevons est différente de la Révélation transmise par Mohammed. Aucune comparasion n'est possible à ce niveau. Mais, en decà de la différence, n'y a-t-il pas une unité fondamentale qui s'exprime ensuite dans cette différence ?

La reconnaissance de l'autre, en tant qu'autre, dans sa différence, n'est possible que s'il existe une base commune, qui nous permet de nous comprendre et de comprendre cette différence. Le Dieu de l'univers, le Seigneur des mondes que les musulmans reconnaissent et que nous reconnaissons dans le Créateur du Ciel et de la Terre, est bien le Créateur de tous les hommes. Et je le retrouve dans les autres. Les chemins qui nous mènent vers Lui sont différents. Ils insisteront sur des aspects différents. Mais une collaboration peut s'établir dans cette recherche même, point de départ d'une véritable fraternité.

Les relations demeurent sur un plan académique, mais cette exigence académique souligne le sérieux de la recherche et la rend plus profonde. En fait, cette culture académique est secondaire par rapport à une véritable entente spirituelle. Car celui que notre quête poursuit, au-delà de la différence, par des voies différentes, c'est bien celui qui a créé l'homme à son image et à sa ressemblance. Il y a en chacun de nous un élément essentiel commun qui nous permet de nous retrouver et de nous comprendre.

Déjà, à la fin de notre première année de travail commun, nous pouvions écrire ensemble: «Croyants des deux religions, musulmans et chrétiens, nous nous sommes retrouvés, non comme des sédentaires satisfaits de ce qu'ils possèdent, mais comme appartenant à la race des bédouins, vivant sous des tentes, des itinérants guidés par l'Esprit de Dieu, fils d'Abraham le nomade. Nous nous sommes reconnus, non pas comme possédant la Vérité divine, mais comme possédés par cette Vérité qui guide, entraîne et libère chacun dans sa ligne propre, plus attachés encore à sa propre Foi».

Car il faut bien reconnaître que nous sortons de cette recherche commune plus attachés, l'un et l'autre, les uns et les autres, à notre propre Foi. Comment expliquer un tel résultat? On m'a souvent traité de naïf. Et pourtant ne sommes-nous pas, les uns et les autres, créés à l'image et à la ressemblance du même Dieu Unique? Si nous sommes, les uns et les autres à la recherche de ce même Dieu Vivant, ne sommes-nous pas pénétrés par le même Esprit-Saint qui inspire toute recherche de la Vérité, lui qui est «Seigneur et qui donne la Vie», qui inspire en nous cette soif et qui nous lance sur le chemin de l'Absolu. C'est ce même Esprit de Dieu qui nous permet dès lors de nous comprendre et de pouvoir avouer ensemble que nous ne comprenons pas encore le terme de notre recherche. Oui, dans la mesure où nous sommes nous-mêmes liés par cette même recherche, et nous nous retrouvons, l'Esprit-Saint manifeste sa présence agissante en nous. Peut-être est-ce là notre place dans le dessein universel de salut que Dieu a conçu.

Los rostros de Cristo en el Sínodo de América

Javier García, L.C.

Introducción

Impresiona profundamente el hecho de que todos los sínodos continentales que se han venido celebrando en preparación del Jubileo del Año 2000 se hayan centrado de forma explícita en Jesucristo. Se puede constatar ya en el título de los mismos: Africa (1994): *L'Eglise en Afrique et sa mission evangelisatrice vers l'an 2000. «Vous serez mes temoins»* (Hch 1,8); América (1997): *Encuentro con Jesucristo vivo, camino para la conversión, la comunión y la solidaridad en América*; Asia (1998) *Jesus Christ the Saviour and His mission of love and service in Asia. «...Thath they may have life, and have it abundantly»* (Jn 10,10); Oceanía (1998) *Jesus Christ and the peolples of Oceania: Walking his Way, telling His Truth, living His Life*; Europa (1999), *Jesucristo viviente en su Iglesia, fuente de esperanza para Europa*. También la 10a. Asamblea Ordinaria del Sínodo de los Obispos (2000) tendrà como tema: *El obispo, servidor del Evangelio de Jesucristo para la esperanza del mundo*. Y la Asamblea Especial para el Líbano (1995), había tenido como tema: *Le Christ est nôtre Espérance. Renouvelés par son esprit, solidaires nous témoignons de son amour*.

El hecho es tanto más significativo, cuanto que las iglesias particulares de los diversos continentes se encuentran con una realidad social, cultural y religiosa muy compleja de sus pueblos: pobreza, pluralismo religioso, culturas diversas, o bien, secularismo, indiferentismo, relativismo, ignorancia religiosa, proselitismo compulsivo de sectas, violencia, corrupción en la vida pública, etc. Problemas complejos y urgentes, que reclaman una respuesta inmediata y eficaz.

Ante tal situación y aunque los obispos no sean especialistas en sociología, uno esperaría un análisis «técnico», de la misma, y soluciones eficientes. Sin embargo, lo primero que hacen los pastores de las iglesias particulares es «volver a sus raíces»: mirar a Jesucristo como al único Modelo, escucharlo como al único Maestro, renovar su confianza en él como el único Salvador del hombre. Y desde esta actitud esperanzada y confesante, de autoconciencia de la propria identidad cristiana, analizan la realidad de sus iglesias particulares y trazan una estrategia pastoral para el nuevo milenio.

No es restauracionismo ni fuga hacia atrás, miedo a los retos presentes o negativa a mirar el futuro. Es observar la estrella polar para ajustar la brújula momentos antes de iniciar la próxima singladura hacia un siglo que comienza. Estamos ante una Iglesia confesante y en marcha hacia el nuevo milenio, cuyo programa global es la nueva evangelización, cuyo faro para navegar por la historia es solo Cristo.

Tal es el espíritu que palpita en los documentos del Sínodo de América y tal fue la actitud de los padres sinodales durante la celebración del Sínodo. Nosotros ahora queremos resaltar y comentar esta «anakephalaiosis» o «re-capitulación» paulina de las reflexiones y documentos del Sínodo en la persona de Cristo.

Sobre la centralidad de Cristo en el Sínodo, baste un texto de Juan Pablo II en la exhortación apostólica postsinodal *Ecclesia in America*:

> «*Encuentro con Jesucristo vivo, camino para la conversión, la comunión y la solidaridad en América*». El tema así formulado expresa claramente la centralidad de la persona de Jesucristo resucitado, presente en la vida de la Iglesia, que invita a la conversión, a la comunión y a la solidaridad. El punto de partida de este programa evangelizador es ciertamente el encuentro con el Señor» (n. 3).

De hecho en la asamblea sinodal alguno de los padres propuso que la exhortación se llamara «*Christus in America*», para dar voz a la fe del pueblo americano, profundamente centrada en Cristo, expresión de la cual es su religiosidad, más aún, su misma cultura.

Y nos proponemos presentar esta síntesis de la cristología de Sínodo de América[1], a través de la categoria del **rostro de Cristo**. La pregunta de fondo, sobreentendida en todo este trabajo es: ¿Qué rostro de Cristo nos transmiten los obispos de América?

Varias razones nos inducen a este planteamiento. Ante todo, creemos que corresponde a aspiraciones legítimas, más aún, a necesidades de contextualización muy sentidas en América, en el momento en que se lleva a cabo la nueva evangelización: hemos de presentar no a un Cristo teórico y puramente espiritualista, sino a un Cristo encarnado en las diversas culturas de los pueblos de América, expresado según su sensibilidad, que responda a las preocupaciones y aspiraciones del hombre y de la mujer del Continente americano de hoy. Un Cristo con **un rostro inculturado**. Ya el Vaticano II había enunciado, en la *Gaudium et Spes*: «La inculturación es la ley de la evangelización cristiana»[2]. La historia de la evangelización ha sido y debe seguir siendo un proceso continuo de «adaptación cultural», de «diálogo con las culturas», de «intercambio vital con los diversas culturas de los pueblos»[3].

Otra razón es el planteamiento y el tono de los documentos del Sínodo de América, que no son teóricos, sino **pastorales**, no ofrecen una cristologia abstracta, sino una «confessio fidei» y un «kerigma» vivos. Corresponde mejor al kerigma un «icono» o imagen viviente de Cristo más que unos enunciados especulativos.

---

[1] En adelante nos referiremos al mismo como «Sínodo de América». Los Documentos de este Sínodo son los siguientes: *Lineamenta* (1996). *Instrumentum laboris* (1997). *Relatio ante disceptationem. Relatio post disceptationem* (ambas de 1997). Mensaje (1997). Las Propositiones o sugerencias conclusivas de los miembros del Sínodo llevan la sigla «sub secreto» y están destinadas exclusivamente al Santo Padre. El broche de oro final del Sínodo de América es la exhortación Apostólica Postsinodal, de Juan Pablo II, *Ecclesia in America*, firmada en México, a los pies de la Virgen de Guadalupe, en su santuario del Tepeyac, el 22 de enero de 1999.

[2] La *Gaudium et Spes* lo expresa con otro término: "Verbi revelati *accommodata praedicatio* lex omnis evangelizationis permanere debet" (n. 44), pero del contexto se deduce que está hablando de la inculturación, aunque entonces no se conocía el término en esta acepción.

[3] GS 44; 58. Cfr. también *Catechesi Tradendae*, n. 53.

Por otro lado, todo hombre y toda mujer que cree en Cristo y toda comunidad que le sigue, están emplazados a responder a la pregunta de Cristo: *¿quién decís vosotros que soy yo?* (Mc 8,29). A pregunta personal y concreta, respuesta personal y vital; cada cual ha de presentar su experiencia del Cristo viviente, su imagen y rostro de Cristo.

Por añadidura, el hombre contemporáneo, moderno y aun postmoderno, ha llegado a ser *homo mediaticus* y *homo comunicator*, habituado al lenguaje icónico de la comunicación. Sin embargo, la misma abundancia de imágenes, predominantemente banales, está terminando por obturar los canales de comunicación entre hombre y hombre. El *homo comunicator* se nos está quedando en *homo incomunicatus* a nivel profundo, no tanto a nivel de sentidos – mensajes coloridos, acompañados de estrépito, que le lanzan impulsos a sus instintos prerracionales, pero le dejan vacío el corazón y entorpecida la mente. Por esto, ¿qué mejor labor de reeducación personalista, más aún, ¿qué mejor terapia espiritual, que lo prepare para el diálogo con el Trascendente, que presentarle una imagen, más aún, un rostro que es *el icono del Dios invisible* (Col 1,15)?

Dividiremos el artículo en dos partes, en la primera, recordaremos, sólo de paso, el tema del rostro de Dios en la Biblia, que en Cristo, rostro visible del Padre, alcanza su expresión más plena. En la segunda, recorreremos el rostro o, quizá mejor, «los rostros» de Cristo en los documentos del Sínodo de América.

I. El rostro de Dios en la S. Escritura

En el Antiguo Testamento el término hebreo *pânîm* aparece varios cientos de veces, y se traduce como «*próspon*» en griego, y como «*persona*» en latín; como «rostro» en español. Se habla repetidas veces del rostro de Yavé. Ahora bien, así como la mano, la voz, el nombre, el corazón, en el Antiguo Testamento indican a Dios mismo, así el rostro de Dios indica a Dios mismo. El rostro de la persona indica la unidad entre la parte que se ve y lo que ella es realmente, es decir, la unidad total del ser. Hablar del rostro de Dios es afirmar la teofanía y revelación de Dios.

Sin embargo, en el Antiguo Testamento, tanto a nivel lingüístico, cuanto a nivel de experiencia religiosa, hay una paradoja al respecto: por un lado, el fiel israelita anhela contemplar **el rostro de Dios**, que es la felicidad del hombre: (Sal 42,3;6); y por eso le ruega: «vuelve tu rostro hacia nosotros y seremos salvos» (Sal 80,4.8.20). Moisés, el amigo de Dios, habla con él cara a cara, como un hombre habla con otro hombre (Ex 31,11; Num 12,8; Dt 34,10). Por otro lado, hay la prohibición de hacer cualquier imagen de Dios (Ex 20,4; Dt 5,8). Prohibición, por lo demás justificada ante el pecado de idolatría no sólo de los pueblos vecinos, sino también de Israel que había caído repetidas veces en el mismo (1Re 6,5; 1Sam 6,5). Moisés, en un momento de gran intimidad con Yavé, le pide: «muéstrame el esplendor de tu rostro, muéstrame tu gloria» (Ex 33, 18,23). A lo que el Dios le dice que sólo verá su espalda. ¡Tan grande es el abismo que separa la santidad de Dios de la indignidad del hombre que sólo ver a Dios podría causarle la muerte![4].

Tendrán los hombres que aguardar a los tiempos mesiánicos, en el Nuevo Testamento, para poder ver el rostro de Dios en la cara del Hijo encarnado, pues *«la gloria de Dios resplandece en el rostro de Cristo»* (1 Cor 4,6). *«Él es el icono del Dios invisible»* (Col 1,15). Por eso, a los griegos, que expresaron un deseo análogo al que presentara Moisés a Yavé, – *«queremos ver a Jesús»* (Jn 12,20-26) – sí les fue concedido: vieron su rostro precisamente en el momento en que Jesús se disponía a mostrarlo al mundo en todo el misterioso esplendor de su «hora» de sufrimiento, pasión y resurrección.

Y es que en el Nuevo Testamento se dan dos momentos culminantes de la **gloria** del rostro de Cristo, en el rostro transfigurado del Tabor y en el rostro del hombre de dolores.

La gloria del **rostro transfigurado de Jesús** brilló y se mostró en el monte Tabor: por un momento la *morphè tou theoù* en que Él existe y subsiste, rasga el velo y traspasa la *morphè tou doùlou* y el «*schêma tou anthrôpou* (la «figura de hombre»)

---

[4] Cfr. más ampliamente este tema en Michelina Tenace, *Prefigurazioni del Volto di Cristo nell'Antico Testamento*, in «Il volto dei volti. Cristo», ed. Velar, Gorle (BG) 1997, 24-30.

en que vive su existencia terrena (Flp 2,6-7): «*El aspecto de su rostro se mudó, y sus vestidos eran de una blancura fulgurante*» (Lc 9,29). Es la anticipación del rostro de Cristo resucitado.

La gloria del rostro del Siervo Paciente de Yavé se revela cuando Pilatos, desde el pretorio lo muestra a la muchedumbre y al mundo, escupido, tumefacto, ensangrentado, coronado de espinas, azotado, y pronuncia aquella frase elíptica y pregnante: «*Ecce homo!*», «*¡He aquí al hombre!*» (Jn 19,5). No era «un hombre» más, uno de entre tantos condenados, era el Hombre por antonomasia, elegido por Yavé para representar a su pueblo en el sufrimiento, como lo había cantado Isaías: «*No tenía apariencia ni presencia; (lo vimos) y no tenía aspecto que pudiéramos estimar. Despreciable y desecho de hombre, varón de dolores y sabedor de dolencias, como uno ante quien se oculta el rostro, despreciable y no le tuvimos en cuenta*» (Is 53,2-4).

He aquí, pues, los dos rostros de Cristo, el rostro humano de Dios y el rostro divino del hombre (*Ecclesia in America* n. 67): el cristiano que contempla a Cristo, en él ve el rostro del Padre, como lo dice el mismo Jesús: «*quien me ha visto a mí, ha visto al Padre*» (Jn 14,9). Y en él también ve el rostro del hombre, sobre todo del hombre más débil, es decir, el rostro del hambriento, del sediento, del peregrino, del desnudo, del enfermo, del encarcelado (Mt. 25,31-40,44-45), del pobre, oprimido y marginado. La visión de fe del rostro de Cristo es inseparable de la visión de amor del rostro del hermano más débil[5].

No en vano uno de los filósofos más leídos hoy en día es Emmanuel Levinas que invita a redescubrir en el rostro del otro el misterio de la trascendencia, que nos merece un respeto sagrado, pues nos lleva al umbral del Otro. Nos referimos sobre todo a su obra más representativa, *Totalité et infini. Essai sur l'exteriorité* (1961). El rostro, siguiendo a Levinas, es lo originario, el ser mismo, lo que da sentido. En el diálogo «cara a cara» se encuentra al otro, que es, en realidad, el Otro. De aquí

---

[5] Cfr. Giovanni Marchesi, «Il volto di Cristo nel Nuovo Testamento», en «**Il volto dei volti. Cristo**», Velar Ed. 1997, p. 36-40 passim. Cf. AA.VV., *Cristologia. Volti africani, latinoamericani e asiatici di Cristo*, ed. EMI, Bologna 1997. Cf. también Eloy Bueno, *Los rostros de Cristo*, ed. BAC, Madrid 1997.

su sanidad y su inviolabilidad. La epifanía del rostro es un hecho ético, lleva inscrito ontológicamente el «no matarás». Por otro lado, en ese «cara a cara» se encuentra el rostro de la viuda, del huérfano y del extranjero, es decir, el ser humano en su máxima vulnerabilidad y desamparo. Y sin embargo, el rostro del la viuda, del huérfano y del extranjero, en su vulnerabilidad lleva inscrita su in-vulnerabilidad. Su mirada refleja su trascendencia ontológica, su ser-más-allá de la violencia, que ningún poder puede destruir.

Su vulnerabilidad, su hambre, apelan a mi responsabilidad, que se hace bondad. Mi encuentro con el Otro suscita mi responsabilidad: no puedo permanecer indiferente ante el rostro de la viuda, del huérfano y del extranjero.

De aquí que Levinas vea el esplendor, la gloria, el señorío, a la vez que la humildad y la vulnerabilidad en el rostro de la viuda, del huérfano, del extranjero; por eso, en ese rostro descubre el Otro.

Nosotros vemos el esplendor y la humildad, la soberanía y la debilidad en el rostro del Hijo de Dios encarnado, que es el Siervo de Yavé de Is 53, 2-3. Aquí nos parece estar el fundamento místico-ontológico de la identificación del rostro de Cristo con los rostros de los más desamparados de entre los hombres (Mt 25, 31-46). Y de aquí parten los obispos de América cuando en los *Lineamenta* describen el rostro de Cristo en los rostros de los más «pequeños de América»[6].

---

[6] Escriben los obispos en los *Lineamenta*: «Por la acción del Espíritu Santo, el misterio de su muerte y de su resurrección se hace presente en la vida actual de la Iglesia, no sólo en su conjunto, sino también en cada uno de sus miembros, pues lo que se haga a los más pequeños de sus hermanos – hambrientos, desnudos, enfermos, sin techo, forasteros, encarcelados – a Él se le hace (Mt 25, 34-46)» (n. 29). Y prosiguen: «El rostro de Cristo sufriente y crucificado tiene hoy, en América, los rasgos de los pobres en las inmensas ciudades, de los desempleados, de los migrantes, de los margnados por distintas causas, de los niños no nacidos, de los niños de la calle y de aquellos que quedan sin escuela, de los jóvenes sin trabajo y sin guía, de las mujeres menospreciadas y explotadas, de los ancianos abandonados, de los enfermos, especialmente de los afectados del SIDA, de los encarcelados. Es también el rostro de las minorías étnicas marginadas, de los indígenas y de los afroamericanos, de los campesinos y de los habitantes de las barriadas periféricas de las grandes ciudades, en el Norte, en el Centro y en el Sur del continente» (n. 30). En el n. 31 describen también el rostro de Cristo resucitado como brilla en las comunidades cristianas de América. Cfr. También *Instrumentum laboris*, n. 62.

No es mera extrapolación o transposición de rasgos por vía metafórica, simbólica o mitológica. Es descubrimiento de las comunes raíces místico-ontológicas del rostro del hombre americano y del rostro de Cristo, *forma Dei y forma servi*, Hijo de Dios y Varón de dolores.

II. Los rostros de Cristo en América

Vengamos ya a los diversos «rostros americanos» de Cristo como los podemos deducir del Sínodo de América. Entre otros, destacamos el rostro del Cristo vivo, el rostro «inculturado» de Cristo, que a su vez comprende el rostro indígena, el rostro afroamericano, el rostro mestizo de la religiosidad popular, el rostro moderno y postmoderno de Cristo. Está también el rostro de Cristo reconciliador, el rostro de Cristo creador de comunión, el rostro de Cristo solidario.

No debería llamarnos la atención esta multiplicidad de «rostros», pues en realidad no es Cristo quien se atomiza en mil rostros culturales, como la imagen reflejada en un espejo roto, sino que son las mil culturas que reflejan el perfil del único Hijo de Dios encarnado, con su propia tonalidad y genio. Ya Pablo lo había expresado: «donde no hay griego y judío, circuncisión e incircuncisión; bárbaro, escita, esclavo, libre, sino que Cristo es todo y en todos» (Col. 3,11). Por otro lado, ya lo hemos dicho, imposible expresar la densidad del misterio de Jeuscristo, con un solo planteamiento, con un solo rostro; cada nuevo perfil presenta una nueva faceta del misterio fascinante del Hijo de Dios que es también el Hijo del hombre.

1. *El rostro de Cristo vivo*

Ante los grandes retos a los que se enfrenta la Iglesia que camina en América -evangelización y misión, justicia y solidaridad, cultura cristiana y secularismo-, los padres sinodales, con Juan Pablo II a la cabeza, responden mostrándole a Jesucristo vivo, sugiriendo un «método» o modo -*meta-hòdos*, camino- para contactarlo, el encuentro personal de cada hombre y de cada mujer con Cristo, y unas metas, la conversión, la comunión y la solidaridad. Como los Evangelios nos narran los encuentros con él de la Samaritana (Jn 4,5-42), de Zaqueo (Lc 19,1-10), de los primeros discípulos, y después de la resurrección, el encuentro de María Magdalena (Jn 20,11-18), de los dos discípulos de Emaús (Lc 24,13-35), de Simón Pedro (Jn 21,1-23), de Saulo en la vía de Damasco (Hch 9,3-30 par).

El primer rostro de Cristo en el Sínodo de América es, pues, el rostro de Cristo vivo, resucitado, que por medio del Espíritu Santo acompaña hoy a la Iglesia en su camino por la historia, es esta la primera certeza vital, germen de todas las demás: *él sigue viviendo y actuando entre nosotros*: «*He aquí que yo estoy con vosotros todos los días hasta el fin del mundo*» (Mt 28,20). «*Esta presencia misteriosa de Cristo en su Iglesia es la garantía de su éxito en la realización de la misión que le ha sido confiada*»[7].

Jesucristo vivo es el Hijo de Dios, que en la encarnación se ha unido en cierto modo con todo hombre[8]. Dimensión histórica e importancia de su humanidad: Cristo es el nuevo Adán que revela plenamente el hombre al hombre y le manifiesta la grandeza de su vocación (ibid. ad sensum).

El rostro de Cristo vivo es, pues, lo contrario de un pietismo desencarnado; en coherencia con el mejor hacer teológico americano de las últimas tres décadas, los obispos de América nos invitan a tomar en serio la santa humanidad del Señor, de su existencia terrena, en un tiempo y un lugar determinados, en Nazaret, al inicio de nuestra era, existencia que culmina en la cruz «para liberar al a humanidad del pecado y del mal»[9].

Sin embargo, la muerte no representa para él el último capítulo de su vida histórica; mediante la resurrección vence la muerte, renovando gloriosamente su humanidad y, en ella, nuestra existencia corporal y terrena, abierta a la trascendencia (Flp 2, 6-11). Se trata de Jesucristo muerto y resucitado, que vive actualmente cerca del Padre y que acompaña a su Iglesia peregrina, donándole el Espíritu de vida[10].

---

[7] Cfr. *Ecclesia in America*, n. 7.
[8] Cfr. *Gaudium et Spes*, n. 22.
[9] Cfr. *Lineamenta*, n. 6.
[10] Cfr. *Lineamenta* n. 6.

Este es el primer esbozo del rostro de Cristo, se trata de una persona viviente y la Iglesia de América contempla el rostro de Cristo resucitado y viviente hoy.

Por esto los obispos quieren acercar al hombre y a la mujer de América, a través del encuentro, categoría antropológica acendradamente personalista: no se encuentra uno con una idea o con un fantasma ilustre del pasado; se encuentra uno como el discípulo con su maestro, el enfermo con el médico, el amigo con el amigo. Intuitivamente los obispos perciben que el hombre postmoderno necesita más que maestros y teorías, ejemplos de vida, testigos, y Jesucristo «es el testigo fiel» (Apoc 1,5). El encuentro tiene también dimensión teológica, en él está toda la historia de la salvación, con su dialéctica de invitación de Dios y de respuesta libre del hombre.

Muestran los obispos también los lugares donde se encuentra hoy a Cristo vivo en la iglesia, como es la lectura de la Palabra de Dios, la liturgia y en la liturgia, como nos dice la *Sacrosantum Concilium* (n. 7), los múltiples modos de presencia de Cristo, que van del celebrante a la comunidad, de la proclamación de la Palabra a los sacramentos, sobre todo a la Eucaristía, sin olvidar a los pobres[11].

Señalan asimismo los efectos del encuentro con Jesucristo vivo, como los que se produjeron en los diversos personajes del Evangelio cercanos a Cristo: fuerza de transformación personal, conversión, comunión, solidaridad, aunque también hubo sus resistencias, como efectos del pecado y de una plena libertad que, herida por el pecado, puede rechazar la oferta de amistad de Cristo: «vino la luz al mundo, mas los hombres prefirieron las tinieblas a la luz, porque sus obras eran malas» (Jn 3,19).

2. *El rostro de Cristo contextualizado o inculturado:*

La *cristología «en contexto»*, parte de la originalidad histórica y cultural de una determinada zona eclesial e intenta una interpretación «inculturada» del misterio de Cristo. En Améri-

---

[11] Cfr. *Ecclesia in America*, n. 12.

ca los rostros del Cristo inculturado son múltiples, tantos cuantos contextos culturales crean los diversos grupos humanos o nacionales. Aquí subrayamos algunos: los rostros de «Cristo indígena», de «Cristo afroamericano», de «Cristo mestizo», de «Cristo moderno y postmoderno, el rostro de Cristo pequeño y pobre (Mt 25,31-46)», come veremos más abajo.

»Evangelizar al hombre significa evangelizar su cultura, su ética y sus valores, sus ideales de justicia y de verdad»[12]. En el esfuerzo por llevar al hombre a encontrarse con Jesucristo, los obispos hablan de la cultura, que es la obra en que el hombre proyecta su alma. Propiamente 'se encuentran entre sí' personas y no culturas; pero las personas non viven en la campana vacía de una existencia sin historia, sino en una cultura que es como matriz de sus valores y de sus ideales. En su propio «lenguaje cultural» el hombre expresa su visión de Dios, del mundo, de sus semejantes y de sí mismo. Cuando el hombre ha sido evangelizado, y se ha encontrado personalmente con Cristo, luego expresa esta experiencia según su sensibilidad, en múltiples formas, del arte a la literatura, de la liturgia a la espiritualidad, de la filosofía a la teología, de las instituciones a las tradiciones. Así van surgiendo los diversos «rostros inculturados» de Cristo según las diversas culturas de los grupos humanos y de las naciones.

En el continente americano hay variadísimas etnias y grupos humanos culturalmente diferenciados, por ejemplo, esquimales de Alaska, algonquinos, iroqueses y atapascos de Canadá, pimas, cheroquees y navajos en EE.UU., siguiendo por las diversísimas etnias indígenas de México, Centro, Sudamérica y el Caribe, afroamericanos, mulatos, mestizos y criollos, emigrantes europeos o asiáticos. América, más que cualquier otro continente, tiene una vocación de crisol de las principales razas y culturas del planeta. Ya lo había intuido el ensayista y filósofo mexicano José Vasconcelos, que, en su obra *La raza cósmica*, ponía el centro de esa fusión racial y cultural precisamente en Brasil.

---

[12] Cfr. *Instrumentum laboris* n. 9.

Los obispos desean ofrecer al hombre americano el rostro de Cristo encarnado en su cultura. Y como se trata de numerosas culturas, no será un rostro 'plano', sino pluridimensional y de múltiples facetas.

a) El rostro indígena de Cristo:

De los indígenas, subraya el *Instrumentum Laboris* (n. 14), con la tradición iniciada por Medellín, y continuada por Puebla y Santo Domingo, el gran amor a la tierra, el respeto hacia los antepasados y hacia las tradiciones comunitarias, el sentido de lo sagrado, la sabiduría de la vida, la austeridad y sencillez de vida. La consideración de Cristo como Jefe, Anciano, Antepasado, Hermano Mayor, Sanador, facilita mejor la comprensión de Jesús y su misterio salvífico. En este rostro de Cristo los indígenas contemporáneos encuentran la respuesta a su búsqueda de dignidad, de identidad, de reconocimiento, de pertenencia, de fraternidad, de paz, de felicidad. Los indígenas veneran al Santo Niño, al Cristo en la cruz, al Cristo-sol, imágenes en las que ven realidades-símbolos de su propia cultura.

Aquí y allá en América se oyen voces de tiempo en tiempo sobre «teología india» o «teología indígena», que expresaría su visión cristiana de la vida, del mundo, de la comunidad y del individuo. En realidad hay que decir que, hoy por hoy, es un título excesivo e inadecuado, pues no hay una reflexión sistemática de fe cristiana hecha a partir de su idiosincrasia y tradiciones culturales. Los mismos indígenas, en el «Tercer Encuentro-Taller de teología india», celebrado en Cochabamba (Bolivia), en 1998, terminaron prefiriendo hablar de «sabiduría», más que de «teología india».

Por otro lado, hay que recordar siempre que no se puede pretender agotar a Cristo en categorías autóctonas o encualesquiera otras categorías culturales, sin empobrecerlo y hacerlo perder su originaria y perpetua novedad. Por esto, nos parece reductiva, y, por lo menos, inexacta, la traducción que hace la revista «Christus», de México (1993), del *lógion joanneo: Kaì Lògos sarks egèneto* (Jn 1, 14), por «Y el Verbo se hizo indio». En Cristo debe permanecer una irreductible e intraducible alteridad. Es, pues, mucho más precisa y diciente la expresión literal de Juan: «*Y el Verbo se hizo carne*», es decir, humanidad completa, cuerpo y alma, concreta e histórica, que siendo humanidad del Verbo Divino, de alguna manera se identifica con todos los hombres (*Gaudium et Spes,* 22): por eso el Verbo se hizo indio, pero también africano y mestizo y criollo y migrante, como se ha venido haciendo asiático o como también se había hecho judío, romano, griego y gentil, germano, celta o franco.

La *Ecclesia in America* indica a la comunidad internacional el deber de «respetar las tierras y los pactos contraídos con ellos (con los indígenas); igualmente a atender a sus legítimas necesidades sociales, sanitarias y culturales» (n. 64). Y quizá mirando al caso de los indígenas de Chiapas, con el guerrillero Marcos y los zapatistas alzados, pero también de algunas zonas andinas, invita a «recordar la necesidad de reconciliación entre los pueblos indígenas y las sociedades en las que viven» (ibd.).

b) El rostro afroamericano de Cristo:

De los afroamericanos el *Instrumentum laboris* – que como se sabe es la síntesis auténtica de las respuestas de los obispos al cuestionario de los *Lineamenta* –, destaca asimismo su sentido comunitario, su respeto a los antepasados y ancianos, su enorme capacidad de sufrimiento, su alegría de vivir expresada en cantos, danzas, ritmos, música y amistad, su gran sentido familiar, su desprendimiento de los bienes materiales, la creencia en una vida ultraterrena (n. 14).

Aquí encontramos también el rostro de Cristo Anciano, Antepasado, Gran Jefe, Sabio, en el que los afroamericanos veneran cuanto de más grande tienen en sus tradiciones. El alma afroamericana es telúrica, emotiva, vital, como el clima y la tierra del Caribe y de la costa donde viven; es expansiva y abierta. En la vivencia de su religiosidad participa toda la persona del afroamericano, alma y cuerpo, con todos sus sentidos: los ojos en el colorido de las fiestas y cultos, de las imágenes de los santos Cristos, la lengua y el oído en los cantos, la música y las plegarias, el tacto en las imágenes que toca con devoción, todo el cuerpo en el ritmo y la danza, en las ofrendas que lleva, toca, entrega, en las promesas que hace y cumple.

Aquí también recuerda la *Ecclesia in America* los rasgos sufrientes de este rostro afroamericano de Cristo por los prejuicios étnicos... olvidando que toda persona de cualquier raza y condición ha sido creada por Dios a su imagen (n. 64).

c) *El rostro del Cristo moderno y postmoderno*:

El proceso de urbanización, con su amenaza de desertificación cultural y cristiana, su estilo de vida anónimo, secularista y pragmático, ha creado las ciudades y megalópolis donde se está gestando la cultura moderna y postmoderna[13].

Los obispos quieren presentar el rostro de un Cristo dinámico, que rescata todos los valores del hombre moderno, tanto científicos o técnicos, como humanísticos: sentido de la dignidad de la persona, de la libertad, de la justicia, la solidaridad, el respeto hacia la creación, la busqueda de sentido y trascendencia; valores de socialidad y comunicación, de democracia y participación.

Los pastores quieren presentar el rostro de un Cristo en el que brillan en grado máximo la dignidad del hombre, al que el mismo Cristo comprende y libera de cuanto lo encadena, el pecado, el egoísmò, la codicia, la concupiscencia y el orgullo. Cristo non sólo no es contrario al progreso del hombre ni mucho menos es el rival del hombre, sino el que posibilita su crecimiento, al fundarlo en la verdad de su ser humano, al purificar su inteligencia, al rectificar y fortalecer su voluntad mediante el don de su gracia.

Tanto los *Lineamenta* como el *Instrumentum laboris* retoman, después de la «*Redemptoris Missio*», la invitación a evangelizar los «modernos areópagos»: el mundo de la comunicación, del desarrollo y de la liberación de los pueblos, del compromiso por la paz, por los derechos de los hombres y de los pueblos, de la promoción de la mujer y del niño, de la salvaguardia de la creación, de la cultura, la economía, la investigación y la ciencia. Sin temor a las burlas y al escepticismo del hombre moderno, el papa y los pastores, como San Pablo en el areópago de Atenas, vuelven a presentar a Cristo a los constructores de la sociedad[14].

Empiezan reconociendo los valores del hombre moderno y postmoderno, como son tantos progresos humanos en cam-

---

[13] En la exhortación apostólica postsinodal *Ecclesia in America* se describen algunos rasgos negativos de esta urbanización alocada y sin planificación (n. 21).
[14] Cfr. también *Ecclesia in America*, nn. 56, 67.

po científico y técnico, en campo de libertad y derechos humanos, su anhelo de libertad y responsabilidad, el sentido de la dignidad de la persona, la socialidad y solidaridad, la autenticidad y sinceridad. Y a la vez, no pueden dejar de ver sus límites y antivalores, como el desarrollo económico con grandes costos sociales, el escepticismo filosófico y el relativismo moral, el traspaso de los límites éticos en campo científico y biogenético, la contaminación y agotamiento de recursos naturales.

El rostro moderno y postmoderno de Cristo ha de presentársele al hombre americano como el de Aquél que da sentido a la vida, como el ejemplar máximo del hombre, como «el que revela el hombre al hombre»[15].

Dentro del «rostro contextualizado de Cristo», está el «rostro mestizo de Cristo», que venera la mayoría de los pueblos de América Latina, y que corresponde al Cristo de la religiosidad católica popular.

3. *El rostro de Cristo de la religiosidad popular*:

El rostro popular de Cristo es el rostro que, en su fe sencilla pero esencial, el pueblo católico de América, sobre todo en el Sur y en el Caribe, venera y adora.

El teólogo protestante Saúl Trinidad afirma que al pueblo pobre de América Latina, indígena, campesino o marginado en las grandes metrópolis, sólo le son posibles tres cristologías:

– una *cristología de resignación*, simbolizada en el Cristo crucificado y en la Madre dolorosa. Cristología en la cual la impotencia del oprimido es interiorizada como inevitable y sirve, por tanto, para sacralizar el sistema de conquista y opresión;

– una *cristología de dominación*, simbolizada por un Cristo glorioso, rico y poderoso, adornado con oro y plata y una imagen de la Virgen como conquistadora. Cristología inevitable, debida al hecho de que el dios de los indios no fue capaz de impedir la profanación de su santuario por los vencedores.

– una *cristología de marginación*, simbolizada en el «Niño marginado», vgr. el Niño de Belén. Es una cristología que juz-

---

[15] *Gaudium et Spes* n. 22.

ga al indígena y al campesino pasivo y conformista, siempre débil e inmaduro y, por tanto, siempre necesitado de protección por «benefactores».

En todo esto, ¿dónde está el «otro Cristo», de Lc. 4, 16-21?, se pregunta Saúl Trinidad. En la misma línea se sitúan los teólogos, protestantes y católicos, que escriben conjuntamente en el libro *«Jesús: ni vencido ni monarca celestial. (Imágenes de Jesucristo en América Latina)»*, coordinados por José Míguez Bonino, profesor en la Facultad Evangélica de Buenos Aires[16].

Parecida opinión desde la óptica antropológica, tiene Richard Nebel, antropólogo alemán americanista, refiriéndose al caso de México; el pueblo pobre proyecta su situación de postración, humillación y pobreza en las imágenes de Cristo sufrientes y «vencidos». De aquí el predominio en la religiosidad popular de devociones a Cristos crucificados, azotados, sangrantes y muertos. A esto se añade la simbiosis con elementos precolombinos que aún sobreviven en la religiosidad popular de México: bajo las formas de los Cristos sufrientes y agonizantes, el indígena y el campesino de México siguen viendo a sus antiguas divinidades Huitzilopchtli, Tezcatlipoca, Xipe Totec, etc. El elemento que los une es el ser dioses vencidos y sobre todo el sacrificio y la sangre. Estaríamos ante una religiosidad sincretista[17].

Sobre la interpretación de Saúl Trinidad, hacemos tres observaciones: entre líneas se lee la descalificación tácita del culto católico a las imágenes – de antigua datación en el debate teológico, la disputa sobre las imágenes, superada por la afirmación de la real encarnación de Cristo, como afirmó el Concilio de Nicea II, en el año 787, y que renace con la Reforma luterana –; la interpretación «psicologista» de proyección de los propios

---

[16] Ed. Tierra Nueva, Buenos Aires 1977. Lo otros autores que colaboran en el volumen son Jaci C. Maraschin, Leonardo Boff, Joâo Dias de Araujo, Saúl Trinidad, Juan Stam, Pedro Negre Rigol, Geroges Casalis, Ignacio Ellacuaría, Segundo Galilea, Severino Croatto, Hugo Assmann, Raúl Vidales, Lamberto Schuurman.

[17] Cfr. Richard Nebel (Bayreuth), *Aspectos cristolólogicos en la religiosidad popular antiguo mexicana-cristiana en el México de hoy*, en K. Kohut y A. Meyers (eds.), «Religiosidad popular en América Latina», Eichstätt, Vervuert Verlag 1988, 178-192.

traumas del pueblo católico en imágenes sagradas de Cristo sufriente o de María como Madre dolorosa, que tubo cierta aceptación en la primera mitad del siglo XX por su una apariencia 'brillante', hoy en día es obsoleta del todo, se demuestra superficial y ha quedado desmentida por los hechos.

En efecto, una observación más completa, en el mero nivel de descripción fenoménica, tendría que haver llevado a estos teólogos y antropólogos 'psicologistas' a incluir entre las «cristologías del pueblo pobre», también la cristología de Resurrección y Señorío, simbolizada por el culto a imágenes de Cristo resucitado y glorioso – por ejemplo, en la devoción a la Eucaristía, tan arraigada en el pueblo –, y en su culto tan difundido a Cristo como Rey y Señor del Universo.

En cuanto a la resignación del pueblo católico pobre, hay que recordar el dato – que pertenece ya a la historiografía universal – de la rebelión del pueblo católico, campesino e indígena, de México, de 1926 a 1929: al grito de *¡Viva Cristo Rey!*, se alzó en armas contra el gobierno masón del general Plutarco Elías Calles, quien pretendía aplicar una legislación antirreligiosa y anticatólica en el país, prohibiendo el culto público a Dios, cerrando templos, seminarios y casas religiosas, expulsando del país a obispos, limitando el número de sacerdotes, encarcelando, ahorcando y fusilando a sacerdotes y fieles por practicar su religión. El grito de rebelión y de guerra de los campesinos católicos, los «cristeros», era justamente: «¡Viva Cristo Rey!», y su distintivo, un Crucifijo colgado al cuello No vemos aquí a un pueblo pobre, resignado y pasivo, ante un Cristo crucificado, sino un pueblo que defiende bravíamente los derechos de Cristo, Rey y Señor del mundo[18].

La religiosidad popular de la que nos hablan los *Lineamenta (n. 62), el Instrumentum Laboris (nn. 17-19) y la Eccle-*

---

[18] El gran historiador francés Jean Meyer ha descrito esta guerra cristera como una verdadera epopeya en su obra de dos volúmenes *La Cristiada*, ed. Siglo XXI, México, D.F., 1994, 14a. edición. Se puede leer también el conmovedor testimonio de uno de los cristeros, joven estudiante que anduvo entre los campesinos católicos alzados y que fue muerto arteramente por agentes gobiernistas cuando el conflicto ya había terminado, Luis Rivero del Val, *Entre las patas de los caballos*, ed. Jus, 1992, 3a. ed.

sia in America (n. 16) vive una cristología mucho más rica y completa de lo que algunos antropólogos perciben. Se caracteriza, entre otros, por los siguientes elementos[19]:

– pone el énfasis en **la humanidad de Jesús**, como camino hacia su divinidad y como modelo de vida y de una existencia humana plenamente realizada.

– Presenta una **exigencia de inculturación** que general múltiples cristología en contexto.

– Está en **diálogo con el mundo contemporáneo**, no se queda en el pasado ni sólo en el ámbito privado, o abstracto e idealista, sino que establece un diálogo entre los problemas y aspiraciones del mundo que le rodea y el contenido de su fe en Cristo. Diálogo que también suscita multitud de ópticas interpretativas del misterio de Cristo.

– Es movida por una **exigencia existencial y práctica** de armonizar ortodozia y ortopraxis, fe y vida.

Todo ello lleva a una multiplicidad de visiones cristológicas que costituyen una verdadera riqueza teológica y pastoral y que desmiente la visión reductiva y superficial de algunos autores como los arriba aludidos. Así tenemos el Cristo Liberador, el Cristo Reconciliador, los Cristos inculturados que acabamos de ver, etc. La cristología de la liberación ve en los gestos salvíficos de Cristo con los pobres y marginados el centro del mensaje cristiano y la realización suprema del reino de Dios. La cristología que ve en **Cristo el Liberador** por antonomasia está en pleno desarrollo, una vez que el Magisterio de la Iglesia introdujo las oportunas precisiones teológicas, recuperando y encauzando la fecunda intuición de los teólogos latinoamericandos. Esta es la cristología que ha venido cobrando mayor desarrollo y hondura teológica en el Continente americano.

La cristología de liberación se ve completada por la cristología de reconciliación que subraya el papel de **Cristo Reconciliador** de los hombres pecadores con Dios y de los

---

[19] Cfr. Comité para el Jubileo del Año 2000, *Jesucristo, Salvador del mundo*, BAC, Madrid 1996, pp. 51-64 ad sensum. Cf. también Cristián Park, *Otra lógica en América Latina. Religión popular y modernización capitalista*, ed. FCE, México 1993.

hombres entre sí, perdonando con su sangre y comunicándoles la gracia y el Espíritu de caridad y vida nueva[20]. Cristo ayuda al hombre herido y dividido a superar las cuatro rupturas fundamentales que sufre después del pecado: ruptura de la comunión con Dios, con los demás, con el mundo y consigo mismo[21]. Lejos de excluirse, el Cristo Liberador y el Cristo Reconciliador se complementan mutuamente, viniendo a añadir cada titulo un nuevo ángulo de visión del único e insondable misterio de Cristo.

La *cristología religioso-popular* trata de redescubrir el significado profundo, teológico y pastoral, de las múltiples tradiciones de la religiosidad cristiana del pueblo. Como dejamos dicho más arriba, el misterio de Cristo es el elemento central de la religiosidad popular. He aquí algunos rasgos del perfil del **Cristo popular:**

– Es un Cristo vivido, escuchado, amado, acogido, seguido por el pueblo cristiano.

– Aunque a veces un poco desfigurado y pobre, desde el punto de vista de las motivaciones, es un Cristo que ilumina y sostiene la existencia global del pueblo, es portador y garante de sus valores más nobles y de sus aspiraciones más auténticas.

– Prueba de ello es la práctica sacramental asidua, sobre todo de la Eucaristía, la celebración de las grandes fiestas litúrgicas cristológicas, como Navidad, Epifanía, Semana Santa, Pasión, Resurrección, Corpus Christi; y la práctica de devociones cristológicas como la Eucaristía, el Sagrado Corazón, Cristo Rey; su presencia protectora en las casas, con imágenes, altarcitos y estatuas.

El Cristo popular asume los rostros humildes de las imágenes históricas y artísticas que el pueblo venera: Cristos cruci-

---

[20] Mns. Fernando Vargas Ruiz de Somocurcio, arzobispo emérito de Arequipa, presenta un panorama bastante completo del desarrollo de la teología de reconciliación en su reciente obra, «Congresos de la reconciliación. Historia y balance», ed. Vida y Espiritualidad, Lima 1997.

[21] Cfr. «Temas para una teología de la reconciliación», en Fernando Vargas Ruiz de Somocurcio, o.c., p. 47.

ficados realistas de la iconografía barroca del México, Cristos crucificados serenos de Ecuador, Perú o Brasil (El Crucifijo de San Francisco, en Bahía; el Señor de Bon Fim, también en Brasil; Cristos yacentes o caídos, de Colombia (El Señor Caído, de Monserrate, en Bogotà); Santos Niños (además de los tradicionales Santo Niño de Atocha, Niño Jesús de Praga, está el Santuario del Niñope, en Texcoco (México), el Niño Jesús de Curiepe, en el Barlovento venezolano, etc.); Cristo Rey entronizado en tantos hogares; Cristo Señor del Universo, en el Santuario del Cerro del Cubilete, en México, en los Andes o el Cristo de Corcovado, en Río de Janeiro; el Sagrado Corazón de Cristo sufriente y resucitado, en toda la geografía religiosa de América; el Cristo de la Eucaristía, que se ofrece como alimento a los hombres y mujeres en peregrinación hacia la patria definitiva.

Dentro de la religiosidad popular encontramos también **el rostro mariano de Cristo**: donde está el Hijo no puede faltar la Madre. La religiosidad popular de América sabe unir, con certero instinto de fe, con 'sabiduría cristiana', lo divino y lo humano, Cristo y María, espíritu y cuerpo, comunión e institución, persona y comunidad, fe y patria, inteligencia y afecto (Documento de Puebla 448; 913). El rostro de Cristo en América Latina va acompañado o ha ido precedido, por el rostro materno de María. Por esto los obispos la llaman Primera Evangelizadora de América, Estrella de la primera y de la nueva Evangelización. En América, como en Caná de Galilea, María anticipa y apresura la «hora» de Cristo: «Haced lo que él os diga» (Jn 2,5)[22], dice Ella a las multitudes de fieles que acuden a sus santuarios de Guadalupe, de Coromoto, de Chiquinquirá, de Copacabana, de la Asunción, del Carmen o de Luján, de Caacupé, de Bien Aparecida o de Maipú, reconduciéndolas hacia Cristo en una práctica sacramental intensa, sobre todo de la reconciliación y la Eucaristía. En el rostro del Cristo americano se leen al trasluz los rasgos de su Madre, la mujer María de Nazaret.

---

[22] Cfr. *Ecclesia in America* (cf. n. 11).

III. El rostro de Cristo Reconciliador

El título mismo de la Tercera Parte de los *Lineamenta*, de la Segunda Parte del *Instrumentum Laboris* y del Capítulo IV de la *Ecclesia in America* nos da un nuevo trazo del rostro de Cristo que nuestros pastores presentan a América: «*Jesucristo vivo, camino para la conversión*», es decir, **Jesucristo vivo Reconcliador**. Aunque en alguna parte de estos documentos se diga «la conversión a Jesucristo», en realidad, es conversión a Dios en Jesucristo y mediante su sangre derramada en la cruz. En efecto, Dios Padre tuvo a bien «reconciliar por El y para El todas las cosas, pacificando mediante la sangre de su cruz (de Cristo), lo que hay en la tierra y en los cielos» (Col 1,20). «Todo proviene de Dios, que nos reconcilió consigo por Cristo y nos confió el ministerio de reconciliación. Porque en Cristo estaba Dios reconciliando al mundo consigo, no tomando en cuenta las transegresiones de los hombres, sino poniendo en nosotros la palabra de la reconciliación» (2Cor 5,18-19). Podemos, pues, hablar con propiedad de Cristo Reconciliador, que mediante su muerte en la cruz, derribó el muro de separación (Cf. Ef 2,14-18).

Reconciliación ante todo del hombre con Dios mediante el perdón de los pecados, reconciliación del hombre consigo mismo, mediante la conversión y la gracia, *metánoia* o íntima y total transformación y renovación de todo el hombre, de todo su sentir, juzgar y disponer[23]. Reconciliación con los demás, para vivir la plenitud del Evengelio en el mandato nuevo del amor, reconciliación también a nivel social, para hacer frente a las «estructuras de pecado» mediante «estructuras de amor».

Reconciliación, pues, como **don** que viene de Dios, «rico en misericordia» (Ef 2,4), y se ofrece a los hombres en Jesucristo, mediador de perdón y de gracia[24]. Y al hablar de reconciliación, viene la imagen y el icono de Jesucristo, Buen Pastor, que busca la oveja perdida y que da su vida por el rebaño.

---

[23] Pablo VI, Const. Apostólica *Paenitemini*, 17 de febrero de 1966; I: AAS 58 (1966) 179.
[24] *Lineamenta* n. 20; cfr. También Jn 3,16.

De este Cristo Reconciliador la Iglesia se declara continuadora. Por ello, siguiendo el llamado del Santo Padre en preparación para el Gran Jubileo del 2000, los pastores de América invitan al pueblo de Dios a hacer un examen de conciencia tanto individual como social, en ámbito eclesial y civil.

Frente al panorama americano, cuya convivencia social frecuentemente es tensa y crispada – corrupción en la administración pública, diferencias económicas clamorosas de clases sociales dentro de un país o entre país y país, violencia de guerrilla, narcotráfico, violencia urbana –, la Iglesia quiere llevar el anuncio reconciliador de Cristo: presenta la Buena Nueva de un Cristo Reconciliador, invitando a una conversión continua, a un nuevo estilo de vida, a una irradiación de este estilo también en ámbito social, para que desaparezcan los «pecados sociales que claman al cielo», como son entre otros, el comercio de drogas, el lavado de las ganancias ilícitas, la corrupción racial, las desigualdades entre los grupos sociales, la irrazionable destrucción de la naturaleza (*Ecclesia in America*, n. 56).

IV. El rostro de Cristo, creador de comunión

Otro rasgo del perfil total de Cristo que nos proponen los pastores en los Documentos sinodales de América es el de Cristo «*Creador de comunión*» o '*Koinonióphoros*'. Cristo creador de comunión hace de la comunión objeto de su oración filial al Padre inmediatamente después de instituir la Eucaristía y poco antes de ir a la pasión y a la muerte: «*como tú, Padre, estás en mí y yo en ti, que ellos también sean uno en nosotros, para que el mundo crea que tú me has enviado*» (Jn 17, 21-26).

Se trata de una realidad trinitaria: el concepto de comunión se encuentra «en el corazón del autoconocimiento de la Iglesia, en cuanto misterio de la unión personal de cada hombre con la Trinidad divina y con los hombres, iniciada por la fe y orientada a la plenitud escatológica en la Iglesia celeste, aún siendo ya una realidad incoada en la Iglesia sobre la tierra»[25].

---

[25] S.C. para la Doctrina de la Fe, «Carta a los obispos de la Iglesia Católica sobre algunos aspectos de la Iglesia considerada como comunión», 28 de mayo de 1992, 3.

Los Documentos sinodales nos recuerdan algunas imágenes de esa comunión del creyente con la Trinidad por medio de Cristo: son la vid mística y los sarmientos, el cuerpo, su cabeza y sus miembros, el edificio de piedras vivientes y la piedra angular *(Lineamenta* 29; cf. LG 6-7). La comunión trinitaria es la culminación de la obra de reconciliación que Dios realiza por medio del Cristo *Koinonióphoros* o «Comunionificador».

No se puede concebir una realización más completa del propósito y de la misión del Verbo Encarnado: una vez que haya introducido a sus discípulos en el círculo trinitario, viviendo de la misma vida divina, aunque en forma participada, y gozando de la contemplación eterna del Padre y de Hijo en el Espíritu (Jn 17,3), estamos ya en la fase de la eterna bienaventuranza; cuando Cristo haya introducido en el seno de la Trinidad al último discípulo, entonces entregará el reino al Padre y se entregará El mismo al Padre (1Cor 15,24-28).

Esta comunión escatológica con la Trinidad queda incoada en la vita presente de cada discípulo en la historia, por su vida teologal, y por su pertenencia a la comunidad eclesial, que es la comunión o unión de los diversos miembros en un mismo cuerpo y bajo una misma Cabeza, que es Cristo. En efecto, por la gracia santificante que recibimos desde el momento del bautismo, empezamos a vivir la realidad de la comunión de vida y amor con Cristo resucitado, y por medio de El con el Padre, con el Espíritu Santo y con todos los miembros de la Iglesia militante, purgante y triunfante.

Comunión trinitaria que ha de tener su irradiación en la historia personal de cada discípulo, transformando su vida en coherencia con el ejemplo y las enseñanzas del Maestro, sobre todo en las relaciones con su prójimo dentro de la comunidad eclesial y civil. Comunión tan real y concreta que los *Lineamenta* describen los rostros de este Cristo con el cual se encuentran cada día en América:

> Los «rostros que Cristo sufriente y crucificado *tiene, hoy, en América, son los rasgos de los pobres en las inmensas ciudades, de los desempleados, de los migrantes, de los marginados, de los niños no nacidos, de los niños de la calle y de aquellos que quedan sin escuela, de los jóvenes sin trabajo y sin guía, de las mujeres menospreciadas y explo-*

tadas, de los ancianos abandonados, de los enfermos, especialmente de los afectados del Sida, de los indígenas y de los afroamericanos, de loa campesinos y de los habitantes de las barriadas periféricas de las grandes ciudades, en el Norte, en el Centro y en el Sur del Continente» (n. 30).
Y «también son los rasgos de Cristo resucitado, *cuyo Espíritu produce numerosos signos de vida nueva, vencedora del pecado, de la muerte y de las fuerzas del mal»* (Ib. 31).

Entre esos rasgos, los *Lineamenta* enumeran los testimonios de santidad de tantos miembros de la Iglesia, de martirio, de misión y voluntariado, tanto de religiosos cuanto de laicos, el ejemplo de los esposos fieles y los laicos entregados a su tarea de santificar el mundo y de llevar el reino de Dios a la sociedad.

Por eso, los pastores invitan al pueblo de Dios de América – obispos, presbíteros, diáconos, consagrados y consagradas, jóvenes, niños y, sobre todo, a la mujer –[26], a convertirse en operadores de comunión en los diversos sectores y para seguir creciendo en ella como lo desea el Maestro. Prestan atención particular a la comunión con los hermanos de las iglesias separadas o de otras confesiones religiosas no cristianas, con los hermanos judíos, impulsando el diálogo interreligioso y el diálogo con todos los hombres de buena voluntad.

Comunión que también se ha de ir traduciendo en la historia como un ideal y una meta de progresiva integración y unidad entre los pueblos. De hecho, tanto en el nivel cultural, cuanto en el económico y político, la humanidad va caminando lentamente hacia esa integración, reflejo pálido, pero genuino, de la comunión trinitaria última de toda la familia humana: son los grandes bloques políticos, económicos y culturales que se empiezan a formar, como la Comunidad Europea, el Mercosur, el Tratado de Libre Comercio entre Canadá, EE.UU y México, el bloque del Sudeste Asiático.

«Es ya un hecho, dicen los obispos en los Lineamenta, *la unidad que están obrando los medios de comunicación social, los cuales van logrando, poco a poco, hacer de nuestro*

---

[26] Cf. *Ecclesia in America*, nn. 36-48.

planeta una «aldea global». Basta sólo pensar en la «Internet» (como pista de información y comunicación internacional) y en la programación de ciertas actividades a nivel internacional, como el turismo, el deporte, la cultura, la ciencia, la técnica, el comercio, la economía, etc. Estos y otros son signos de una marcha lenta, pero grandiosa e imposible de detener, que contribuye a la unidad de la familia humana. Usando todos los elementos mencionados se promueve la unidad, la Iglesia prepara el encuentro con Cristo. Cuando Él haya reunido en su Cuerpo resucitado a todos sus miembros, entonces entregará el Reino al Padre y Dios será todo en todos (cf. 1 Cor 15,24-28). Esta es una grandiosa tarea y un enorme desafío que tiene la Iglesia en América: trabajar por la comunión mientras se dispone a cruzar el umbral del Tercer Milenio de la era cristiana»[27].

V. El rostro de Cristo solidario

Despúes de recordar los obispos que desde el Antiguo Testamento la fe en Dios Creador del universo es fe en un Dios que se revela como solidario con el hombre en medio de las tribulaciones de la historia (Gen 3,15; Ex 20,1-7), y que recomienda especial atención a los pobres, débiles, huérfanos y viudas (Am 5,7-11; Mi 3,1-4; Ez 18,21), nos presentan el rostro de Cristo solidario al leer «la encarnación del Hijo de Dios como la expresión más grande de la solidaridad del Dios de la Alianza con la humanidad pecadora» (Jn 1,14)[28].

Jesús conserva y afina aún más el imperativo veterotestamentario del amor a Dios y al prójimo: «Y este es su mandamiento: que creamos en el nombre de su Hijo Jesucristo, y que nos amemos unos a otros tal como nos lo mandó. Quien guarda sus mandamientos permanece en Dios y Dios en él; en esto conocemos que permanece en nosotros, por el Espíritu que

---

[27] *Lineamenta* n. 27, También la *Ecclesia in America* dedica una atención particular a los medios de comunicación social como instrumentos de comunión y cultura, n. 70.

[28] *Instrumentum laboris* nn. 50-51.

nos dio» (1Jn 3,23-24; Mt 5,17; Mc 12,28-34; cf. Lev 19,18), encarnándolo en el propio ejemplo de dar la vida por amigos y enemigos (Jn 15,13) y dando al ejercicio de la misericordia hacia los más pequeños relevancia escatológica (Mt 25,31-46).

El continente americano se presenta como un mundo dividido por chocantes contrastes sociales de países superdesarrollados, al Norte, con otros en vías de desarrollo, subdesarrollados o en el extremo de la escala de los países más pobres del mundo; por contrastes entre clases sociales dentro de un mismo país, en el que conviven personas catalogadas por la revista *Forbes* en el elenco de los más grandes millonarios del mundo e inmensas mayorías de personas que viven en pobreza y aun en miseria; por contrastes entre el peso de una deuda externa que es como un par de grilletes en los pies de los países del Sur del continente que impide dar pasos hacia su desarrollo, y los intereses de esa misma deuda que benefician exorbitantemente a los países y sociedades acreedoras del Norte; por los efectos negativos de la globalización cuando es estimulada sólo por el lucro al margen del servicio a las personas y grupos más débiles.

Ante este panorama de contrastes y tensiones, los obispos presentan el rostro de Cristo solidario como testimonio y exigencia para el pueblo cristiano de América. Tal exigencia tiene su traducción y su cauce de actuación en la Doctrina Social de la Iglesia, ese conjunto orgánico de sabiduría operativa en campo social, de criterios evangélicos, de principios de antropología cristiana y de derecho natural o positivo, de reglas objetivas del actuar económico del conocimiento preciso de las circunstancias de cada tiempo y lugar, de cada situación humana por remediar[29].

Lejos de ser un rostro desencarnado de Cristo el que los obispos nos ofrecen, el rostro solidario es el rostro más concreto, más tangible y más humilde (Mt 25,31-46): son los pobres y pequeños, los niños de la calle, las mujeres, los enfermos del Sida, los indígenas despojados de su habitat humano y cultural, los parados, los habitantes de las barriadas periféricas de grandes ciudades, los afroamericaos, los grupos humanos y países subdesarrollados que se debaten en extrema pobreza.

---

[29] Cfr. *Ecclesia in America* n. 54.

Y dentro de la comunidad eclesial, el rostro de Cristo solidario es también el rostro de los pastores que invitan a los laicos, sacerdotes, religiosos, a los matrimonios, a los teólogos, a la comunión. Es el Cristo que invita a los mismos pastores a la cooperación fraterna entre las iglesias particulares del Norte y dal Sur en recursos espirituales, humanos, culturales económicos; es el Cristo solidario que invita a toda la comunidad católica a trabajar por las necesidades, espirituales y materiales, de todo grupo humano, sin importar lengua, raza, religión o posición social, y a recomponer la túnica inconsútil de la unidad de su Cuerpo por medio del diálogo ecuménico, la oración, el amor, la comprensión mutua y, sobre todo, por el testimonio de la santidad.

Conclusión

Recogiendo los diversos «motivos» en una cláusula sinfónica final, podemos decir que el Sínodo de América nos presenta un rostro de Cristo con los rasgos de nuestras culturas americanas. Se pueden reconocer en él los pueblos autóctonos e indígenas de América, los afroamericanos, los pueblos culturalmente «mestizos» que han forjado el Cristo de la religiosidad popular, los criollos y los habitantes de las grandes ciudades, creadores de una cultura moderna y postmoderna.

A unos y otros los obispos presentan un Cristo Viviente y Reconciliador, que nos reconcilia con Dios, con los demás hombres y mujeres, con nosotros mismos y con la creación, un Cristo creador de comunión trinitaria, eclesial y social, un Cristo solidario en un continente atravesado por tensiones y desigualdades, que camina hacia la integración cristiana de corazones hecha justicia, liberación, participación y opción preferenzial por los más pobres y débiles.

Como argumento último de reconciliación, comunión y solidaridad entre todos los pueblos de América, los pastores nos invitan a los cristianos a tomar en serio el misterio de la encarnación del Hijo de Dios y, sobre un horizonte escatológico, nos recuerdan que ese rostro encarnado de Cristo nos sale al encuentro todos los días en los más débiles y pequeños de entre los hombres y mujeres de América, pues *«lo que hicisteis a uno de estos hermanos míos más pequeños, amí me lo hicisteis»* (Mt 25,40-45).

John Paul II's message to the VI FABC Plenary Assembly

In preparing for this meeting with the Pastors of the Church in Asia I have prayed to be an apt instrument of the Holy Spirit who at all times and in every place gives life to the Church and, according to Christ's promise, leads her into all the truth (cf. Jn. 16.13). I have prayed to be able – in the words of the Psalm – to sing "his praise in the assembly of the faithful" (Ps 149:1). It is certainly with a song of praise and thanks-giving to God in my heart that I join you in marking the happy occasion of the *Silver Jublee of the Federation of Asian Bishops Conferences*.

I have been deeply touched by Archbishop Rozario's warm words of welcome and I also wish to thank the other Bishops for their thoughtful remarks on the vital questions of proclamation, life and ecology, which form the subject of your reflections during these days.

The Assemblies of your Federation – of which this is the Sixth – not only provide a forum for exchanging pastoral experiences and discussing issues of common interest. More signficantly, they give expression to the profound *ecclesial communion and affective collegiality* which unite the bishops of South, Southeast and East Asia with one another and with the See of Peter. Together with our brother Bishops throughout the world we feed the one flock which Christ has redeemed with his precious blood *(Cf. 1 Pet 1:19)*. With one accord, therefore, let us give thanks to God for the "bonds of unity, charity and peace" that link us with each other under "the chief Shepherd *(1 Pt. 5:4)*, whose servants we are.

Our meeting is taking place against the background of the *Tenth World Youth Day*, which has just concluded. We are all, witnesses of the generous response of the young to the Church's summons to take up the pilgrim Cross of Christ. In this context, tribute must be given to the Filipino Bishops, who gave close attention to the spiritual preparation of the young people taking part. Yet, in a real sense, it is these young people, and others like them all over the world, who are calling the Church – inviting the Pastors of the Church – to ever greater efforts to present Christ to them in the fullness of his grace and truth. My words therefore are meant to be a fraternal encouragement, exhorting you as Saint Paul exhorted Titus: that as he had already made a beginning, he should also compete the gracious work of his ministry *(Cf. 2 Cor8:6)*. It is your ministry as Bishops, and the situation in which it is exercised, that is the underlying theme of these thoughts, which I share with you.

Since the establishment of your Federation twenty-five years ago, rapid technological progress and economic growth have *revolutionized the face of Asia*. While affirming the benefits of this development, the Church must nevertheless make a realistic assessment of the price paid for this modernization and confront those aspects which pose "an immense threat to life: not only to the life of individuals but also th that of civilization itself" *(Letter to Families, 21)*. Even more striking than Asia's recent material progress has been the *transformation of the spiritual landscape* of the Continent. Religious indifferentism and exaggerated individualism now threaten the traditional values, which, generally speaking, bestowed meaning and harmony on the life of individuals and on the communities they composed. The forces of secularization tend to undermine your rich religious and cultural heritage. *This great Continent is at a spiritual crossroads*.

Such a moment can only confirm the Church's resolve to carry out her *primary mission*: the proclamation of Jesus Christ, and the promotion of the values of God's Kingdom *(cf. Redemptorist Missio, 34)*. And in cooperation with every force for good, Catholics on this continent should feel the urgency of building up "*the civilization of love*, founded on the universal values of peace, solidarity, justice and liberty, which find their full attainment in Christ" *(Tertio Millennio adveniente, 52)*.

Jesus Christ, the God-Man, Crucified and Risen, is the hope of humanity. He is the foundation of our faith, the reason for our hope and the source of our love. The Incarnate Word, the Savior and Mediator between God and man *(cf. I Tim 2:5)*, is "the only one able to reveal God and lead to God" *(Redemptoris Missio, 5)*. And Christ alone can fully reveal the ultimate grandeur and dignity of the human person and his destiny *(cf. Gaudium et Spes, 22)*. The mystery of God's saving love revealed in Jesus Christ is a doctrine of faith, not a theological opinion. *And this Good News impels the Church to evangelize!* It impels Bishops to foster evangelization as a primary task and responsibility of their ministry.

The magna charta of evangelization remains the Apostolic Exhortation *Evangelii Nuntiandi* of Pope Paul VI, with the complement of the Encyclical *Redemptoris Missio*, which I wrote in 1990 in order to deepen and promote the concept of "missionary evangelization" (No. 2), or the mission *Ad Gentes*, which seemed to have lost appeal and even validity in the eyes of some.

Paul VI's notion of evangelization faithfully re-states Christ's tradition, and the insights of the Second Vatican Council. It is a comprehensive notion which avoids the pitfall of over-emphasis on one or another aspect of this complex reality to the detriment of others: In Pope Paul's view, evangelization includes *those activities that dispose peolpe to listen to the Christian message, the proclamation of the message itself, and the catechesis that unfolds the riches of truth and grace* contained in the kerygma. Moreover, evangelization is directed not only to individuals, but also to cultures, which need to be regenerated by contact with the Gospel. Human development and liberation are integral parts of this evangelizing mission, but they are not identical with it, and they are not the end of evangelization. Paul VI was clear about the fact that evangelization cannot be reduced to a merely temporal project of human betterment. It must always include a clear and unambiguous proclamation of Jesus Christ as Lord and Savior, who brings that abundant life" *(Jn 10:10)* that is no less than eternal life in God.

Allow me to make some general remarks about evangelizing this continent. A first requirement of this ecclesial task is *the renewal of the Catholic community at every level* – Bishops, priests, Religious and laity – so that all may contribute to spreading the faith, in which we stand. Our prayer must be that the priests, Religious and laity in your pastoral care will never lose heart in accomplishing the *prophetic mission entrusted to each one*. "Every disciple is personally called by name; no disciple can withhold making a response: "Woe to me if I do not preach the Gospel' *(1 Cor 9:16) (Christi-fideles Laici, 33)*. Indeed, to repeat something I once said to the Italian Bishops, the new evangelization "is not born of the will of those who decide to become propagators of their faith. It is born of the Spirit, who moves the Church to expand" *(Address to Italian Bishops on a Liturgical Course,* 12 February 1988). Everyone who has received the Spirit, every person who is baptized and confirmed, is called to be an evangelizer.

Without forgetting other important components of this renewal, "the signs of the times" urgently call for *"enabling the laity to assume their specific role"* in bringing the truths and values of the Gospel to bear on the realities of the temporal sphere. In fact, when we try to imagine the future of evangelization on this continent, do we not see it as the *irradiation of a vibrant, living faith* practiced and declared by individual Christians and Christian communities, big or small, which, with few exceptions, form a *pusillus rex* in the midst of numerically superior "hearers" of the word?

To "irradiate" the faith implies the highest standards of Christian living – a rich life of prayer and sacramental practice, and moral integrity – on the part of everyone. To proclaim to others "eternal life in Christ Jesus our Lord" *(Rom 6:23)* demands of each member of the Church the holiness and integrity of one for whom "to live is Christ" *(Phil 1:21)*. Proclamation becomes credible when it is accompanied by *sanctity of life*, sincerity of purpose and respect for others and for the whole of creation. The Encyclical *Redemptoris Missio* exhorts the Church's members: "You must be like the first Christians and radiate enthusiasim and courage, in generous devotion to God and neighbour".

In a word, you must set yourselves on the path of holiness. Only thus can you... re-live in your own countries the missionary epic of the early Church" (No. 91).

Herein lies a great challenge that confronts each Bishop, as a principal teacher and guide of the faithful in truth and holiness of life. But here too we have the source of our certain hope and of our optimism. The Church's future will not be *solely* the result of our human efforts, but, more fundamentally, the result of the workings of the Divine Spirit, whom we must not impede but assist.

A further consideration is the cultural framework in which evangelization in Asia has to be carried out. The religious traditions of very ancient cultures remain powerful forces in the East, and present you with particular challenges. The Church esteems these spritual traditions as "living expressions of the soul of vast groups of people. They carry within them the *echo of thousands of years of searchings for God*, a quest which is incomplete but often made with great sincerity and righteousness of heart" *(Evangelii Nuntiandi, 53)*. While the Church rejects nothing of what is true and holy in the great religions *(Nostra Aetate, 2)*, she can only hope that one day this preparation for the Gospel will come to maturity in ways that are fully Christian and fully Asian. As Bishops of the Churches in Asia, part of your concern must be to stimulate the growth of the seeds of truth and goodness found in those religions.

Under your pastoral supervision efforts are being made to increase understanding, respect and cooperation between Christians and followers of other religious traditions, and in many cases, in collaboration with the Pontifical Council for Inter-religious Dialogue, various forms of dialogue are now taking place and bearing fruit. *Inter-religious dialogue* should not remain only a matter of theological discussion. Where possible, it must reach to the grass-roots, correcting misunderstandings that communities have with one another, and fostering solidarity in the building of a more just and human society. This "dialogue of life" must go forward with balance, sincerity and openess *(cf. Redemptoris Missio, 57)*, always in the conviction that authentic dialogue is achieved only by "speaking the truth in love" (Eph 4:15).

Furthermore, as Bishops you have the demanding task of accepting Saint Paul's invitation to become all things to all men" *(1. Cor 9:22)*, identifying yourselves with the life and traditions of your people so that the perennial truth of Revelation can be expressed in ways that are meaningful and convincing. On you rests responsibility for fostering with wisdom and fidelity the most suitable means for communicating the Gospel to the various Asian cultures. The more you take into account the questions, religious formation, language, signs and symbols of those whom you wish to lead to Christ, the more effectively you will serve the cause of evangelization *(cf. Evangelii Nuntiandi, 63)*.

However arduous this task of authentic inculturation, we can take consolation from the experience of the early Church. Although the preaching of Christ Crucified and Risen ran counter to the religious culture of those, to whom the Gospel was first preached, the Holy Spirit guided the Church's growth. Beginning at Pentecost and continuing from generation to generation, the *Spirit of Truth has ever accompanied the Church's proclamation*, leading its hearers to the "obedience of faith" *(Rom 1:6)*, which has then purified and elevated their way of life, imbuing customs and behaviour with a Christian outlook and spirit.

Another recurring aspect of your pastoral activity is *the relationship between proclamation and human developmant*. Briefly, let us acknowledge that no human need, no human suffering can leave Christ's disciples indifferent or insensitive. Yet, the Church does not have and cannot claim to have a "tecnical" solution to all the ills that afflict humanity. Rather the Church herself, like a pilgrim in a foreign land, presses forward amid the difficulties and in the consolations of God *(cf. Lumen Gentium, 8)*. At the same time it is her duty always to seek to make her voice heard in the conscience of individuals and the consciousness of society, defending the dignity of every human person, created in the image and likeness of God, and upholding the principles and values of faith, truth, freedom, justice, and solidarity. She knows that the terrible evils, which affect humanity, have their source not only in man's injustice towards man but in man's radical injustice in the sight of God. In fulfilling her evangelizing mission, therefore, the Church cannot neglect the needs of the poor, the hungry, the defenseless, the oppressed, and the culturally deprived. But those involved in that mission must know that their responsibility goes far beyond healing the wounds of this life. They must also communicate the "new life" that comes through the grace of Jesus Christ. The Church's mission and destiny is to save man, the whole man. At this level there is no distinction of persons, neither Jew nor Greek *(cf. Rm. 10:12)*, neither rich nor poor. All are offered God's word and the grace of redemption, because all are sinners *(cf. Rom 5:12)*.

Dear Brother Bishops, if ever you feel discouraged by the seemingly impossibile task of a more effective evangelization – perhaps due to the fact that some Asian cultures seem disinclined to listen to the Gospel message – I urge you to remember that, when you proclaim "Christ the power of God and the wisdom of God" *(1 Cor 1:24)*, "it is not you who speak, but the Spirit of your Father speaking through you" *(Mt. 10:20)*.

At the same time, you have to make it clear that the act of faith, and reception into the communion of the Church through Baptism, must always be entirely free *(cf. Catechism of the Catholic Church, No. 160)*. *Evangelization must never be imposed.* It involves love and respect for those being evangelized. While ever insisting on the Church's right and duty to proclaim with joy the Good News of God's mercy, Catholics must carefully avoid any suspicion of coercion or devious persuasion *(cf. Dignitatis Humanae, 4)*. On the other hand, accusation of proselytism – which is far from the Church's genuine missionary spirit – and a one-sided understanding of religious pluralism and tolerance should not be allowed to stifle your mission to the peoples of Asia.

Before I end, I wish to appeal to you to do all you can to foster what is generally called the mission *ad gentes*. Despite the fact that some try to minimize this holy duty, the Church cannot renounce her vocation to "make disciples of all nations" *(Mt 28:19)*. She can never be content as a small minority or an inward-looking community. Indeed, the Church firmly believes that every person has "the right to know the riches of the mystery of Christ – riches in which we believe that the whole of humanity can find, in unsuspected fullness, everything that it is gropingly searching for concerning God, man and his destiny, life and death, and truth" *(Evangelii Nuntioandi, 53)*. As the dawn of the Third Millennium draws near, it is "particularly in Asia, towards which the Church's mission *ad gentes* ought to be chiefly directed" *(Redemptoris Missio, 37)*. The mission ad gentes, which often implies the idea of setting out towards new lands and new peoples, today implies above all setting out towards new areas of *Asia's human geo-*

graphy: towards those sectors of society made up of the urban poor, migrants and their often abandoned families, refugees, young people, and the modern areopagus of the media of social communication.

I ask you to pay careful attention to missionary evangelization in all your pastoral planning: in catechesis, preaching, priestly formation, the training of Religious, the apostolate to families and youth, the allocation of personnel, the sharing of resources, and in the prayer, which Christians must always offer for the propagation of the faith. All individuals, associations and communities should ask themselves if there is more that they could do in order to open wide to Christ the doors of Asia.

In these years of preparation for the Great Jubilee of the Year 2000, your particular Churches are fully committed to giving a *fresh impulse to the evangelization of Asia.* Just as in the first millennium the Cross was planted on the soil of Europe, and in the second on that of the Americas and Africa, we can pray that in the Thrid Christian Millennium a *great harvest of faith* will be reaped in this vast and vital Continent. If the Church in Asia is to fulfill its providential destiny, evangelization as the joyful, patient and progressive preaching of the saving Death and Resurrection of Jesus Christ must be your absolute priority.

In your work you are strengthened by the example and intercession of the *great host of Martyrs* who have given life to the Church in Asia through the shedding of their blood. Ablaze with love of Christ and his Church, those great men and women – from China, Japan, Korea, the Philippines, Vietnam and elsewhere – were baptized "with the Holy Spirit and with fire" *(Lk 3:16).* With your missionaries and the saints who have born witness to the Gospel, they became the seed of Christianity in your lands.

In closing, I make my own the memorable words spoken by Pope Paul VI twenty-five years ago here in Manila: "Jesus Christ is our constant preaching; it is his name that we proclaim to the ends of the earth *(cf. Rom 10:18)* and throughout all ages *(Rom 9:5).* Remember this and ponder on it: the Pope has come among you and has proclaimed Jesus Christ" *(Homily,* 29 November 1970).

To you, dear Brothers, this grace has been given in South, Southeast and East Asia: "to preach to the Gentiles the unsearchable riches of Christ" *(Eph 3:8)*. I entrust you, your pastoral endeavours and all your people to Mary, Mother of the Redeemer and Star of the New Evangelization, and I gladly impart my Apostolic Blessing.

* * *

The issues of Proclamation, Life and Ecology were presented to the Holy Father as the immediate concerns of the FABC

PROCLAMATION

Holy Father:

Asia has changed radically since the Manila visit twenty-five years ago of your predecessor of holy memory, Paul VI, an event which also occasioned the birth of the Federation of Asian Bishops' Conferences – the FABC. In the sixties, Asia was a sleeping economic giant whose people's daily life was bounded by the slow rhythm of villeage culture and ancient traditions.

Today, in the nineties, Asia is the growth center of the world. Technology has captured the Asian soul, transforming peasants into slum dwellers and migrant workers alienated from their cultural and spiritual roots. The economic impulse has introduced into Asian societies what your Holiness has termed "economic, financial and social mechanisms" that accentuate the situation of wealth for some and poverty for the rest[1].

We who stand at the threshold of the Third Millennium must ask ourselves how to proclaim the Gospel in the face of a new world economic order that has replaced orbis christianus

---

[1] Soilicitudo Rei Socialis, no. 16.

with a technocratic society. It is a technical civilization that unleashes new forms of poverty and slavery -a poverty which corrupts the human spirit in a degradation worse than material poverty. It is a slavery which chains man to unbridled passions that threaten to destroy families and cultures. Indeed, Asia has awakened but its journey towards growth can lead to a highway of despair if it is not at the same time also a spiritual advance.

True, Asia is home to ancient religions, the "living faiths of mankind"[2], which also reflect the divine light of the hidden Christ in our midst. But historical reality leads us to recognize the limits of their spiritual capacities to heal the schisms in the soul of Asia and to satisfy the deeper yearnings of its peoples.

This then is a picture of the Asian Areopagus. Like the Apostle, we must proclaim the Unknown God[3] to peoples who worship the gold and silver of untrammeled material progress. To a generation possessed by the spirits of consumerism and secularism, we must proclaim with clarity "Jesus, the God-Man, crucified and risen"[4] as humanity's hope.

The FABC has tried to meet this challenge of a New Evangelization by trying to understand who Jesus is in the Asian context[5]. Who is this Christ whose death can ignite the hearts of Asia's martyrs in Vietnam, Korea, Japan, China, the Philippines and India? Who is this Son of God whose words can inspire an increasing number of Asian-born missionaries and religious to give him undying fidelity? Who is this Jesus whose personality is so attractive to Asia's youth in search of a model on whom to pattern their lives?

Our search for an answer to this question brought us to encounter the Lord in His poor. Like the Baptist, we were directed to find the Christ among the rejects of society, the despised misfits of a technocratic order. And once again we

---

[2] Toward a New Age in Mission. International Congress on Mission, Manila, 2-7 December 1979, Vol. I-II, p. 35.
[3] Acts 17:23-28.
[4] Inauguration of African Synod, Pope John Paul II, no. 5.
[5] Journeying with the Spirit into Fuller Life. FABC, April 1994, no. 25.

hear the mandate of the Master to proclaim the Good News to the poor[6].

But proclamation will not produce commitment and renewal unless accompanied by prophetic witnessing. The evangelizer's own life must give splendid testimony to the moral truth and value of his message. The ancient sages and spiritual guides of Asia were renowned for their practice of detachment and asceticism. Shall we, children of God's light, instead be like reeds swaying in the breeze leading undisciplined and luxurious lives?

As you stated in your homily two tears ago in Denver, the gospel must be proclaimed through the power of one's witness[7]. And the strength of that witness depends on the knowledge and love of Jesus Christ – this is the same Lord, whom we have heard, whom we have seen, whom we have touched in the midst of his chosen poor. Thus it is in Christ's total giving of Himself for suffering mankind that our discipleship finds its meaning and mission.

Holy Father, because of your arduous apostolic journeys and because of your personal sufferings, which served to unite you more closely with the mystery of Christ's cross and with suffering humanity – you have become our principal evangelizer. Your words and your life help us to understand the mentality and attitude of modern Asia and how to illuminate our people with the clear and vigorous proclamation that the Lord Jesus Christ is our saviour and the answer to Asia's search for unity and meaning.

LIFE

One of the hallmarks of Christian civilization is respect for life: human life – this is the second pressing concern of the FABC. The student of history will agree that the presence of

---

[6] Luke 7:22-23.
[7] Mass with Youth Forum Delegates, Denver, 14 August 1993.

the Church in Asia ushered into its cultures the life-giving values of compassion, self-sacrifice and loving mercy. The proclamation of the Good News in its frontiers by courageous missionaries opened a new chapter in Asia's history which untill then the only knew ancient creeds with their tendency towards self-centered and passive religiosity. With Christianity came hospitals and orphanages, colleges and schools for the poor, congregations of religious men and women dedicated to charity. They served not only to heal broken bodies, but to give Asians a new vision of values and practices leading to "a civilization of love"[8] and life.

Yet we can ask today: "Is Asia home to cultures of life based on love?" For, as Asia surges forward towards industrialization, there are increasing signs of practices hostile to life. These the FABC enumerated in its Fifth Plenary Assembly[9] as: militarization, exploitative tourism, discrimination against women, unjust treatment of migrant workers, and the continuing pervasive poverty.

Living in Asia, we have also become aware that as the use of the instruments of violence declines in international affairs, it gains greater appeal at the national level. This is confirmed by the media's glorification of violence, by the alliance of criminality and politics, by the promotion of abortion in the name of selfish prosperity. Our streets have become zones of danger, our children are brutally abused and, while the value of our properties increases, that of human life is diminished.

But our study should not stop with statistics no matter how startling they are. We should study the causes of the phenomena we experience in accordance with the proverb of your country: "Do not punish a blind sword, but rather the hand"[10]. Both in your interview in La Stampa and in your homily inaugurating the Synod for Africa, your holiness has pointed out that the cause for the serious social and human

---

[8] Prayer for Archdiocese of Denver, 14 August 1993.
[9] Held in Bandung, Indonesia, 27 Luly 1990 under the theme: "Journeying Together Toward the Third Millennium".
[10] By the polish poet, Mickiewics which the Pope quoted in his "La Stampa" interview, L'Osservatore Romano, 17 November 1993, 6/7.

problems facing the world today is the anti-life culture of unbridled capitalism[11].

This then is the Leviathan against which we must struggle. In its degenerate form this economic system readily sacrifices the human spirit at the altar of efficiency and progress. Its ensemble of technical and psychological instruments can reach every town and village in Asia, changing behaviors, poisoning imaginations, controlling relationships, thereby creating a new culture, where death rather than life triumphs – not death merely in its grosser forms of murder and assassination, but a death which drains the human spirit of its nobility and destiny. It is a death daily experienced by street children in our poluted environment. It is a white death endured by Asia's poor who are forced to adopt "practices hostile to life" in favor of economic systems "which serve the selfishness of the rich"[12].

The struggle for Asia's soul is between two cultures – one that brings in its wake, death; and the other, life. We must therefore be involved in a cultural transformation. This is brought about by inserting gospel values to guide the criteria by which Asians make decisions, to reorient the educational systems which influence their children's minds, and to humanize the processes by which they are governed. In this struggle, our faith assures us that ultimate victory belongs to those who defend life and who act in the service of life. He who said: "I came that they may have life, and have it more abundantly" (Jn.10:10) will not be denied the full realization of His prayer to the Father. It is the proclamation of Jesus Christ as the Way, the Truth, and the Life that is our best response to the culture of death that has surfaced in the Asian continent.

Holy Father, in this perilous journey towards life, we have in you a compassionate and understanding brother-pilgrim. You understand us for you yourself come from a country which fought hard for its freedom, a country subjected to the influence and aggression of its neighbors. It is no wonder that your heart spontaneously reaches out to side with the

---

[11] L'Osservatore Romano, 17 November 1993, 6/7.
[12] Homily inaugurating the Synod for Africa, Pope John Paul II, number 3.

poor, the defenseless, the marginalized. We make our own prayer of thanksgiving:

"Thank you, Lord Jesus Christ, for life... Thank you, thank you for the life you gave us and that you are giving us, and you are permitting us. Thank you through your Mother, our Lady... Amen"[13].

Ecology

Holy Father:

Our third concern is for ecology. The thread that unites this concern with the first two, namely, proclamation and human life – is the theme of God's gift of life: supernatural life as proclaimed by the Church, human life given us by the Creator, and now, planetary life linked to the integrity of creation. Placing these three concerns under one unifying theme is in itself an indication of our new awareness of their essential interrelationship. We have come to realize that the achievements of the human community must be used to heal and nourish the earth rather than to denude or destroy it.

Asia was once a vast biological treasure house whose environmental riches have been subjected to massive levels of destruction. For example, in our host country, the Philippines, there used to be 17 million hectares of rain forests. Today there remain only 984.000 hectares or the equivalent of only 5 years of wood supply[14]. The extent of the ecological damage all over Asia was outlined by a 1993 FABC Colloquium on Faith and Science. Its participants noted what they termed "serious distortion of the cycles in the entire ecosystem"[15] namely: deforestation, depletion of nonrenewable energy resources, destruction of coral reefs, contamination of food by pesticides, and loss of fertile land through excessive use of chemical fertilizers.

---

[13] Final Homily to Youth, Denver, 15 Autust 1993.
[14] Business World, 26 december 1990.
[15] "Root Causes of the Environmental Crisis" FABC Colloquium, January 31 – February 5, 1993, Tagaytay City, Philippines.

The Chruch in Asia has come to the defense of our beautiful but fragile planet from whose seasonal changes our liturgy draws some of its insights on birth and death, on decline and regeneration. Some of these initiatives are the following: early in 1988, the Catholic Bishops Conference of the Philippines issued a pastoral letter on ecology under the title:

> "What is Happening to Our Beautiful Land?" In 1989, the Indonesia Bishops" Conference issued its own pastoral letter entitled: "Promotion of Underprivileged Development: to Respect and to Develop Environment". And in 1993, the Office of Education and Student Chaplaincies of the FABC organized a Colloquium which called for replacing the concept of humanity as "master of the universe" with the "concept of stewardship".

The Church is not alone in this concern. The Eastern religions have made contributions to increasing man's awareness of his harmony and unity with nature. Ecumenical groups have formed solidarity movemens between industrialized Japan and its neighobors to promote environmental protection. But in this vital issue, we might once more run the danger of seeing only symptoms rather than of searching for their root causes – we might then be punishing the sword and not the hand. The problems of the environment will not be solved merely by funding campaigns to save the ozone layer, or to use environmentally friendly products instead of plastics. We need a serious moral shift in favor on an integral rather than a fragmented approach.

Towards this end, we found guidance in the 1990 World Day of Peace Message of your Holiness. This message, entitled "Peace with God the Creator, Peace with All Creation" clearly situated the ecological crisis as a moral problem. We quote: "When man turns his back on the Creator's plan, he provokes a disorder which has inevitable repercussions on the rest of created order" (n. 5).

Among these disorders are the immoral application of disrespect for life, that promotes the reckless exploitation of natural resources as well as the more than 3,000 persons in Bhopal, India, who died 11 years ago in an industrial accident that could have been prevented.

What moral responses can we give to the actuations of a Leviathan guided not by moral principles but by blind technological factors? Here, your Message gives us a formula to follow. It cautions us against repeating the errors made in the past by the industrialized economies. It urges us to address the structural forms of poverty. It inspires us to adopt a more simple, moderate and disciplined way of life.

In the face of a culture of profligacy and destruction, we must with courage and faith put forward a counter-culture of sacrifice and compassion. In conclusion, Holy Father, we thank you for your fraternal patience and solicitude in listening to our contemporary concerns. Your journey has not only traversed the many miles from Rome to Manila, it has routed you deeply into the centers of the Church in Asia whom you have illumined with the radiance of your faith and love. Beloved pilgrim, our foremost evangelizer whom Christ chose to bring His Church to the next millennium – from the hearts of all Asia – thank you!

* * *

CHRISTIAN DISCIPLESHIP IN ASIA TODAY: SERVICE TO LIFE (FINAL STATEMENT OF THE SIXTH FABC PLENARY ASSEMBLY JANUARY 10-19, 1995 MANILA, PHILIPPINES)

INTRODUCTION

1. To our God of love and life, Father, Son and Holy Spirit, we give praise and thanks!

In the same city of Manila, where 25 years ago in the inspiring presence of the Pope Paul VI, the dream of actualizing the communion of Asian Churches began, we, the bishop-delegates of twenty-one countries and territories, gather in Manila for the Sixth Plenary Assembly of the Federation of Asian Bishops' Conferences. We are deeply blessed by the active participation in our Assembly of a numer of dedicated lay persons, priests, religious and brothers[16].

---

[16] We note with pain the absence of delegates from some countries. We hope for the day when conditions would allow them to celebrate with our ecclesial communion in a fuller way.

On this occasion a singular grace for us is likewise the moving presence of Pope John Paul II. With him we not only celebrate the 25th anniversary of the resolution to form a structure that would later become the FABC, but also the 25th year of Radio Veritas Asia, the 400th year of the Archdiocese of Manila and its 3 historic suffragans: CEBU; CACERES and Nueva Segovia, and especially the 10th World Youth Day. Indeed these festivities are peak moments of God's grace to the Church in Asia, in communion with one another and with the Holy Father – at the service of life.

2. Remembering with gratitude the beginnings of FABC, we are impressed by the vigor of the creative energies that gave it birth and life. We also recognize that the history of FABC is but a short chapter in the continuing saga of the Asian Churches solicitude for life, whose individual and collective stories are about promises already realized, if yet waiting to be fulfilled.

This remembrance of blessings past is both comfort and strength. For we realize that the spring from which FABC draws its vigor is the God who has blessed us in Jesus Christ with every spritual blessing (Eph 1:3). We thank our God in our remembrance (Phil 1:3).

A. 25 YEARS OF FABC COMMITMENT TO LIFE

3. Through its past five plenary assemblies, FABC tried to discern the current "life-context" of the Asian pastoral situations that inevitably consist of death-dealing as well as life-serving realities. The initial bishops meeting in Manila in 1970 already indicated the expectations of Asians for "a better and fuller life for themselves and their children" (ABM, 10). For this reason, the Church in Asia must foster a threefold dialogue: with the many different faiths of Asia, with the cultures of Asia, and with the poor multitudes of Asia. We believe that fullness of life can be realized "only in and through Christ and his Gospel, and by the outpouring of the Holy Spirit" (FABC I, 1974).

For the Church and its mission in Asia, whose peoples are characterized by traditions of deep religiosity, prayer has to be "the river of life". Prayer is absolutely indispensable if the Christ-life is to dwell within Christian participation in life-giving liberation and development (FABC II, 1978). This inner life of prayer builds the Church into a credible community of faith, rooted in the life of the Trinity and turned resolutely toward the construction of a fully human future for Asian peoples (FABC II, 1982).

This is why the laity must act as an evangelizing and liberating force in the struggle for fullness of life (FABC IV, 1986). Our unique contribution is our vision of Jesus Christ, and our Christian spirituality manifested through dialogue, discernment and deeds. As Church, we need to walk in compassion and humility, in accompaniment with all the people's of Asia "as they pray, work, struggle and suffer for a better human life, (in their) search for the meaning of human life and progress" (FABC V, 1990).

Through the years FABC has addressed various concerns that promote social, economic, religious and ecclesial life. Such concerns are: the promotion of justice and integral development particularly in relation to women, migrant workers and indigenous peoples; the building of basic ecclesial communities and basic human communities; the promotion of interreligious dialogue, especially the dialoge of life; leadership formation and specialized formation of priest-formators, youth chaplains, bishops and lay leaders; the conscientization and organization of basic sectors of society; and a more effective use of media for evengelzation.

The overall thrust of activities in recent years had been to motivate the Churches of Asia towards "a new way of being Church", a Church that is committed to becoming "a community of communities" and a credible sign of salvation and liberation.

4. Yet on this the 25th anniversary of FABC we have to confess humbly that the goal of conscientizing the local Churches and building a communion of our Asian Churches is still far from being reached, despite the truly remarkable advances already made in this regard.

We are glad to recall, even if only briefly, the extraordinarily rich story of FABC. It is the story of a listener attentive to the perils of life, to the visions of life, to celebratory songs of life and who wants to share his singular wealth, which is the memory of the person named Jesus, who is for us the Way the Truth and the Life.

5. The theme for this Sixth Plenary Assembly of FABC is most fitting. We take as our theme "Christian Discipleship in Asia Today: Service to Life," in order that we may recommit ourselves to the promotion of life in Asia.

B. A VISION OF LIFE AMID ASIAN REALITIES

6. "Life Vibrant life pulsating from the fecundity of Asia" (FABC International Theological Colloquium, 1994). How do the disciples of Jesus in Asia view this life that is welling up from the depths of Asian peoples, their histories, their habitats and their cultures? What service can the disciples of Jesus in Asia offer to affirm, enhance, defend, and promote this life?

Our response begins with a rapid scan of Asian realities, not so much to repeat the already substantive analyses that previous FABC assemblies and a great number of FABC seminars and workshops have done, as simply to situate more clearly the struggle of Asia for life.

7. We turned our attention to whatever threatens, weakens, diminishes and destroys the life of individuals, groups or peoples; whatever devalues human beings as conceived, born, infant, old; whatever socio-cultural, religious, political, economic, or environmental factors that threaten or destroy life in our countries. We identified some of these forces of death at work in Asia. And we concluded that as promoters of life, we could only denounce them.

We were alarmed at how the global economy is ruled by market forces to the detriment of people's real needs. We considered the insecurity and vulnerability of migrants, refugees, the displaced ethnic and indigenous peoples, and the pain and agonies of exploited workers, especially child laborers in our countries.

We became more aware of the forces of death depriving women and girls of their dignity, freedom, personhood, and fuller humanity. We realized how the same forces undermine the family, the basic cell of society and the Church, through liberalist, anti-life, anti-child, anti-woman, anti-family policies and values and pose many threats to wholeness of life in the area of health care, especially of the poor.

We recognized the growing violence, terrorism, conflicts and nuclear proliferation fueled by the arms trade and greed for profit, all of which violate people's rights. They threaten participative democracy, humane governance and a just and peaceful society. We also noted with pain that our sisters and brothers in some countries are still denied their right to religious freedom.

In the area of religious pluralism, we reflected on the growing fundamentalist extremism and fanaticism discriminating and excluding people who belong to other religious traditions, thus destroying the harmony of people's lives and their solidarity already witnessed to in a dialogue of life.

As we reflect on these negative areas, we could not ignore the immense damage to the ecosystem of our planet which offends justice and the rights of people.

We say "no" to these death-dealing forces.

8. In this scenario of shadows, we were also encouraged by areas of light. We became aware of the many signs of hope in the histories and cultures of our peoples, as seen in peoples'- movements and the initiatives of groups, peoples, and the Churches in Asia for the service of life. We identified with great joy these expressions of life powerfully at work in Asia. We resolved to affirm them, encourage them, celebrate them, and unite our efforts to them.

Noteworthy among them are the growing consciousness regarding human dignity and empowerment of the poor, the growing voices of groups and peoples for humanized development, and the cries of marginalized groups for participatory and democratic governance.

We dwelt also on the movements for the protection of the environment and ecosystem linked to justice, and the solidarity of committed groups and peoples in the struggle for the rights of women, children, especially young girls, and those of indigenous peoples. Truly remarkable is the increasing number of young people moving towards solidarity and community, and seeking a deeper spirituality. We were consoled by efforts of many groups to foster dialogue with people from other faiths. We did not miss the value of mass media for the promotion of values and support of peoples' movements and rights.

To these life-giving forces, we give a reounding "yes".

9. From the dynamic forces at work in Asian realities a basic vision of life emerges. In the living heritage of cultures and religious traditions of Asia we discern values and their expressions in symbols, stories and art forms, that embody a vision of life; while we are critically aware of the distortions that have entered into these traditions. In these cultural and religious traditions we also discover the responses to life given by past generations of Asian peoples, which in turn become resources for our contemporary response.

We Asians are searching not simply for the meaning of life but for life itself. We are striving and struggling for life because it is a task and a challenge. But life is a gift too, a mystery, because our efforts to achieve it fall far too short of the ultimate value of life. We speak of life as a *becoming* – a growing into, a journeying to life and to the source of life.

10. So what might this vision be?

In the rich diversity of ancient Asian cultures and faiths there is a vision of *unity in diversity, a communion of life* among diverse peoples. In this context we seek to become persons of dialogue.

Ours is a vision of *holistic life*, life that is achieved and entrusted to every person and every community of persons, regardless of gender, creed or culture, class or color. It is the fruit of integral development, the authentic development of the whole person and of every person.

We envision a life *with integrity and dignity, a life of compassion* for the multitudes, especially for the poor and the needy. It is a life of *solidarity* with every form of life and of *sensitive care* for all the earth. It is thus a life that unites us Asians among ourselves and with the whole of creation into one community life.

Fo us to live is to live with integrity and dignity, in peace and justice, in freedom and participation, in mutuality and complementarity. It is to live in simplicity and friendship.

At the heart of our vision of life is the Asian *reverential sense of mystery and of the sacred*, a spirituality that regards life as sacred and discovers the Transcendent and its gifts even in mundane affairs, in tragedy or victory, in brokenness or wholeness. This deep interiority draws people to experience *harmony and inner peace* and infuses ethics into all of creation.

11. Such is a broad sketch of an Asian vision of life. With the eyes of the heart, with our faith, we need to understand it as the work of the creative Spirit of the God of Life, who in all things and among every people is healing, renewing, and recreating in ever new, ever mysterious ways.

What can we, and how can we, as disciples of Jesus, contribute to the shaping and achieving of such a vision of life in Asia, with our Asian peoples and for Asian peoples? How can the Churches of Asia participate, as Churches and as Asian, in the common global search for life? What does Christian discipleship in Asia mean, if it is to truly serve life?

Our response leads us to Jesus, the Life that we are following and that we share with others.

C. Life in the Footsteps of Jesus

12. All life is related to the active presence of the Creator Spirit. No wonder Jesus, confessed as Messah and Lord, is Spirit-filled. He who is the Life is dependent on the Spirit. Conceived in the virgin's womb by the Spirit's power (Lk 1:35, Mt 1:20), anointed by the Spirit at his baptism in the Jordan (Mk 1:10), driven into the wilderness by the Spirit to be prepared for his mission (mt 4:1), sent to preach the good news of salvation by the Spirit's action (Lk 4:18-19), Jesus ushers in the new creation, the fullness of life in God. As the Risen One, he

breathes the Holy Spirit on his disciples (Jn 20:22f), making them partakers of his life and mission.

What vision of life emerges from the Spirit-filled Jesus?

13. JESUS AND THE KINGDOM OF THE GOD OF LIFE, "I came that they may have life, and have it abundantly" (Jn 10:10). With these simple words, Jesus describes his mission. But it is also depicted as the mission of announcing and inaugurating the Kingdom of God (Mk 1:15), the hope of subjugated Israel for the fullness of life in God. Jesus teaches what life in the Kingdom consists in.

13.1 *Communion with Abba*: Jesus identifies the ultimate source of life, the God whom he intimately calls Abba. In Abba Jesus finds his whole life. "I am in the Father and the Father in me" (Jn 14:11). In Abba he finds the resting place of his life's journey. "Father, into your hands I commend my spirit" (Lk 23:46). Who Jesus is, what he does, where he ends up, are all found in a passion for communion with Abba.

13.2. *Liberating and Recreative Communion among Neighbors*. In compassionate love, Jesus makes his own the struggles and aspirations of Israel for life. Assuming their humanity, he incarnates Abba's life-giving actions of old: creation of all the living out of sheer love, liberation of the chosen people from the bondage of Egypt, mutual belonging within the covenant. Like Abba, Jesus brings life through a new creation, a radical liberation and a renewed communion.

At his word, demons flee, sinners are liberated. At his touch, the sick are healed. He frees the victims of society from the evil and sin that shackle them. He restores them to communion. He breaks down barriers set up by greed, pride, discrimination, lopsided social norms and even religious distortions. Outcasts become sisters and brother. Sinners are worthy of compassion. The hungry, the thirsty, the prisoners, the naked bear the divine presence. And God is our Father. In the freedom and communion that Jesus offers, a new creation dawns. The human community is reborn. Indeed the time of fulfillment has come. Life in abundance is in our midst. The Kingdom is here (Lk 17:21).

13.3. *Death for the Life of the Many*. In his passion for life, Jesus courageously confronts death. But like all defenders of life, He catches the wrath of the "friends of death" and suffers humiliating death. In the meal he shares with his friends before being crucified, he portrays his death as an act of self-giving for the life of others: "my body is given for you" (Lk 22:19), "my blood is to be poured out for the many" (Mk 14:24). And he commands his disciples to remember this supreme act of love. On the cross, Jesus unites himself with every person seeking life. On the cross, life is poured out from the love and strength that dare to be weak for Abba and neighbors. On the cross, Jesus wins life by offering his own life in death.

13.4. *The Risen One Conquers Death*. Jesus' rising from the dead tells the whole of humanity and creation that God is the Master of life. In the resurrection of Jesus, death has been stripped of its definitive role in shaping history. History belongs to life! God offers hope to the whole world and its teeming millions searching and struggling for life through the Risen One, Word of Life, and the Author of Life.

13.5. *The Gift of the Spirit of Life*. Jesus promises and gives the Spirit, "the Lord, the Giver of Life". The Spirit that enabled Jesus to be the life-giving Messiah, will enable the community of disciples to remember him, to follow him, and to participate in his life. The followers of Christ, individually and corporately, are to be comforted and rejuvenated in their following of Jesus by the Spirit of Life.

This image of Jesus – man of the creative Spirit, friend of God, person of interiority, bringer of harmony, lover of the poor, healer and liberator, bold prophet, suffering companion, victor over death, and sharer of his Spirit – resonates with the Asian peoples' vision of life.

14. DISCIPLESHIP IN THE SPIRIT OF LIFE. It is the Spirit of Jesus that creates the community of disciples. And it is in the power of the Spirit that we believe in him (1 Jn 4:2f), remember him (Jn 14:26), communicate with him (Acts 8:39) and live by him (2 Cor 12:13). Discipleship is living by the

Spirit of the Risen Lord and by the demands of the Kingdom of Life. The peoples of Asia will be drawn to Jesus if his disciples abide in his life (Jn 15:4).

14.1. *"Solidarity" with God.* As Jesus immersed himself in the depths of Abba's life and love, so the community of disciple has to immerse itself totally in the life of the Triune God and live by communion, so that it might more credibly share the love and life of God with others and more effectively bring the forces of God's Kingdom of Life to bear on the death-dealing realities of Asia.

In order to be in solidarity with God, prayer is indispensable. Prayer expresses our inner spirit and impels us towards ever deeper communion and intimacy with God. This communion is at the core of life-giving spirituality. In Jesus' own example, mission and service draw their energy and power, their very life, from solidarity with Abba and lead back to this solidarity. If the disciples of Christ are steeped in prayerful encounter with, and in the service of, Abba, they will strike a chord in the heart of Asia where traditions of spirituality and prayer abound.

14.2 *Liberating and Recreative Communion Among Neighbors*: Like Jesus, we have to "pitch our tents" in the midst of all humanity building a better world, but especially among the suffering and the poor, the marginalized and the downtrodden of Asia. In profound "solidarity with suffering humanity" and led by the Spirit of life, we need to immerse ourselves in Asia's cultures of poverty and deprivation, from whose depths the aspirations for love and life are most poignant and compelling. Serving life demands communion with every woman and man seeking life and struggling for it, in the way of Jesus' solidarity with humanity.

Our solidarity requires a resolve to work with our Asian sisters and brothers in liberating our societies from whatever oppresses and degrades human life and creation, most especially from sin. We offer radical freedom of life in Christ. In a special way, we will follow Jesus in his "preferential journey" with the poor and will assist in the liberation of the materially poor, indigenous peoples, displaced persons, victims of misguided economic and political development, victims of wars and divisions, and victims of sex tourism. We will more actively assist in the integral development of women, children and the youth, who cry out for liberation from many dehumanizing and oppressive situations and for their rightful place in society and in the Church's mission to serve life.

With our Asian sisters and brothers, we will strive to foster communion among Asian peoples who are threatened by glaring economic, social and political imbalances. With them we will explore ways of utilizing the gifts of our diverse religions, cultures and languages to achieve a richer and deeper Asian unity. We will build bridges of solidarity and reconciliation with peoples of other faiths and will join hands with everyone in Asia in forming a true community of creation.

14.3. *Dying for the Many.* Immersion in Asia's cultures of poverty is a dying to ourselves so that we may live for God and for others. It is a dimension of the spirituality that stems from Jesus himself for whom the giving of life to others happens in the giving of the very self. That is why the love of the Father, Son and Spirit, the self-giving of God to all humanity, especially on behalf of the poor, is at the heart of all genuine service to life.

It is this love that impels us as the disciple-community of Jesus to confront and act against death-dealing realities, oppression and injustice, discrimination and exploitation, the destruction of the ecosystem, and the tampering with life. As disciples we cannot serve both life and death! Just as Jesus worked as a prophet of new life and died to usher it in, so we in Asia today must prophesy on behalf of the God of life. Refusal to prophesy and speak against the forces of death is to fail in serving life!

We may hesitate because we are minority group. Indeed we are a little flock in Asia. But it is from this position of weakness that God's gift of divine life in Jesus Crucified, the power and wisdom of God, is most significant. Triumphalism and displays of pomp and human power do not witness to the abnegation of Jesus on the Cross. It is often from our weakness that God's love as life-giving grace is more clearly made manifest.

We memorialize Jesus' total self-gift around the Eucharistic table. We partake of the very life of Jesus, the Bread of Life broken and shared. We drink of the Cup of the new covenant with God. We join Jesus in serving life by washing the feet of our neighbors. We celebrate the new creation when simple fruits of the earth and work of human hands become the presence of Jesus in our midst. We look to that promised banquet where all will sit as brothers and sisters around the Good of Life.

14.4. *Living in the Risen One*. Faith in the Risen One demands that his disciples in Asia be symbols of hope. Because Jesus is risen, we realize that the promise of life is not empty. Our common search will not end in senselessness, but in life. The resurrected life, proclaimed in word, deeds, presence, community and service by the disciples of Christ, can help assure Asians that in the various arenas of death, life still pulsates and flows; life is a promise that is being realized and will be fulfilled in Jesus and His Spirit.

14.5. *Walking by the Spirit of Life*. The gift of the life-giving Spirit makes men and women disciples of Jesus. "Living by the Spirit, walking by the Spirit", (Gal 5:25) is concretely seen in a life marked by the fruits of the Spirit: "love, joy, peace, patience, kindness, goodness, faithfulness, gentleness, self-control" (Gal 5:22f). These values, which are opposed to the "fruits of the flesh", need to be infused into the Church's lifestyle, policies, programs and communal life.

The Spirit is the powerful breath animating the mission of the disciples of Christ. Whether in explicit proclamation of the Gospel or in the silence of prayer, whether in the warmth of personal contact or the burden of liberative action, the Spirit of life guides, sanctifies and unifies the disciple-community for the world and humanity. The deepest communication of the Church to Asia is its Spirit-filled and multiform mission of sharing Christ as the Way, the Truth and the Life.

14.6. Our reflection on discipleship cannot be complete without invoking Mary, the woman who gave Jesus to the world. She who is the Mother of Life is also the foremost disciple of Life. Her example teaches us that discipleship involves attentive listening to the word of God and the freedom to respond to it (Lk 1:26-38) She regards herself a servant in solidarity with her people Israel, celebrating God's mercy for the lowly and the hungry (Lk 1:46-55). She courageously suffers with her Son at the foot of the cross and from that wood of life becomes the mother of us all (Jn 19:25-7). With the early disciple-community, she prays, awaiting the promised Spirit of Life (Acts 1:12-14). Now with her Son in glory, she enlivens the hope of all for eternal life. In Mary we find not only a mother but also a model and companion in our pilgrimage to life.

14.7. In the final analysis of the question that we have asked about our Christian contribution to the struggle for full life in Asia, our answer is brief, but profoundly committed. Our answer is Jesus and his Gospel of Life. Our answer is the sharing of Abba's liberating and reconciling life and love with others. Our answer is authentic discipleship in the creative Spirit of Jesus, the Spirit of Life.

15. MAJOR PASTORAL AREAS OF DISCIPLESHIP. The above reflection on a theological-pastoral basis of discipleship leads us to its concrete implications for our pastoral mission. Many, indeed, are our pastoral concerns: dialogue with peoples of other faiths, dialogue with the poor, dialogue with the cultures of Asia; justice and integral development mediated by the social teachings of the Church, formation and education, the apostolate of the media and the arts. We have deliberated on all these very important and interconnected concerns. The results will be pubblished.

But in the light of our faith-reflection, we believe that five concerns require special pastoral focus.

15.1. *The Asian family* is a microcosm of Asian society. It is bombarded on all sides by anti-family forces of dehumanization and disintegration, ranging from material and moral poverty to secularistic values, and external pressures leading to anti-life types of bioethics and practices of abortion and contraception. Children, as in many other areas of life, become the unwilling and innocent victims. Young girls and boys are also exploited through illegal labor practices and sex tourism. Discipleship in Asia then has to denounce such anti-life and anti-family pressures, policies, and practices and foster bioethics that is in accord with God's law and the Church's teachings in order to promote the family as a "sanctuary of life" and a school of life.

15.2. The complex issue of *women and young girls* in Asia has to be one of the major concerns. Already our Fourth Plenary Assembly, in Tokyo, 1986, raised the issue to the level of the whole Asian Church. We cannot effectively promote our Christian vision of full life unless the Church as a communion of communities will credibly expend its moral and spiritual energies towards the conversion of mentalities, the transformation of structures, and the eradication of practices that deny women and young girls in Asia their God-given dignity. An urgent pastoral imperative is for women to exercise their right to coresponsibility and mutuality with men – in society and in the Church.

15.3. On the occasion of the 10th World Youth Day, the Church likewise confronts the reality of Asia as the continent of *youth*. As in other FABC forums, we stand in solidarity with their struggles for authentic life. We share their concern and alarm in the face of misguided polcies and structures that are already laying the foundations of their future. We wonder with them if the earth will still be preserved for them and their children at the rate it is being misused now. We commit ourselves to accompany their life-giving movement in their aspiration to transform themselves and our societies towards fuller life.

15.4. *Ecology* is once again brought to our pastoral attention, and urgently so, since we see in the countries of Asia the continuing and unabated destruction of our environment – waters, forests, plant and animal life, air – and the support system of all created life. Life, especially in a Thrid World setting, is sacrificied at the altar of short term economic gains. The Lord, the Giver of Life, calls our discipleship in Asia into question on the time-bomb issue of ecology. Choosing life requires our discipleship to discern and act with other faiths and groups against the forces of ecological destruction.

15.5. Special attention is given to *the displaced* in our societies: political and ecological refugees and migrant workers. They are marginalized and exploited by the system, denied of their place in society, they must go elsewhere to seek a dignified life. In welcoming them we expose the causes of their displacement, work toward conditions for a more human living in community, experience the universal dimension of the Kingdom (Gal 3:28), and appreciate new opportunities for evangelization and intercultural dialogue.

Though our pastoral directives for action touch on many issues of concern, we appeal for a particular pastoral focus on these five major challenges.

Conclusion

16. As we end our deliberations, we do so as we began – with a prayer of thanks, hope and commitment.

Prayer of Service to Life in Asia

Loving and life-giving God, at the beginning you called us in Asia into life, enriched us with an astonishing variety of cultures, ways of living, believing, and worshiping. As sisters and brothers in your one Asian family, we thank you and praise you.

Among us are the poorest of the poor, the poor with their many faces of misery and pain, millions who seek not only a better life, but the full Life that only you can give. We hear your call to serve them, the way your Son Jesus served others in total love, in utter selflessness, eucharistically.

Send us your Spirit of Life, that together with other communities, we may respond to the anguish of our sisters and brothers with courageous and generous love, and with them come to the Life that never ends.

May our Mother, Mary, the voice and Mother of the Poor, who announced the liberation of the lowly, be our companion. May she as the mother and model of all disciples lead us to the Way, the Truth, and the Life in your Kingdom forever and ever. Amen.

Catechesis as an instrument of Evangelization: reflections from the perspective of Asia

Peter C. Phan

It is unmistakable from Pope John Paul II's many writings that the church's evangelizing mission has been one of his major and abiding concerns[1]. Among these papal publications two stand out in importance: the Apostolic Exhortation *Catechesi Tradendae* (october 16, 1979) and the encyclical *Redemptoris Missio* (December 7, 1990)[2]. These documents enunciate, among other things, the important principle that catechesis is an essential part of the evangelizing mission of the church and must be understood in that context. Furthermore, in his Apostolic Constitution *Fidei Depositum* on the publication of the *Catechism of the Catholic Church* (1992)[3], no doubt one of the lasting legacies of his pontificate, John Paul II urges the church's pastors and the Christian faithful to "receive this catechism assiduously in fulfilling their mission of proclaiming the faith and calling people to the Gospel life"[4].

---

[1] In 1979, John Paul II wrote: "Catechesis has always been a central care in my ministry as a priest and as a bishop" *(Catechesi Tradendae*, 4). We might now add, as a pope. What is meant by mission, evangelization, and catechesis, will be made clear in the course of the essay.

[2] *Catechesi Tradendae* will be cited as *CT* and *Redemptoris Missio* as *RM*, followed by the number of the paragraph. English translations of both documents are available from Pauline Books & Media, Boston.

[3] The text will be cited as *CCC*, followed by the number of the paragraph. Its English translation, copyrighted by the United States Catholic Conference, is available from Paulist Press, New York, 1994. For good introductions to the *CCC*, see *Introducing the Catechism of the Catholic Church: Traditional Themes and Contemporary Issues*, ed. Berard Marthaler (New York: Paulist Press, 1994) and *Commentary on the Catechism of the Catholic Church*, ed. Michael J. Walsh (Collegeville: Liturgical Press, 1994).

[4] *Fidei Depositum*, Section 3.

The purpose of this essay is to study the link between evangelization and catechesis and to examine how catechesis, and in particular the catechism, are to function within the church's mission of evangelization. The sources for reflection include not only the three documents mentioned above but also, and especially, the recent *General Directory for Catechesis* (1997)[5]. The essay will first briefly review the development of the church's official teaching on evangelization and catechesis from the *General Catechetical Directory* (1971)[6] to the *Catechism of the Catholic Church* (1992). The second part of the essay will focus on this theme as elaborated by the *General Directory for Catechesis*. The final part will reflect on the role of the catechism as an instrument of evangelization, especially for the churches of East Asia.

Evangelization, Catechesis, Catechism: from 1971 to 1992

1. **The *General Catechetical Directory*.** In compliance with Vatican II's mandate that a "directory for the catechetical instruction of the Christian People"[7] be drawn up, the Congregation for the Clergy prepared the *General Catechetical Directory*, which was approved by Paul VI and promulgated on April 11, 1971. Its intent is "to provide the basic principles of pastoral theology... by which pastoral action in the ministry of the word can be more fittingly directed and governed" whereas its immediate purpose is "to provide assistance in the production of catechetical directories and catechisms"[8].

---

[5] Congregation for the Clergy, *General Directory for Catechesis* (Vatican City: Libreria Editrice Vaticana, 1997). Henceforth it will be cited as *GDC*, followed by the number of the paragraph.

[6] Congregation for the Clergy, *General Catechetical Directory* (Washington, DC: Publications office, United States Catholic Conference, 1971). Henceforth it will be cited as *GCD*, followed by the number of the paragraph.

[7] *The Decree on the Pastoral Office of Bishops in the Church (Christus Dominus)*, 44.

[8] Foreword.

The *GCD* distinguishes four closely related forms of the ministry of the word: evangelization, or missionary preaching, catechesis, liturgy, and theology (17). By evangelization the *GCD* understands the activity which "has as its purpose the arousing of the beginnings of faith... so that men will adhere to the word of God" (17). Catechesis proper, which generally presupposes evangelization, is "that form of ecclesial action which leads both communities and individual members of the faithful to maturity of faith" (21). Since the focus of the *GCD* is catechesis proper, it does not have much to say about evangelization as such but devotes its pages entirely to the elaboration of catechesis as a ministry of the word (its nature, purpose, and efficacy), its criteria, message, methodology, and plan of catechetical action[9].

With regard to the catechism, which it considers as one of the "catechetical aids", the *GCD* says: "The greatest importance must be attached to catechisms published by ecclesiastical authority. Their purpose is to provide, under a form that is condensed and practical, the witnesses of revelation and of Christian tradition as well as the chief principles which ought to be useful for catechetical activity, that is, for personal education in faith. The witnesses of tradition should be held in due esteem, and very great care must be taken to avoid presenting as doctrines of the faith special interpretations which are only private opinions or the views of some theological school. The doctrine of the Church must be presented faithfully" (119).

2. Evangelii Nuntiandi. The *GCD*'s narrow definition of evangelization as the first proclamation of the Gospel to those who have not yet known Jesus is vastly enlarged by Paul VI's encyclical *Evangelii Nuntiandi*, a veritable *magna carta* for evangelization[10]. Seen as a much more complex process than the verbal proclamation of the Good News, it is said to be

---

[9] It is not the purpose of the essay nor is it possible to summarize the teaching of *GCD* on these points here. Interested readers can consult parts two through six of the document.

[10] English translation is available from St. Paul Books & Media. The encyclical will be cited as *EN*, followed by the number of the paragraph.

composed of seven intimately intertwined elements: "Evangelization... is a complex process made up of varied elements: the renewal of humanity, witness, explicit proclamation, inner adherence, entry into the community, acceptance of signs, apostolic initiative. These elements may appear to be contradictory, indeed mutually exclusive. In fact they are complementary and mutually enriching. Each one must be seen in relationship with the others" (24).

Among the many methods of evangelization *EN* lists witness of life, preaching, liturgy of the word, catechesis, utilization of mass media, personal contact, sacramental celebrations, and popular piety. With regard to catechesis it is said that through "catechetical instruction" people learn "the fundamental teachings, the living content of the truth which God has wished to convey to us and which the Church has sought to express in an ever richer fashion during the course of her long history. No one will deny that this instruction must be given to form patterns of Christian living and not to remain only notional"(44). Further, concerning the catechism, *EN* affirms that "the effort for evangelization will profit greatly... if those giving catechetical instruction have suitable texts, updated with wisdom and competence, under the authority of the bishops" (44). Finally, *EN* vigorously insists on the necessity for evangelization to "translate" or "transpose" the Gospel message, "without the slightest betrayal of its essential truth", into the various conditions of the anthropological and cultural language in "the field of liturgical expression, and in the areas of catechesis, theological formulation, secondary ecclesial structures, and ministries" (63).

3. *Catechesi Tradendae.* John Paul II's Apostolic Exhortation *Catechesi Tradendae* develops further Paul VI's teaching on catechesis. *CT* acknowledges the complex character and the several elements of evangelization, of which catechesis is a "stage", and affirms that "there is no separation or opposition between catechesis and evangelization. Nor can the two be simply identified with each other. Instead, they have close links whereby they integrate and complement each other" (18). For *CT*, the specific difference of catechesis lies in its aim, namely, "the *teaching* and *maturation* stage, that is to say, the

period in which the Christian, having accepted by faith the person of Jesus Christ as the one Lord and having given Him complete adherence by sincere conversion of heart, endeavors to know better this Jesus to whom he has entrusted himself: to know His 'mystery', the kingdom of God proclaimed by Him, the requirements and promises contained in His Gospel message, and the paths that He has laid down for anyone who wishes to follow Him" (20, italics added).

As for catechisms, *CT* states that the task of preparing them can be undertaken "only with the approval of the pastors who have the authority to give it, and taking their inspiration as closely as possible from the General Catechetical Directory, which remains the standard reference" (50).

One important new addition in *CT* is its recommendation that catechesis be joined with the church's work for ecumenical unity. It urges that catechesis give "a correct and fair presentation of the other Churches and ecclesial communities that the Spirit of Christ does not refrain from using as means of salvation" (32). More significantly, it suggests that in situations of religious plurality it is necessary "to have certain experiences of collaboration in the field of catechesis between Catholics and other Christians, complementing the normal catechesis that must in any case be given to Catholics" (33).

4. *Redemptoris Missio.* John Paul II returns to the theme of evangelization in his encyclical *Redemptoris Missio*. Here, however, the operative word is "mission" rather than evangelization, since one of the pope's intentions is to affirm the legitimacy and urgency of the mission *ad gentes,* and not only evangelization in general. *RM* distinguishes three situations for the church's activities. First, there are "peoples, groups and social contexts in which Christ and his Gospel are not known, or which lack Christian communities sufficiently mature to be able to incarnate the faith in their environment and proclaim to other groups". Here the church exercises the "mission *ad gentes* in the proper sense". Second, there are "Christian communities with adequate and solid ecclesial structures" with Christians who bear "witness to the Gospel in their surroundings and have a sense of commitment to the universal mission". Here the church exercises its "pastoral care". Thirdly, there is

"an intermediate situation, particularly in countries with ancient Christian roots, and occasionally in the younger Churches as well, where entire groups of the baptized have lost a living sense of the faith, or even no longer consider themselves members of the Church, and live a life far removed from Christ and his Gospel". Here the church exercises a "new evangelization" or a "re-evangelization" (33).

Besides its emphasis on the necessity of the mission *ad gentes*, *RM* is noted for its teaching on the Holy Spirit as the "principal agent of mission" (chapter three) and on the various "paths of mission," in particular ecclesial basic communities (51), inculturation (52), and interreligious dialogue (53). On catechesis as such, *RM* has little to say explicitly, but it is implicit in its emphasis on the necessity of "forming local churches" which is the goal of the mission *ad gentes*: "The mission *ad gentes* has this objective: to found Christian communities and develop churches to their full maturity" (48). Of course, one of the effective means to achieve this goal is catechesis. Again, *RM* does not say anything about catechisms, but no doubt the composition of these texts must be an important part of the task of inculturation by which "the Church makes the Gospel incarnate in different cultures and at the same time introduces peoples, together with their cultures, into her own community" (52)[11].

---

[11] After the publication of *RM* in 1990, the Congregation for the Evangelization of Peoples and the Pontifical Council for Interreligious Dialogue issued a joint document entitled *Dialogue and Proclamation (DP)* on May 19, 1991. This document seeks to clarify the relationship between these two activities as components of the one evangelizing mission of the church: "Interreligious dialogue and proclamation, though not on the same level, are both authentic elements of the Church's evangelizing mission. Both are legitimate and necessary. They are intimately related, but not interchangeable: true interreligious dialogue on the part of the Christian supposes the desire to make Jesus Christ better known, recognized and loved, proclaiming Jesus Christ is to be carried out in the Gospel spirit of dialogue. The two activities remain distinct but, as experience shows, one and the same local Church, one and the same person, can be diversely engaged in both" (77). Obviously, this document has profound implications for catechesis and catechism. For both the texts of *RM* and *DP* and excellent commentaries on them, see *Redemption and Dialogue. Reading* Redemptoris Missio *and* Dialogue and Proclamation, ed. WILLIAM R. BORROWS (Maryknoll, NY: Orbis Books, 1993).

5. **The *Catechism of the Catholic Church*.** Paul VI's and John Paul II's concerns for evangelization and catechesis, appropriated especially by the extraordinary assembly of the Synod of Bishops in 1985, produced a concrete fruit in 1992: the *Catechism of the Catholic Church*. In his Apostolic Constitution *Fidei Depositum* introducing the catechism, John Paul II describes it as a "reference text" for "a catechesis renewed at the living source of the faith", as "a sure norm for teaching the faith and thus a valid and legitimate instrument for ecclesial communion", and as "a sure and authentic reference text for teaching catholic doctrine and particularly for preparing local catechisms" (3). John Paul further notes that the catechism "is not intended to replace the local catechisms duly approved by the ecclesiastical authorities, the diocesan Bishops and the Episcopal Conferences, especially if they have been approved by the Apostolic See. It is meant to encourage and assist in the writing of new local catechisms, which take into account various situations and cultures, while carefully preserving the unity of faith and fidelity to catholic doctrine" (3).

On the theme of mission, the *CCC* reiterates the teaching of and quotes abundantly from *RM*. References are made to the essentially missionary nature of the church, the Holy Spirit as the principal agent of mission, the tasks of inculturation and interreligious dialogue, and ecumenical collaboration (849-86).

On catechesis, the *CCC* relies extensively on *CT*, and speaks of it as built on a number of elements of the church's pastoral mission, such as "the initial proclamation of the Gospel or missionary preaching to arouse the faith; examination of the reasons for belief; experience of Christian living; celebration of the sacraments; integration into the ecclesial community; and apostolic and missionary witness" (6). The *CCC* affirms that Jesus is "the heart of catechesis" with reference to whom everything else is taught (426-29). It refers to the liturgy as "the privileged place for catechizing the People of God" (1074). With reference to moral catechesis, it says that "*catechesis* has to reveal in all clarity the joy and the demands of the way of Christ" in so far as it has to deal with the Holy Spirit, grace, the beatitudes, sin and forgiveness, human virtues, Christian virtues, and the twofold commandment of love (1697).

On catechisms, the *CCC* stresses the necessity of particular catechisms to adapt the presentation of Christian doctrines to local conditions. The *CCC* "does not set out to provide the adaptation of doctrinal presentations and catechetical methods required by the differences of culture, age, spiritual maturity, and social and ecclesial condition among all those to whom it is addressed. Such indispensable adaptations are the responsibility of particular catechisms and, even more, of those who instruct the faithful" (24).

6. In summary, in the two decades from the *GCD* to the *CCC* important developments have taken place with regard to catechesis and catechism. It would be useful to list here some of the most significant points:

(1) Catechesis is an essential component of the church's evangelizing mission and must be understood and carried out within that perspective, not in opposition or separation from evangelization.

(2) The concept of evangelization or mission itself has been vastly broadened to include not only verbal proclamation of the Good News but also all other activities of the church, such as personal witness of life, preaching, liturgy of the word, sacramental celebrations, popular piety, ecumenical dialogue, fostering social justice, inculturation, and interreligious dialogue.

(3) Carried out in intimate connection with these church activities, catechesis is still understood as *teaching* of Christian doctrine directed toward the *maturation* of the faith.

(4) Catechesis is also an important part of the mission *ad gentes* the necessity of which is strongly reaffirmed.

(5) Local catechisms are not made redundant by the existence of a universal catechism; on the contrary, their necessity and usefulness is strongly and repeatedly affirmed.

(6) However, local catechisms should not be simply abbreviations or simplifications of the *CCC*, but they should be composed as part of the process of the church's evangelizing mission, namely, ecumenical dialogue, inculturation, and interreligious dialogue.

GENERAL DIRECTORY FOR CATECHESIS: A SYNTHESIS AND GUIDE FOR THE FUTURE

1. The *General Directory for Catechesis*. The *GDC* proposes to achieve a balance between the principal requirements for catechesis posited by two decades of catechetical reflections: "– on the one hand the contextualization of catechesis in evangelization as envisaged *by Evangelii Nuntiandi;* – on the other hand the appropriation of the content of the faith as presented in the *Catechism of the Catholic Church*" (7). Clearly then, according to the new directory, the two issues that should guide contemporary catechesis are inculturation and the appropriation of the teachings contained in the *CCC*, or to join the two issues together, the challenge for contemporary catechesis is how to inculturate the teachings of the CCC^{12}.

2. *Evangelization*. Compared with its 1971 predecessor, the *GDC* stands out in its resolute and consistent placing of catechesis within the church's mission of evangelization. Indeed, its entire first part (a third of its total of 300 pages!) focuses on catechesis as an intrinsic and integral task of evangelization. Here lies the relative novelty as well as the significance of the new directory. Repeating the teachings of Paul VI and John Paul II, the *GDC* sees evangelization as a complex process of transmitting divine revelation composed of "stages" or "essential moments" (47-49) among which the "ministry of the word" is "a fundamental element" (50). The functions of the ministry of the word in evangelization are fivefold: (1) "the

---

[12] For studies on the *GDC*, see CATHERINE DOOLEY, "The *General Directory for Catechesis* and the Catechism: Focus on Evangelizing", *Origins* 28, no. 3 (1998): 33, 35-39; idem, "Baptismal Catechumenate: Model for All Catechesis", *Louvain Studies* 23 (1998): 114-23; MICHAEL HORAN and JANE REGAN, *Good News in New Forms: A Companion to the* General Directory for Catechesis (Washington, DC: National Conference of Catechetical Leadership, 1998); CESARE BISSOLI, "*Il Direttorio generale per la Catechesi:* Origine, contenuti, confronto", *Salesianum* LX (1998): 521-47; MARIA PIERA MANELLO, "Un nuovo *Direttorio Generale per la Catechesi*", *Rivista di scienze dell'educazione*, 35, 3 (1997): 425-39; and the journal *The Living Light* 34, nos. 2 and 4 (1997-98).

primary proclamation", directed to non-believers, those who have chosen unbelief, those Christians who live on the margins of Christian life, and those who follow other religions; (2) pre and post baptismal catechesis: the catechesis of non-baptized adults in the catechumenate, the catechesis of baptized adults who wish to return to the faith, or of those who need to complete their initiation, and the catechesis of children and the young; (3) "permanent catechesis" for those Christians who have been initiated into the basic elements of the Christian faith, but who need constantly to nourish and deepen their faith throughout their lives; (4) the homily in the celebration of all the sacraments; and (5) theology, which is "the systematic treatment and the scientific investigation of the truths of the Faith" (51).

Within the process of evangelization catechesis is intimately related to the "primary or first proclamation." Between these two forms of the ministry of the word there is a "complementary distinction": "Catechesis, 'distinct from the primary proclamation of the Gospel,' promotes and matures initial conversion, educates the convert in the faith and incorporates him into the Christian community" (61). Nevertheless, the *GDC* acknowledges that "in pastoral practice it is not always easy to define the boundaries of these activities" (62) and not rarely these two forms of evangelization do need to take place simultaneously.

After this first proclamation follows the "catechesis at the service of Christian initiation" which is "an essential 'moment' in the process of evangelization" (63). This "initiatory catechesis" must be comprehensive and systematic, includes not only instruction but also an "apprenticeship of the entire Christian life", and prepares to incorporate the catechized person into the community.

In addition to this initiatory catechesis, there is catechesis at the service of ongoing formation in the faith. This "continuing catechesis" can take different forms: study of the Bible, study of the social teaching of the church, liturgical catechesis, occasional lectures, spiritual formation, and theological instruction (71).

Lastly, there is catechesis and religious instruction in schools. This instruction too is evangelization in so far as "it is called to penetrate a particular area of culture and to relate with other areas of knowledge. As an original form of the ministry of the word, it makes present the Gospel in a personal process of cultural, systematic and critical assimilation" (73).

Whatever form catechesis takes, however, its fundamental tasks are: promoting knowledge of the faith, liturgical education for a full, conscious and active participation in the liturgy, moral formation, and initiation to prayer (85)[13]. Besides these fundamental tasks, catechesis must also perform two additional tasks: educating the catechized "to live in community and to participate actively in the life and mission of the church", including its ecumenical dimension, and initiating them into the missionary work of the church, including interreligious dialogue (86). All these tasks, the *GDC* insists, are necessary and mutually interdependent, each realizing in its own way the object of catechesis (87).

3. *Inculturated Catechesis.* Compared with the old directory, the *GDC* has a brand-new part in which, instead of listing the basic Christian doctrines to be communicated in catechesis, it discusses how the contents of the *CCC* should be inculturated into local churches. Obviously, this part is of great interest to our essay, since it speaks at great length on how catechesis should be carried out and especially how the catechism should be composed at the local level. The *GDC* insists that the Gospel message is christocentric (98) and trinitarian (99), and that it is this "trinitarian christocentricity" that determines the internal structure, the pedagogy, and the practical implications of catechesis (100). In light of this trinitarian christocentricity, the message of the Gospel must be presented as a message of both salvation (101) and liberation (103).

This message of salvation and liberation must be inculturated, a "profound and global process and a slow journey": "It is not simply an external adaptation designed to make the Christian message more attractive or superficially decorative. On the contrary, it means the penetration of the deepest strata of persons and peoples by the Gospel which touches them

---

[13] These four tasks correspond to the four "pillars" of the *CCC*.

deeply, 'going to the very center and roots' of their cultures" (109).

There are two basic principles governing this process: "compatibility with the Gospel and communion with the universal Church" (109). With regard to catechesis, there are four concrete tasks: (1) relying on the local church as the principal factor of inculturation, especially the catechist; (2) drawing on local catechisms which respond to the demands of different cultures; (3) making use of the catechumenate and catechetical institutes, incorporating, with discernment, the language, symbols, and values of the cultures; and (4) offering an effective apologetics to assist the faith-culture dialogue (110).

Compatibility with the Gospel, which is one of the two principles governing inculturation, is further explained in terms of integrity or authenticity, comprehensiveness, and hierarchialism. By integrity or authenticity two things are meant: first, "intensive integrity", that is, a presentation of the Gospel message "without ignoring certain fundamental elements, or without operating a selectivity with regard to the deposit of faith"; and secondly, "extensive integrity", that is, a presentation that "gradually and increasingly proposes the Christian message more amply and with greater explicitness, in accordance with the capacity of those being catechized and with the proper character of catechesis" (112). By comprehensiveness is meant a coherence which is achieved by organizing the contents of the faith "around the mystery of the Most Holy Trinity, in a christocentric perspective" (114). By hierarchialism is meant harmony which is achieved by observing the "hierarchy of truths", that is, by adhering to the fact that "some truths are based on others as of a higher priority and are illumined by them" (114)[14].

4. *Contexts of Inculturation.* This inculturation of catechesis is both a need and a right of every Christian individual and

---

[14] The *GDC,* 115 argues that this "hierarchy of truths" is present in the way the history of salvation is told (with Jesus Christ as the unifying center), the Apostles' Creed is formulated (with the doctrine of the Trinity as its structure), the sacraments are understood (with the Eucharist occupying a unique place), moral theology is organized (with the double commandment of love of God and neighbor as its summary), and prayer is taught (with the Our Father as its heart).

Christian community and involves the community as community (167-68). There is the need to adapt catechesis first according to age, i.e., adults, infants and young children, young people, and the aged (171-88), and then according to special conditions such as the disabled and the handicapped, the marginalized (e.g., immigrants, refugees, nomads, traveling people, the chronically ill, drug addicts, prisoners), professionals (e.g., workers, artists, scientists, university students), and rural and urban people (189-92).

The remaining two categories to which catechesis should be adapted are of special importance for catechesis in Asia. The first refers to the religiously plural context, and here the *GCD* speaks of catechesis on the one hand and popular devotions, non-Catholic Christians, Jews, followers of other religions, and new religious movements on the other. The *GDC* acknowledges that "Christians today live in multi-religious contexts; many, indeed, in a minority position" (200). It stresses that in this context catechesis has three tasks: deepening and strengthening the identity of believers; helping Christians not only discern the elements in those religions which are contrary to the Christian message but also accept the seeds of the Gospel which are found in them and which can sometimes constitute an authentic preparation for the Gospel; and promoting a lively missionary sense among believers (200).

The last category is the socio-cultural context, and here the *GDC* discusses inculturation proper. In this context catechesis is charged with six tasks: knowing in depth the culture of persons and the extent of its penetration into their lives; recognizing the cultural dimension in the Gospel itself; proclaiming the conversion demanded of cultures by the Gospel; witnessing to the transcendence of the Gospel over cultures; promoting a new expression of the Gospel in accord with the culture being evangelized; and maintaining the content of the faith integrally (203).

Catechetical inculturation follows a series of methodological steps: "a listening to the culture of the people, to discern an echo... of the word of God; a discernment of what has an authentic Gospel value or is at least open to the Gospel; a purification of what bears the mark of sin (passions, structures of evil) or of human frailty; an impact on people through stimulating an attitude of radical conversion to God, of dialogue, and of patient interior maturation" (204).

The *GDC* also points out that catechetical inculturation must not be restricted to a few experts but must involve the whole People of God; that it must be guided and encouraged, and not forced; that it must be an expression of, and mature in, the community, and not exclusively the result of erudite research; and that it requires the cooperation of all the agents of catechesis (206).

One important element of inculturation is language. The *GDC* states that though catechesis must make use of the forms and terms proper to the culture, nevertheless it must "respect and value the language proper to the message, especially biblical language, as well as the historical-traditional language of the Church *(creed, liturgy)* and doctrinal language *(dogmatic formulations)*.... In the process of inculturating the Gospel, catechesis should not be afraid to use traditional formulae and the technical language of the faith, but it must express its meaning and demonstrate its existential importance" (208).

5. *Local Catechisms.* Lastly, as concrete steps toward catechetical inculturation, the *GDC*, following its predecessor, suggests three: a socio-cultural and religious analysis of the state of the diocese, developing a plan of action, and elaboration of instruments and didactic aids for catechetical activity (279-83). Among these, "catechisms excel all others. Their importance derives from the fact that the message transmitted by them is recognized as authentic by the Pastors of the Church" (284). These local catechisms are declared to be "invaluable instruments for catechesis" since through them "the Church actualizes the 'divine pedagogy' used by God himself in Revelation, adapting his language to our nature with thoughtful concern" (131).

Every catechism adopted by the local church must have three characteristics. First, it is official, and as such it is qualitatively different from other catechetical aids, such as didactic texts, non-official catechisms, and guides. Secondly, it is "a synthetic and basic text, in which the events and fundamental truths of the Christian mystery are presented in an organic way and with regard to the 'hierarchy of truth". Thirdly, it is "a reference point to inform catechesis" (132).

The *GDC* insists that in elaborating this kind of catechism the local church should exercise a "mature creativity" (134). It makes it clear that an inculturated local catechism is not "a mere summary of the *Catechism of the Catholic Church*" (134) because the latter lacks genuine adaptations to the local conditions. Such local catechisms can be diocesan, regional or national in character. Furthermore, they can be structured in different ways, e.g., they can be organized according to a trinitarian structure, or the stages of salvation, or a biblical theme, or an aspect of the faith, or the liturgical year (134).

In summary, the *GCD* represents a comprehensive and organic synthesis of the teachings of Paul VI and John Paul II on evangelization and catechesis. Its long-term influence and significance do not lie in any new doctrine but in its fundamental approach to catechesis as an intrinsic moment of the evangelizing mission of the church and in its strong insistence on the necessity of local catechisms that both creatively and faithfully inculturate the contents of the faith as presented by the *CCC*.

CATECHESIS AND CATECHISM FOR ASIA IN THE NEXT MILLENNIUM

From the recent history of the Asian churches, it is obvious that they are a stranger to neither inculturation nor inculturated catechesis. A cursory reading of the documents of the Federation of Asian Bishops' Conferences (FABC) will quickly dispel any doubt that evangelization and catechesis, especially in their triple form of inculturation, interreligious dialogue, and solidarity with the poor, have been the staple themes of their reflections and publications in the last three decades[15]. This last part of this essay will first review what the

---

[15] See *For All Peoples of Asia. Federation of Asian Bishops' Conferences. Documents from 1970 to 1991*, ed. GAUDENCIO ROSALES and C.G. ARÉVALO (Maryknoll, NY: Orbis Books, 1992). Henceforth, *For All.*

FABC and the recent synod of Asian bishops have said about catechesis as an essential element of evangelization and will then, by way of conclusion, make some suggestions, in the light of the teachings of both the Roman documents examined above and of the FABC as well as of the synod of Asian bishops, regarding the composition of inculturated catechisms for East Asia.

1. *Evangelization and Catechesis in Asia.* That evangelization is a first-priority concern of Asian bishops is demonstrated by the fact that the theme of the FABC's first plenary assembly held in Taipei, Taiwan in 1971 was "evangelization in modern-day Asia". The assembly dramatically affirmed the urgency of evangelization: "...the preaching of Jesus Christ and His Gospel to our peoples in Asia becomes a task which today assumes an urgency, a necessity and reaches the magnitude unmatched in the history of our Faith in this part of the world"[16].

Evangelization was studied again during the international congress on mission held in Manila, Philippines on the occasion of the 400th anniversary of the foundation of the diocese of Manila in December 1979, co-sponsored by the Sacred Congregation for the Evangelization of Peoples and the Pontifical Mission Aid Societies of the Philippines. The congress had nine workshops, and their titles alone indicate the scope and richness of the discussions: Toward a theology of mission for Asia today; local Asian churches and the tasks of mission: inculturation; dialogue with other religious traditions in Asia; the Gospel, the kingdom of God, liberation and development; basic Christian communities and local ministries; prayer, spirituality and formation for mission; co-responsible evangelization; mission and education; and media and evangelization[17].

Evangelization was also the focus of the FABC's fifth plenary assembly in Bandung, Indonesia, July 1990, the title of which was "Journeying Together Toward the Third Millen-

---

[16] *For All*, 13.
[17] See *For All*, 125-63.

nium". The theme of evangelizing mission of the church in contemporary Asia was discussed at length[18]. Besides plenary assemblies (which generally met every four years) and occasional congresses, the FABC also had six offices relating to various aspects of church life, one of which is mission or evangelization. Until 1991 there have been five "institutes" on missionary apostolate, that is, conferences in which a number of bishops, priests, religious and laity participated and issued final statements[19].

As can be gathered from its manifold documents, the FABC's theology of evangelization is extremely rich and varied and resists a comprehensive summary. Indeed, it is itself already an instructive example of an Asian theology of mission. The following statements attempt to represent its essential points:

(1) The church's evangelizing mission and activity must be informed by the sociopolitical, economic, cultural, and religious contexts of modern Asia. Hence it must be preceded by a careful and accurate analysis of these contexts to respond to the "signs of the times"[20].

(2) The proclamation of Jesus Christ is "the center and the primary element of evangelization without which all other elements will lose their cohesion and validity"[21]. With the proclamation of Jesus Christ, the kingdom of God, which was his message, becomes the goal of evangelization[22].

(3) The primary focus of evangelization in Asia today is "the building up of a truly local church"[23]. This local church must have its proper autonomy within the communion with the

---

[18] See *For All*, 279-89.
[19] See *For All*, 93-108; 291-94; 335-47.
[20] See *For All*, 3-5; 30-31; 57-59; 68-69; 179-83; 275-79; 335-37.
[21] See *For All*, 292.
[22] See *For All*, 342: "... The reign of God is a universal reality, extending far beyond the boundaries of the Church. It is the reality of salvation in Jesus Christ, in which Christians and others share together .... Seen in this manner, a 'regnocentric' approach to mission theology does not in any way threaten the Christo-centric perspective of our faith. on the contrary, 'regnocentrism' calls for 'christo-centrism' and vice versa ...".
[23] *For All*, 14.

universal church: "... In our Asian context we are in the process of re-discovering that the individual Christian can best survive, grow and develop as a Christian person in the midst of a self-nourishing, self-governing, self-ministering and self-propagating Christian community"[24]. Hence, evangelization will lead to gathering together a believing community, the church.

(4) Mission will practice dialogue as its essential mode in its threefold and interrelated forms: dialogue with the religions of Asia (interreligious dialogue), dialogue with the people, especially the poor (liberation), and dialogue with the cultures of Asia (inculturation)[25].

(5) The acting subject of mission in Asia today is the local church: "Local Churches, servant and inculturated, are the subject of the evangelizing mission"[26]. It is the members of the local church that discern and work out the most effective ways in which the Gospel is proclaimed, the church planted, and the values of the kingdom of God realized in their own place and time[27].

(6) Every local church in Asia must be both a "receiving church" and a "sending church." Every local church is responsible for its mission and co-responsible for the mission of its sister-churches[28].

(7) Evangelization in Asia must be the particular responsibility of the laity, especially in the roles of evangelist, catechist, preacher, and religion teacher[29]. The FABC's fifth ple-

---

[24] *For All*, 77.

[25] See *For All*, 23; 138-48. For studies of these aspects in FABC's documents, see STEPHEN BEVANS, "Inculturation of Theology in Asia: The Federation of Asian Bishops' Conferences, 1970-95", *Studia Missionalia* 45 (1996): 1-23 and PETER C. PHAN, "Human Development and Evangelization", *Studia Missionalia* 47 (1998): 205-27.

[26] *For All*, 343.

[27] See *For All*, 130.

[28] See *For All*, 130.

[29] See *For All*, 79. It is interesting to note that the "Asian Colloquium on Ministries in the Church" (Hong Kong, March 1977) spoke *first* and at great length of the ministries of the laity before dealing (relatively briefly) with those of deacons, priests, and bishops, contrary to the practice of most Roman documents. For further teachings of the FABC on the laity, see the statement of its fourth plenary assembly (Tokyo, September 1986), the title of which is "The Vocation and Mission of the Laity in the Church and in the World of Asia", in *For All*, 177-98.

nary assembly declares: "... The lay faithful should take upon themselves as their specific responsibility the renewal of Asian society according to the values of the Gospel. They are the primary evangelizers of culture and cultures, and of the whole fabric of life in society"[30].

(8) Evangelization must make use of all possible means at the disposal of the church in Asia, particularly "grassroots ecclesial communities"[31], schools and universities as well as nonformal education[32], and the media of communication[33].

(9) Among the means of evangelization catechesis stands out in importance. It is true that the FABC has not spoken extensively and *explicitly* on catechesis as the work of teaching Christian doctrines aimed at maturating the faith. Nevertheless, catechesis is implied in the FABC's numerous statements on evangelization, education, and ministries in the church. The FABC explicitly stated that "[a] more thorough-going renewal is called for in catechesis"[34] and spoke of 13 kinds of specialized catechizing ministry for the laity[35].

(10) In sum, for evangelization to succeed in Asia, what is needed is not merely a new approach to evangelization, but a new way of being church: "We dream of a servant Church: servant of God, servant of Christ, servant of his plan of salvation; servant of the Asian peoples, of their deep hopes, longings and aspirations; servant of the followers of other religions, of all women and men, simply and totally for others"[36].

The Asian Synod of Bishops, convoked by John Paul II to prepare for the third millennium, met in Rome in April-May 1998, and had as its theme "Jesus Christ the Savior and his mission of love and service in Asia". The synod's *instrumentum laboris*, which collates the responses of various Asian

---

[30] *For All*, 283.
[31] See *For All*, 148-52.
[32] See *For All*, 156-61.
[33] See *For All*, 162-63.
[34] *For All*, 79.
[35] See *For All*, 79-81.
[36] *For All*, 340.

Bishops' Conferences to the *lineamenta*, devotes its final chapter to the theme of mission in Asia[37]. It represents the concerns of Asian bishops for "a new evangelization in Asia": "Evangelization today has acquired a wider meaning than in the past. Evangelization is a complex reality and has many essential elements such as witnessing to the Gospel, working for the values of the Kingdom, the struggle for human promotion, dialogue, a mutual sharing of God-experiences, inculturation and dialogue with other religions, to mention a few"[38].

The document speaks of the liturgy as the wellspring of mission, the importance of the Bible in evangelization, missionary spirituality, the role and formation of the laity for mission, the family as the agent and the first place of catechesis, youth as evangelizers, prayer and contemplation as the source of power for evangelization, various forms of dialogue (interreligious dialogue, inculturation, human promotion), service to creation, and the means of social communication[39].

2. *Local Catechisms as an Instrument of Evangelization in Asia.* Interestingly enough, neither the documents of the FABC nor those of the Asian Synod have explicitly mentioned the need of composing local catechisms for Asia. Yet the history of catechisms written both in and for Asia is rich as well as varied. The names of Francis Xavier, Roberto di Nobili, Alessandro Valignano, Michele Ruggieri, and Matteo Ricci and their catechisms need no introduction[40]. The catechism by Alexandre de

---

[37] The English edition of the *instrumentum laboris* is available from *Libreria Editrice Vaticana*, Vatican City, 1998. The document will be cited as *Instrumentum*, followed by the number of the paragraph.

[38] *Instrumentum*, 47.

[39] See *Instrumentum*, 40-53.

[40] For a history of early catechisms in Asia, see PETER C. PHAN, *Mission and Catechesis. Alexandre de Rhodes and Inculturation in Seventeenth-Century Vietnam* (Maryknoll, NY: Orbis Books, 1998), 111-121 and J. JENNES, *Four Centuries of Catechetics in China. Historical Evolution of Apologetics and Catechetics in the Catholic Mission of China from the 16th Century until 1940* (Taipei: Fujen University, 1975). For a detailed history of catechisms from 1450 to 1870, see PIETRO BRAIDO, *Lineamenti di storia della catechesi e dei catechismi. Dal "tempo delle riforme" all'età degli imperialismi (1450-1870)* (Turin: Editrice Elle Di Ci, 1991). For a comprehensive and readable history of catechisms, see BERARD MARTHALER, *The Catechism Yesterday & Today* (Collegeville, Minn.: The Liturgical Press, 1995).

Rhodes entitled *Cathechismus pro iis qui volunt suscipere baptismum, in octo dies divisus,* in Vietnamese and Latin, less known than those of his Jesuit colleagues, was no less influential[41].

Recently, a national catechism for the Philippines was approved by the Congregation for the Clergy, the first to receive this honor since the publication of the CCC[42]. The *Catechism for Filipino Catholics (CFC)* was begun in 1984, completed in 1994, and approved by the Vatican in 1997. The *CFC* claims to be truly Christ-centered and trinitarian, and solidly grounded in the Bible, Church teaching, and human experience. Furthermore, it claims to respond to the particular needs of Filipino catechesis as sketched in the National Catechetical Directory of the Philippines (approved by Rome in 1984) and to be truly inculturated in the context of Filipino cultural and religious values and traditions.

The *CFC* is divided into three parts, flanked by the introduction called "Foundations" – which discusses the identity of the Filipino Catholic and the themes of revelation, faith and unbelief – and the epilogue, a commentary on the Our Father. The three parts are entitled "Christ, our Truth", "Christ, our Way", and "Christ, our Life" respectively. The first part deals with doctrine, speaking of believing in God the Father (head and faith); the second with the moral life, speaking of following Christ (hands and love); and the third with worship and sacraments, speaking of trusting in the Holy Spirit (heart and hope). Each chapter seeks to achieve three goals: integration, inculturation, and community formation, and is composed of five sections: introductory text, context, exposition, integration, and questions and answers.

All in all, the *CFC* is an impressive achievement. Its most notable features include a conscious and consistent effort at bringing about genuine inculturation (by an almost ubiquitous

---

[41] For a short presentation of de Rhodes' catechism and his catechetical method, see PETER C. PHAN, "Catechesis and Catechisms: Alexandre de Rhodes' Mission in Vietnam", in *The Echo Within: Emerging Issues in Religious Education,* ed. CATHERINE DOOLEY and MARY COLLINS (Allen, Texas: Thomas More, 1997) 103-28.

[42] See *Catechism for Filipino Catholics* (Manila: ECCCE and Word & Life, 1997).

reference to the Filipino context and by citing the teachings not only of the magisterium of the universal church but also that of the Filipino church), integration (by linking the three parts of doctrine, moral life, and worship together), and orientation toward praxis (by stressing the communal and social dimensions of faith). The *CFC* is intended not as a textbook but as a proximate source book for the preparation of catechetical materials, religion textbooks, and other guides.

No doubt both the method and structure of the *CFC* can serve as a useful guide for the composition of other national catechisms in Asia. Of course the fact that the *CFC* is written in English makes the first stage of inculturation, i.e., translation of Western theological categories, somewhat simpler. This is not the case when the catechism is presented in other languages such as Chinese or Vietnamese in which such fundamental vocabularies as God, Holy Spirit, grace, sin, salvation, and sacrament can, as history has shown, cause serious difficulties. Furthermore, the fact that Christians form the great majority in the Philippines vastly simplifies the task of interreligious dialogue, which again is not the case with countries such as India, China, Vietnam, Korea, Japan, and others. Finally, the Filipino church has at its disposal several Catholic universities with a copious corps of experts in relevant sacred disciplines, whereas in some other Asian countries such as China and Vietnam even an elementary level of theological education has not been available, not even to the clergy, for several decades.

With regard to national catechisms in countries such as China, Japan, Korea, Taiwan, and Vietnam that share similar religious traditions (mainly Buddhist, Confucian, and Taoist), similar socio-political condition (socialist and Communist, except Japan, South Korea, and Taiwan), and similar Christian minority status (in all of the countries mentioned), some suggestions may be offered here, though unfortunately only in the most cursory fashion.

(1) Before embarking upon a national catechism, it would be useful for the churches of these countries to compose first national catechetical directories in the light of the recently promulgated *GDC*. These directories will supply concrete norms for the composition of national catechisms later.

(2) Selective use should be made of the *CCC* in catechesis, which by now has been translated into the languages of these countries. Indeed, summaries of the *CCC* should be used in the meantime, though it must be remembered that these summaries cannot be regarded as equivalents of inculturated local catechisms still to be composed. The advantage of these summaries is that they begin the process of incorporating the essential contents of the *CCC* into local catechesis as well as into local languages.

(3) The composition of the national catechisms will of course proceed in stages, perhaps following the three parts adopted by the *CFC*. In the composition of this national catechism, the collaboration of non-Catholic Christians will be actively sought, especially in countries where non-Catholics Christians are numerous, e.g, South Korea and Japan. In this way not only ecumenical unity will be served but also the danger of using different sets of vocabularies for the same theological terms among Catholics and Protestants (e.g., in Vietnam) will be avoided.

(4) It would be useful to attempt to express key Christian concepts in terms of the cultural and religious heritage of the country and subject these attempts to a wide and searching critique by experts of the same country and culture. For example, how can the concept of the reign of God be expressed in the Confucian framework?[43]. How can Jesus Christ be understood in the context of the veneration of ancestors?[44]. How can ecclesiology be elaborated talking account of the concept of family? How can Christian ethics be structured around filial piety? Once validated, these interpretations may be used as signposts for the process of inculturating Christian doctrines into the culture of each country.

(5) A wide variety of Asian sources must be pressed into service, especially sacred texts and religious practices of non-Christian religions (far more so than in the *CFC*) so that a genuine interreligious dialogue becomes an essential part of catechesis[45].

---

[43] See, for instance, PETER C. PHAN, "Kingdom of God: A Theological Symbol for Asians?" *Gregorianum* 79/2 (1998): 295-322.

[44] See, for instance, PETER C. PHAN, "The Christ of Asia", *Studia Missionalia* 45 (1996): 25-55.

[45] For a discussion of these sources, see PETER C. PHAN, "Jesus the Christ with an Asian Face", *Theological Studies* 57/3 (1996): 403-405.

At the threshold of the third Christian millennium the church is challenged to undertake new forms of evangelization. Nowhere is this challenge as urgent as in Asia. Within this new evangelization catechesis understood as the teaching of Christian doctrines and practices for the purpose of maturing the Christian faith is a necessary and vital part. And a powerful instrument for evangelization the catechism has been and will continue to be.

Asian Saints and Blessed, and the New Evangelization

FRANCIS X. CLARK, S.J.*

Asian Saints and Blessed of the Catholic Church now number over 450. All of them are martyrs, except three. They died from 1597 to 1946. They are sons and daughters of eight Asian cultures: China, India, Japan, Korea, Philippines, Sri Lanka, Thailand, Vietnam[1].

Unfortunately, Catholics in Asia know little about them. Although the eight individual cultures are conscious of their own saints and blessed, rarely have they even heard of those of other countries. If this is true of Asia, much less do Catholics of Europe, the Americas and Africa realize that they exist.

A book is in preparation on these Asian Saints and Blessed; it will hope to make their lives available to readers everywhere. Meanwhile, however, this article, although it touches only the surface, can present something about them and their possible role in the new evangelization.

---

* The author of this article was born in New York City, is now a naturalized citizen of the Philippines. For seventeen years he was a staff member of the East Asian Pastoral Institute connected with the Ateneo de Manila University. Conversations there with participants from practically every Asian country first uncovered data about Asian Saints and Blessed; further research resulted in an eighty-page booklet on them in 1979, and in a chapter in his book, *Introduction to the Catholic Church of Asia*, in 1987. Because the last two decades have seen new Saints and Blessed, a book about them is imperative. He has also personally visited shrines and museums about the Asian Saints and Blessed, as Nagasaki in Japan, Seoul in Korea, Thailand, Kerala (Sister Alphonsa and Father Chavara), Taipei in Taiwan, in addition to areas of Sri Lanka and Saigon where no specific shrines exist.

[1] Asia geographically can be understood in different ways. Here it will mean Japan to Pakistan, Indonesia to Mongolia.

The first part of the article will attempt a brief survey of the martyrs of China, Japan, Korea, Vietnam; from these four countries come the overwhelming majority of the martyrs. It will offer reasons why Asian men and women should both venerate and imitate them: a) they are truly *Asians*; b) they are genuine *witnesses* to the gospel of Jesus; c) by far the majority are *laity*; d) many of these laity are *women*; e) they form part of *story theology*; f) they exemplify, to an astounding degree, human *courage* for a transcendent ideal.

The second part will attempt to view globally the main persecutions of China, Japan, Korea and Vietnam. Why did Asians then cruelly persecute and put to death their fellow Asians? How should the world now evaluate the mentality at that time of both persecutors and persecuted? What lessons can even modern nations learn from those experiences?

A third section will present some data about the martyrs of India, the Philippines and Thailand, and about the three nonmartyrs of Sri Lanka and India.

1. A SURVEY OF THE MARTYRS OF CHINA, JAPAN, KOREA, VIETNAM

a) *Asian*. These Saints and Blessed are truly Asians. They were born in Asia, they lived their lives completely in Asia, they were part of the culture, the language, the habits and customs of their people. Although without doubt often the bishops and priests who *first* brought the faith to them arrived from Europe, yet Chinese, Japanese, Korean and Vietnamese priests were ordained after a time and were also the shepherds who died with their flocks.

b) *Witnesses*. Many are aware that "martyr" derives from an original Greek word meaning to testify, to be a witness. Yet not so many realize the English roots of "witness". It comes from "–ness", a suffix which can join itself to adjectives, and occasionally nouns, to express a certain state or quality of a thing. Thus there are scores of words like gladness and sadness, willingness and unwillingness, hardness and softness. The first part of wit-ness, namely, wit, derives from an old English expression meaning to know[2]. Traces of it are still found today, as when people say "a keen wit", "to be frightened out of one's wits", "to wit," and even less charitably "half-wit" and "nitwit". The basic meaning therefore of wit-ness is a state of knowing, a confidence that I know that I know, and so firmly that I am willing to stand up to be counted and even, when needed, to lay down my life. The Asian martyrs are conspicuous for such faith, "I know that I know".

Those who read through the acts of their martyrdoms, their trials before judges, their appearances before Mandarins and other government officials, marvel at the wisdom and constancy given to them to reply to the needs of the moment. Some examples can illustrate.

In China during the Boxer persecution of 1900, a young man named Peter Tciu, nineteen years old, stood before an army general with power to order death sentences. Because of severe previous pressure and punishment, Peter was weak and in rags. The general, somehow compassionate, strove to induce him again and again to apostatize. Peter responded: "Great man, you cannot disown your father and your mother; for the same reason I cannot deny God, my heavenly Father". The general, full of disdain, shouted: "Get out of here, stupid" and had him beheaded[3].

In Korea, a judge asked a girl: "Did you see God"? She answered: "No, I didn't. Can't a country man, who has never seen the king, believe there is a king? When I see all the creatures on earth, I know there is a Creator"[4].

In a bloody persecution in Japan, a Filipino married man was captured with Spanish Dominican missioners. When the Japanese executioners proposed the final question: "Therefore, if we grant you life, will you renounce your faith"? Lorenzo answered: "That I will never do, because I am a Christian, and

---

[2] *The Oxford English Dictionary*, v. 7, 98; v. 12, 205.
[3] GIUSEPPE WANG, *Martirologio della Chiesa Cattolica in Cina* (Città del Vaticano: Edizione Alma Mater, 1968) 88-89.
[4] KIM CHANG-SEOK THADDEUS, *Lives of 103 Martyr Saints of Korea* (Seoul: Catholic Publishing House, 984) 56.

I shall die for God, and for him I will give many thousands of lives if I had them"⁵.

In Vietnam a married man stood before his judges. Incessantly they tried varied methods to get him to deny his faith. Finally, he remarked to them: "Why do you make such attempts? You take us perhaps for children, who would let themselves be convinced to offend God through fear of suffering⁶.

c) *Laity*. If one gathers together all the Asian priests, religious Brothers and Sisters, seminarians, any at all who can be counted as living a life set apart for more intense service of God and the Church, in round numbers they total 100. Yet the laity number over 350, more than three times as many. Korea, for one example, has only one priest and ninety-two lay people. Another example can be Vietnam; it has thirty-seven priests but fifty-nine lay men and women. These laity are from all strata of ordinary family fathers and mothers, those engaged in various trades and occupations of urban and rural communities.

This proportion of Asian laity to Asian clergy and religious invites comparison with Europe. Some modern authors complain about the European Saints and Blessed; why among them so many clergy and religious, why so few laity?⁷.

d) *Women*. In round numbers again, of over 350 laity over 100 are women. This again fits in well with a new evangelization, where women are gradually receiving the acceptance and the role due to them in the Church and the world. Specific examples can be multiplied. Asian mothers were killed with their children. Asian maidens won the double crown of virgin and martyr. Valiant Asian women mothered also a male lineage of Saints and Blessed, especially in Korea where even three

---

⁵ FIDEL VILLAROEL, *Lorenzo de Manila. The Protomartyr of the Philippines and his Companions.* (Manila: Saint Paul Publications, 1979) 108.

⁶ Benedictines de Paris. *Vies des Saints et des Bienheureux* (Paris: Letouzey, 1935-1959), v. 13, 173.

⁷ "One group which is clearly underrepresented is the laity". KENNETH WOODWARD, *Making Saints: How the Catholic Church Determines Who Becomes a Saint. Who Doesn't, and Why* (NewYork: Simon and Schuster, 1996) 336; LAWRENCE CUNNINGHAM, *The Meaning of Saints* (San Francisco: Harper & Row, 1980) 50-52.

generations of one family, grandfather, father and son, all suffered martyrdom.

e) *Story Theology*. Today story theology is a justifiable and effective manner of making Christ and the faith known. These Asian martyrs offer many inspiring narratives; in a variety of cultures and situations, they chose to die rather than to surrender to either the promised rewards or the imminent threats of the persecutors[8].

f) *Courage*. Finally, on the general principle that all people admire courage for a worthwhile cause, wherever it may appear in human life, these martyrs merit surpassing admiration. These are some few of multiple examples.

In China Blessed Si, eighteen years old, was still only a catechumen. Captured and commanded to prostrate himself before a pagoda, he refused. At the place of torture, he knelt, made the sign of the cross and said: "Do with me what you wish". They cut off his right arm. He shouted: "Courage, go on; cut me in as many pieces as you wish and you will see that every piece is Catholic"[9].

From Korea comes the story of Columba (Kim Nyo-im). Columba's mother and six children converted to the Catholic religion. Two of the six, Columba and Agnes, resolved not to marry. In a trial the officials therefore asked: "Why are you not married"? They replied: "Because we want to worship God, the Creator of all things, with clean body and heart, and save our souls".

Tortures followed. For example, to make her indicate where Catholics were hiding and where Catholic books were kept, they twisted her legs, burned her body with heated charcoal, penetrated her skin with needle like instruments. Finally, police used a method which was unthinkable even in pagan lands.

They stripped Columba and Agnes of their clothes, took them from the jail for women, threw them into a prison of

---

[8] WOODWARD, *Making Saints*, 13; CUNNINGHAM, *Meaning*, 5 says: "Hagiography is Christianity from below".
[9] WANG, *Martirologio*, 98.

criminal men, allowing these prisoners to do anything they wanted. Although for two full days this continued, a power from above protected Columba and Agnes; no man approached them. Later Columba vehemently complained to the chief judge about this treatment: "You can kill us, but you have no right to do that kind of thing to us". The judge agreed, and punished the police responsible. The officials attempted three final beatings to force her to deny her faith, without success. They then cut off her head[10].

Louis, a catechist of the Franciscans in Japan, was crucified for the faith at Nagasaki when he was only twelve years old. Both Christians and other bystanders stood entranced at the joy he showed from his cross, as he kept saying: "Paradise, Paradise; Jesus, Mary"[11].

In Vietnam a Father Dominic Drach, a Dominican priest, confronted that devastating dilemma which the Vietnamese rulers had learned from the Japanese. They placed a crucifix on the ground, then commanded Catholics to approach and step on it. If they did so, they were freed; if they refused, they were tortured and killed. At this decisive moment Fr. Drach proclaimed: "This is the image of the cross on which my Lord died; it is the emblem of the faith... I adore it and will rather die than profane it". Ultimately he was beheaded[12].

Through the last 130 years one reaction to these narratives is the following: "How like they are to the martyrs of Rome!" For a few samples, a book in 1870 compares the martyrs of Korea and Vietnam to those of Rome, step by step showing the similar words and actions of the victims widely separated by time and distance[13].

In 1929 Paul Dudon, after hearing of the heroism of Korean martyrs, wonders why the world and the Church are

---

[10] KIM, *Lives of 103*, 86-87.
[11] LUIS FROIS, *Relación del Martirio de los 26 Cristianos Crucificados en Nangasaqui el 5 Febrero de 1597*. (Roma: Pontificia Universidad Gregoriana, 1935) 115.
[12] GUY-MARIE OURY, *Le Vietnam des Martyrs et des Saints* (Paris: Le Sarment Fayard, 1988) 126.
[13] *The New Glories of the Catholic Church*. Translated from the Italian by the Fathers of the London Oratory. London: Thomas Richard and Son, 1870.

so much aware of the Roman martyrs for Christ and so little of equally admirable Koreans[14].

In 1939 the first chapter of a book remarks:

> When studying the immense field of martyrdom in China, we are surprised to meet at every step striking resemblances between the martyrs of the East and those of the West. No one would expect to find Agnes and Sebastian, Felicitas and Tarsicius, living again in China[15].

In fact, proceeding even a step further, do not these martyrs in some aspects even surpass the Roman martyrs? Rome was not far distant from the Holy Land where Christ lived. If anyone wished to verify the facts about Jesus, his apostles, the beginning of the Church, a trip to the Holy Land was possible. Further, the culture and daily life of Mediterranean countries, Rome and Greece and Judea included, contained many similarities. All of them had bread and wine, fig trees, sheep and shepherds, a similar climate.

But the cultures of China, Japan, Korea and Vietnam, with the veneration of ancestors, the rice and tea, the languages with characters, the daily life, were incalculably different. Further, for anyone from Asia who wished to verify the facts of the life of Christ, difficult and dangerous indeed was the voyage. Yet somehow these martyrs so deeply interiorized the truths brought from afar that they became steadfast witnesses for them unto torture and death.

2. Why the persecutions? How evaluate them now?

Before presenting abstract reasons, four concrete samples from history can offer some background.

In Korea Andrew Kim protested to his judges: "If I have been in touch with foreigners it was because of my religion; it

---

[14] Paul Dudon, "Martyrs de Corée 1838-1846", *Etudes* (1925) 541-550.
[15] P.X. Mertens, *The Yellow River Runs Red: A Story of Modern Chinese Martyrs.* (St. Louis: Herder, 1939) 1.

was for my God; it is for him that I die"[16]. In Japan Paul Miki, close to ordination as a Jesuit priest, was hanging on a cross in Nagasaki when he proclaimed these final words to his countrymen: "I did not come from the Philippines. I am a Japanese by birth, and a brother of the Society of Jesus. I have committed no crime, and the only reason why I am put to death is that I have been teaching the doctrine of Jesus Christ"[17].

In Vietnam, the governor violently attacked Saint John Dat:

> Wretched man, why have you taken up with a foreign religion? Whose is the rice you eat? Who rules the country you live in? If you want to worship the Portuguese king [Jesus Christ], why don't you go to Portugal? As for the rest of you Christians, go home, and do not dare to follow your religion; worship as we do, or your death will be the penalty.

Saint John answered loudly: "Christians, we must obey our ruler when his orders are just; but we must honour and obey God first[18].

Again in Vietnam, a Christian deacon dialogues with a learned Mandarin. The Mandarin:

> Let Europeans follow the religion of Jesus, that is good for them. But you, Annamites, ought to follow that of your country. To leave the national religion in order to adopt a foreign one, that is to be a bad citizen. Even more, it is to be rebellious and liable to punishment. It is to disobey the laws of the State and our sovereign, who forbids us to follow any other religion except his.

The deacon:

> Our religion is nowhere a stranger. It is not circumscribed in any one point of the universe. It is for all peoples and all cultures, because it is of God. You blame us for not

---

[16] JOSEPH CHUNG-MUN KIM and JOHN JAE-SUN CHUNG, *Catholic Korea Yesterday and Today* (Seoul: St. Joseph Publishing Co, 1984) 218.
[17] FROIS, *Relación*, 102.
[18] DONALD ATTWATER, *Martyrs from St. Stephen to John Tung* (New York: Sheed and Ward, 1957) 181.

following the national religion, but what is that religion? The learned have their own, the religion of Confucius, but it is at bottom only a pure ceremonial; it treats only of morality and of rites. It is silent about what is more important for us to know, namely, what man becomes when this terrestrial habitation is dissolved. or is the national religion that of the ordinary folk? But each one for his inclination can take the object which pleases him[19].

From these samples three reasons can be extracted. There reigned a religions resisted, the concomitant political/commercial colonization atmosphere could confuse.

Concerning first the xenophobia, Korea was called the "Hermit Kingdom"; any foreigner could face a death sentence. China had a similar law; St. Francis Xavier was willing to risk it, but ship captains were not, and that is why he died on Sancian island, off the southern China coast. Japan, after two centuries of seclusion, opened to the world only in 1854.

Second, much more did these civilizations resist a foreign religion. Why exchange now, they asked, our cults and religions of several thousand years because of these strange intruders from Europe?

Thirdly, due to the conditions of that era, the religious missionaries from the West necessarily arrived in the same vessels with military, government and commercial envoys searching for territories and fortunes. Correct in their suspicions but wrong in their conclusions, many Asian government officials confused the two distinct motivations. The martyrs, however, clearly discerned the difference; one was from God.

Surely everyone must admit that China, Japan, Korea and Vietnam had their own solid reasons for their reactions at that time; everyone must somehow sympathize with their reasoning. For China, for one instance, the "foreign concessions" were humiliating.

But several centuries later, what is the situation? South Korea can be an example. Although at that time it was the

---

[19] OURY, *Le Vietnam*, 119.

"Hermit Kingdom", and foreigners were liable to death, today a highly efficient tourist bureau's one task is to attract as many visitors as possible into Korea. Korean students are studying in the United States and Europe. Korean tourists themselves are free to visit other countries. Catholics are fully cooperative citizens. In other words, Korea now has accepted freedom of religion, human rights, freedom of conscience, normal contacts with other nations. But at the time of persecutions those Catholics whom they tortured and killed already had accepted and wanted to propagate that very same freedom of conscience, freedom of religion, human rights.

Japan is basically like Korea, and grants the same freedoms. It also has the concern for tourists from abroad and for sending its own students and tourists to other countries.

Somewhat different from Korea and Japan, however, are China and Vietnam. Although these two countries also invite tourists and send students abroad to study, at the same time they severely restrict freedom of religion, freedom of conscience and human rights. These limitations do not arise from the Chinese or Vietnamese national character itself, but from atheistic Communism. If Communism were not ruling there now, most probably they would allow the freedom of religion, the freedom of conscience and human rights common in Korea and Japan.

The question becomes inevitable: Who was correct then at the time of the persecution? The governments had might on their side, but not right, as they themselves have discovered in the intervening years. Perhaps this truth and the experience behind it can help other countries too.

The Martyrs of India, Philippines, Thailand; the Non-Martyrs of Sri Lanka and India

India. Gonzalo Garcia led a fascinating life, from India to Japan to Macao to Manila to Japan. Born near Bombay, as a teenager he went to Japan to help Portuguese Jesuit missioners as a catechist. After some years he left Japan for Macao to interpret for the Portuguese and Japanese traders. Then in Manila he joined the Franciscans as a Brother. When the Franciscans sent priests from Manila to Japan, Gonzalo accompanied them and interpreted before even Hideyoshi, absolute ruler of Japan. He was crucified in 1597 at Nagasaki[20].

Philippines. The already mentioned Lorenzo Ruiz, a father of three children, had a strange story. "I could not stay in Manila because I had a quarrel with a Spaniard"; he feared a trial or mistrial that might end in a death sentence. He accompanied the Dominican missionaries departing from the Philippines; when they landed in Japan, he there surrendered his life for the faith[21].

Thailand. The martyrs here are unique. First, they died for Christ only in 1940. Secondly, although there was then a persecution in Thailand, it was far less severe and universal than in China, Japan, Korea, Vietnam. Yet in their particular village in north Thailand it was intense: the police challenged them to give up their faith or die.

The leader of the group, a married man with five children, was the catechist of the village and responsible for the Catholics there after the French priest was expelled. The police ambushed and killed him in a separate incident.

The other six died together, shot by the police in the cemetery. They were two Sisters of the congregation of the Lovers of the Cross, their middle-aged housekeeper, and three teenagers who lived and worked with the Sisters. Pope John Paul II beatified them in 1989[22].

In this obscure village Thai Catholics have constructed a beautiful shrine on a large area of land between the Mekong river and the cemetery. What makes these martyrs still more distinct is that people are alive who recall the martyrdom. For example, a brother, now seventy, of one of the teenage girls was twelve when it all happened.

---

[20] J.H. GENSE and A. CONTI, *In the Days of Gonzalo Garcia*. Bombay: St. Xavier's College, 1957.

[21] VILLAROEL, *Lorenzo de Manila*, 23.

[22] THAREN, *Canonizationis Servarum Dei Agnetis Phila et Luciae Khambang Ex Instituto Amantium Crucis Cum Quattuor Sociabus Et Servi Dei Philippi Siphong Onphithak Catechistae In Odium Fidei. Uti Fertur. Interfectorum. Positio Super Martyrio*. Roma; Tipografia Guerra s.r.l., 1987.

The Non-Martyrs. The three confessors of Asia, although so few, are very important. They are the beginning of what can and must expand in the decades and centuries to come. Just as European Christians had their martyr St. Sebastian and also St. Francis of Assisi, their martyr St. Agatha and yet also their St. Teresa of Avila, so Asian men and women are needed not to die for the gospel but to live it so integrally that they will become a model of culture and faith. Asia almost everywhere present moment hears and speaks about "inculturation". But inculturation is basically an abstract term. Inculturated confessor saints will be its supreme form in reality.

Sri Lanka. Joseph Vaz was born in Goa, entered the seminary, was ordained priest. After a few years he heard of the situation of the Catholic people in Sri Lanka. During Portuguese rule for about 150 years many had become Catholics. But now the Dutch Calvinists had taken over the island; because no priest was allowed to enter, the faith was in peril. Joseph Vaz offered himself for this threatening task. He entered Sri Lanka as a beggar, worked in secret for many years, visiting the different Catholic settlements, keeping their faith alive. In addition to his own apostolate, he brought in other Oratorians to supplement and continue the work after his death in 1711. His life was truly heroic. Pope John Paul II beatified him in 1992 in Sri Lanka[23].

India. In south India lies the state of Kerala, where Francis Xavier himself labored. Fr. Kuriakose Elias Chavara was the founder of the congregation of the Carmelites of Mary Immaculate, and an indefatigable apostle. He was beatified in Kerala itself by John Paul II in 1986[24]. His followers have constructed a shrine on the top of a hill, where a tomb contains his body and where several adjacent buildings display all kinds of records of his life, even the skiff which he used on the rivers of Kerala.

---

[23] An older life of Blessed Joseph Vaz is still recommended. S.G. PERERA, *The Life of the Venerable Father Joseph Vaz, Apostle of Ceylon.* Galle: Loyola House, 1953.

[24] *Cyriaci Eliae Chavara. Sacerdotis Confundatoris Congregationis Fratrum Carmelitarum Mariae Immaculatae* († 1871). *Positio Super Introductione Causae Et Super Virtutibus Ex officio Concinnata.* Typis Polyglottis Vaticanis, MCMLXXVII.

Sr. Alphonsa belongs to the Clarists, a well-known congregation in India. As a young girl she had a great desire for holiness and to imitate St. Therese of Lisieux. In God's plan sickness was locked into her life. For many years confined to bed and bearing intense pain, on that pain she built even higher holiness. After her death people recognized her sanctity; they prayed at her tomb and were inspired to imitate her. She died only in 1946, just after World War II, and therefore is the latest of all Asian Saints and Blessed. Her congregation has constructed on the top of a hill an imposing shrine; in its chapel lies her body entombed. Nearby a museum exhibits photos, documents and relics of her life[25].

---

[25] CHEVALIER K.C. CHACKO, *Sister Alphonsa*. Bharananganam: Vice Postulator, 1990 is a well known book about Sister Alphonsa.

The Transformation of Culture as New Evangelization (for the Third Millennium in Oceania)

PHILIP GIBBS, SVD

1. INTRODUCTION

As the peoples of Oceania approach the third millennium, what is required for a new evangelization of the region at this time? The life of a community in Melanesia, and the interventions at the recent Special Assembly for Oceania of the Synod of Bishops will provide fresh points of reference for this paper[1]. Synod participants rightly pointed out that the crisis of faith experienced today occurs in the midst of a crisis of culture, and that new evangelization requires a transformation of culture-hardly a simple matter amongst the cultural complexity of the region. This paper argues that, if evangelization is to be culturally and morally relevant in Oceania in the coming decades, then the Church, through dialogue, must contribute a Christological dimension to the life-giving elements found in the wider society. In particular, compassion, community and care of creation will be essential components in any attempt to re-express the truth of the Gospel.

2. FRAGMENTED COMMUNITIES

I had been looking forward to getting established in my new family in the village. It was a special opportunity to try a

---

[1] References to "the Synod" in the text refer to the recent Special Assembly for Oceania of the Synod of Bishops (22 November-12 December 1998).

different form of missionary outreach. For years I had lived on mission "stations" which have structures that often insulate one from the common people. Then I had been teaching at the Seminary, which tends to isolate one even more. Now there was an opportunity to stay with a family for several months, hopefullly a chance to learn at first hand the daily realities that people face.

My arrival coincided with a crisis in the Kaiap community. The family I was to stay with have four girls, and one of them had been attacked by a group of young men, high from smoking marijuana. She is a very strong girl and had managed to beat off her assailants, but suffered a badly bitten hand in the process because, in order to prevent one of her attackers from calling out, she had tried to pull out his tongue. That was only one of a whole series of crises that I experienced in the community. In the first week there we had to deal with a case of incest, drunken brawls, and accusations from one group in the splintered community against another. Except for one Seventh Day Adventist and one Baptist, the community is Catholic and their religiosity has been behind some of the tensions. One group claimed that they were seeing apparitions of the Blessed Virgin, and inferred that others were not able to have the experience because they were too sinful[2].

These are the sort of realities faced by communities in the Papua New Guinea Highlands as they move towards the dawn of the third Christian millennium. For nineteen centuries people there had been unaware of the Christian Gospel. The first evangelization began only fifty years ago. People embraced the new Gospel enthusiastically at first. However, now, after fifty years, a new generation of young people – educated and rather critical – find themselves caught up in a crisis of faith. Changes have fragmented the community. Fundamentalist preaching stirs up fears about the year 2000 and the coming millennium. In such a situation, what forms of evangelization are appropriate?

---

[2] Funding for the research in the Kaiap community was provided by the Research Enablement Program, a grant program for scholarship supported by the Pew Charitable Trusts, Philadelphia, PA., U.S.A., and administered by the Overseas Ministries Study Center, New Haven, CT, U.S.A.

3. Oceania in the Twilight of the Second Christian Millennium

The account above is a particular example from Papua New Guinea. However, it illustrates several features common throughout Oceania: a very recent history of evangelization and dramatic and rapid social change.

Geographically Oceania spans almost one third of the earth's surface. As Cardinal Tomko noted during the recent Synod, Oceania is sometimes called the "water" or "floating" continent because apart from Australia, it is made up of islands and vast expanses of sea[3]. The bishop of Toowoomba noted how his diocese alone is two and a half times the size of Italy, and a former bishop of Rarotonga described his diocese as little dots sprinkled over an area of water the size of Western Europe. The vast distances, resulting in isolation and dispersion of communities, and the mosaic of different cultures and languages, make communication a very real challenge.

The Church "born under the Southern Cross" is relatively young. Christianity came to the region only in the late eighteenth and early nineteenth centuries[4]. In Australia the Catholic Church arrived in 1788 along with the first convicts sent from Ireland. The official beginning of Catholic evangelization in New Zealand coincided with the arrival of Bishop Pompallier in 1838. The nationality and denominational background of the missionaries left a lasting impact on the development of Christianity in the Pacific. A few islands are predominantly Catholic, but throughout most of the Pacific the Catholic Church followed after the previously established denominations of Protestant origin[5].

---

[3] Synodus Episcoporum - *Bulletin*, 10 - 26.11.1998 - 4.
[4] There were some isolated early mission efforts, but they left little lasting impact on the region. See J. GARRETT, *To Live Among the Stars – Christian Origins in Oceania* (Geneva and Suva: World Council of Churches in association with the Institute of Pacific Studies, 1982) 3.
[5] See M. ERNST, *Winds of Change: Rapidly Growing Religious Groups in the Pacific Islands* (Pacific Conference of Churches, Suva/Fiji, 1994).

In recent times there have been dramatic and rapid social changes which leave a lasting effect on Christian faith. Unemployment and migration from the Islands to Australia and New Zealand lead to the breakdown of families. Drift to the cities and urban growth provide opportunities for the rise of new religious groups. Burning issues today include poverty, the physical and sexual abuse of children, the unjust taking of life, the low status of women, the neglect of youth, the problem of drugs, the exploitation of workers, the policies of transnational companies, the rights of indigenous people, and the destruction of the environment.

Today, a tidal wave of secularism, sweeping across the Pacific, is testing the vitality of church life. Worse than antagonism comes indifference. In Australia, weekly mass attendance has fallen from 50% in 1960 to 20% now. In New Zealand the number of those who declare themselves as having "no religion" has increased from 27.2% of the population in 1991 to 37% at the present time[6]. Clearly, many people are facing a crisis of faith in institutional religion.

The problems and challenges notwithstanding, the Church in Oceania offers a unique contribution to the Universal Church. Among these are the following:

- Richness of cultures, languages and ways of expressing faith.
- Laity involved and taking responsibility in church life.
- Closeness to the environment.
- Freshness. The region is the most recent to receive the Gospel
- Multicultural societies
- Tradition of small communities
- Australian and New Zealand societies exhibit the value of tolerance.
- Societies in Papua New Guinea and the Pacific value relationships and hospitality.
- Indigenous spiritualities as an expression of the sacred

---

[6] Source of statistics: intervention of Archbishop George Pell at the Synod, and the address by Cardinal Tomko to the New Zealand Bishops, reported in the *NZ Catholic*, Nov. 29, 1988, p. 8.

	Oceania
Area: 8,508,769 sq.km	Diocesan Priests 2,813
Population: 28,829,000	Religious Priests 2,296
Catholics: 8,047,000	Brothers 2,085
Missionaries sent 1,255	Women Religious 11,872
Missionaries received 1,647	Catechists 12,658

Source: International Fides Service. Nov. 13 and Dec. 11, 1998, pp. 721 and 794.

4. Crisis of Faith – Crisis of Culture

The importance of evangelising culture was noted by Paul VI in *Evangelii Nuntiandi* (1975): "What matters is to evangelise man's culture and cultures (not in a purely decorative way as it were by applying a thin veneer, but in a vital way, in depth and right to their very roots), in the wide and rich sense which these terms have in *Gaudium et Spes,* always taking the person as one's starting-point and always coming back to the relationships of people among themselves and with God" *(EN* 20).

In most parts of Oceania the culture that was the object of the first evangelization no longer exists as such. People today live in a completely different world. How does one proclaim the Gospel in a way that resonates with the local experience of a people's culture and history, in a time of rapid change? The *Instrumentum Laboris* from the recent Synod notes: "The crisis of evangelization is more than just a crisis of faith; it is also a crisis of culture. A number of responses state quite explicitly that the faith has not sufficiently penetrated the culture in question so as to call it and lead it to Christ"[7].

Consider again the people in the Kaiap community. Life is changing rapidly in the Papua New Guinea Highlands. Children go to school and learn about a world quite different from that of their parents. The boys no longer live in the "men's" house, and the initiation rites are abandoned or radically changed. Traditional culture seems outdated – belonging to

---

[7] Synod of Bishops, Special Assembly for Oceania, *Instrumentum Laboris* #21.

those who have died. Village life is "hard". One spends a lot of time gathering firewood, fetching water, and preparing food. In urban areas, for those who have the means, gas cookers, running water, and electric appliances save a lot of time and trouble. However, usually, the gas stove and the television come along with many other trappings of modern Western culture. The religious symbols attuned to a rural tribal way of life begin to lose their meaning in a modern urban setting.

The changes have fuelled an intense debate in the community about traditional cultural values. Some argue that Christians must distance themselves from anything to do with traditional culture and its values, and lead a life guided by "Christian" values and principles. For example, they argue that people who decorate their bodies with feathers and other traditional finery are making a deliberate display of themselves and are guilty of the sin of pride. The element of truth in such thinking conceals the mistaken notion that culture is an extrinsic separable reality, that one can abstract the "essence" of the Gospel, and that traditional cultural values and Christian values share nothing in common. Such ideas easily lead to a separation of faith and life typical of the dualism found in the Western scientific world view[8]. This state of affairs is hardly conducive to a healthy resolution of the cultural crisis in the community.

In New Zealand and in Australia, the crisis of faith for many Catholics is associated with the breakdown of the former Irish Catholic subculture. While the older people experience the collapse of a culture that once nurtured and supported them, young people find themselves hung up between the modernity of the scientific-technological world and post-modern relativism with its questioning of dogmatic certainties. With new found individualism, mobility and competition people are searching for new identities and relationships. In a world deeply suspicious of claims to truth, Christian faith

---

[8] See H. JANSSEN, "Changing Communities in the Context of Changing World View", *Catalyst* 24.1 (1994) 47.

becomes a personal option. The church is feeling the strain of trying to transmit the Gospel to such an evolving new world[9]. What sort of vision can the Church propose in this situation?

In his report, at the Synod, Archbishop Hickey of Perth, asked: "Have we a vision of an evangelised culture or society? What then are the signs of an evangelised culture?" He then replied in terms of Mt. 11:4-5, the vision Jesus gave in response to the questions of John the Baptist's emissaries: "Go back to John and report what you hear and see; the blind recover their sight, cripples walk, lepers are cured, the deaf hear, dead people are raised to life, and the poor have the Good News preached to them". The Archbishop added: "our region will only be successfully evangelised when we are able to repeat these words of Jesus"[10].

5. Evangelization of Culture

The Apostolic Exhortation of Paul VI, *Evangelii Nuntiandi,* helps us realise that evangelization is a complex process. Essentially, however, evangelising means "bringing the Good News into all the strata of humanity, and through its influence transforming humanity from within and making it new" (EN 18). Now one hears frequent reference to the "new" evangelization. Pope John Paul II declares that it is new in its enthusiasm, its methods, and its expression[11].

Firstly, the new evangelization is noted for its evangelical boldness whereby the agents of evangelization show an irrepressible enthusiasm for the task of announcing the Gospel. Since evangelical boldness has its source in the Spirit, since the new evangelization requires a clear appreciation of ways that

---

[9] See Synod of Bishops, Special Assembly for Oceania, *Lineamenta* #17.
[10] Synodus Episcoporum - *Bulletin,* 04 - 23.11.1998 - 18.
[11] According to Avery Dulles these three aspects of the "newness" of the new evangelisation were first mentioned in the pope's address to the bishops' council of the Latin American churches at Port-au-Prince, Haiti, on March 9, 1983. See *Origins* 12 (March 24, 1983): 659-62, at 661, referred to in A. DULLES, "The New Evangelization: Challenges for Religious Missionary Institutes", in S. BEVANS and R. SCHROEDER, eds., *Word Remembered, Word Proclaimed* (Steyler Verlag, Nettetal, 1997) 19, f. n. 3.

the Spirit can inspire a hopeful vision of society in Oceania, based on a revived sense of human dignity. That vision will be accomplished only with Christ (2Cor 5:17).

Secondly the new evangelization should use methods that will "make the Church present at the cultural cross-roads of our time"[12]. This is easier said than done. In many ways the Church throughout Oceania is becoming marginalised from the mainstream culture. The new evangelization does not mean helping people to overcome their indifference to a past Christian culture, but presenting the Good News in a way that offers a life-giving alternative to the dehumanising effects of modern technical culture. Being present at the cultural cross-roads may mean adopting different models of mission and methods of evangelization. The first evangelization accompanied the colonial take-over by European powers. The new evangelization must present the Church not as a power over against the world, but as a sacrament of God in the world. This requires communicative methods, especially collaboration in life situations.

Thirdly, the new evangelization expresses the Gospel News in unaccustomed ways to contemporary audiences. At the Synod, Bishop Walker of Broken Bay asked: "Is the life of the Catholic community a genuine embodiment of our traditional faith which speaks meaningfully and relevantly to the society of which it is a part?"[13]. Offering the gifts of faith in a language and form that are true to tradition yet responsive to modern cultures is a particularly challenging task in Oceania with its great diversity. The more traditional societies must deal with issues of inculturation, while the more modern secularised cultures must take on the challenge of helping people rediscover the sacred dimension of life[14].

---

[12] "Opening Address of the Holy Father", #22, in *Santo Domingo and Beyond: Documents and Commentaries from the Fourth General Conference of Latin American Bishops*, ed. A.T. Hennelly (Maryknoll, NY.: Orbis, 1993) 54.

[13] *L'Osservatore Romano* (English edition) n. 49 - 9 December 1998, p. 18.

[14] There are moves in this direction, for example, the attempt in the Sydney Archdiocese, in a project entitled "A Sense of the Sacred", to revise the curriculum of Catholic Secondary schools. It hopes to affirm what Catholic schools aim to achieve – young people and teachers committed to transforming the world and sharing the Good News.

Dialogue entails both challenging and listening. While every effort must be made to be sensitive to culture and cultural change, at times evangelization means being counter-cultural. To evangelise is to confront not only personal sin, but social and structural sin where there are abuses of power and "cultures of deceits" contrary to the spirit of the Gospel. Agents of evangelization cannot hide from or ignore sinful realities. Cardinal Ratzinger warned the bishops against any false sweetening of the figure of Jesus, and pointed out that the Lord wanted his disciples not to be sugar, but rather the "salt" of the earth[15].

Pope Paul VI reminded us that the Church as agent of evangelization must begin by being evangelised itself (EN 15) The principal source of such evangelization is the Spirit of God. However, the Spirit may well work through elements of the surrounding culture. For example, in Oceania, the traditional cultures can share values including the integral character of indigenous spiritualities, a sense of the sacred, of community, sharing and communal ownership. Modern cultural values include the promotion of the dignity of the person, the contribution that all should make to decision making and the ecological movement. From an ecclesiocentric perspective, culture is too often viewed merely as a *praeparatio evangelica*. However, the divine mission goes far beyond the confines of the Church, and sometimes cultural resources may help to re-express the Gospel in unexpected ways.

6. Credible and Relevant Witnesses

While the first evangelization was relatively successful in Oceania, most would agree that the official Church at least is losing ground in keeping abreast of changes and in influencing the agents of cultural transformation. At the Synod, Cardinal

---

[15] In the summary of Cardinal Ratzinger's intervention, the *L'Osservatore Romano* (daily edition) Saturday 28 November, 1998, p. 8, refers to "un falso addolcimento della figura di Gesù".

Williams of Wellington said that in the more Europeanised local churches of Oceania, the shepherds' joy has turned to grief and anxiety because their flocks are diminishing.

The new evangelization in Oceania must shy away from attempts to restore a form of Christendom–presenting the Church as a powerful force over against the world. Salt or leaven are more appropriate images. The Church does not have a monopoly on evangelization. If evangelization entails bringing the Good News into all the strata of humanity, and through its influence transforming humanity from within and making it new, then there will most likely be other agents of evangelization besides church-going Christians. Church members surely offer an indispensable contribution in giving witness to Christ. But is Christ limited to the Church?

One must be open to the possibility of the Good News being shared by other agents. Where would one find such dialogue partners? They will be found where one finds witness to values such as community, compassion and care of creation.

These values are singled out for three reasons. Firstly, they run counter to many of the dehumanising effects of modernity. Secondly, for some in the wider society, the present performance of the Catholic Church with regard to these values is a source of scandal; as agent of evangelization, the Church may need a conversion of consciousness in these areas. Thirdly, these three values are elements from the surrounding culture in Oceania that can help to re-express the Gospel today. Community, compassion and care for creation surely have meaning in other regions of the world, but they are particularly important for the transformation of culture required for the new evangelization in Oceania.

7. COMMUNITY

God is calling the world to a *communio* of right relationships with the created world and with all people regardless of culture, nation, age, gender, or race. Jesus is the perfect example of this communion (Eph 2: 13-18). He extended a welcome to all, particularly the poor and marginalised, and he left a memorial meal as a way of expressing his commandment of love.

Today throughout Oceania many people are experiencing the undermining and collapse of traditional structures of family and society. Yet the faith is lived and shared primarily through communities and the domestic church – the family. Hence the importance of stressing the communal dimension of Christianity as leaven within existing groupes.

If the Church is to be effective, it must be perceived as demonstrating *communio*. Often this is not the case. For the Catholic Church in Oceania to show greater cohesion and a spirit of communion, a number of issues need to be faced realistically. For example, it is important for the local church to be able to celebrate the liturgy with appropriate liturgical texts in the language and culture of the people. Issues such as the perceived view of the Church on women and on sexual morality must be confronted honestly. More needs to be done in dialogue with other Christian churches and with non-religious currents in society. While there is an evangelical desire within Oceania to progress in these areas, sometimes such initiatives are blocked by outside influences.

Those outside of the region can hardly imagine the immense distances separating small pockets of population throughout much of Oceania. With so few priests, it is increasingly difficult to maintain the dimension of ecclesial union central to Catholic communities – the celebration of the Eucharist. At the Synod, Bishop Kiapseni of Kavieng said that it seems the right of the community to celebrate the Eucharist has become a privilege and a rare one at that. Celebrations of the Word with Holy Communion distributed by a catechist or non ordained religious is no substitute for the celebration of the Eucharist[16]. This is an important issue for the healthy growth of Catholic communities in Oceania. Again, proposed solutions are often considered unacceptable by people outside of the region.

---

[16] Synod Intervention, reprinted as "Tradition and Inculturation" in *General Bulletin msc*, 6/1998 - December, pp. 9-10.

Nevertheless, there are many factors in favour of the communal dimension of a new evangelization in Oceania. There is a widespread desire for participation by all in the life, decision-making processes and ministries of the local Churches. This is apparent, not only in modern societies, but also in traditional tribal cultures as well.

In the Archdiocese of Wellington in New Zealand, there is a Commission for Evangelisation with a full time co-ordinator. An important insight for the church in Wellington is that evangelization is the task not just of the individual but also of the faith community as a whole. Much effort is put into stressing that being Catholic is personal but not private. In a society which increasingly claims no need for faith in the transcendent, there is a renewed effort not to impose impossible obligations, on people but to present the Christian community as one of compassion and companionship. One important area is to reach out to non-practising parents of children in Catholic schools. Also young people are being encouraged to contribute to parish life in active and leading roles[17].

At the Synod, Bishop Gilles Cote of Daru-Kiunga argued for the importance of building Church upon the strengths of culture: "The only way to build the Church, Mystery of Communion, in our Melanesian Society, is to build it with the participation of all, making sure that the key values of the culture become somehow the key values of our process of evangelization.... our efforts and our methods used for evangelization need to make it possible for the Catholic faith to immerse itself in our Melanesian culture and to be re-expressed according to the legitimate forms of that culture. Will the Institutional Church allow Jesus to walk the way of the people of Melanesia, just like he did in Palestine, challenging the truth of their own religious experiences, purifying and enriching their lives, not from outside or from the top, but from within?"[18].

---

[17] See *Response of the Archdiocese of Wellington to the Lineamenta*, published by the Archdiocese of Wellington, January 1998.
[18] Synod Intervention, summary in *L'Osservatore Romano* (English edition) n. 48 - 2 December 1998, p. 15; quotation from type-written manuscript by Bp. Côté.

The church in Oceania will be a credible and relevant witness to *communio* only if it be allowed to grow and flourish as a community. For communion to be a way of life, the church must deal with the obstacles identified by people who have left the practice of the faith. The evangelisers must be prepared to build upon the cultural, ecclesial, and technological strengths that are already present. Communities of the future need not necessarily be physical communities, but could be linked into networks through electronic media. Even if communities are not able to share the Eucharist, they could share in a communion of witness and prophetic action. Christians in Oceania may find existing communities which will welcome the leaven of faith-filled people intent not simply on expanding church membership, but on being effective witnesses to the transforming action of God in the world.

8. Compassion

The media so often portrays the Catholic Church as rigid and judgmental rather than as welcoming and compassionate. This leads to a very real difficulty for the Church in terms of its credibility in the wider community. In Oceania, people are generally very tolerant, but not towards hypocrites. At the Synod, Bishop Patrick Power of the Archdiocese of Canberra and Gouburn noted, "As Church entering a new millennium, we must find new ways of embracing those people closest to the heart of Jesus so that authentically we may 'walk his way, tell his truth and live his life"[19].

In his intervention at the Synod, Cardinal Williams of Wellington spoke about why some people choose not to be members of the Catholic Church. In New Zealand, religiously mixed homes outnumber homes where both spouses are Catholic in the ration of 2 to 1. In such mixed marriages the faith of both the Catholic spouse and the children is perilously at risk because the spouse who is not Catholic finds no welcome in

---

[19] Synodus Episcoporum - *Bulletin* 06 - 24.11.1998 - 4.

the Catholic Church. Pastors witness families choosing reluctantly and painfully to withdraw from allegiance to the Catholic Church in favour of joining another where all the family members can celebrate their unity as a family. The second example given is related to marriage breakdown. In New Zealand only 45% of school age children are being reared in two-parent families. After marriage breakdown some Catholic single parents are faced with the choice of marriage outside the church, or hardship for both themselves and their children. They end up on the periphery of the worshipping community or they join ecclesial communities "where the words of our Saviour, 'Come to me all of you who are heavily burdened and I will give you rest,' appear more credible and comforting." The Cardinal acknowledged the scriptural, theological and canonical bases for the position of the Catholic Church but added, "I simply draw attention to the pastoral consequences, and plead for the development of a pastoral praxis characterised by compassion both for the poor as we usually understand that term and for the 'ecclesially' impoverished"[20].

For a credible and relevant evangelization of culture in Oceania, the evangelisers must follow a lifestyle more explicitly marked by charity and compassion. Several areas stand out for special attention. In Australia and New Zealand, many women, some highly qualified in ecclesial sciences, feel they can find no home in the church. The new evangelization must challenge elements of culture that demean women and, where necessary, challenge practices of the church itself. Youth are another group that warrant particular attention. They are calling the church to witness to the Good News. As Bishop John Dew of Wellington noted at the Synod, young people are struggling with life issues and the church is called to give hope and life to them by proclaiming the Gospel of Jesus Christ: "Our world is not going to be changed by ideas, words, sermons or books. Our world will be changed by the witness of holy lives"[21].

---

[20] Synod Intervention, summary in *L'Osservatore Romano* (English edition) N. 48 - 2 December 1998, p. 16; quotation from type-writen manuscript by Cardinal Williams.
[21] Synodus Episcoporum - *Bulletin* 06 - 24.11.1998 - 5.

The socio-economic sphere is another area of particular concern for discovering the compassionate face of Christ in the transformation of culture in Oceania. Evangelisers need to propose alternatives to the economy-driven model of society which dominates current policy. They must challenge the Darwinian model of survival of the fittest with another in which compassion figures prominently.

In order to break down some of the negative images of the church at present it may be necessary to seek forgiveness of those who have been hurt by its behaviour. It is important to tell the truth, even when this involves the truth about past wrongs and the need for reconciliation. Besides dealing with the blocks to receiving Christ's message of love and compassion, people in Oceania, as they enter into the third millennium, need religious images that touch their deepest aspirations for a truly human society. Bishop Peter Cullinane of the NZ Bishops' Conference said that "we need to re-imagine, re-image, and re-form the church around the theme of discipleship – the church as a community of disciples"[22].

Among the signs in Jesus' proclamation, there is one of particular importance: the humble and the poor are evangelised, become his disciples and gather together "in his name" (EN 12). Witnesses to the Good News in Oceania, following in the footsteps of Jesus, are called to present this compassionate face to the world and in so doing to call people into communion with his Body[23]. This will be an essential part of the new evangelization of culture in Oceania.

9. CARE OF CREATION

People in Oceania find that their resources are being sought after by other nations, for example, in nuclear testing and dumping, logging, and mining. Yet Pacific people are custodians of the ocean which contains over one half of the earth's

---

[22] Synodus Episcoporum - Bulletin 06 - 24.11.1998 - 8.
[23] See "Message to the People of God" #28. Special Assembly for Oceania of the Synod of Bishops, 1998.

total supply of water. Its continued health is important for everyone. With environmental changes and the prospect of rising sea levels, some Pacific islanders are starting to think about finding a new place to call home.

In recent years the question of a nuclear free Pacific has captured the attention of people in Oceania in a way that few other issues have done. It has been admirable to see nations being prepared to sacrifice economic gain and military power in an effort to ensure a life-giving environment for future generations. The church has played an important role in supporting the moral dimension of such questions. However, there are many incentives to find a way to promote respect for creation as the next millennium, draws near.

Traditionally in most parts of Oceania, the land did not belong to the people, but "the people belonged to the land". Today the idea should be stressed that the earth is an expression of the providence of God. The earth and its resources are a challenge to the industriousness, skills and intelligence of the human being taken individually or socially. The task is to promote a life-giving environment for the present generation and their descendants.

Evangelisers in Oceania need to consider the cost to the human environment of "development" which ignores human suffering, and which destroys community values and beliefs. They must challenge models of development that are deeply unevangelical in their squandering the world's resources. As the Papua New Guinea and Solomon Islands bishops have said, "The ultimate determining factor will not be science and technology, but human persons recovering a sense of the unity in creation and arriving at a consensus about what are the right choices to ensure the common good"[24].

The church must also challenge the dualistic world-view that considers nature as helplessly fallen. How can one love and respect what is perceived as sinful? Unfortunately while people are being liberated from fear of demonic inhabitants of the reef

---

[24] "Creating an Environment for Tomorrow" in PNG/SI Catholic Commission for Justice, Peace and Development, ed. *Justice and Development inside Papua New Guinea*, Boroko, Papua New Guinea, n.d. p. 48.

and forest, they are also losing their sense of the sacred significance of the natural world. The challenge is to build upon indigenous spiritualities that help people in Oceania understand that they are part of creation, and at the same time enable them to be citizens of modernity. They are called not only to live in harmony with nature, but also to assure that natural resources lead to fuller human life. This is accomplished through culture - by which they humanise the world and give it meaning.

Evangelisers must promote a culture of life. Respect for creation and "life" issues go together. Archbishop Adrian Smith of Honiara pointed out at the Synod how the Church would achieve much more success in its promotion of the dignity of human life if it were done in the language and context of creation as a whole[25]. Promoting a culture of life demands a cultural transformation that affects people's system of values. It would lead to a spirituality that opposes competition for scarce resources, and promotes the fullness of life for all. It would mean communities of people who believe in the power of the Spirit more than in that of the economy. The new evangelization will dare to promote such an audacious dream.

10. Culture of Life

I began this paper with an account of my first day in the Kaiap community. Reference was also made to the debate going on there concerning traditional cultural values. A former member of the community described the place as a battle ground of satanic forces. With government assistance, a leader in the community had opened an outlet for liquor sales (one of only three in the province), so the hills often resounded to the noise of drunken singing and the uproar from the occasional brawl. In addition, it seems that some "prophets" had introduced the youth to what was called a "faith test" in which boys and girls would sleep in close proximity; the test being whether they could control their desires. Not surprisingly, many "failed" the test. These and other misguided ventures resulted in a very unhealthy community.

---

[25] See Synodus Episcoporum - *Bulletin* 09 - 26.11.1998 - 3.

With my encouragement, the community leaders, elected a new chairman, and began to plan a program of renewal. The program of catechesis, worship and works of service would involve everyone: from the elementary school children, and the youth, to the mature men and women, and the elderly and sick. The leaders were also to press for liquor sales at the Lodge to be restricted to live-in guests only.

There were special healing events, including communal celebration of the sacrament of the sick, and of reconciliation, and even a charismatic mass with fire symbolising the power of the Spirit. However, the high points of the renewal were "bush" experiences; one for the women and another a month later for the men. Although seldom practised in recent times, the men have a tradition of going to an isolated place deep in the forest for rites of growth and purification. For the women it was a new experience. Because of the stories about moral laxity in the community, the leaders decided to conduct sessions on what it means to be a Christian woman today. Mature women instructed younger ones in traditional rituals and lore which they felt had given them pride and dignity as women in the tribe. Many of the young women experienced ceremonies that they had only heard about before. The days of seclusion ended in a procession with a statue of our Lady (dressed in the ceremonial costume of a woman of the clan) and a special celebration of the Eucharist. Reconciliation figured prominently for the men, who after their time of seclusion performed a ceremony in which a spokesman publicly confessed their wrongdoing and then shot an arrow off the mountainside into the valley below as a symbol of their desire to rid themselves of sin.

The account here is just one example of evangelization in a small community in Papua New Guinea. Community life, reconciliation (compassion) and the fullness of life were the prominent themes in this experience of culture expressing the values of the Gospel. I noticed the life-giving effect of people reinterpreting traditional cultural values so they could be meaningful today. For example, women took the symbols of their traditional menstrual seclusion (food taboos and symbolic plants) and incorporated them into prayer and instruction on Christian womanhood. The men reinterpreted the symbols from their purification rituals, applying them to Christian manhood. The symbols had mostly to do with well-being and the fullness of life. At the end of six months, the change was so pronounced that even outsiders were commenting on the community. Symbols in isolation would have little power, but associated with faith in Christ and the power of the Spirit, they helped bring about a renewed way of life for the community.

11. Conclusion

What is required for a new evangelization in Oceania as the third millennium approaches? This paper has argued that amidst the cultural complexity and the rapid changes occurring in Oceania, a new evangelization will mean a cultural transformation. At present the Church is becoming marginalised from the mainstream in the secularised cultures, and is caught up in the separation of faith and culture in the traditional societies. To have an influence, evangelisers do not have to seek after power or privilege for Church institutions. Rather, the most urgent challenge for evangelization in the next millennium entails entering into dialogue, challenging the forces of death, listening to the Spirit working within the culture, infusing life-giving values that are shared by the Gospel. Evangelisers can work together with these elements in the wider culture and contribute a christological dimension to them. They will respectfully listen, challenge, and invite people to make their own the fullness of the truth which is revealed in Jesus Christ.

What will be the signs of an evangelized culture in Oceania? An evangelized culture will be regenerated by its encounter with the Gospel. In particular, community, compassion, and care of creation will be essential components in the new culture of life. These three values run counter to the dehumanising forces experienced today. Values such as these will anchor the delicate and charming canoes of oceanic cultures to Christ the rock of salvation.

> "Let his praise be sung from remotest parts of the earth
> by those who sail the sea and by everything in it,
> by the coasts and islands and those who inhabit them...."
> (Is 42.10).

The African Synod and the powerful word of God in evangelization at the threshold of the Third Millennium

RT. REV. PETER K. SARPONG

Preamble

As we head for the Third Millennium, we in Africa cannot but be worried in a way.

Humanity finds itself entangled in supreme contradictions. Human beings have reached the moon and are trying to explore Mars; human beings make machines talk and "think"; a machine can beat the best chess player in the world. The tremendous advances in communications have brought the world together as a global village.

What happens 8,000 miles away at one moment is almost at the same moment known auricularly or even visually the whole world over.

In spite of all this, human beings are strangers to themselves, not being able to talk to one another; we are not able to use our intelligence to realise the needs of one another. We are insensitive to the plights of one another. The behaviour of human beings towards one another negates the biblical truth that God created us all in his own image and likeness. Many people are worried about their weight; they have too much food, and millions of others are dying of hunger.

Slogan

It was, no doubt, to correct this anomaly that well-meaning organisations and individuals, at the beginning of this last decade of our century, came up with catchy slogans meant to captivate the imagination of humankind: *Food for all by the year 2000, Water for all by the year 2000, Education for all by the year 2000, Health for all by the year 2000.* These slogans called for human beings to do something about the stark inequalities and inequities surrounding us.

But what has the year 2000 got to do with all this? A lot; indeed everything. The year 2000 has meaning only in Jesus Christ, the object, the Means and the Final End of evangelisation. He is the Second Person of the Most Blessed Trinity, the most ancient of all Mysteries, who took upon himself our human nature and became like us in all things but sin (Phillippians 2:7). He is our Saviour, the Unique Mediator between us and God, our only Light, Life, Way and Truth. He became a human being to liberate us from the shackles of iniquity and oppression, or so our faith tells us. Our faith tells us that Jesus is meaningful in each and every situation of our life.

Evangelisation

All history revolves around him. His importance is acknowledged even by non-Christians. Time itself is reckoned with regard to him and his existence. We talk of the year before Christ *(B.C.)* and of the year of the Lord *(Anno Domino)*.

This Master of history has commanded us, his followers, to preach him, to bear witness to him. Preaching Jesus is the core of Evangelisation. It is to make him present in our hearts so that we can make him present in the hearts of others.

Call by Vicars of Christ

That is why at the beginning of this last decade of this century, Pope John Paul 11 called upon all believers to adopt a new evangelisation that would make Jesus indeed relevant in the present-day situation and prepare us for a worthy celebration of his 2000th birth year. This evangelisation was to be new in its method, its intensity and its expression.

Pope Paul VI had earlier called for a new Pentecost. The Pentecost event is a practical, historical synonym of evangelization. The Holy Spirit, the Principal Agent of evangelization, is the Chief Actor on Pentecost. He destroys that antithesis of Pentecost, the Tower of Babel, that edifice of pride, insensitivity and sheer folly (Gen. 11:8). When the apostles preached on Pentecost day, each one of their multi-lingual audience heard them in his or her own tongue (Acts 2:6). The Holy Spirit had brought that freedom that is the result of true evangelization, the disentanglement of oneself from bondage of whatever type.

African Synod

The African Synod was summoned, in response to this call, to adopt a new evangelization and a new Pentecost. It was meant to invoke the Holy Spirit to help Africa destroy the innumerable towers of evil dotted around the whole face of our continent, towers of arrogance, greed, selfishness, ethnocentrism, irreligion and excessive particularism; towers of callousness, power-drunkenness, bribery and corruption, intolerance, vendetta; towers of hedonism, sadism, atrocities of untold proportion and insensitivity to the plight of one another; in short, towers of death, against which we have been urged by His Holiness the Pope, in his Encyclical, *Evangelium Vitae*, to promote, proclaim and consolidate the Gospel of Life in our culture of death.

This was the way the African Church thought it could pave the way for the reign of Christ in the hearts of Africans. It was a kind of very tall order given by Africa to itself. Under the title, *The Church in Africa and her Evangelising Mission Towards the year 2000: You shall be my witnesses (Acts 1:18)*, the Synod Fathers discussed the sub-themes: *Proclamation of the Word, Inculturation, Dialogue, Justice and Peace* and *Social Communication*. The aim was to address the actual situation on the African continent.

Hunger for the Word of God

For this, we acknowledge and rely on the powerful Word of God, that Word that liberates and cleans, as contained in the

Bible. For we Africans have come to accept the Bible as important to us. We are eager for the Word of God as a result of our traditional belief in the supremacy of God. That is why many of us will stop buying or selling to listen to the "evangelist" or "prophet" preaching the Word in market places. We believe in the power of God's Word and have no problem making the Word of God in the Bible central to life. Evangelisation by Word comes readily to us because of our desire to share what we have with others in a spirit of community.

INTERPRETATION

However, whilst acknowledging the supremacy of the pride of place of the Word of God in evangelization, the Synod Fathers could not close their eyes to the fact that there is a problem with authentic interpretation of Scriptures in Africa. The task of giving an authentic interpretation of the Word of God has been entrusted to the living teaching of the Church alone. Its authority in this matter is exercised in the name of Jesus. Many, however, go in for their own personal, literal interpretation which often results in the *'worship of the Bible as book'* to the neglect of life situations. The consequence of this fundamentalist approach to the interpretation of the Bible has been religious conflicts of all forms: Christians against Christians, Christians against Muslims, Christians against followers of Traditional Religion whom they uncharitably accuse of being idolatrous and superstitious.

The different interpretations of the Word of God have worked against the very evangelization we want to promote. For religious intolerance and violence is an unfortunate state of affairs no matter where it is found.

CHALLENGES ARISING FROM THE NEW SITUATION

The Synod was fully aware that this problem is compounded by the newness in the world around us manifested in diverse ways: the advancement of science and technology which affects our conception of the nature of God and the human person; the ever more serious danger of total destruction of the environment; ethnic and excessive tribal particularism which calls for new relationships between peoples of different cultures; the empowerment of women resulting in the awareness of their equality with men in all aspects of life. These changes engulf us as we grapple with the age-old problems of ignorance, ethnic conflicts, poverty, disease and ignorance.

All these are causing the emergence of a totally new world order which is beyond our expectations.

The changes and newness around us, the problems that we face today, indeed call for a new evangelization, a new way of facing reality. We need to discover afresh the newness of the Gospel message in order to realise that the *"Word of God has such force and power that it can serve the Church as her support and energy, the strength of faith for her children, the food for the soul, the pure and everlasting source of spiritual life"* (*Dei Verbum 21;* Catechism of the Catholic Church 131).

The Synod Fathers realised that the situation in Africa requiring this force and power of the Word of God was manifold, complex and frightening.

Situation

Religiously, just as in the bibiical account of the relationship between God and his people, the Israelites, we are told that that latter, again and again, abandoned their God and went after gods that did not exist, gods that had ears but could not hear, eyes but could not see, mouths but could not speak, so also Africa is fast sinking into the abyss of irreligiosity. The wonderful faith all African peoples had in a Creator Supreme Being, for whom each African ethnic group had a name that was unique to him, is mercilessly being eroded. The Supreme Being is gradually being pushed away from the centre of the African's life to the periphery. In the past, we Africans were wise because we feared God and Holy Scripture teaches *"The fear of the Lord is the beginning of wisdom"* (Prov. 9:10). That solidified wisdom of our forefathers is nowadays, alas, liquified by all kinds of worldly, some often un-African, values and is evaporating with alarming velocity.

Secularism is eating its lethal way into our social bones. Especially in the urban situations, Africans are losing a sense of the ultimate, the sense of Deity. In the past, we would, out of fear and respect for God, refrain from committing inhumanities that are currently the bread and butter of many an African society. A soldier who kills an enemy in war had to be ritually cleansed afterwards. When somebody did anything bad, he or she would be told, *"Don't you fear God?"* It appears the African's fear of the Lord has been very badly shaken.

Morally, the African is left in a limbo. We are fast losing hold of our traditional ways of life and yet have not been able to adopt the noble aspects of modernity. Our sense of morality that was dynamic and related horizontally to the neighbour, with whom we live, before being elevated vertically to God has completely lost its power. Crimes that were unthinkable in the "good old days" are now committed almost with masochistic glee. Evils like prostitution, abortion, and daylight robbery are daily haunting our cities. Sin is no longer looked upon with the disgust it deserves. Selfishness, greed and pride have become endemic; we can kill without qualms. South Africa won the sympathy of the world in its apartheid days because the life of the African was not valued by the minority racists. Yet South Africa now has legalised abortion and is reported to be on the way to legalising euthanasia. The evil of brutal, sadistic, sometimes cannibalistic practices of certain traditional secret cults is showing its ugly head again. The horrible phenomenon of devil worship, previously unknown in certain parts of Africa, is now gaining ground in many parts of Africa. The one term that appears most appropriate to describe the current African moral scene now is *decadence* or *depravity.*

Culturally, we are losing our identity with undesirable alacrity. Our cultures once contained and, in many cases, still contain, wholesome values that were the mainstay of our honourable life. As members of a given family or clan, we were known for our communal life; we were hospitable, we loved one another, we cared for our brothers and sisters, we partook in ceremonies and rites; we shared triumphs and defeats. Ideally, we practised collective ownership and corporate responsibility. Our ethnicity, a great gift of God, gave us

Our dignity and a point of reference. It afforded us our security; we were welcomed at home. It was not possible for somebody to be entirely destitute. The clan was always there to lend a much-needed helping hand in times of personal or social crisis. We were proud to be what we were – Mende, Luo, Hausa or Igbo.

These wonderful values of ethnicity have, unfortunately, been turned into ethnocentric absurdity. Ethnocentrism is a perversion of ethnicity; it makes us look in on ourselves; it makes us forget that other people are human beings just as we are, that other people have the right to their dignity and our respect. Ethnocentrism makes us support evil and condone crime. We stand behind "our people", even when they are wrong; it makes us gang with demonic intentions against others. In sum, ethnocentrism is a negation of the humanity and existence of people we do not regard as our own.

There is no doubt that ethnocentrism is the cause of many devastating conflicts in Africa; it is the root cause of many of the atrocities that are taking place all over our continent. In its worst form, it has caused the unceasing wars, intractable inhumanities, and sometimes near genocide that Africa has been witnessing in Rwanda, Burundi, Kenya, Liberia, Sierra Leone, Democratic Republic of the Congo, Somalia, Sudan, Algeria, to name just these few.

Culturally too, we have lost the respect that is due to our elders, the aged and the sacred. We have lost the sense of the decency of human life and we have intensified our oppression of the woman.

Our once proverbial respect for life is gradually giving way to an incredible *"culture of death"*. We tenaciously stick to certain cultural imperatives that are simply outmoded and should be forgotten. No matter what good function they may have had in the past, surely such customs as female circumcision, the disposal of children with disabilities, the killing of twins, human sacrifice and such similar customs cannot now be condoned. That worse practices can be found in Europe, America and everywhere is no excuse for not doing something about them.

Individualism is steadily gaining the upperhand over the African's renowned communal sense.

Politically, Africa has only exchanged colonial servitude with indigenous oppressive terror. Political stability is the exception. This has resulted in one coup after another which, in turn, creates fratricidal wars, tyranny and sheer intimidation.

Political deceit is rampant, vote rigging is taken for granted, political favours are granted without compunction; politics has, indeed, become a dirty game. It has introduced senseless executions, incredible and flagrant violations of human rights in the form of imprisonment without trial, torture, massacre of innocent Africans, suppression of freedom of the press and of association, as well as religious intolerance. The political situation causes favouritism and nepotism and breeds hatred, antagonism and animosity.

Megalomania threatens citizens who do not toe the party line. Self-made godfathers tenaciously cling to power for decades even in the face of worsening socio-economic conditions. They usually manipulate the electoral process to maintain a firm grip over power, usually seen as a personally acquired property.

Here one must commend the exemplary decision of President Nelson Mandela to hand over power to a younger person.

Socially, the state of affairs cannot but create an atmosphere of horror and fear.

There is discrimination everywhere. Internecine conflicts make life impossible for millions. The phenomena of street children, child labour, girl and boy combatants, in some cases, child slavery, are destroying the future of our youth. Rural youth feel lost, are deprived of their identity and, in search of non-existent jobs, flock to the cities where they lack any solid orientation in life. Many of them, in search of greener pastures, abandon their homeland for countries in Europe and America where they are not wanted anyway, and some of them end up as criminals.

The huge number of young people aimlessly roaming the streets of our cities is simply frightening. This has contributed to a large extent to drug abuse and alcoholism. We are being subjected to huge urban situations with all the attendant problems, not the least of which are joblessness, crime, overcrowding, even shelterlessness. The anonymity in the big cities means that the child grows up to become an adult, having lost all appreciation of his origin, traditions, law and culture.

Economically, all this is due to abject poverty that makes life miserable.

Unemployment has taken over in societies where hard work was once prized above any other value. Everywhere, as a result of the political instability, social flexibility and uncertainty, disease reigns, bringing in its wake helplessness and wretchedness. Hunger stares us in the face. The rate of child mortality is frightening. Added to all this is the incidence of refugeeism, which results in hardships more cruel than its demonic causes.

Legally, most African countries are observing the law of the jungle. There seem to be two types of laws: one for the privileged, the other for the underdog. People can be imprisoned and disgraced for stealing one tin of sardines when others can steal or misappropriate $10 million and breathe freely the air of liberty. Laws may be enacted against social evils, like the desecration of the environment, but not be applied because those who break them are men and women of power or influence.

At the *international* level, Africans continue to produce raw materials whose ridiculous prices are fixed by the rich, powerful nations. our nations must continue to grapple with the huge debts imposed on us by the state of our unacceptable indigence. In this context, the movement to have the debts of the poorest countries cancelled is to be commended. However, care must be taken to ensure that it is the poor, and not the rich, who mainly benefit from this cancellation. Moreover, it is for the Governments of the poor countries themselves to see to it that the internal factors contributing to the debts are decisively tackled.

Environmentally, our very source of existence is being depleted at an alarming rate. The jungles of Africa, sensationally described in books written by adventurers in the 17th and 18th centuries, are fast disappearing. Operations of mining companies often cause disease. Environmental degradation is happening everywhere.

Educationally, many African children have no way of going to school. The school may not be there and where it is, the poverty is such that people cannot send their children to it.

In most countries, at best fewer than 70% of school-going children actually do go to school. Many of these are forced to study under trees or in buildings that are death traps. Ignorance, therefore, is a real problem.

Psychologically, Africans have been made to accept an inferior position in their thinking and action. They have been told for centuries that their culture and institutions are inferior and not in any way comparable to those of Europe, and have imperceptibly come to accept this humiliation *de facto* as a reality. Hence many young people look down upon their own culture, spurn it and, wittingly or unwittingly, seek to replace it with foreign habits. What is worse, some even do not know that culture and do not care to know it.

Health-wise, infant mortality remains very high; babies die of the simplest curable diseases. Drugs that have expired are dumped on Africa; African hospitals, in most cases, have become graveyards; doctors that African universities produce at very great sacrifice to themselves flock to Europe and America for greener pastures.

The Role of The Bible

We could go on and on but to what purpose? The situation is sombre. We have not fully described its disastrous effect on the ordinary African. That is the more reason why the Church today *"forcefully and specifically exhorts all the Christian faithful ... to learn 'the surpassing knowledge of Jesus Christ' (Phil. 3:8), for ignorance of the scriptures is ignorance of Christ"* (Dei Verbum 21; Catechism of the Catholic Church 122; St. Jerome).

Love

The Synod presents the Bible to Africans to remind us of and to impress upon us the power of love. It underlines the immeasurable value of love and helps us in our efforts at constructing the *Civilisation of Love* in which there is no discrimination, neither Greek nor Gentile, slave nor free person, man or woman (Gal. 3:28).

The Bible reminds us of the need to live in community. The Bible is the Word of God and the Word of God is powerful; it penetrates into the innermost recesses of the person; it presents God to us as our only source of peace, our only cause of satisfaction. The Bible reminds us of our collective filiation in the common Creator, our Father. It, therefore, reminds us that we are brothers and sisters. The Tutsi and the Hutu, the Kikuyu and the Masai, the Bemba and the Shona, the Zulu, the Asante, all have the same origin and, therefore, must love and not kill one another.

The Bible vividly presents the truth that, in Jesus Christ our Lord, we have a common Saviour. Jesus is at the centre of Evangelisation. He is the Reconciler *par excellence*. Jesus has reconciled us to ourselves and, collectively, to God.

Hope

Jesus summed up His evangelising mission, in the Gospel of Luke, when he went to His own town, Nazareth. He was handed the Scroll and He opened it and read:

"The spirit of Lord Yahweh is on me
for he has anointed me
to bring the good news to the afflicted.
He has sent me to proclaim liberty to captives,
sight to the blind,
to let the oppressed go free,
to proclaim a year of favour from the Lord.... (Lk. 4:18-19).

He then folded the Scroll and said: *This text is being fulfilled today even while you are listening* (Lk. 4:21).

Jesus indeed liberates. He came to establish a Kingdom and he founded a Church to be at the service of the Kingdom, to be its instrument, a means to it and its sign. The Church then is the assembly of men and women who believe in the Lordship of Jesus Christ and who have sealed that belief in baptism. By reason of this baptism, they have become one family, a family that knows no bounds.

In the person of Jesus, therefore, the Bible brings hope to the African; it gives us the certainty of liberation from the bondage of sin. For the Bible exhorts us that in Jesus Christ we should all see a common dignity, and impels us to honour and protect it.

The Bible warns us against the tragedy of vendetta and places before us the sublimity of forgiveness and reconciliation.

It affirms and confirms what is noble and praise-worthy in our cultures and challenges those elements in our way of life that result in debasing behaviour and, indeed, in cruelty.

The Bible teaches the need for Africa to have holy politicians and saintly heads of state if Africa is to be saved.

New Methods

Faced with these tremendous challenges, we need new methods. In order to be able to evangelise, we must allow ourselves to be evangelised so as to experience, through radical obedience (Hb. 5:8; Phil. 2:8) in a new and gratuitous way, the friendly face of God who makes life arise from death (Phil. 3:10-11; Eph. 1:18, 23), and to experience that Jesus is the Lord (Acts 2:31; Phil. 2:11). Therefore, we have to listen to the living Word that God speaks to us in order to be able to proclaim it.

Hence the need for holy priests who offer acceptable sacrifices to God and, by the quality and character of their lives, become effective agents of evangelization.

We in Africa need priests who understand clearly the words of the Lord (Mt. 9:37,38). For, alas, the words of Pope St. Gregory the Great appear to be applicable to Africa now more than ever before: "there *are only a few labourers for a harvest so plentiful, a fact we cannot mention without deep sorrow, because, although there are many who would hear the good news, no one is there to tell it to them. Look how the world is full of priests, yet only very rarely is one of them to be found at work in God's harvest, for although we have well and truly received the offce of a priest, we do not carry out the tasks affached to that offce"*. (2nd Reading of Office of Readings of the Feast of St. Luke).

It is for this reason that realising the role of saintly priests in evangelization, the Synod stressed the need for the proper formation of our priests who would be true labourers.

With such true labourers leading the flock in the various vineyards of Africa, this new experience of God will enable us to look back with profound gratitude for the wondrous deeds of God in the life and history of our people and help us discern and understand God's presence and actions today. From this new experience of God is born the courage to proclaim the Word of God and become authentic witnesses of Jesus Christ.

The Scriptures by themselves do not necessarily open our eyes. What makes us perceive the presence of the resurrected Christ is the concrete gesture of sharing in a vibrant community of believers.

Eucharist

The highest expression of this communion is the Eucharist which reveals to us the sacramental dimension of the Word of God. The New Evangelization opens our eyes and makes us discover the presence of the Good News of the Resurrection in our life.

Inculturation

The Synod Fathers stressed that the Bible pushes us to enter every corner of our society to reform it and to animate it. This is demanded by evangelization whose chief instrument is inculturation. Inculturation, in turn, is the incarnation of the Christian message and Christian life in a particular cultural context in such a way that the experience not only is expressed by elements proper to the culture in question but becomes the principle that animates, guards, vivifies, purifies and directs that culture, transforming it in such a way that there is a new creation. (*Proposition 28 of the Synod of Bishops*).

Even a cursory look at the account of salvation history makes it clear that the Bible would want the Christian life to be a part of each and every culture. There is no super-culture whose traits must be adopted by universal Christianity. on the contrary, every culture has elements that are noble and praise-worthy and can enrich the Christian message and be enriched by the same.

To enable the Christian message to permeate and enrich our cultures, it is important that the Bible be translated into the various languages and also be made easily available to these cultures. This fact was stressed in a particular way by the Synod.

Elements

Obviously, there are cultural elements that are unwholesome and, in the light of modern reality, obsolete. These, naturally, must be abolished, substituted for or else purified. There are other elements that are indifferent and can be turned to good or, if not well-handled, to evil.

Evangelisation in Africa should clearly distinguish between these elements. The idea of a Creator God, Supreme in everything, Cause of everything, Just, Eternal, Kind, Fatherly, Provident, Giver of everything that is found in all African societies and cultures, is an excellent platform from which to launch our inculturation satellite into the orbit of evangelization. But the spirit of retaliation that has become endemic everywhere in Africa is clearly contrary to biblical aspirations. When it comes to institutions such as initiation ceremonies, dancing and so on, it is what one makes of them that matters.

The Bible has a Book of Proverbs. We need to have our own book of proverbs talking about God and the African values of morality, good life, obedience, kindness, mercy, compassion, love, unity, justice and peace and so on. The so-called life cycle ceremonies do resemble and, in many parts coincide with aspects of all the Sacraments. It has been said innumerable times, for example, that polygyny and divorce are cultural in Africa. But it can be shown also that, for example, in Asante, whereas polygyny may indeed be part of the actual culture, in reality it is against the ideal culture.

Church as family of God

The Synod of Africa stressed the image of Church as Family of God. The wholesome elements in the African Family, well utilised, could be a great asset in our search for solutions to some of the problems of Africa. By baptism we become members of the Church and form one family. Why can't we use the good values of the African family to nourish this Christian family?

Action

Here it is good to note that we have gone far beyond the stage of justifying inculturation, We have reached the stage of action and should be thinking in specific terms of what actually to do. We bear in mind that inculturation does not deal only with dancing and singing, as some Fathers of the Synod thought, nor should we think that inculturation has no relevance to issues of justice and peace. If we were truly inculturated, those issues of injustice and violence would not even arise.

Inculturation is not a glorification of the past. It deals with the present, the actual situation of the African. It is a contextualised theology touching the felt needs of the African.

Obsession with Spirits

And here we enter the whole area of obsession with the spirit world. All over Africa, people live in daily dread of witches and magicians and other spirits or semi-spiritual beings. Has evangelization nothing to say here? What about the power of Christ? Of course, there could be an exaggeration in emphasising the power of Christ to deliver us from evil at the expense of the presentation of Christ as a Person of love, humility, compassion, concern, of purity, of holiness and of justice to be imitated.

This is how the Bible portrays Jesus Christ to be. Secondly, where and how does the Holy Spirit fit in in the African cosmology? What is the relevance of the invincible sanctifying, recreating Spirit to an environment replete with demonic spirits?

Book for the World

The Bible must become a book for the world because we cannot understand the Bible without the human reality in need of salvation, nor can we understand the human reality without the Bible.

Our biblical apostolate in the new evangelization should question our deformed world. The light of the Gospel should enable us to discover and destroy the idols we have made and dispel the shadows that prevent human beings from walking in the light of God (Rev. 21:24)

The New Evangelisation to which we have committed ourselves *"demands from us new ways of reading and proclaiming the Word, in continuity with the sound tradition of the Church. We should start with the reality in which we actually fnd ourselves today, and allow the Word of God to throw light on this reality. This would entail, on our part, affentive listening to the God who speaks through the Scriptures, through the Church and through the human situation. Such a reading will reveal to us the true face of God, not the God of abstract philosophy, who remains unmoved by the events of the world, but the God and Father of our Lord Jesus Christ, whose face in Christ, and through the coming of the Kingdom of God, is turned in loving compassion and concern for all those who suffer in every age and are struggling to fnd meaning in their lives"* (CBFIV Plenary Assembly, Bogota 1990, Final Statement 7.1).

STRATEGY

The Fathers of the Synod realised that for all this there should be a strategy. It has been noticed that in most Dioceses in Africa only between 10 and 20% of Catholics take part in Church services. Up to something like 80% of all the children baptised in Church are illegitimate. Church services are often experienced as boring, especially by the youth. In many places, the Church is fast losing the young.

We can hardly, therefore, follow the programme sketched above without some definite plan. What is needed in order to answer the challenge of the Synod are small cells of vibrant Christian life, especially among the young. A way should be found of raising up Christians with the spiritual quality of the early Christians of the Acts of the Apostles and the Letters of St. Paul and with the quality of the Martyrs of Uganda.

The Jesus Method

How do we get such Christians? We suggest that it is not through the Sunday Eucharist nor is it through homilies or programmes designed for the crowds. It would appear that in the circumstances serious formation of small groups of "disciples" is what is needed. We have to adopt the "Jesus method". He chose a small group of committed apostles and entrusted the gigantic task of evangelization to them.

Schools of Evangelisation

It is for this reason that the Schools of Discipleship and Evangelisation are becoming popular in Africa as a follow-up to the African Synod. These Schools of Evangelisation are the result of an international organisation called "Youth with a Mission". This programme has been taken over by the Charismatic Renewal in many different African countries. Latin America is reported to have more than 300 such Schools or operations within the Catholic Church.

Formulae

The simplest formulae to use to understand and realise the objectives of such Schools are the following:

1. There is a novitiate for lay people, men and women. This novitiate is not preparing people for entry into a religious community but for entry into the Christian life in the midst of the world: of family, of job and of civic responsibility. The focus of the formation given is not to acquire head knowledge but heart understanding. The emphasis is not on talks, lectures and conferences but on one to one exchanges that will ensure

the basic character formation of the "novices". There is a heavy emphasis on prayer, study of Scripture and other holy writings and manual work. In this way, the students are together initiated in a practical way into a deeper Christian life. Again, the emphasis is on the practice of Christian life, not on the theory of it.

2. In an ideal situation, the Schools should be staff intensive, with about two or three students to a member of staff. In some places, the School is expected to last for six months. It comprises four months of basic discipleship training in the light of the Gospel. This is followed by one month field work. The students are sent out, as Jesus sent out his disciples, to apply the training given and test their spiritual strength and weaknesses.

3. Then follows another month spent on return to the School. This helps to integrate the practical experiences gained with the more theological knowledge acquired earlier.

4. This School deliberately has both men and women. It is essential that students work through the problems and tensions and come to an option for the way of holiness. In accordance with the words of Scripture: *Speak* to *the whole community of Israelites and say: 'Be holy, for I, Yahweh your God, am holy'*". (Lev. 19:1-2)

5. Once the students have completed their six months training, they are expected to be multipliers of Gospel life. Some will simply return to their situation which they left, be it prayer groups or parishes or sodalities and be "vision carriers" there. Others are employed full-time to reach out to different groups of people.

Follow-up

Each year the former students are brought back for deepening courses and retreats. Some will reach out to various groups of people who require sympathetic attention, such as victims of AIDS and their families, praying for and with them and leading them to conversion and a holy death in Christ. In every way, every graduate of the School is expected to be a lay apostle in the deepest sense of the word, except that they are better prepared than lay apostles of past generations. It is hoped that they will bear mutual fruit to revitalise the Church and bring the vision of a deeper Christian life to many, the vision of an evangelising Christianity, as it was in the early Church.

Kumasi Diocese

Kumasi Diocese has benefitted enormously from these Schools of Evangelisation in the past eight years. Some of the graduates of the Schools have been able to make scores of converts in villages that did not have a single Catholic. They are indeed involved in primary evangelization in its strictest sense of the word.

Biblical Foundation

It is essential that these graduates are trained in the biblical apostolate. It is expected of them that they bring the power of the Word of God to bear on their work.

Crusade Against Bribery and Corruption

It is only then that we hope that the programme, such as the Bishops of Ghana have launched to prepare Ghanaians for a worthy entry into the Third Millennium, can have any hope of even a partial success.

Ghana, like all African countries, is plagued with the evil of bribery and corruption which has eaten its way into every fibre of our society. It was felt that the Church had to do something concrete about the situation. Therefore, on July the 10th, the Bishops declared a crusade against bribery and corruption. The thrust of the crusade, in the words of the Bishops themselves, is:

"We hereby declare a crusade against bribery and corruption and appeal to the whole Church, clergy, religious, and lay, to begin it right away with intensive prayer. Let us celebrate Masses, use Novenas, hold prayer meetings, organise pilgrimages, adoration of the Blessed Sacrament, symposia, etc., all for that purpose.

We further suggest that at the end of every Mass, a special prayer be said for Ghana. Initially, the pastor will decide on the form of the prayer to use. At a later stage, we will compose a brief prayer for this. We call on all Christ's faithful to form small units and cells of people committed to honesty and probity, to wage a relentless war on dishonesty and impropriety.

It is not going to be easy. Those who are so committed to the defence of their compatriots and the promotion of justice in this country should be prepared:

i) never to give bribes, under any circumstance whatsoever, no matter what their needs may be;

ii) to vow never to demand or accept bribes, even if this will deprive them of a job to which they are entitled,

iii) to commit themselves to combating any acts of bribery and corruption that they notice or that comes to their attention.

In doing this, they should be ready to be condemned; they may be imprisoned; they may be fined heavy sums of money; they will be hated; they will be persecuted; they will be disgraced. However, they should always remember the words of the Lord: "Blessed are those who are persecuted in the cause of uprightness: the kingdom of Heaven is theirs" (Mt 5:10).

We charge the Justice and Peace Commission on parish and diocesan levels with this grave responsibility. We, your Bishops, pledge our support to all who shall be victimised in this exercise.

We appeal in a special way to our Catholic young men and women to direct their energies to this crusade. We plead with them to tackle this problem ecumenically with their brothers and sisters of the other Christian Churches. We make a passionate appeal to our Muslim brothers and sisters and the followers of traditional religion, all of whom believe in the paternity of God and our filiation in him, to join in this campaign to deliver our nation from the clutches of the bane of corruption".

Conclusion

In conclusion, many Bishops' Conferences of Africa, in preparation for the Great Jubilee, realise that there is need for every Diocese to establish a special Biblical Apostolate. In line with the thinking of Vatican Council ll, we realise that we should be especially attentive to the context and unity of the whole Scripture, that we should read the Scripture within the living tradition of the Church, that we should be attentive to the analogy of faith and the coherence of the truths of faith among themselves and within the whole plan of Revelation.

We realise that:

1) "The Bible is a book that deals with our relationship with God in the context of a believing community and not a book that gives scientific explanation of the world".

2) There is a "gradual unfolding of the pedagogy of God in the Bible. Therefore, in interpreting texts the total content and the global dynamism of God's plan which culminates in Christ must be taken into account".

3) "Since the Bible uses a variety of literary devices, care should be taken, in its interpretation, to explain them using a proper methodology".

4) "It is not possible to read the Bible and understand its message independently of the community and the historical context in which it lives".

We also realise that a new way of reading the Bible should give a new thrust to the biblical apostolate towards a more effective evangelization:

1) A thrust from the book to the Word: through Bible reading, the Word of God should become alive in the hearts of all people.

2) A thrust from a private reading to a transforming presence in the world: In our private reading of the Bible, we need to be inspired by the Spirit of God to transform our society.

3) A thrust from Church to the Reign of God: The Church, like Jesus, is a servant. Her fulfilment is derived from humble service to the world as she gathers humanity in a new community of love around Christ.

In order that the Bible take its righfful place in the evangelising mission of the Church, we realise that it is necessary to ensure that the Bible is not only owned and read but also believed.

In response to the call to return to the Bible, the faithful are encouraged to organise and participate in biblical activities such as Enthronement of the Bible, the celebration of Bible Sunday and Bible Week especially in parishes where this is not a practice.

The Christian family life is urged to have its centre of unity and strength in the Word of God. To this end, we propose that family prayer become an occasion for reading and reflecting on the Word of God. Marriage and Family Life Formation groups like "True Love Marriage and Family Life Ministry" are encouraged to emphasise the use of the Bible at meetings and in the home.

The catechesis of the youth who are the evangelisers of today and tomorrow is to be based on the Bible. Preparation for the reception of Sacraments of Initiation and Marriage are to be biblically orientated.

Women are especially encouraged to become agents of evangelization. Bible-based programmes are to be planned for women's groups so that the Word of God can empower them for effective evangelization.

At the first Pentecost all those who received the Spirit became prophets of the Word. They were sent into the world to begin the creation of a new heaven and a new earth. We believe that the same Spirit is in our midst today, inviting us to be prophets of the New Evangelization.

Finally, we pray that through the intercession of the Blessed Virgin Mary, Star of Evangelization, we realise the vision of the Church to have an organised biblical-pastoral response to the many challenges of this Evangelization Mission of the Bible in Africa as we head for the Great Jubilee.

Les Eglises d'Afrique et la «nouvelle Evangélisation»

RENÉ LUNEAU

Même si, à la fin de l'année 1975, dans une exhortation apostolique demeurée célèbre: *Evangelii nuntiandi,* le pape Paul VI avait magistralement ouvert le chemin de la «nouvelle évangélisation», l'histoire retiendra que le pape Jean-Paul II en a été l'infatigable artisan. Pendant les deux dernières décennies (1978-1998), ne ménageant ni son temps ni sa peine, il aura parcouru en tous sens les cinq continents, afin qu'une fois encore, Pierre pût «confirmer ses frères dans la foi» (Lc 22, 32).

C'est, à ma connaissance, en Haïti, au début de l'année 1983, et au cours de la 19ème Assemblée plénière du Conseil épiscopal latino-américain (CELAM), alors que se préparait la célébration du cinquième centenaire de l'Evangélisation de l'Amérique (1492-1992) que Jean-Paul II évoqua pour la première fois, de manière explicite, la nécessité d'une «nouvelle évangélisation»: «La commémoration du demi-millénaire d'évangélisation, déclara-t-il aux membres du CELAM, aura sa pleine signification dans la mesure où elle est un engagement pour vous, comme évêques, avec vos prêtres et vos fidèles; un engagement non de réévangélisation, mais d'une *nouvelle évangélisation.* Nouvelle en son ardeur, dans ses méthodes, dans son expression»[1].

L'expression connut d'emblée une grande fortune et constitua depuis lors l'un des axes majeurs du pontificat. Mais alors que dans le monde occidental, la «nouvelle évangélisation» se proposait surtout d'exorciser les méfaits de sociétés à ce point

---

[1] In *Documentation Catholique (DC),* n° 1850 (17 avril 1983), p. 438. (Je souligne).

sécularisées qu'elles n'accordent plus aucune place à la dimension religieuse de l'homme, il semble qu'en Afrique, on ait vu en elle, essentiellement, une autre manière d'exprimer la nécessaire *inculturation* de la foi dont on débattait abondamment depuis quelques années déjà. Ainsi, au cours de l'été 1985, le pape Jean-Paul II, évoquant, devant des intellectuels camerounais réunis à Yaoundé, l'enracinement de la foi en terre africaine, leur disait: «C'est à vous laïcs et prêtres africains qu'il appartient de faire que cette graine (de l'Evangile) produise un fruit original, authentiquement africain, de permettre de faire lever toute la pâte chez vous. C'est tout l'enjeu de la *seconde évangélisation* qui est entre vos mains»[2]. Deux ans plus tard, en mai 1987, il reprenait les mêmes propos, en présence cette fois des évêques malgaches venus à Rome en visite *ad limina*: «Vous avez souligné, leur disait-il, l'enjeu de l'inculturation. On peut parler à ce propos d'une *nouvelle évangélisation* qui est désormais entre vos mains; elle vise à produire, à partir de la sève authentiquement chrétienne reçue d'en Haut, des fruits authentiquement malgaches, en union avec les autres églises particulières du continent africain et avec l'Eglise universelle[3]. «Il n'y a donc pas lieu de s'étonner que les *Lineamenta*, préparant le Synode africain, et publiés en juillet 1990, évoquent «une évangélisation primaire (ou première proclamation)» à laquelle «doit s'ajouter une indispensable évangélisation *renouvelée* pour ceux qui sont déjà baptisés»[4].

On peut ainsi légitimement tenir pour équivalent, en contexte africain, *inculturation* et *nouvelle évangélisation* – et il en va sans doute de même dans les autres continents où le message évangélique rencontre des univers culturels et religieux qui lui ont au départ profondément étrangers. Toutefois une difficulté demeure: que faut-il entendre au juste par *inculturation*? Le pape Jean-Paul II a souvent parlé de cette question

---

[2] In *D.C.* n° 1903 (6 octobre 1985), pp. 914-915. (Je souligne).
[3] In *L'Osservatore Romano,* 22 mai 1987, p. 4 (Mots en italiques dans le texte).
[4] *Lineamenta*, «L'Eglise et sa mission évangélisatrice vers l'an 2000». «Vous serez mes témoins». Cité du Vatican, 1990, n° 19, p. 25. (Mot en italiques dans le texte).

controversée rnais il n'est pas toujours facile d'harmoniser l'ensemble de ses discours[5].

On se souvient peut-être que, dès 1979, quelques mois après le début de son pontificat, dans une allocution adressée à la Commission biblique pontificale, Jean-Paul II avait déclaré: «Le terme acculturation ou inculturation a beau être un néologisme, il exprime fort bien l'une des composantes du mystère de l'incarnation»[6]. Le pape y revint longuement l'année suivante lors de sa première visite à l'Eglise du Kenya: «L'acculturation» ou «l'inculturation» que vous promouvez à juste titre, disait-il aux évêques rassemblés, sera justement un reflet de l'incarnation du Verbe, lorsqu'une culture, transformée et régénérée par l'Evangile, produit à partir de sa propre tradition *vivante*, des expressions *originales* de vie, de célébration et de pensée chrétienne»[7]. Trois ans plus tard, en avril 1983, recevant cette fois des évêques zaïrois en visite *ad limina*, Jean-Paul II ne craignait pas d'évoquer devant eux ces premiers siècles de l'histoire chrétienne ou cohabitaient «des Eglises judéo-chrétiennes, des Eglises orientales et des Eglises latines. Cette diversité, disait-il, a parfois été accentuée jusqu'à des tensions et des schismes. Il n'empêche que la coexistence de ces diverses Eglises reste la manifestation la plus typique et à bien des égards la plus exemplaire d'*un légitime pluralisme dans le culte, la discipline, les expressions théologiques*»[8]. Lui-même avait souligné avec force dans la Lettre de fondation du Conseil Pontifical pour la Culture, qu'«une foi qui ne devient pas culture est une foi qui n'est pas pleinement accueillie, entièrement pensée et fidèlement vécue»[9]: il déclarait en outre en 1987, lors d'une assemblée de ce même Conseil: «Ce néologisme (l'inculturation) découvre un enjeu capital pour l'Eglise, surtout dans les pays de traditions non chrétiennes. En entrant en contact avec les cultures, l'Eglise doit accueillir tout ce qui dans les traditions des

---

[5] Je crois utile de reprendre ici, parfois très librement, quelques pages que j'ai consacrées à cette question dans mon livre *Paroles et silences du Synode africain, 1989-1995*, Paris, Karthala, 1997, pp. 49 ss.
[6] In *D.C.*, n° 1764 (1979), pp. 455-456.
[7] In *D.C.*, n° 1787 (1.6.1980) p. 534 (Je souligne).
[8] In *D.C.*, n° 1854 (19.6.1983) p. 604 (Je souligne).
[9] In *D.C.*, n° 1832 (1982) pp. 146-148.

peuples est conciliable avec l'Evangile pour y apporter les richesses du Christ et pour *s'enrichir ellemême de la sagesse multiforme des nations de la terre* (..) L'inculturation engage l'Eglise sur un chemin difficile mais nécessaire»[10].

Il suffisait d'ailleurs à Jean-Paul II d'interroger sa propre tradition. Lors de sa première visite en Pologne en juin 1979 le premier pape slave de l'histoire avait affirmé, face à la foule rassemblée dans la cathédrale de Gniezno, qu'«il devait venir un moment où les successeurs des Apotres auraient commencé à parler également la langue de nos aïeux et à annoncer l'Evangile au peuple qui ne pouvait le comprendre et *l'accepter* que dans cette langue[11]. «Ainsi la langue et la culture qui la porte lui apparaissaient-elles comme une sorte de *passage obligé* dans la transmission de la foi, faute de quoi la foi ne serait ni comprise ni, surtout, acceptée».

Or, il semble bien que, face à ce discours qui voit dans l'inculturation «l'incarnation de l'Evangile dans les cultures autochtones et *en meme temps* l'introduction de ces cultures dans la vie de l'Eglise»[12], et cela pour un enrichissement mutuel, il y en ait un autre d'une *tonalité sensiblement différente*. J'ai évoqué plus haut ce discours du pape aux intellectuels camerounais dans lequel il leur confiait, en quelque sorte, la tâche de la *nouvelle évangélisation*. Evoquant les fruits qu'on peut légitimement attendre d'une inculturation de la foi en terre africaine, le pape poursuivait: «Ces fruits représenteront une nouvelle richesse pour votre pays comme pour l'Eglise entière qui les attend de grand coeur pour être toujours plus «catholique». Et d'ajouter: «On peut observer aussi qu'ils auront forcément des points communs avec ceux produits dans l'Eglise catholique. Les exigences du Seigneur sont les mêmes en matière d'amour, de pardon, de paix, de pureté. Le Credo est le même. La tradition vivante de l'Eglise exprime la façon dont cet Evangile et ce Credo ont été vécus, avec l'Esprit-Saint et le Magistère, dans la trame d'une histoire concrète certes, mais en réponse à des

---

[10] In *D.C.*, n° 1935 (1.3.1987) p. 242 (Je souligne).
[11] In *D.C.*, n° 1767 (1.7.1979)p. 611 (Je souligne).
[12] Lettre encyclique *Slavorum Apostoli* in D.C. n° 1900 (21 juillet 1985), p. 724.

questions vraies de l'esprit et du coeur humain qui rejoignent une *expérience universelle*. Il y a un donné théologique qui est le *chemin obligé* d'un approfondissement *ultérieur* dans les cultures. Il importe que les chrétiens de ce pays et de ce continent étudient à fond ce donné qui caractérise leur propre histoire, pour tracer une voie sûre et profitable, en communion avec toute l'Eglise»[13].

Et c'est ici que le bât blesse! Car, outre le fait que le travail propre de l'inculturation semble remis à plus tard, puisqu'il ne s'agit que d'un «approfondissement ultérieur», quelles peuvent bien être les chances du «chrétien camerounais», fut-il «intellectuel», d'étudier à fond ce donné théologique qui seul le rend possible? Faut-il croire que l'inculturation de la foi reposera essentiellement sur la seule érudition des clercs?

Or il ne manque pas de textes pour conforter cette manière de voir, tel ce discours du pape aux évêques zaïrois le 23 avril 1988: «Tous ceux qui travaillent à cette oeuvre («exprimer le mystère chrétien selon le génie africain») doivent *d'abord* approfondir la Bible, les Conciles et les documents du Magistère. Assimilant dans la foi le message universel chrétien, ils pourront l'intégrer dans leur culture[14]. «Le discours d'avril 1983 évoquant la cohabitation d'Eglises judéo-chrétiennes, orientales, latines et un «légitime pluralisme dans le culte, la discipline, les expressions théologiques» ne semble plus de saison». Certes, chacun sait bien que l'inculturation de la foi dans la tradition religieuse du peuple évangélisé ne peut être qu'une oeuvre de longue haleine mais quelle part en revient à l'humble *peuple de Dieu* qui témoigne, par sa vie même, de la foi qu'il a reçue? Doit-il attendre patiemment, dans l'ombre, qu'on lui dise ce qu'il doit vivre et penser?

Et pourtant, dans l'homélie prononcée le jour même où s'ouvrit le Synode (10 avril 1994), le pape Jean-Paul II revint

---

[13] In *D.C.* n° 1903 (1985), p. 915. J'ai longuement commenté ce texte dans un article de la revue *Etudes* de mai 1989, article intitulé «Une tradition africaine de la foi?» (pp. 657-667).
[14] In *D.C.* n° 965 (3 juillet 1988), p. 652. Certains passages de ce texte ont été repris *in extenso* dans une adresse de Jean-Paul II à la Conférence épiscopale du Bénin le 3 février 1993 (in *D.C.* n° 2068 (21 mars 1993), p. 253.

avec insistance sur cette autre manière de concevoir l'inculturation: «Il *faut*, déclara-t-il, *que l'Assemblée du Synode pour l'Afrique s'inspire de tout le Magistère de l'Eglise*; il faut qu'elle lise en profondeur et de son point de vue personnel, toutes les vérités que contient le nouveau *Catéchisme de l'Eglise catholique*, récemment publié. Après cette phase romaine de travail, le Synode doit se déplacer en Afrique avec le patrimoine acquis et là, partout où il le jugera utile, il devra témoigner de sa naissance africaine»[15]. Semblable rappel s'imposait-il à l'ouverture d'un Synode d'évêques, qui sont en raison même de leur charge, «docteurs de la foi» et à qui incombe en tout premier lieu, la responsabilité de la nouvelle évangélisation de leur continent? Leur faudra-t-il trouver une expression africaine adéquate aux 2865 articles que compte le *Catéchisme de l'Eglise Catholique*? Ne s'agit-il que d'acquérir et d'assimiler un enseignement élaboré, pour l'essentiel, sous d'autres latitudes, qu'on s'efforcera, avec plus ou moins de bonheur, de traduire et d'adapter aux nécessités du lieu? Le Peuple de Dieu qui est en Afrique n'est-il là que pour accueillir, applaudir, célébrer? N'a-t-il rien à dire de sa propre expérience de la foi? Comment ne pas remarquer que les Eglises dites du Tiers-Monde sont *totalement* absentes *du Catéchisme de l'Eglise catholique*? Est-ce un hasard si, parmi les 54 références répertoriées dans la rubrique «les Documents ecclésiaux» *une seule* concerne ces Eglises[16]? N'ont-elles rien écrit, rien dit qui mérite d'être retenu alors qu'elles constituent pourtant près des 2/3 de la Communion catholique dont le nouveau Catéchisme entend exprimer la foi aujourd'hui[17]?

Il n'est donc pas surprenant que le Synode africain (1989-1995), si bien intentionné soit-il[18], ne soit pas parvenu à clari-

---

[15] In *D.C.* 2094, (15.5.1994), p. 475. Mots en italiques dans le texte.

[16] Il s'agit en l'occurrence du document de Puebla (Mexique, 1979) à propos de la «religion populaire» (n° 1676).

[17] Cf. RENÉ LUNEAU, «Qui écoute ce que l'Esprit dit aux Eglises»? in «Les nouveaux appels de la Mission», *Revue Africaine des Sciences de la Mission*, 1994/1, pp. 271-283.

[18] J'ai noté ailleurs (in *Paroles et silences...* pp. 51-54) les changements très sensibles que le *Document de Travail* (février 1993), préparatoire au Synode, apporte à ce que les *Lineamenta* (juillet 1990) avaient écrit à propos de l'inculturation.

fier sa pensée en matière d'inculturation. Lorsque viendra l'heure des *propositions* soumises par l'assemblée à Jean Paul II, il rappellera avec force la nécessité d'une réelle inculturation «*l'un des plus grands défis de l'évangélisation pour les Eglises d'Afrique et de Madagascar, à l'aube du troisième millénaire.* Elle (l'inculturation) est l'expression de communauté (prêtres, religieux, laïcs, théologiens, artistes, etc.) qui fait porter du fruit à chacun selon ses talents»[19] (prop. n° 33). Dans le même temps, il mettra en exergue les deux critères qui jugeront en dernier recours la qualité de l'oeuvre entreprise: «la compatibilité avec le *message chrétien* (...) la communion avec l'Eglise *universelle*». Il aura à coeur d'«utiliser les aspects les plus nobles de la culture» et «d'abandonner ceux qui sont contraires aux valeurs chrétiennes»[20] (prop. n° 31).

Or, ce qui, en première lecture paraît aller de soi, se révèle, à la réflexion, moins clair qu'il n'y paraît. «Message chrétien» qu'est-ce à dire? S'agit-il de l'Evangile, de la charte des Béatitudes, ou faut-il en étendre le champ à «toutes les vérités que contient le nouveau Catéchisme» et à chacun de ses articles? Qui dessinera les frontières d'une Eglise «universelle» dont on subodore, non sans raison, qu'elle est pour l'essentiel *latine* alors qu'on sait, depuis Vatican II, qu'elle est d'abord le fruit de la communion de ces Eglises locales «*en qui et par qui* existe l'Eglise catholique une et unique»[21]? L'inculturation requiert-elle autre chose que l'intangibilité du lien qui, dans la foi et dans la charité, doit exister entre toutes les Eglises, au service desquelles l'Eglise de Rome exerce son charisme de communion et d'unité? Que dire de ce vocabulaire instrumental qui ne renonce pas à «utiliser» «les aspects les plus nobles de la culture», fut-ce à des fins d'évangélisation, et qui déprécie les autres? Au nom de quels critères *évangéliques*? N'avait-on pas reconnu que l'inculturation n'était pas dissociable de l'évangélisation ellemême et qu'en elle se révélait aujourd'hui le mystè-

---

[19] Cf. M. CHEZA (éd.), *Le Synode africain. Histoire et textes*, Paris, Karthala, 1996, p. 255.
[20] Id. p. 254.
[21] Cf. Constitution dogmatique *Lumen Gentium*, 1964 (n° 23) in *Documents conciliares. Concile Oecuménique Vatican II*, t. 1, Paris, Centurion, 1965, p. 74.

re même de l'incarnation de Jésus-Christ? A-t-on oublié *qu'Ad Gentes* 22 avait déclaré «*nécessaire* que, dans chaque grand territoire socio-culturel, comme on dit, soit encouragée une *réflexion théologique* telle que, à la lumière de la Tradition et de l'Eglise universelle, les faits et les paroles révélés par Dieu, consignés dans les Saintes Lettres, expliqués par les *Pères* de l'Eglise et le *Magistère*, soient soumis à un *nouvel examen*...». Force est de constater que ce dernier tarde à venir, même si les *Lineamenta* soulignaient en leur temps que «cette réflexion théologique n'est pas *facultative:* elle est une *nécessité*, une exigence du mystère de l'incarnation»[22]. En fait, on aimerait pouvoir concilier la nécessité d'une *évangélisation renouvelée* et l'affirmation sans cesse reprise d'un donné théologique, immuable en ses formulations fondamentales et «chemin obligé d'un approfondissement *ultérieur* dans les diverses cultures»[23]. Comment ne pas voir qu'à la vérité, *l'essentiel a déjà été dit* et que l'inculturation dont on nous parle n'en est, au mieux, que la mise en images, l'illustration, rien qui soit réellement important? En douterait-on que les propos tenus naguère par le Cardinal B. Gantin, alors préfet de la Congrégation des Evêques nous enleveraient toute illusion: «Avant l'inculturation, disait-il, il y a l'évangélisation. Jésus-Christ s'incarne. En soi, l'évangélisation est une culture. Si maintenant on parle d'inculturation, c'est qu'il s'agit en fait d'un *approfondissement* pour une bonne *adaptation* de l'Evangile dans la culture locale»[24]. Retour à la case-départ. Il faut s'y résigner mais reconnaître qu'on a perdu en route la «nouvelle évangélisation» et toute la créativité qu'elle nous promettait. On ne parvient pas à entrer dans la logique propre de l'inculturation et à *exorciser* tout à fait une tentation qui, à terme, la réduit à une *nouvelle méthodologie missionnaire*. Déjà, lorsque le *Document de Travail* préparatoire au Synode abordait le «monde de la communication, à la fois culture à évangéliser et (..) instrument puissant qui pourrait servir à l'évangélisation», il estimait

---

[22] *Lineamenta*, in *op. cit.* n° 51.
[23] Id. n° 53.
[24] In La *Croix* 7 février 1990. Je souligne.

nécessaire d' «étudier ce monde» pour voir comment *l'utiliser* aux fins de l'évangélisation[25]. «Qui ne voit que, s'il ne s'agit que d'utiliser les richesses propres au monde que l'on évangélise pour le mieux «subvertir», il n'y aura jamais d'inculturation et de «nouvelle évangélisation». Dans son Incarnation, Jésus n'a pas «utilisé» la nature humaine, fût-ce pour la sauver; il s'est fait homme.

Est-ce la peine d'ajouter que la question posée ici n'est pas spécifiquement africaine? Lors du Synode asiatique qui se sera tenu à Rome en avril-mai 1998, on aura entendu le Rapporteur général de ce Synode, le Cardinal Paul Shan Kwo-hsi (Taiwan) affirmer que les Eglises d'Extrême-Orient «ont un sérieux besoin d'inculturer la foi dans les cultures de l'Asie et de perdre leur aspect de copie carbone des Eglises des sociétés occidentales»[26], tant il est vrai qu'elles apparaissent encore «culturellement étrangères en Asie». Certains évêques japonais ne sont pas moins sévères, tel Mgr Toshio Oshikawa, évêque de Naha: «En dépit des fréquentes exhortations en faveur de l'inculturation, il me semble que la norme pour la vie chrétienne, la discipline ecclésiale, l'expression liturgique et l'orthodoxie théologique reste celle de l'Eglise occidentale, (ce qui constitue) un blocage très efficace de tout effort pastoral visant à créer, pour nos Eglises jeunes et minoritaires, un processus de croissance dans la foi, la spiritualité et la vie morale»[27]. Même requête chez Mgr Joseph Suwatan (Indonésie): «Nous avons besoin d'une Eglise ouverte au dialogue et à la collaboration avec toutes les personnes de bonne volonté, une Eglise inculturée dans la société où elle vit»[28].

Les évêques d'Asie sauront-ils mieux se faire entendre que certains de leurs collègues africains, qui avaient demandé explicitement, lors de leur Assemblée synodale, la reconnais-

---

[25] Cf. «L'Eglise en Afrique et sa mission évangélisatrice vers l'an 2000» «Vous serez mes témoins», *Document de travail*, Synode spécial des évêques pour l'Afrique, Paris, Centurion I Cerf, n° 20, p. 20. (Je souligne).

[26] «L'inculturation s'impose dans les travaux du Synode» in La *Croix*, 23 avril 1998.

[27] Id. *Ibid.*

[28] Id. *ibid.*

sance d'un droit propre aux Eglises d'Afrique, à l'instar de ce qui existe pour les Eglises orientales[29]? On peut raisonnablement en douter en écoutant le cardinal Secrétaire d'Etat Angel Sodano déclarer solennellement aux Pères du Synode asiatique qu'«il serait curieux qu'au moment où l'on va vers une «globalisation» toujours plus grande de l'humanité, l'Eglise soit mue seulement par une force centrifuge. (..) Si le Seigneur a voulu que son Eglise soit «une» autour de Pierre, principe visible d'unité, il faut que le magistère du Pape soit toujours plus fidèlement écouté et que les normes qu'il établit avec son gouvernement pastoral soit toujours suivies, dans un esprit filial»[30].

On le voit, le malentendu est total. La «globalisation» qu'on se garde bien de définir est-elle exigence d'uniformité? Est-ce manquer d'esprit filial que de quitter la maison maternelle et de revendiquer son chez soi quand le temps de la vie adulte est venu? Force est de reconnaître que l'Eglise latine[31] continue, bien à tort, à s'estimer universelle et qu'elle ne se résoud pas à prendre au sérieux la singularité d'Eglises nées sous d'autres cieux, riches d'autres cultures et qui sont, à leur manière, l'Evangile en son commencement.

Faut-il le dire clairement? La question de l'inculturation demeurera sans vraie réponse tant que les Eglises africaines et asiatiques ne disposeront pas, à l'égal des Eglises orientales, d'un droit qui leur soit propre et qui les soustraira aux normes et aux usages d'une Eglise essentiellement latine.

Et il ne faudrait plus tarder. Dans quelques années, les deux-tiers des fidèles appartenant à la communion catholique seront issus de sociétés non-occidentales et les Eglises africaines, asiatiques, y pèseront très lourd, ne serait-ce qu'en raison de leur croissance démographique rapide[32]. Chaque année, les Eglises africaines baptisent près de quatre millions de catéchu-

---

[29] Cf. *Paroles et silences*. pp. 111-127.
[30] In *La Croix*, 30.4. 1998, p. 11.
[31] Non sans raison, René Jaouen écrit: «Les textes conciliaires souffrent continuellement de l'emploi de trois termes considérrés comme équivalents alors qu'ils sont distincts: Eglise, Eglise romaine, Eglise latine» in *L'Eucharistie du mil. Langages d'un peuple, expressions de la foi*, Paris, Karthala, 1975, pp. 250-251.
[32] Voir «1978-1998. Le centre de gravité de l'Eglise s'est déplacé vers le sud» in *La Croix*, 11-12 octobre 1998, pp. 12-13.

mènes et en l'espace de 18 ans seulement (1978-1996) elles auront doublé le nombre de leurs fidèles qui sera passé de 54,8 millions à 109,3[33]. Qui dit mieux? Mais comment assumeront-elles, au sein de la communion ecclésiale, l'héritage énorme qui leur a été transmis, quand l'effondrement de la démographie en Occident entraîne une moindre influence des Eglises qui, jusqu'alors, cumulaient richesses, savoirs et pouvoirs? Qui ne voit dès à présent que la mise en oeuvre *urgente* d'une inculturation qui ne se contente plus de mots, commande, pour une large part, l'avenir même du catholicisme au cours du siècle prochain?

Si l'on tarde trop, on verra proliférer en Afrique, pour ne parler que d'elle, ce qui est déjà très largement amorcé: des milliers et des milliers d'Eglises afro-chrétiennes conjuguant avec plus ou moins de bonheur la parole reçue des Eglises missionnaires et des traditions séculaires héritées des anciens. Le Document de Travail publié un an avant les Assises synodales africaines était tout à fait conscient de la séduction que ces Eglises exercent sur nombre de chrétiens et estimait par ailleurs qu'en l'an 2000, elles compteraient 60 millions de fidèles avec un taux de croissance de 1,5 million par an[34], ce qui est, à tout prendre, très important. Le Rapporteur général du Synode, le cardinal H. Thiandoum, archevêque de Dakar, avait insisté fort opportunément sur la nécessité d'un dialogue avec ces Eglises:

> «Leur progression, disait-il, nous invite à revoir nos méthodes d'évangélisation et d'attention pastorale. Ne devons-nous pas reconnaître le secret de leur réussite: zèle et conviction profonde, attention aux besoins individuels du corps et de l'âme, organisation efficace en petits groupes, le caractère festif, chaleureux et joyeux de leurs célébrations? S'il arrive que des oppositions acharnées contre l'Eglise se manifestent, une attitude chrétienne pacifique est toujours possible; elle est de règle dans un esprit de dialogue»[35].

---

[33] Id. ibid.
[34] Cf. *Paroles et silences...* p. 161
[35] Rapport du cardinal H. THIANDOUM, in D.C. n° 2094 (15.5. 1994), p. 482
36 cf. *Paroles et silences.* pp. 157-167.

Or, paradoxalement, ni le Message adressé par le Synode Africain aux Eglises, ni les 64 propositions soumises à l'attention du Saint Père, ni *Ecclesia in Africa,* ne feront la moindre allusion à un dialogue éventuel avec les Eglises afrochrétiennes. Quoiqu'il en soit des raisons de cet étonnant silence[36] et même si, à l'évidence, toutes ces Eglises ne sont pas «chrétiennes» au meme titre, la *créativité* dont elles témoignent devrait inciter les Eglises à la réflexion. Car, comme le constate le théologien burkinabé Sidbe Semporé:

> «L'exemple des églises afro-chrétiennes force à admettre que nous pouvons disposer, dès aujourd'hui, du personnel suffisant pour le gouvernement des communautés et le travail d'évangélisation; nous pouvons avoir sur place les moyens de former et d'entretenir nos responsables; nous avons sur le continent tout ce qu'il faut pour célébrer notre foi dans le culte et les sacrements, pour répondre à tous les besoins pastoraux, pour poursuivre le service théologique de notre Eglise. A condition de pratiquer en tout la politique de nos moyens et de renoncer à etre des copies qu'on s'essouffle à revoir et à corriger pour les maintenir dans la conformité. A condition surtout qu'une petite Pentecôte vienne ébranler l'Edifice et instiller dans les coeurs la «parrèsia», ce precieux don d'audace et d'assurance qui permet aux bâtisseurs de retirer l'échafaudage et de tirer l'échelle sans peur de l'effondrement et de la dérive»[37].

Les Eglises africaines sont-elles réellement conscientes du défi auquel elles seront affrontées dans les décennies à venir? Peut-être leur faudrait-il relire une page souvent cité depuis lors, écrite en 1971 par le théologien allemand Joseph Ratzinger – il n'était pas encore cardinal et préfet de la Congrégation pour la Doctrine de la foi:

> «Dans l'unité de l'unique Eglise, il doit y avoir place pour la pluralité des églises, car seule la foi est indivisible et la fonction unificatrice de la primauté lui est subordonnée.

---

[36] Cf. *Paroles et silences,* pp. 157-167
[37] Sidbe SEMPORE, *Propositions pour un Synode et après...,* Cotonou, 1994, p. 56 (souligné dans le texte).

Tout le reste peut et doit être divers, ce qui suppose l'existence de fonctions directives indépendantes, telles qu'elles étaient réalisées, par exemple, dans les «primats» ou «patriarcats» de l'ancienne Eglise (..). L'image d'un Etat centralisé que l'Eglise catholique offrit jusqu'au Concile, ne découle pas tout simplement de la charge de Pierre mais bien de l'*amalgame* qu'on en fit avec la tâche patriarcale qui fût dévolue à l'évêque de Rome pour toute la chétienté latine, et qui ne fit que croître tout au long de l'histoire. Le droit ecclésial, la liturgie unitaire, l'attribution unitaire faite par le centre de Rome des sièges épiscopaux, tout cela sont des choses qui ne font pas partie nécessairement de la primauté en tant que telle; elles résultent de la concentration de deux fonctions. Par suite, la tâche à envisager serait de distinguer à nouveau, plus nettement, entre la fonction proprement dite du successeur de Pierre et la fonction patriarcale; en cas de besoin, de *créer de nouveaux patriarcats détachés de l'Eglise latine* (..).
Finalement, on pourra peut-être, dans un avenir pas trop éloigné, se demander si les Eglises d'Asie et d'Afrique, comme celles de l'Orient, ne pourraient pas présenter leurs formes propres en tant que «patriarcats» ou «grandes Eglises[38]».

Même si, de toute évidence, le propos n'est plus à l'ordre du jour, doit-il pour autant être oublié? Si l'opportunité semble avoir changé au cours des dernières années et s'il est peu probable que l'auteur de ce texte le signerait aujourd'hui, a-t-il pour autant perdu sa pertinence? Combien d'Eglises souhaiteraient que les suggestions au demeurant fort raisonnables, formulées il y a près de trente ans par un théologien de grand renom, soient progressivement mises en oeuvre?

---

[38] J. RATZINGER, *Le nouveau peuple de Dieu*, Paris, Aubier, 1971, pp. 67-69. Le mot *amalgame* est souligné dans le texte, le reste l'est par moi (in *op. cit.* p. 60). On peut voir également à ce propos: cardinal Y.M. CONGAR, *Eglise et Papauté*, Paris, Cerf, 1994, p. 19 ss; J.M. TILLARD, *L'évêque de Rome*, Paris, Cerf, 1982, pp. 70-84; C. DUQUOC, *Des Eglises provisoires. Essai d'ecclesiologie oecuménique*, Paris, Cerf, 1985, 101-110.

Au fond, l'inculturation et la nouvelle évangélisation que tous appelient de leurs voeux demandent à l'Eglise-Mère qui, la première, porta la Parole, de se convertir à la *nouveauté* de la vie qu'elle a engendrée même si, dans le premier moment, elle a quelque peine à se reconnaître dans l'enfant qu'elle a mis au monde. Semblable en cela au paysan dont nous parle l'évangile de Marc : «Il en est du Royaume de Dieu comme d'un homme qui jette la semence en terre; *qu'il dorme ou qu'il soit debout,* la nuit et le jour, la semence germe et grandit, il *ne sait comment. D'elle-même,* la terre produit d'abord l'herbe, puis l'épi, enfin du blé plein l'épi (Mc 4, 26-29). On transmet la Parole, on ensemence. Cela fait, on demeure en retrait, présent silencieusement à ce qui naît et rendant grâce pour l'éternelle nouveauté de l'Evangile. Quant aux nouvelles communautés, suscitées par l'Esprit, en profonde communion avec les Eglises qui les ont appelées à la Vie et ne peuvent préjuger de ce qui va naître, elles ne disent plus seulement ce qu'elles ont appris, ainsi qu'elles l'ont fait pendant si longtemps, *elles découvrent des choses nouvelles,* et témoignent de la nouveauté de ce qu'elles vivent en Jésus-Christ. Par là, elles nous offrent la chance *d'apprendre quelque chose de neuf* à propos d'un Evangile que nous pensions si bien connaître. Le mystère pascal ne dit pas autre chose qui invite à mourir à un certain âge du monde et de l'Eglise pour toujours commencer une nouvelle Pâques; il faut s'en persuader: Jésus ne cesse de nous précéder en Galilée (Mt 26, 32; 28, 7).

Les organisations internationales catholiques et les dèfis de la nouvelle évangélisation au troisième millénaire

J. JOBLIN

La vie associative aura encore une place au XXIème siècle; elle est en effet liée au phénomène humain; l'homme n'existe que relié à des groupes; c'est au sein de la famille ou d'associations de substitution que, dès sa naissance, il assure sa survie; c'est en s'intégrant dans des groupes de jeunes puis regroupant des individus selon leurs affinités ou leurs intérêts qu'il prend conscience de sa personnalité et la forme. Cette loi générale se vérifie dans l'Eglise où existent de nombreux types d'associations. Tout homme est pris dans un réseau de relations sans lequel il ne pourrait se développer; aucune histoire individuelle ne peut être dissociée de celle des communautés que ce soit dans la société civile ou religieuse.

Les formes associatives ont changé au cours des siècles; celles qui existent actuellement ne pourront y échapper elles aussi. Etroitement dépendantes de la philosophie sociale de l'Occident, elles ne semblent pas préparées à aborder les problèmes de société (comme ceux des libertés publiques, du statut personnel etc...) avec un esprit nouveau; or sans rien sacrifier de leur raison d'être, il leur faudra prendre part à l'effort de la communauté intemationale de s'entendre sur des valeurs ayant le même sens pour tous. Les OIC sont dès maintenant au défi d'être actives dans un contexte international nouveau. Il leur faut non seulement se maintenir au niveau technique qu'ont atteint les problèmes internationaux mais participer dans des conditions nouvelles à l'annonce de l'Evangile. L'avènement du troisième millénaire est l'occasion pour les OIC de prendre conscience du défi devant lequel elles se trouvent. A quelles conditions seront-elles en mesure de participer à la croissance humaine des sociétés? La question n'a rien d'iconoclaste. Des formes associatives originales apparaissent à chaque époque; il en est qui se développent et perdurent dans le temps; d'autres ont une fonction plus brève; à laquelle de ces deux catégories appartiennent les organisations catholiques qui existent actuellement? Comme il n'est pas possible de répondre de manière exhaustive à une telle question dans les limites d'un article, celui-ci tentera d'éclairer le cas des professionnels catholiques et de leurs associations: celles-ci ont-elles encore un sens dans un monde qui s'ouvre au pluralisme, c'est à dire à un moment où l'on tente de faire collaborer sur un pied d'égalité des mouvements sociaux issus de familles philosophiques et religieuses différentes? Les luttes doctrinales que mènent certaines associations catholiques n'appartiennent-elles pas à une forme périmée de présence de l'Eglise au monde lorsqu'était contesté son droit à intervenir dans les affaires sociales ou même son droit à l'existence? Certes, les hommes se sont toujours regroupés pour relever les enjeux de la société quand ceux-ci dépassaient leur capacité d'intervenir; mais les défis changent et il se pourrait que les associations de professionnels catholiques ne soient plus la forme qu'il convienne de choisir pour apporter une réponse d'Eglise à la société présente. Il ne suffit pas de dire que les professionnels catholiques et leurs associations doivent prendre part à la solution des problèmes de société mais de montrer quel apport spécifique ils peuvent faire dans les débats qui s'instaurent à ce sujet.

I. Ambivalence du phénomène associatif

Le phénomène associatif a pris des formes si diverses et parfois si éphémères au cours de ces deux derniers siècles qu'on le juge volontiers secondaire; or il est omniprésent car inhérent à la vie des sociétés.

Aucun pouvoir ne peut s'exercer de manière durable s'il ne repose sur le consensus d'une population. Les associations sont la charnière qui les unit. Plus une société est étendue, moins ses dirigeants peuvent établir un contact direct avec ceux qui la composent; il est alors demandé à des associations de type politique, économique, religieux, culturel ou autres de l'assurer. Qu'il s'agisse de la société civile ou ecclésiastique ces réseaux de contact peuvent prendre des formes extrêmement diverses. Ils peuvent faire communiquer les populations et les autorités de deux manières différentes. Une charnière peut en effet avoir une double fonction: elle peut resserrer la dépendance des deux éléments qu'elle réunit ou au contraire la distendre. Une association syndicale, par exemple, peut être étroitement contrôlée par le gouvernement ou par le comité central du parti unique (comme il en était dans les pays communistes); elle est alors un instrument aux mains du pouvoir pour imposer sa politique à une population qui n'a pas été consultée; par contre, la loi et les traditions sociales, comme il en est dans les pays dits démocratiques, peuvent garantir la liberté d'organisation et d'action de leurs dirigeants, librement élus; ceux-ci représentent alors la masse des travailleurs et prennent part à ce titre aux négociations entre les diverses forces sociales et politiques sur les orientations de la société. Ainsi le phénomène associatif se retrouve-t-il dans toutes les sociétés, mais le rôle qui lui est dévolu peut être dit ambigu puisqu'il dépend de la philosophie sociale de chacune d'elles. Il en est de même dans l'Eglise, mais d'une manière qui lui est propre.

La société internationale a connu au cours de ces trente dernières années une évolution au cours de laquelle la référence éthique a fait de moins en moins de place à la dimension religieuse et spirituelle de l'existence[1]. Il fut relativement aisé aux premiers Secrétaires généraux de l'ONU comme Dag Hammarskjold ou U'Than de souligner l'inspiration religieuse ou spirituelle qui était à la base de l'entreprise des Nations Unies; il n'en est plus de même aujourd'hui où d'autres familles de pensée font sentir leur poids.

La société où travaillent les professionnels catholiques et leurs associations est fortement influencée par ceux qui souhaitent limiter l'emprise de la religion à la seule vie privée; il leur

---

[1] J. JOBLIN, *Non credenza e realtà religiosa nelle istituzioni internazionali* in *Civiltà Cattolica* 1977 I pp. 545-555; d°, *Diritti dell'uomo, ateismo e Istituzioni culturali cristiane* in *Civiltà Cattolica* 1981 III pp. 118-132.

faut donc justifier qu'elle ait sa place dans la vie publique; par ailleurs, au moment où les religions non chrétiennes (paganismes divers et islam) contestent l'interprétation donnée par l'Occident à plusieurs dispositions de la Déclaration Universelle des Droits de l'Homme de 1948 au nom de leurs traditions religieuses et culturelles, il leur faudra trouver des voies nouvelles pour contribuer à l'ouverture réciproque de blocs que chaque civilisation constitue par rapport aux autres.

II. Les professionnels catholiques et le laminage des valeurs spirituelles

Quelles que soient les époques, les croyants se sont toujours trouvés confrontés au problème de l'incroyance, c'est à dire au fait qu'un certain nombre d'hommes affirment inutile d'entrer dans l'Eglise comme d'adhérer à des croyances religieuses pour vivre vertueusement et inscrire les valeurs de fraternité, de droiture et de solidarité dans la société; même si au Moyen-Age et à la Renaissance, un certain nombre de personnes vivaient éloignées de la pratique religieuse, l'incroyance était alors un phénomène individuel qui ne mettait pas en péril les principes chrétiens qui étaient à la base de la vie sociale et politique. Au cours du siècle dernier, l'incroyance a commencé à devenir un phénomène collectif dans les pays de civilisation occidentale, en ce sens que les relations sociales y furent réglées de plus en plus en ignorant le rôle spécifique des forces spirituelles dans la vie publique[2].

Le passage de l'incroyance de type individuel à celle de nature collective s'est effectué progressivement; il a eu des incidences sur la pratique associative dans l'Eglise; en bref, on ne s'est plus seulement préoccupé de protéger et de sauvegarder la foi qu'on jugeait menacée par les nouveaux mouvements sociaux et politiques en leur opposant des oeuvres et des associations dites «catholiques»; le souci s'est imposé d'évangéliser

---

[2] E. POULAT, *Liberté et laïcité. La guerre des deux France et le principe de la modernité* Cerf/Cujas Paris 1987 p. 440.

une société laïcisée et indifférente aux valeurs religieuses. La participation aux activités socio-politiques a permis de soutenir ce qu'il y avait de juste dans ses aspirations tout en critiquant ses limites du fait de l'anthropologie sur laquelle elles s'appuyaient; la lutte contre l'incroyance s'est alors inspirée de deux stratégies différentes.

Un exemple typique de l'attitude de réserve à l'égard du monde se trouve dans les associations Kolping, du nom du prêtre de Cologne (1813-1865) qui les lança dans les années 1848; elles regroupaient, au moment de leur fondation, les jeunes apprentis chrétiens arrivant en ville; elles sont restées fidèles à cette première vocation; le fait qu'elles sont présentes encore aujourd'hui dans plus de 40 pays montre que ce type de réponse à l'athéisme a toujours sa raison d'être. Tandis que l'évolution des associations Kolping a été minime depuis leur création, celle des groupes qui ont formé les syndicats chrétiens a suivi une trajectoire totalement différente; un mot, quelque peu barbare, la résume, celui de «déconfessionnalisation». Cette histoire est celle des «Labre» dont les membres jouèrent une part essentielle dans la fondation de la Confédération internationale des syndicats chrétiens (CISC).

Un frère des Ecoles chrétiennes, le frère Hiéron, regroupa dans les années 80 de jeunes employés dans une association sous le patronage de St Benoît Labre; d'où le nom qui leur fut donné. Seuls des catholiques pratiquants et s'astreignant à une régle de vie sévère pouvaient en faire partie. Lorsque la liberté syndicale fut instaurée en France, ils fondèrent le SECI (syndicat des employés du commerce et de l'industrie) en s'appuyant sur les mêmes principes; c'est ainsi qu'un certificat de bonne conduite délivré par le curé de la paroisse était exigé pour en faire partie. A l'issue de la guerre de 1914, ses dirigeants (Zirnheld, Tessier...) rassemblèrent les nombreux syndicats catholiques qui existaient au plan local en une organisation unique; mais, en 1919, le problème se posa de savoir quelle attitude adopter vis à vis des syndicats chrétiens d'Alsace-Lorraine qui, eux, regroupaient catholiques et protestants. En décidant de les accueillir, la base syndicale fut élargie mais, en même temps, l'esprit confessionnel allait s'estomper. La référence à la doctrine sociale de l'Eglise contenue dans les statuts céderait la place, après la deuxième guerre mondiale, à un humanisme spirituel et, finalement, le congrès d'Evian (1964) voterait la déconfessionnalisation; seule une minorité restant fidèle à l'inspiration primitive des fondateurs[3].

L'évolution qui a affecté le syndicalisme chrétien n'est pas un phénomène isolé. Il ne fut pas possible, à l'issue de la deuxième guerre mondiale, de reconstituer des syndicats chrétiens dans divers pays de l'Europe de l'ouest (Allemagne, Italie) et bien que de création récente, les organisations régionales de la CISC en Amérique latine et en Afrique[4] se laïcisèrent après quelques années; finalement le secrétariat international lui-même passa de l'appellation de CISC à celle de CMT (*Confédération Mondiale du Travail*). Le fait que l'organisation des patrons catholiques (UNIAPAC) ait connu une évolution semblable oblige à constater que des professionnels catholiques ont senti à un certain moment le besoin de se démarquer de l'Eglise[5]; ils n'entendaient pas rejeter ses enseignements; leur choix ne manifestait aucune hostilité mais ils estimaient que les valeurs humaines et chrétiennes qu'ils défendaient seraient mieux perçues s'il était entendu que leur acceptation n'impliquait pas nécessairement leur entrée dans l'Eglise visible.

L'image de la charnière revient ici pour interpréter l'évolution qui vient d'être retracée. Si des catholiques qui se regroupèrent à l'origine dans des associations professionnelles confessionnelles éprouvèrent par la suite le besoin de poursuivre leur service de l'Eglise en s'ouvrant sur l'extérieur, d'autres, notam-

---

[3] F. LAUNAY, *La CFTC, origines et développement 1919-1940* Publication de la Sorbonne Paris 1986 p. 488; F. BRANCIARD, *Histoire de la CFDT. 70 ans d'action syndicale* La Découverte Paris 1980 p. 366; B. DUMOUR, *Catholiques en politique* DDB Paris 1993 pp. 93 et sq.

[4] A. LECOMTE, *Nouvelles étapes du panafricanisme syndical* in Revue de l'Action Populaire 1962/159 pp. 673-689; L. BOVY, *Histoire du mouvement syndical africain d'expression française* LGDJ Paris 1968 pp. 111-130.

[5] A l'inverse le cas de la Confédération Vietnamienne des Syndicats Chrétiens doit être ici signalé. Elle était la plus importante du pays; elle comptait environ 10% de chrétiens, les autres membres étaient bouddhistes et le président lui aussi; ce qui montre que la référence chrétienne peut ne pas être perçue comme un obstacle à l'adhésion de non chrétiens dans certaines circonstances.

ment celles formées par les professions de santé, restèrent fidèles au modèle d'Action catholique. Les unes et les autres ont cependant en commun de réagir à la laicisation croissante de la vie. Bien qu'empruntant deux voies différentes, toutes deux refusent de renouer avec les luttes doctrinales d'antan qui leur apparaissent avoir été trop souvent génératrices d'injustices et de manque de solidarité. Refusant de faire de leurs différences religieuses et philosophiques la raison d'un désaccord permanent, elles sont alors conduites à joindre leurs efforts à ceux des autres mouvements ou «forces d'idéal» qui travaillent à la solution des problèmes sociaux; mais elles sont alors mises au défi de rendre compte de l'actualité de leur foi dans un monde pluraliste.

III. REPONSE DES PROFESSIONNELS CATHOLIQUES A L'INCROYANCE DE LEUR MILIEU

L'incroyance se répand à tous les niveaux de la vie sociale. La passivité des populations occidentales contre la propagande et les mesures en matière de natalité, d'euthanasie, de recherches biologiques comme l'absence de réaction en face du divorce, le retard apporté au baptême des enfants, la baisse de la pratique religieuse... sont autant de signes que les règles et rites qui étaient communément acceptés il y a seulement un demi-siècle ont perdu une grande part de leur signification pour l'homme occidental[6]. Cette perte du sens explique son silence devant les violations des droits de l'homme ou les discriminations et persécutions dont souffrent les chrétiens dans de nombreux pays ou au moment de la constitution de pouvoirs économiques, judiciaires ou autres qui modifient progressivement et sans opposition réelle les fondements éthiques des sociétés où ils vivent[7]. Si la foi est ébranlée, c'est qu'un divorce existe entre la philosophie qui inspire les comportements courants des individus et la doctrine de l'Eglise.

---

[6] J. JOBLIN, *Christianisme et sécularisation* in Gregorianum 77, 3 (1996) pp. 471-500.
[7] J-B. D'ONORIO (sous la direction de), *Le respect de la vie en droit français*, Téqui Paris 1997 p. 296.

L'athéisme

Un athéisme pratique s'est répandu en Occident. Bien qu'il coexiste encore avec le maintien de formes religieuses dans la vie sociale, il est une forme de rationalisme qui, enfermant l'homme dans le présent, émousse l'idée que l'existence puisse avoir un sens[8]. Il est le refus de reconnaître qu'il y a au-delà des rapports humains fondamentaux avec la nature ou les autres hommes «une réalité dont (l'individu) ne peut disposer et qui lui fait toucher la présence d'une transcendance». Il prétend rompre avec tout le passé de l'humanité pour lui apporter une libération de «l'opium»[9] qui l'endort et la prive d'être elle-même.

L'athéisme contemporain nous met au coeur d'un débat qui porte sur la nature religieuse ou non de l'existence. Tandis que pour les uns la conscience d'un Absolu que l'homme ne peut atteindre mais conditionne son existence est à l'origine d'une relation de la personne avec la divinité et donne naissance à un ensemble de croyances et de rites que l'on englobe sous le nom de sacré, pour d'autres le sacré est une illusion et la religion une construction de l'esprit propre aux formes primitives de civilisation et dont il convient maintenant de se débarrasser. L'opposition fut vive entre ces deux points de vue durant les derniers siècles; elle donna lieu à de nombreux conflits. Une des premières tentatives en vue d'instaurer la paix sociale eut lieu en convenant de faire abstraction de toute référence aux motivations religieuses ou idéologiques des uns et des autres chaque fois qu'il s'agirait d'un objectif d'intérêt général qui ne pourrait être atteint sans le concours de tous. Constatant que les valeurs supérieures dont s'inspirent les acteurs sociaux ne font pas obstacle à ce qu'ils collaborent dans des entreprises communes mais limitées, on est passé de là à une conception de l'action sociale qui demande à chacun

---

[8] A. JEANNIERE, *Les fins du monde* Aubier Paris 1987 p. 168
[9] «La religion est l'opium du peuple». K. MARX a usé de l'expression dans le deuxième article qu'il a publié dans les *Annales franco-allemandes* publiées à Paris en 1844; cf. A. LUCIANI, *Cristianesimo e movimento socialista* Marchio Venezia t. II p. 330.

de renoncer à faire intervenir des considérations doctrinales, religieuses ou non, dans la vie publique[10]. Or une telle généralisation repose sur un illogisme puisque, au nom de la liberté individuelle et de la paix sociale, elles impose progressivement l'incroyance comme credo aux sociétés occidentales; de plus, elle contient le germe de nouvelles luttes doctrinales car les tenants d'une religion, surtout monothéiste, ne peuvent admettre d'enfermer ses manifestations dans la sphère du privé.

Les professionnels catholiques et leurs associations face au laminage de la dimension religieuse de l'existence.

La crise que les professionnels catholiques et leurs associations doivent affronter ne pourra être surmontée si l'on ignore le contexte historique dans lequel elle est née; elle est en effet le résultat d'une évolution historique due au renouvellement des problèmes sociaux.

1. *Les OIC face aux «forces d'idéal» non chrétiennes*[11]. L'attitude que prend chaque OIC face à l'incroyance dépend beaucoup de son histoire. Les plus anciennes d'entre elles ont été créées pour protéger la foi de leurs membres ou venir

---

[10] Les manuels scolaires de plusieurs pays de l'Occident ignorent le fait religieux; on en est même venu à juger contraire à la liberté due à l'incroyance d'ériger un sapin de Noël dans un lieu public alors qu'il s'agissait d'une ancienne tradition. Cf. R. BRUCE DOUGLAS & D. HOLLENBACH, *Catholicism and Liberalism. Contribution to American public Philosophy* Cambridge Un. Press 1994 p. 352; J. DAVIDSON HUNTER, *De l'humanisme laïque in Dialogue* (ed. française) Washington 1991/2 pp. 65-71; F. ONIDA, Clausole religiose del 1° Amendamento del Bill of Rights, free exercise and establishment della religione in F. MARGIOTTA BROGLIO e altri, *Religioni e sistemi giuridici* Il Mulino Bologna 1997, pp. 227-253.

[11] F. RUSSO, *La place des Organisations internationales catholiques dans l'Eglise* in Etudes oct. 1964 pp. 438 449; H. DE RIEDMATTEN, *Le fait non-gouvernemental dans l'Eglise catholique* in Civitas (CH) XXX 1974-1975, pp. 85-95; J. JOBLIN, *Pourquoi encore dans les années 90 l'existence d'associations catholiques professionnelles* in Medicina et morale 1990/3 pp. 525-540; S. GEBS (sous la direction), *Les OIC dans la vie internationale. Présence au monde participation aux projets majeurs des Nations-Unies, collaboration à la mission de l'Eglise* Secrétariat de la Conférence des OIC Genève 1997 p. 18; A. SCHAFTER, *Une session au coeur de l'actualité* CCIG Genève 1997 p. 6 (miméographié); R. SUGRANYES DE FRANCH, *Le Christ dans le monde* Fayard Paris 1972.

en aide aux plus démunis. Un tournant fut pris à l'issue de la première guerre mondiale sous l'influence de la réflexion sociale de précurseurs comme Jaurès ou don Sturzo puis de ceux qui firent entrer l'Occident dans la phase pluraliste de son histoire. Albert Thomas, socialiste et premier directeur du Bureau international du Travail, Mgr Nolens, président du parti catholique aux Pays-Bas et membre du Conseil d'administration du BIT, Gaston Tessier et Georges Serrarens, respectivement président et secrétaire général de la Confédération internationale des syndicats chrétiens (CISC) jouèrent ici un rôle considérable que Pie XI appuya; ils insistèrent les uns et les autres sur l'opportunité et la nécessité de la collaboration des «forces d'idéal"[12] s'inspirant aussi bien d'un humanisme laïcque de la doctrine sociale de l'Eglise. En 1926, Albert Thomas s'adjoignit un prêtre pour développer les relations du Bureau avec les mouvements religieux[13], en 1927, les présidents des OIC d'action sociale prirent l'habitude de se réunir à Fribourg (CH) pour étudier les programmes de la Société des Nations (SDN) et s'accorder sur les moyens d'insérer leurs organisations dans la vie internationale; onze d'entre elles s'y associèrent. La Conférence des organisations catholiques internationales devait naître de cette initiative en 1951. Les OIC empruntaient alors une voie nouvelle, celle de la collaboration ponctuelle; mais elles ne pouvaient prétendre au titre d'interlocuteur qualifié sur la scène internationale sans se voir reconnaître une compétence professionnelle; ainsi, par exemple, lorsque fut créé en 1933

---

[12] L'expression est commune à Sturzo et à Thomas. Cf. L. STURZO, Leone XIII e la civiltà moderna in *Sintesi sociali* Roma 1906, pp. 96, 122; A. THOMAS, Message lu sur la place St Pierre à l'occasion des cérémonies destinées à commémorer le quarantième anniversaire de *Rerum Novarum* in A. ARNOU, *Les Catholiques et l'Organisation internationale du Travail* Spes Paris 1937 p. 19; d'autres formules semblables furent employées par Thomas, par exemple celle de «forces spirituelles» dans un discours à l'Alliance universelle (Genève 1928) in BIT, *Albert Thomas et la politique sociale internationale* BIT Genève 1947 p. 151 ou celle de «vigoureuses forces morales» dans son message aux Semaines sociales de Besançon in BIT, *Dix ans d'organisation internationale du Travail* BIT Genève 1931 p. 462; cf. J. JOBLIN, *Essere Chiesa nella società pluralista* in *Civiltà Cattolica* 1979 III pp. 345-357.

[13] Un protestant occupa une position similaire pour assurer les relations avec les mouvements sociaux relevant de cette tendance.

le Comité International Catholique des Infirmier(e)s et Assistant(e)s médicaux-sociaux (CICIAMS) insista-t-on sur la nécessité d'une formation technique sérieuse pour les personnels de santé comme d'un perfectionnement continu de leurs connaissances.

La politique de collaboration menée par les divers mouvements sociaux a été mise en doute par certains secteurs de l'opinion publique car elle n'a pas empêché la diffusion de l'incroyance pratique; aussi plusieurs se sont-ils demandés s'il convenait de la poursuivre. Une réponse positive doit être donnée à cette question; encore faut-il que les professionnels catholiques et leurs associations se placent dans la perspective adoptée par le Concile Vatican II dans les documents sur l'apostolat des laïcs (*Apostolicam Actuositatem*) et L'Eglise dans le monde de ce temps (*Gaudium et Spes*).

Les OIC professionnelles sont l'un des points de rencontre privilégié entre l'Eglise et le monde. Elles inscrivent la «loi de Dieu dans la cité terrestre"[14]; elles sont situées à la «rencontre de la vie et de la conscience chrétienne avec les situations du monde"[15]; elles incitent leurs membres et les professionnels catholiques, comme dit encore Jean-Paul II dans le même passage, à donner aux enseignements de la foi leur «application dans l'histoire». L'intervention des OIC dans la vie professionnelle répond au devoir de tout chrétien de prendre part à l'aménagement de la société afin de créer les conditions les plus favorables au «progrès matériel et développement spirituel"[16] de «tout homme et de tout l'homme"[17]. Leur engagement n'est pas le résultat d'une décision de circonstance; il est le fruit d'une doctrine[18] qui est vie. Leur participation au développement, à la promotion ou à la défense des droits de l'homme doit alors être telle qu'elle laisse apparaître la logique de leurs motivations et leur carac-

---

[14] *Gaudium et Spes* § 43.2.
[15] *Centesimus Annus* § 59.
[16] *Déclaration de Philadelphie* 1844.
[17] *Populorum Progressio* § 14.
[18] *Populorum Progressio* § 39.

tère transcendant. Les professionnels catholiques et leurs associations doivent s'avancer dans l'histoire des hommes en fonction de leur logique de foi et non d'une doctrine politique dont les limites apparaissent après une période d'enthousiasme; leur force évangélisatrice vient avant tout de ce que leur vie professionnelle laisse percevoir la vision cohérente de l'existence qui les guide aussi bien pour respecter les «structures sociales consacrées par l'histoire"[19] que pour réformer celles qui engendrent l'injustice. L'action des professionnels catholiques et de leurs associations ne se confond pas avec celle des mouvements politiques s'ils gardent devant les yeux la vision de l'homme qui les inspirent et lui sont fidèles; en discernant dans leur action ce qui favorise l'avènement d'un véritable développement humain de ce qui le contrarie, ils laissent apparaître la source de leur engagement.

2. Nouveau regard sur la collaboration des OIC et des «forces d'idéal» non chrétiennes. Lorsque la JOC fut admise en 1935 à plaider la cause des jeunes travailleurs devant la Conférence internationale du Travail, elle montra que la pauvreté et le chômage dont ils souffraient appelaient à un sursaut de toutes les bonnes volontés; ce faisant, elle appela chacun à trouver dans ses motivations profondes la force de soutenir des initiatives nouvelles; elle sembla utiliser le discours traditionnel des leaders politiques, syndicaux ou patronaux soucieux de remédier à des maux sociaux clairement identifiés; mais en fait, elle ouvrit la voie à une nouvelle approche des problèmes sociaux en montrant que leur solution ne dépendait pas de décisions ponctuelles mais d'une politique globale. Les motifs qui déterminent nos contemporains pour passer à l'action font appel aux valeurs de justice, de solidarité et de paix et non plus à une obligation s'imposant de l'extérieur à la conscience. Cette manière de voir s'est aujourd'hui répandue; c'est en fonction de cette approche que doit être envisagée la

---

[19] PIE XII, *Message Noël 1956*.

question de la collaboration des chrétiens avec les autres forces sociales[20].

Un renversement de perspective s'est produit à l'occasion des deux guerres mondiales; le concours à la réalisation d'objectifs communs à une nation a été perçu comme un devoir justifiant de dépasser les différends idéologiques de ceux qui la composent. Cette manière de voir a eu une incidence sur la manière de porter le témoignage de la foi dans la société. Du moment où les non-croyants n'ont plus regardé les valeurs religieuses comme incapables de contribuer à la solution des problèmes de société mais au contraire y ont vu un *confirmatur* apporté aux politiques nationales, les professionnels catholiques et leurs associations ont été au défi de faire comprendre que si leurs motivations ne les détournaient pas de participer aux tâches concrètes que la société s'était fixées, elles demandaient également d'instaurer un dialogue sur un registre propre qu'il convient maintenant de préciser. Ils ne considéraient pas la doctrine sociale de l'Eglise comme un programme[21] pour la réalisation duquel ils devraient lutter, comme il le fut souvent au début du siècle; elle constitua un cadre les guidant pour formuler des exigences et proposer «des voies nouvelles en partant de la réforme des esprits»[22].

Voir et juger... Il ne s'agit pas pour les OIC de se comporter comme des associations professionnelles revendiquant des avantages matériels pour leurs membres. Il leur faut *voir*

---

[20] Une centaine de jocistes présenta aux délégués une pétition couverte de 85.000 signatures de jeunes travailleurs. «Nous vous l'avouons, Messieurs, quand nous songeons à l'avenir, nous sommes effrayés; la peur de vivre nous bouleverse... on ne connaîtra jamais la douleur qui ronge le coeur des jeunes victimes de ce chômage persistant... C'est pourquoi, Nous les jeunes chômeurs du monde entier, nous nous tournons vers vous, Messieurs les délégués,...Par les liens d'une étroite collaboration internationale qu'établit (la Conférence internationale du Travail), nous croyons en effet qu'elle peut promouvoir des mesures utiles pour combattre le chômage des jeunes. Nous sommes convaincus que vous ferez maintenant tout ce qui est en votre pouvoir pour apporter immédiatement des remèdes à notre situation». cité par A. LEROY, *Les catholiques et l'Organisation internationale du Travail* Spes Paris 1937 pp. 62-63.
[21] *Centesimus Annus* § 43.
[22] *Gaudium et Spes* § 81.2

les situations d'injustice, analyser et comprendre le jeu des «mécanismes pervers» qui entretiennent les situations d'injustice; il ne s'agit pas pour elles de se limiter à dénoncer le manque de liberté religieuse, la faim, la situation dramatique des réfugiés... encore que cela doive être fait car il leur revient de se faire reconnaître comme une source objective d'information par l'opinion. L'une de leur mission est de démonter les «structures de péché» qui ont conduit à inscrire l'injustice sur les causes dans les sociétés, situations que déplorent les médias mais qu'ils ne présentent pas comme des malheurs sur les causes desquels nous pouvons agir. Les professionnels catholiques et leurs associations doivent convaincre l'opinion d'agir; ils veilleront donc à ne pas exprimer leur indignation dans des jugements catégoriques qui ne sont pas réalistes. Il ne suffit pas de dire qu'on condamne la faim, le manque d'habitat ou les violations des droits de l'homme. Il faut voir ce qui peut être fait: mon pays ne peut pas accueillir toutes les misères du monde, disait récemment un chef de gouvernement. Une solution trop hâtive d'un problème peut être à l'origine de plusieurs autres: l'accueil des migrants peut favoriser l'insécurité, désorganiser le système scolaire, s'accompagner d'un manque de logements, être source de chômage... De même le développement du commerce mondial ou un abaissement trop brusque des barrières douanières peuvent avoir des conséquences très négatives sur le petit commerce ou la moyenne industrie... La méthode *a priori* d'aborder les questions sociales doit être réévaluée. Il convient de partir des exigences de justice, de solidarité et de paix que ressentent nos contemporains et que partagent les professionnels catholiques afin d'en «affiner» le contenu[23] et non de prendre position sans nuances.

... **Pour agir**. C'est dans la confrontation pacifique avec les autres mouvements sociaux que les professionnels catholiques et leurs associations peuvent être le témoin des valeurs évangéliques et par là même d'une vision globale de la condi-

---

[23] PAUL VI *Allocution* à la Conférence internationale du Travail, 10 juin 1969.

tion humaine. Ils pensent au progrès de l'humanité en fonction d'une histoire et d'une espérance qu'ils disent fondée sur la vérité de l'homme. Ils sont donc, comme dit Jean-Paul II, à un confluent; ils orientent le devenir des sociétés non pas en cherchant à le conformer à un modèle préétabli mais en le construisant jour après jour et en le considérant comme toujours révisable et perfectionnable. Telle a été la stratégie suivie par les OIC durant les cinquante dernières années; elle n'a pas été sans danger car elle a exposé les professionnels catholiques à se laisser entraîner à trop de concessions vis à vis des idées dominantes du milieu où ils travaillaient et à perdre de vue l'inspiration qui était à l'origine de leur engagement. Le rôle des OIC apparaît ici comme capital. Leur mission dans le monde de plus en plus pluraliste où nous entrons est d'être perçue par leurs membres et aussi les autres professionnels comme des cellules de réflexion offrant une interprétation cohérente et organique des nouvelles manifestations de la vie humaine; elles ont certes à énoncer clairement leur opposition aux dérives de la société actuelle que ce soit en matière d'avortement, d'euthanasie ou de bioéthique comme aussi vis à vis des structures économiques qui aggravent les inégalités sociales ou les politiques d'armement ... mais il leur faut également évaluer les situations du point de vue de la vision religieuse qui est la leur. Les positions qu'elles défendent ne sont pas des thèses abstraites mais elles s'insurgent contre ce qui fait obstacle et défigure la vision de la société qui est la leur: «si le message chrétien d'amour et de justice perd toute efficacité pour la réalisation de la justice dans le monde, il lui sera difficile d'être considéré comme crédible par nos contemporains»[24]; tel est le point central du défi qu'elles ont à relever[25].

L'accomplissement d'une telle mission de la part des OIC demande qu'elles bénéficient du soutien des communautés chrétiennes. Elles sont au contact de l'incroyance; mais pour

---

[24] A. TERGEL, *Human Rights in Cultural and Religious Traditions* AAU Uppsala 1998 p. 154.
[25] T. GAUDIN, *Préliminaires à une prospective des religions* L'Aube Paris 1998 p. 228.

que celui-ci soit fructueux encore faut-il qu'elles bénéficient du concours de spécialistes des questions qu'elles traitent[26], comme aussi de théologiens et d'experts en sciences sociales; il y a là un nouveau domaine d'engagement communautaire qui n'est que trop rarement pris en compte.

Participation pastorale des OIC aux politiques publiques

L'incroyance n'est pas un amoralisme mais elle ne croit pas nécessaire de fonder ses règles de comportement sur un Absolu extérieur à l'homme; elle pense que le consensus des peuples suffit à fonder l'obligation. Les professionnels catholiques et leurs associations veulent faire prendre conscience à leurs contemporains que cette anthropologie conduit l'humanité à un contre-développement car elle ne laisse pas place à un contre-pouvoir face aux autorités politiques.

Les professionnels catholiques et leurs associations adoptent de plus en plus une stratégie qu'on peut appeler socio-éthique[27]; celle-ci part d'un élément commun, qui n'est autre que le contenu des grands documents des Nations Unies. Ces dernières ont en effet obtenu des diverses populations du monde, en dépit de leurs différences culturelles, de considérer un certain nombre de valeurs globales comme devant constituer la base d'une civilisation mondiale; mais reste à préciser leur contenu dans les diverses instances de dialogue de la vie internationale. C'est en ce point que s'insèrent les professionnels catholiques et leurs associations surtout lorsqu'ils jouissent du statut consultatif[28]. Bien qu'aucun débat philosophique n'y ait lieu, la présentation des diverses positions se rattache toujours

---

[26] Il est très évangélique que ce concours soit apporté de manière bénévole dans la plupart des cas, mais ce bénévolat écarte certaines personnes de prendre part au travail des OIC.

[27] J. JOBLIN, *Il movimento cattolico sociale e l'evoluzione di suo metodo di azione* in *Civiltà Cattolica* 1983 III pp. 319-332.

[28] Les OIC ont eu largement recours au statut consultatif durant le demi-siècle qui s'achève. Elles ont créé à cet effet des centres d'information et de documentation qui suivent les activités des Nations Unies à Paris, Genève, New York et Vienne; elles servent de support logistique aux OIC et, souvent, aux Observateurs du Saint-Siège durant les conférences.

à une anthropologie sociale, c'est à dire à une conception de l'humain qui provoque chacun à réexaminer la sienne pour la purifier des apports secondaires qui l'ont recouverte au cours des ans. L'anthropologie chrétienne suppose que tout homme est orienté par nature vers la recherche de la Vérité. Croyants et incroyants se sentent également liés par un devoir qui les dépasse, qu'il considèrent comme absolu et auquel ils se livrent tout entiers. Les uns et les autres se sentent responsables en conscience de travailler au bien de l'humanité; mais ils se séparent sur la source de cette obligation et, à un certain moment, sur les conclusions qui en découlent. Les Déclarations des Nations Unies leur offrent alors une grille de lecture pour clarifier leurs opinions dans le dialogue[29].

Les professionnels catholiques et leurs associations doivent être conscients de ce que leur mission est de faire découvrir le vrai sens de l'homme dans la vie moderne. Ils ont à rendre compte de leur foi en montrant comment elle s'intègre dans une interprétation globale de l'existence humaine. Leur position pourra être rejetée par ceux qui en ont une autre conception; mais ils devront exiger que l'une et l'autre soient également respectées, c'est à dire que rien ne soit imposé qui aille à l'encontre des convictions de l'autre; comme le dit la Déclaration *Dignitatis Humanae*: nul ne doit être obligé d'agir contre sa conscience[30]. Cette affirmation est celle par laquelle se réintroduit la notion d'absolu dans l'existence. Derrière l'affirmation selon laquelle «la dignité de la personne humaine exige que chacun agisse suivant une détermination consciente et libre"[31], il y a autre chose qu'une simple revendication individualiste mais la reconnaissance d'un de ces absolus qui conditionnent toute vie car nul ne peut en modifier les exigences. Le propre des professionnels catholiques et de leurs associations sera de faire reconnaître ce fait. Il se rencontreront souvent dans cette action avec d'autres mouvements laïcs qui luttent pour la vérité dans les relations sociales. Un exemple peut en

---

[29] J. JOBLIN, *Christianisme et sécularisation* in Gregorianum 77,3 (1996) pp. 471-500.
[30] Déclaration *Dignitatis Humanae* § 2, de même *Pacem in terris* § 34.
[31] *Pacem in terris* § 34.

être trouvé dans la lutte commune entreprise par les mouvements humanistes et ceux issus du christianisme social pour faire admettre et respecter la liberté d'association. Il ne s'agit pas, comme certains seraient tentés de le dire, de vouloir imposer la conception occidentale des relations sociales à d'autres pays qui ne la respectent pas ou la rejettent mais de lutter pour la reconnaissance d'une structure fondamentale des sociétés modernes qui doivent être telles qu'elles favorisent la «participation organique»[32] de tous aux prises de décision et à leur application. La conscience que l'homme moderne a pris de sa dignité demande que celle-si soit reconnue dans les faits. Il y a là un de ces impératifs nouveaux par lesquels l'homme confesse dépendre d'un ordre supérieur auquel il est lié par nature. Lorsque les OIC, dans les conférences sur la famille ou sur le développement se font l'écho de certaines revendications, elles luttent certes en vue d'obtenir un résultat mais elles entendent également faire prendre conscience de la dépendance fondamentale dans laquelle se trouve encore l'homme de la civilisation industrielle et télématique. Il en est de même avec les organisations d'aide humanitaire où les organisations catholiques mêlent leurs secours avec ceux beaucoup plus importants mobilisés par les gouvernements et d'autres associations privée.

Une réponse réfléchie à l'incroyance

La réponse des professionnels catholiques et de leurs associations à l'incroyance pratique qui se répand en Occident se fera par la mise en valeur du lien qui existe entre leur foi et leur activité professionnelle.

* *Une constatation.* Il convient de renoncer à toute discussion d'ordre intellectuel ou philosophique avec ceux qui nient la dimension religieuse de l'existence; ces derniers disent ne pas la voir et rien ne peut être fait directement contre une telle assertion. Une telle constatation ne signifie pas que les OIC doivent renoncer à une justification raisonnée de leurs

---

[32] PAUL VI, All. devant la Conférence internationale du Travail 10 juin 1969.

positions; celle-ci est indispensable et c'est une de leurs tâches de permettre aux professionnels catholiques d'intégrer leurs activités dans une vision globale, religieuse et humaine, de l'existence. Les incroyants pourront alors reconnaître dans leur attitude une cohérence et une logique qui invitent à la réflexion.

* *La nature du dialogue.* Une méfiance existe à l'égard du mot «dialogue» car il évoque pour beaucoup l'idée d'un marchandage; sans doute peut-il revêtir cette forme lorsqu'il s'agit de passer aux décisions concrètes; mais celui qui s'arrête à cette image s'interdit de saisir sa nature profonde; ici d'aider ceux qui y participent de bonne foi à découvrir la vérité sur l'homme et la société. Il renvoie tout homme aux motivations profondes qui le déterminent, c'est à dire à l'impératif moral qui le pousse à agir. Ni l'homme politique, ni le savant qui disent refuser toute obligation morale qui leur soit imposée de l'extérieur n'échappent au besoin inné de ia conscience de justifier ses choix moralement. Celui qui revendique la liberté de recherche et y voit son devoir de savant obéit à un impératif moral qui le dépasse; qu'il le veuille ou non, il réintroduit dans sa vie une forme de dépendance qu'il considère comme absolue; il se sent lié par un impératif auquel il se soumet tout entier. Un terrain commun existe donc avec le professionnel catholique; il est constitué par l'obligation morale que l'un et l'autre reconnaissent de suivre les exigences de leur vérité.

* *La conduite du dialogue.* Les divergences qui pourront éclater entre professionnels sur les décisions à prendre pour pousser plus avant leur politique ou leur recherche trouveront leur solution dans l'examen des conséquences de l'une et l'autre position au regard d'un développement humain des sociétés. La recherche de la vérité sur l'homme conduira souvent à des luttes sociales mais c'est au travers de celles-ci, si elles sont menées dans un esprit de collaboration que se construira une société fondée sur un sens plus parfait de l'homme. Le résultat ne sera pas obtenu immédiatement, en un clin d'oeil, mais au terme d'une long processus d'échange de vues, ce qu'on a appelé le dialogue; ce dernier doit permettre à chacune des parties à l'exercice de mieux comprendre la position de l'autre et de découvrir dans la sienne propre des éléments accessoires qui font obstacle à leur compréhension mutuelle[33]. Certes l'une d'elles peut être tentée d'user d'une position de force pour imposer son point de vue mais il y a alors domination d'une thèse par la force et non construction d'un monde plus uni parce qu'il partage les mêmes valeurs; or c'est dans cette direction que s'effectue le progrès de l'humanité.

Les OIC doivent aider les professionnels catholiques à prendre conscience de la dimension religieuse de leur présence dans la vie professionnelle pour qu'ils ne cèdent pas à la tentation de s'identifier avec les politiques décidées par un consensus majoritaire. Leur collaboration n'est pas aveugle car elle relève d'un choix qui s'enracine au plus profond d'eux-mêmes.

Critères d'une croissance humaine

Le simple rappel de la doctrine catholique ne constitue pas la pointe du dialogue avec l'incroyance; il est un élément dans une stratégie globale qui vise à faire reconnaître la relation de l'homme à une réalité transcendante à laquelle les religions monothéistes donnent le nom de Dieu. L'application de cette stratégie semble devoir comporter les étapes suivantes:

* *Faire découvrir l'illusion d'une approche des problèmes de société fondée sur la seule raison.* L'incroyance actuelle de l'Occident doit être considérée à deux niveaux; 1) celle de l'homme de la rue qui n'est pas réfléchie et s'est introduite subrepticement dans les mentalités sous l'effet de la pression sociale; l'individu vit alors au jour le jour et perd le sens d'une destinée qui doit influencer ses choix et comportements quotidiens; 2) celle des «médiateurs sociaux», leaders charismatiques, qui diffusent cette mentalité nouvelle. C'est avant tout avec cette mentalité nouvelle que sont confrontés les professionnels catholiques et leurs associations; Ils sont responsables de réintroduire le sens de l'absolu

---

[33] Les discussions qui s'ouvrent périodiquement au plan international sur la manière d'entendre concrètement les libertés permettent à la fois de comprendre la légitimité de modèles sociaux différents et la nécessité qu'ils se soumettent à des exigences fondamentales; c'est à découvrir celles-ci qu'est ordonné le dialogue.

dans la vie sociale en partant de l'obligation morale à laquelle obéissent les chefs politiques ou les chercheurs quand ils se donnent pour tâche de porter plus avant la croissance humaine.

* *Affirmer que toute croissance n'est pas nécessairement bénéfique* à l'ensemble de l'humanité. Les efforts entrepris pour réglementer l'usage de l'atome en est un exemple. La société présente est donc responsable de faire reconnaître les lignes suivant lesquelles doit se faire le progrès des sociétés. Des critères doivent donc être établis dont le contenu sera précisé peu à peu.

* *Etablir des critères pour mesurer le progrès humain des sociétés.* Leur établissement n'a rien d'extraordinaire puisque toute action humaine engage une doctrine. Ces critères se trouvent dans les documents internationaux: *égalité de tous les* hommes et égal droit de chacun d'eux, sans distinction de sexe, de race ou de religion, de poursuivre son progrès matériel et développement spirituel avec des chances égales; liberté d'association qui permette à chacun de participer d'une manière organique à la vie politique, sociale... des sociétés auxquelles il appartient; *état de droit*, c'est à dire protection des libertés fondamentales par l'autorité publique; *liberté religieuse,* ce qui signifie dans une société pluraliste la non intervention de la religion comme de l'Etat dans le domaine de l'autre. Tel est le point de vue d'après lequel les professionnels catholiques doivent demander que soient appréciés les programmes de recherche, les programmes économiques et financiers, la garantie des libertés civiles et des droits de l'homme. Cet examen se fait en commun; les OIC sont l'une des structures par lesquelles l'Eglise y participe. Elles accomplissent une fonction analogue dans leurs rapports avec les religions non-chrétiennes.

IV. Rencontre des OIC et des civilisations extra-occidentales

Un des défis majeurs que les OIC devront relever dans le siècle à venir sera celui de leur rencontre avec des populations appartenant à des civilisations dont les racines ne plongent pas dans l'humus de la culture méditerranéenne modelé par le christianisme. Elles devront trouver de nouvelles voies pour assurer une présence évangélisatrice auprès de peuples qui ont une vision de l'existence différente de la leur et dont le poids démographique et économique ne manquera pas de grandir. Les OIC doivent dès maintenant se préparer à cette tâche qui leur demandera d'assumer de nouvelles responsabilités.

I. *Rencontre des OIC et des paganismes*

Nouveauté de la situation

L'occidental pense que l'homme a mission de transformer le monde, de le rendre plus humain et plus accueillant pour tous; dans les autres civilisations, chaque individu aura tendance à se considérer comme le gardien de relations qu'il n'aura pas établies avec la nature et les autres hommes. L'occidental se perçoit comme un acteur dans une histoire; celui qui n'est pas marqué par cette civilisation se considère comme soumis à un destin sur lequel il n'a pas prise.

Lorsque les OIC entendaient réagir contre l'incroyance, elles se plaçaient à l'intérieur d'un même système de valeurs que les athées. Les uns et les autres faisaient référence à la dignité de la personne humaine, à l'ordre public, à la non intervention de l'Eglise dans les affaires de l'Etat et réciproquement. Ils s'opposaient sur la manière d'entendre ces valeurs; mais ce qui les rassemblait, c'est que les uns comme les autres se sentaient engagés dans la construction d'une société fondée sur la paix, le justice, la solidarité et l'égalité comme sur la nécessité de renoncer aux antagonismes du passé. Tous étaient fils de la culture méditerranéenne qui remet à l'homme de dominer l'univers, mais ils différaient sur le terme où ils devaient le conduire. Dans cet environnement, les professionnels catholiques et leurs associations se demandaient comment faire percevoir à ceux qui les entouraient la lumière vers laquelle ils se tournaient pour chercher le sens de leur participation au développement de la planète.

Distance des systèmes de valeurs

La plupart des OIC sont fortement marquées par leur origine occidentale au point d'être parfois considérées comme un instrument de la politique de cette civilisation particulière. Elles devront donc être soucieuses de faire reconnaître leur spécificité au milieu de tensions qui ne manqueront pas de naître entre l'Occident fort de la domination qu'il tire encore de sa puissance économique, technique et financière et le grand nombre de pays émergents qui tendront au moins à l'égaler. Les OIC seront un des lieux où se manifestera cette tension, habituées qu'elles sont à ce que l'Europe exerce une influence souvent trop déterminante dans leurs organes de direction; il ne leur suffira pas d'y faire entrer des représentants d'autres parties du monde pour apparaître comme internationales, c'est à dire au dessus des conflits de civilisations; leurs membres doivent apprendre à penser le bien commun universel sans prendre pour normes les préjugés de leur propre civilisation. Il leur faut se mettre à l'école de leurs collègues originaires des pays ou régions où domine une autre philosophie sociale. L'individu n'y occupe pas la place centrale qui lui est attribuée en Occident car il lui est enseigné que son premier devoir est de respecter les traditions des groupes familiaux et sociaux. Alors que la tradition politique occidentale des derniers siècles place l'unité de la nation dans le consensus qui s'établit sur certaines valeurs indépendamment des croyances religieuses ou philosophiques de chacun, la plupart des pays non-occidentaux, non seulement ne dissocient pas les traditions religieuses ou culturelles des traditions sociales et politiques mais encore voient dans cette union la garantie de l'unité de la nation. Ces civilisations ne sont pas ouvertes à l'idée d'universalité car elles y voient un danger pour la sauvegarde de leur identité; les populations de ces parties du monde ont conscience de ce que leurs cultures – et certaines le sont de plusieurs millénaires – sont beaucoup plus anciennes que celles de l'Occident, elles pensent donc pouvoir trouver en elles-mêmes le ressort d'une nouvelle expansion si on les laisse rattraper leur retard économique et technique. Habituées à vivre dans des sociétés profondément inégales, les populations de ces régions ne se sentent pas concernées par le désir de l'occident de créer une civilisation mondiale fondée sur la liberté, l'égalité et la solidarité. Le XXIème sièdé sera celui d'une rupture due à la volonté des peuples émergents de se dégager de l'occidentalisme qui a présidé à la formulation du droit des gens depuis cinq sièdes; nul doute qu'ils lui imposent leur marque en y introduisant des règles nouvelles.

La philosophie individualiste à laquelle a recours la civilisation occidentale pour justifier sa domination sur le reste du monde est aujourd'hui sérieusement contestée d'autant que la situation des nouveaux «dragons»[34] est renforcée par leur poids démographique. La population blanche de l'Europe ne se renouvelle plus à un rythme suffisant non seulement pour compenser la natalité des populations immigrées mais même dans certains pays pour assurer le maintien de la population à son niveau actuel[35]; le recours à l'immigration aggrave ce phénomène. Dans le même temps, la masse des pays extra-européens accroît son poids relatif dans la population mondiale[36] et demande que soit mis un terme à la domination économique et financière qu'exerce une minorité dans les affaires mondiales. Des hommes et des femmes se réclamant de cultures et de religions autres que celles des peuples occidentaux seront de plus en plus nombreux à occuper de postes de responsabilité dans la vie sociale même en occident; nul doute qu'ils exerceront une influence croissante sur la conception des relations internationales. Les idéaux de paix, de liberté, de justice, d'égalité et de solidarité sont aujourd'hui, dira-t-on, largement partagés par les populations non-occidentales; certes, mais elles les entendent dans le contexte culturel qui leur est propre. Les quatre critères qui ont été proposés plus haut comme base du dialogue avec l'incroyance sont pris dans un sens totalement nouveau car le fonds de culture méditerranéenne qui était commun aux croyants et aux incroyants a disparu: que signifie la famille fondé sur la liberté des contractants pour des peuples qui n'ont pas intégré la notion de personne dans leur culture et font du mariage un arrangement

---

[34] E. VOGEL, *The Four little Dragons. The Spread of Industrialisation in East Asia* Harvard Uni. Press 1991 p. 138.
[35] J.D. LECAILLON, *Aspects de la démographie en Europe* in *Familia et vita* (Rome) 1998/3 pp. 149 constate en 1997: «Le solde naturel (naissances-décès) est négatif en Allemagne, en Italie et en Suède et quasiment nul en Espagne et en Grèce; d'autre part, à l'exception de l'Andorre et de la Suisse, l'immigration a été supérieure à l'émigration dans tous les pays de l'Europe».
[36] G-F. DUMONT, *La décélération démographique mondiale* in *Familia et vita* 1998/3 pp. 133-145.

entre deux groupes ? Que signifie l'état de droit garanti par les tribunaux là où l'éducation est orientée à l'intégration de l'enfant dans le groupe pour en faire le serviteur de l'ordre tel que l'entend la collectivité ? Que signifie l'égalité là où l'autorité du chef ne se discute pas et, pire encore, où les inégalités sociales sont le résultat de déterminations venant de la qualité morale d'une vie antérieure ? Que signifie la séparation du religieux et du politique là où la religion est appelée à confirmer l'emprise du pouvoir sur le groupe ? Tandis que les religions monothéistes sont fondées sur une révélation par laquelle Dieu fait connaître son intention salvifique et sa volonté de la réaliser avec le concours de l'homme, les religions païennes ont donné naissance à des civilisations dénuées d'espoir. Alors que les sociétés chrétiennes s'efforcent de libérer les potentialités créatrices des individus, les autres enferment les individus dans le groupe le soumettant à des règles d'inégalité pouvant aller, pendant de longues périodes, jusqu'à confondre l'état de droit avec la volonté du prince ou d'un parti; aussi est-il difficile de penser que l'utopie de l'universel égalitaire répandue par l'Occident depuis cinq siècles sera spontanément acceptée comme telle au plan mondial. Le défi que devront relever les professionnels catholiques et leurs associations durant le XXIème siècle sera d'établir un pont avec ces autres cultures qui, devenues majoritaires, prendront sans doute conscience de la menace que fait peser sur elles l'introduction de nouvelles valeurs dans leur système clos[37].

Les pays dont la culture n'a rien à voir avec celle de la civilisation méditerranéenne sont plus ou moins allergiques à son anthropologie sociale. Alors que les Occidentaux s'avancent dans la société avec la bonne conscience d'accomplir une mission civilisatrice, les pays extra-occidentaux veulent que les relations internationales prennent en compte certains intérêts qu'ils accusent l'Occident d'avoir ignorés. Ils veulent être libérés des valeurs mises par celui-ci à la base de son expansion; ils disent que leur propre culture peut être source d'un authen-

---

[37] S.P. HUNTINGTON, *Le choc des civilisations* Ed. Odile Jacob Paris 1997 p. 402.

tique développement³⁸. Sans doute parlent-ils des droits de l'homme, mais ils disent que ce vocabulaire leur est étranger³⁹, qu'il leur a été imposé et qu'ils ont dû en user pour avoir accès à cette tribune mondiale et à ce gouvernement embryonnaire qu'est l'ONU. Mais les valeurs que cette dernière propage ne sont pas pour eux universelles; elles reflètent les aspirations de la culture où elles sont nées; aussi parlent-ils de «Asian values» qu'on dit difficilement conciliables avec celles de l'Occident⁴⁰ ou les pays d'Afrique préfèrent-ils s'entendre sur une Charte africaine des individus et des peuples⁴¹. La conception unitaire du monde est aujourd'hui contestée; si l'ensemble des peuples admet qu'elle peut exister au plan économique, nombreux sont ceux qui ont conscience de différer des autres par leur système social, leurs traditions culturelles, leurs croyances religieuses, leur doctrine politique, leur niveau de développement et leur conception des droits de l'homme.

La cassure culturelle entre l'Occident et le reste du monde a sa racine dans les *a priori* des structures mentales qui caractérisent chaque civilisation. La culture occidentale est celle du concept et les OIC en sont bien la fille dans leur manière d'aborder les questions sociales; elles ne se contentent pas de recourir à ce qu'on peut appeler le concept pratique qui permet de réfléchir sur l'enchaînement des phénomènes et d'intervenir dans leur déroulement; elles ont fait du concept un instrument d'exploration du réel en vue d'en percer les mystères. Alors que les autres civilisations sont pragmatiques, celle de l'Occident est rationnelle, critique et logique; elle procède par schèmes qu'elle applique au

---

[38] Ainsi le philosophe LIAN SHUMING (1893-1988) qui vécut en Chine populaire rechercha toute sa vie quelles pourraient être les vertus du confucianisme qui feraient sortir l'Asie de son retard.

[39] N. SINGH, L'Asie et les droits de l'homme in K. VASAK, *Les dimensions internationales des droits de l'homme* UNESCO Paris 1978 pp. 702-706

[40] Atty. MA.J.G. SAN-JUAN TORRES, *Regional Protection of Human Rights in Asia* in HARAYA PASS ASA (Manila) 1998/4 p. 3; cf. également les débats auxquels a donné lieu la Conférence de Vienne sur les droits de l'homme en 1993.

[41] La distance entre le point de vue occidental et celui des pays africains in L. KUNHARDT, *Die Universalität der Menschenrechte*. Olzog Verlag München 1987 p. 402.

réel. Un exemple de cette mentalité se trouve dans la *Déclaration de Philadelphie (1944)* dans laquelle les Nations alliées après avoir défini que l'objectif de toute politique sociale est de promouvoir le «progrès matériel et développement spirituel» de «tout homme et de tout l'homme»[42] demandent de juger de ce point de vue les programmes de développement des gouvernements afin que la communauté internationale s'assure que tel est bien l'objectif poursuivi. La politique sociale des pays asiatiques a été établie dans une toute autre perspective. L'homme n'en est pas le terme car il n'a pas la valeur que lui donne l'Occident; des mesures sociales sont adoptées au coup par coup, mais manque ce sens de l'égalité fondamentale des êtres et de leur valeur absolue que le christianisme a tant contribué à développer.

Les individus qui vivent dans les sociétés païennes ne sont pas préparés à pratiquer le jeu démocratique comme il était entendu à Athènes ou à Rome; l'éducation ne les a pas portés à combiner leurs activités spécifiques comme le commerce, l'agriculture ou l'artisanat en des unités conceptuelles qui leur auraient permis de se mouvoir à l'aise dans les réalités sociales et d'imaginer quel pourrait être leur progrès[43]. Le système des valeurs du monde occidental incite chacun à pousser plus loin sa contribution innovatrice à la société; il a été ainsi conduit à mettre de plus en plus en valeur la responsabilité et la dignité inhérentes de tous les êtres humains ainsi que l'égalité de chances qui devait leur être offerte.

La fracture qui existe entre les pays d'Occident et les autres est aggravée dans le cas des pays asiatiques; leurs cultures actuelles ne reposent pas sur l'idée d'un Dieu personnel, maître de l'univers et créateur de l'être humain. Il en résulte que l'idée de personne est étrangère à ces civilisations et que l'individu est privé d'un sens de responsabilité propre vis à vis de la société; il est inséré dans des institutions comme la famille ou la nation dont les chefs ne peuvent accepter de modifier les

---

[42] *Populorum Progressio* § 14.
[43] M.I. FINLEY, L'économie antique p. 20 in F. CHÂTELET et G. MAIRET, *Les idéologies* Marabout Verviers 1981 t. I p. 177.

règles de la tradition qu'après s'être assurées que le changement ne relâchera pas leur contrôle sur les individus[44].

Rôle des professionnels catholiques et de leurs associations

Les professionnels catholiques et leurs associations se trouvent à la croisée des chemins. Au moment où l'interpénétration des civilisations fissure le monolithisme des blocs culturels, les OIC doivent aider les professionnels catholiques à découvrir comment se comporter en chrétiens dans un environnement dominé par les valeurs du paganisme auquel il leur faudra se mêler du fait des conditions de vie moderne.

* Au contact de pratiques qui ne respectent pas la valeur sacrée de la personne, les professionnels catholiques devront prendre leur distance avec elles sans laisser aucun doute sur la vision religieuse du monde qui est la leur[45]. Leurs prises de position doivent apparaître comme des démarches de vie, procédant d'une conscience qui est comme structurée pour percevoir dans les engagements qu'elle prend ce qui contribue le mieux à la croissance humaine dans toutes ses dimensions.

* Les professionnels catholiques comptent parmi les artisans de l'insertion du christianisme dans les cultures où dominent les religions païennes. Ils ont à communiquer «la nouveauté dont (ils) ont fait l'expérience à la suite du Christ aux autres hommes dans la réalité concrète de leurs difficultés, de leurs luttes, de leurs problèmes et de leurs défis»[46] car la lumière de la foi rend plus humaines les situations difficiles; ce faisant ils devront distinguer «ce qu'il y a de vrai et de saint»[47] dans les traditions culturelles non chrétiennes «à la lumière de l'Evangile comme de l'enseignement de l'Eglise et mus par la charité»[48]. Les professionnels catholiques et leurs associations

---

[44] L. SANG-TAEK LEE, *The Catholic Human Rights doctrine and its Encounter with Te Confucian Social Tradition* PUG Roma 1997 pp. 10-22.

[45] *Evangelium Vitae* § 73; J. JOBLIN & R. TREMBLAY (a cura di), *I Cattolici e la società pluralista. Il caso delle leggi imperfette* ESD Bologna 1996 p. 284.

[46] *Centesimus Annus* § 59.

[47] *Nostra AEtate* § 2.

[48] *Apostolicam Actuositatem* § 7.

doivent être conscients qu'ils donnent forme à l'«actualité historique»[49] en unissant dans leurs activités les exigences que comportent l'enseignement des Béatitudes et le souci d'améliorer les conditions de vie et de travail des populations en étroite coopération avec tous les «hommes d'idéal».

Les OIC doivent se préparer à affronter les problèmes qui naîtront de leur rencontre avec les paganismes; elles sont appelées à être aux avant-postes de l'Eglise pour faire connaître le caractère novateur du message de l'Evangile fondé sur l'offre universelle du salut apportée par le Christ. Elles devront trouver des bases de collaboration avec des mondes qui ont une autre philosophie sociale que la leur; il leur faudra savoir distinguer dans le message dont elles sont porteurs ce qui lui est essentiel de ce qui est son incarnation dans une culture particulière, celle du monde méditerranéen[50]. Il leur faudra découvrir ce qui est essentiel à leur anthropologie sociale et le détacher de certaines habitudes de pensée à travers lesquelles il a été perçu. Faisant confiance à la recherche de la vérité qui est inscrite au coeur de tout homme, les professionnels catholiques sauront que c'est la perception de la rectitude inscrite dans leur propre vie qui révélera à ceux qui les entourent l'excellence du message dont ils sont porteurs.

Comme le remarque le cardinal Daniélou, nous ne devons pas avoir peur d'un christianisme où peuvent se mêler encore des traditions païennes alors qu'on en trouve toujours en Occident; mais les professionnels catholiques et leurs associations doivent savoir pourquoi certains points doivent être tenus fermement tandis que pour d'autres il est possible d'en étaler la réalisation dans le temps. C'est ainsi qu'au cours des deux millénaires qui s'achèvent l'Eglise a toujours été intransigeante vis à vis de toute sacralisation du pouvoir conduisant à la soumis-

---

[49] On entend par «actualité historique» chacun des moments où l'homme donne sens à son activité et à son existence par ses décisions libres; cf. G. FESSARD, *De l'actualité historique* DDB Paris 1960 t. I pp. 293-294; M. SALES, *Gaston Fessard (1897-1978). Genèse d'une pensée* Brepols Paris Bruxelles 1997 p. 153.
[50] J. DANIELOU (Cardinal), *Christianisme et religions non chrétiennes* in *Etudes* octobre 1964 pp. 323-336; d°, *Approche de l'athéisme moderne* in *Etudes* novembre 1964 pp. 467-486.

sion du pouvoir religieux au pouvoir politique comme sur le respect de la vie tant physique (avortement, euthanasie) que spirituelle (monogamie et conception chrétienne du mariage) tandis qu'elle savait temporiser sur la participation des peuples au gouvernement ou sur certaines situations sociales marquées par l'inégalité comme l'esclavage ou l'arbitraire avec lequel les autorités s'attribuent le droit de vie ou de mort comme celui de faire la guerre. Les chrétiens doivent développer la conscience qu'ils ont de la dignité de l'homme afin de donner à leur vie une plus grande cohérence[51].

II. Rencontre des OIC et de l'islam

L'islam est l'un des trois monothéismes; chacun d'eux affirme l'existence d'un Dieu unique qui, miséricordieux, désire réunir dans l'unité tous les hommes dispersés et leur offre une voie de salut pour atteindre cette fin. L'islam est à l'opposé des paganismes; il en a même horreur. Leur idolâtrie est la négation même de l'existence du Dieu unique, maître de l'homme et de tout le créé.

Le cas de l'islam doit ici être retenu car c'est avec cette famille religieuse que se rencontreront de plus en plus les professionnels catholiques et leurs associations durant le XXIème siècle. Cette religion est en effet répandue dans le monde entier où elle a été à l'origine de la formation d'Etats confessionnels; de plus, depuis la fin de la deuxième guerre mondiale, on assiste à un brassage de populations qui voit affluer en Occident une immigration musulmane dans des sociétés de tradition chrétienne et, on constate en Afrique une pénétration islamique qui met au contact musulmans, animistes et chrétiens.

L'islam et le christianisme se séparent sur la question de l'anthropologie

L'islam comme le christianisme ont élaboré une morale sociale en fonction de la vue historique qui est la leur d'un uni-

---

[51] F. Koneczny, *On the Plurality of Civilization* Introduction de A. Hilckman, Polonica Publications London 1962 p. 360.

versalisme en construction; mais leur point de départ différent fait qu'ils conçoivent différemment le rôle de l'homme dans l'exécution de ce projet. Tandis que pour le christianisme – et cette vision est à la source de la conception occidentale des droits de l'homme[52] – tout homme, parce que créé à l'image de Dieu est titulaire de droits qu'il tient de sa qualité d'homme, dans la perspective islamique l'homme a par nature des devoirs vis à vis de Dieu son auteur et les droits dont il jouit sont ceux qui lui ont été accordés par révélation divine dans le Coran[53]. L'homme est doué d'une infinie dignité dans les deux traditions mais elle y est entendue différemment. Le principe d'égalité fondamentale et de non discrimination entre les êtres humains du fait de leur création à l'image de Dieu se heurte en islam à la doctrine révélée qui établit des inégalités, entre autres entre hommes et femmes, croyants et non musulmans ou limite la liberté de conscience.

Ressemblances et différences entre les doctrine sociales de l'islam et du christianisme.

Les rapports des professionnels chrétiens et musulmans seront facilités du fait qu'il existe des points de ressemblance entre leurs doctrines sociales respectives[54]; il n'appartient pas à cet exposé de dresser un bilan à ce sujet mais qu'il suffise de rappeler un événement de ces dernières années. Lors de la conférence du Caire (1994) musulmans et chrétiens ont montré qu'ils partageaient certaines positions communes en matière sociale. Les uns et les autres, ayant le sens de la sacralité de la vie, ont ainsi joint leurs efforts pour s'opposer aux tentatives faites pour imposer à la société internationale une conception matérialiste de l'existence. Par contre, un même accord de col-

---

[52] J. JOBLIN, *Regard et perspective d'avenir sur les droits de l'homme* in COMMISSION PONTIFICALE JUSTICE ET PAIX, *Les droits de l'homme et l'Eglise* Vatican 1990 pp. 11-47.

[53] A. PACINI (a cura di), *L'islam e il dibattito sui i diritti dell'uomo* Fondazione Agnelli Torino 1998 p. 5.

[54] DR. MOHAMMAD HADI ABDEKHODA'I, *Essere ambasciatore presso la Santa Sede.* Conférence à l'Associazione Carità politica (Roma), 21 mars 1999, p. 10.

laboration n'a pu être réalisé en ce qui concerne les droits de l'homme car, sur ce point, leurs anthropologies ne coïncident pas. Pour les chrétiens, il existe une fraternité fondamentale entre tous les hommes païens, pécheurs ou croyants; ils sont tous égaux par nature car créés à l'image de Dieu et objet d'un même amour de Dieu qui veut sauver tous les hommes; le Christ considère que ce qui est fait au plus petit d'entre eux, c'est à lui-même que cela a été fait (MT 25). Pour les musulmans, la fraternité n'existe qu'entre ceux qui sont entrés dans *l'ummah* qui se fait par la reconnaissance de la souveraineté d'Allah. La perspective chrétienne voit tout être humain comme progressant de l'état où il se trouve vers une plus grande ressemblance au Christ; celle de l'islam est centrée avant tout sur la pratique des obligations fondamentales (la confession de foi et la prière cinq fois par jour, le ramadan, le pèlerinage à la Mecque, l'aumône et la commémoration du sacrifice d'Abraham)[55]. La volonté de diffuser ces pratiques et de ne pas tolérer ce qui leur est étranger manifeste la soumission à la loi donnée par Dieu et confirme ainsi l'appartenance à la communauté.

Une autre différence des fondements des doctrines sociales chrétiennes et islamiques se trouve dans leurs conceptions de l'autorité. L'anthropologie chrétienne voit dans l'homme un être social que les diverses autorités ont pour mission d'aider à concourir librement au bien commun. Pour l'islam, le salut résulte du rapport direct que chacun entretient avec Dieu; il en résulte que le pouvoir n'est pas essentiel à son anthropologie; il existe pour remédier à la faiblesse humaine; il est responsable de maintenir la communauté des croyants dans la fidélité et de la protéger de toute corruption éventuelle[56]; aussi les non-musulmans qui vivent en terre d'islam ne peuvent jouir d'un statut d'égalité avec les musulmans; ils sont tolérés s'ils appartiennent à une religion du Livre; ils sont des *dhimis*[57]. L'origine de cette divergence entre chrétiens et mu-

---

[55] Une minorité en islam a également développé une tradition mystique, mais elle reste quelque peu marginale.

[56] BAT'YE OR, *Les chrétiens d'orient entre diihad et dhimitude* Cerf Paris 1991; JEAN-PAUL II, *Discours au Corps diplomatique* 13 janvier 1990.

[57] AHMED ISHTIAQ, *The concept of an islamic State*. An analysis of the ideological controversy in Pakistan. Stockholm University, 1985, p. 256

sulmans se trouve dans le fait que l'islam n'a pas affiné son anthropologie en reprenant la notion de péché originel. Celle-ci place la responsabilité personnelle des individus au-delà de l'accomplissement indispensable d'actes extérieurs pour bénéficier de la miséricorde de Dieu; elle demande une conversion intérieure qui conduit à se détacher du péché pour s'attacher, jour après jour, à Dieu. Cette conception théologique de la place de l'homme dans le monde a des conséquences qui séparent la théologie politique des deux religions. Dans le christianisme, le pouvoir politique est un élément naturel de la condition humaine mais l'homme ne peut lui être totalement soumis; il est responsable en dernier ressort de juger de son devoir moral vis à vis des autres hommes pour se diriger avec eux vers la vie éternelle; le domaine strictement religieux échappe au pouvoir politique; il n'en va pas de même dans l'islam où le pouvoir politique n'existe que pour faire appliquer la loi coranique et empêcher qu'elle ne soit violée.

Responsabilité des professionnels catholiques et de leurs associations

Les professionnels catholiques et leurs associations doivent être conscients de la différence qui existe entre les deux théologies sociales du christianisme et de l'islam comme des courants d'interprétation divers qu'on y rencontre; en effet un nombre croissant de travailleurs venant de pays catholiques seront appelés à vivre dans des pays musulmans. Plus le gouvernement sera islamique moins il accordera de libertés à ceux qui ne partagent pas la foi musulmane; le cas extrême étant celui de l'Arabie saoudite où les réunions entre croyants et la célébration de la messe sont rigoureusement interdites. En effet l'universalisme exclusif de *l'ummah* doit être maintenu et ce principe conduit à ce que la communauté musulmane se resserre sur elle-même et cherche à rendre son territoire impénétrable à toute idée nouvelle. Cette solidarité d'un type nouveau pour l'Occidental peut être aisément vérifiée; jamais ou presque, un Etat musulman, une université coranique ou un intellectuel musulman même affichant des idées libérales n'émettent des protestations, même discrètes, contre les violations flagrantes des droits de l'homme qui se produisent dans certains pays frères.

Une conception aussi monolithique de l'Etat religieux a formé la mentalité des masses musulmanes; habituées à voir dans le non musulman un Satan, un pécheur et une menace, leurs structures mentales sont fondamentalement discriminatoires et la grande majorité d'entre elles ne peut pas ne pas apporter cette manière de juger dans les pays où elles émigrent. Leur rêve est de s'y constituer comme des communautés musulmanes vivant selon leurs propres lois civiles et religieuses[58]. Croyant que les hommes sont appelés à former un seul peuple sur la base de l'islam, elles se considèrent comme l'avant-garde de la nouvelle conquête qu'entreprend le monde musulman après plusieurs siècles d'éclipse qu'elles attribuent à la domination coloniale.

La question de l'universel est au centre des divisions entre chrétiens et musulmans. Pour le christianisme, peuples et civilisations construisent leur unité en accueillant librement les valeurs de solidarité, de fraternité et de liberté pour tous sans distinction car il attend la réconciliation de l'humanité d'une conversion du coeur dont tous sont capables. Cette conception a pénétré la mentalité occidentale pour laquelle tous les hommes ont le droit de poursuivre leur progrès matériel et développement spirituel avec des chances égales[59]. Il n'en va pas de même pour l'islam où l'unité du genre humain vient de l'acceptation de la révélation contenue dans le Coran. Dans un cas, l'unité existe du fait que tous les hommes partagent une nature commune et s'actualise dans la mesure où leurs esprits convergent vers la Vérité; dans l'autre, seul l'accueil de la Révélation est source d'unité.

V. L'engagement des OIC

Le contexte dans lequel les professionnels catholiques et leurs associations devront témoigner de leur foi sera de

---

[58] S. BARINGHORST, *Cultural Pluralism and Antidiscrimination Policy. The Experience of The City of Bradford* in D. TRANHARDT (ed.), *Europe a next Immigration Continent. Policies and Perspectives Studies* LIT Münster/Hamburg 1992 pp. 145-165; J.D. DURAND & R. LADOUS, *Entretien avec René Remond* Beauchesne Paris 1992 pp. 57-79.

[59] Déclaration de Philadelphie, 1944.

moins en moins imprégné de valeurs évangéliques. Un jeune philosophe de Chine populaire de retour d'un voyage en Europe et aux Etats-Unis a jugé que cette culture manquait d'horizon spirituel; devenue une sorte de *rock'n roll* qui anesthésiait les âmes, elle lui semblait désormais incapable de répondre aux problèmes du monde[60]. Quant aux civilisations qui sont liées aux religions non-chrétiennes leur conception de l'universel est réduite à leur propre horizon. Ces mentalités sont à l'opposé de celle du professionnel catholique pour lequel le monde est en marche vers son unité, une unité à la fois naturelle et spirituelle qui se construit chaque jour grâce à un processus de réexamen de ses certitudes passées. Cette vue dynamique de l'histoire humaine et cette disposition à accepter de modifier son regard sur le monde mettent en jeu des habitudes de pensée voire des situations acquises, ce que beaucoup de peuples craignent d'entreprendre ayant placé leur identité dans certains modes traditionnels de présence au monde.

Rôle des professionnels catholiques et de leurs associations

Les OIC doivent aider les professionnels catholiques à prendre conscience des situations nouvelles dans lesquelles ils se trouvent et, en conséquence, à réévaluer la vision du monde qu'ils ont reçue du passé[61].

1. *Les OIC doivent offrir aux professionnels catholiques un lieu de d'amitié et de ressourcement spirituel où il découvrent quel est le comportement souhaitable d'un chrétien dans le milieu de vie qui est le leur.*

---

[60] LIU XAOBO, *The inspiration of New York: Méditation of an iconoclast* in *Problems of communism* jan. 1991 pp. 113-118; G. BARME, *Liu Xaobo The broken mirror. China after Tien Anmen* Longman (UK) 1989 pp. 52-99. L. VANDERMEERSCH, *Le Confucianisme* in J. DELUMEAU (sous la dir.), *Le fait religieux* Fayard Paris 1993 p. 609: «Ce que le nouveau confucianisme dénonce dans la culture occidentale ... (c'est) la perte du sens existentiel des valeurs corrélative à l'annihilation de l'eprit religieux, entièrement corrodé par le rationalisme scientifique».

[61] PIE XII, *Message au monde* Noël 1956.

L'OIC doit être le lieu où, grâce à l'expérience d'une foi vécue en commun, un professionnel peut prendre du recul par rapport aux problèmes qui l'assaillent quotidiennement. Ceux-ci sont en effet extrêmement variés; quelques uns peuvent être énumérés qui concernent les professions de santé: ainsi des conditions de travail et d'emploi, des relations professionnelles, de l'accès des plus démunis aux soins médicaux, de la situation des personnes âgées... mais aussi des loisirs, des conditions de logement, de la vie familiale etc... Autant de questions sur lesquelles les chrétiens peuvent prendre position si leur discours s'appuie sur une connaissance des problèmes de l'ensemble de la profession et de ses perspectives d'avenir. Ce qui vient d'être dit ici en s'en tenant aux professions de santé pourrait l'être également des enseignants, des ingénieurs, des travailleurs ruraux, de la jeunesse etc... Les OIC se sont préoccupées avant tout durant la période 1919-1939 de la qualification professionnelle de leurs membres; ce souci n'est plus suffisant aujourd'hui; il doit être complété car, à l'époque de la globalisation, la solution des problèmes à l'échelon local est le plus souvent influencée par des décisions prises à un niveau supérieur voire mondial; elles doivent donc rendre leurs membres conscients des conditions nouvelles auxquelles ils doivent sans cesse adapter leur réponse aux problèmes de société.

2. *Deux illusions guettent les OIC dans leur souci d'adaptation à un monde en voie de globalisation.*

Les OIC doivent développer chez leurs membres un sens de l'homme et du bien commun qui les place au-dessus des intérêts particuliers des Etats, d'un parti ou d'une idéologie. Parce que liés à l'Eglise, les professionnels catholiques et leurs associations doivent être les avocats des intérêts de tous et spécialement des plus faibles au milieu de discussions marquées par la défense des intérêts étatiques ou corporatifs. Les professionnels catholiques sont au défi de confronter les régles éthiques de leur profession avec la vision du monde qui est la leur; ils devront dans certains cas se dissocier du comportement général de leurs collègues. Ils pourront alors être tentés de quitter cette position inconfortable d'intermédiaire entre l'éthique et la morale en minimisant l'importance d'une de ces deux réalités.

* Les uns peuvent souhaiter réduire la contribution technique que les organisations catholiques ont à faire au développement, à la défense des droits de l'homme ou à l'administration de la chose publique. Pour eux, les professionnels catholiques s'égareraient en empruntant une telle voie car ils pactiseraient en quelque sorte avec les tenants de l'incroyance et du paganisme au lieu d'incarner l'Evangile dans des réalisations, limitées certes mais exemplaires. Cette non-participation à la vie publique est à l'opposé de ce que Pie XI appelait en 1927 la charité politique[62]. S'adressant aux membres de la FUCI (*Federazione universitaria dei Cattolici italiani*), il leur faisait remarquer que la plus haute forme de la charité après l'entrée dans la vie consacrée était l'engagement dans la vie politique où l'on «considère les intérêts de la société toute entière»; elle est de ce point de vue, «le champ le plus vaste de la charité, de la charité politique"[63]; en effet, le chrétien y prend part avec les autres mouvements sociaux au «passage, pour chacun et pour tous, de conditions moins humaines à des conditions plus humaines»[64].

* L'autre tentation qui menace les membres des associations catholiques est de se donner tout entiers à l'action sociale, politique ou autre au point d'attendre d'une théorie politique ou d'une idéologie qu'elle détermine ce qui est plus ou moins humain. Le souci de coopérer sans arrière-pensée à la réalisation d'un projet ne dispense pas le professionnel catholique d'examiner si la politique suivie favorise pour tous, dans le *hic et nunc*, une extension de la pratique des droits de l'homme, une amélioration des conditions d'existence ou un plus grand respect de la vie. C'est ainsi que Pie XI argumenta en 1937 pour condamner le nazisme et le communisme en affirmant que la personne humaine ne peut être sacrifiée aux intérêts d'un Etat, d'une race ou d'un parti[65]; opposition intelligente qui n'enferme pas le chrétien dans une tour d'ivoire mais le

---

[62] Pie XI, ALL. aux membres de la FUCI, 18 décembre 1927; A. Luciani, *La Carità politica* San Paolo Cinisello Balsamo (Milano) 1994 p. 355

[63] A. Luciani, *La carità politica* San Paolo Cinisello (Mi) 1994, pp. 354-355.

[64] *Populorum Progressio* § 20.

[65] Pie XI, Enc. *Mit brennender Sorge* contre le nazisme et *Divini Redemptoris* contre le communisme.

pousse à coopérer d'une manière active et critique avec les autres mouvements sociaux; comme le remarquait Jean XXIII: «une doctrine une fois fixée et formulée ne change plus, tandis que des mouvements ayant pour objet des conditions concrètes et changeantes de la vie ne peuvent pas être largement influencés par cette évolution»[66].

3. *A quelles conditions les OIC et les professionnels catholiques peuvent-ils prendre part active à la Nouvelle Evangélisation?*

Les professionnels catholiques et leurs associations engagés dans la vie publique ne peuvent accomplir leur tâche sans recevoir le soutien des communautés catholiques. Ils ne sont pas des aventuriers agissant de manière isolée et qui, tels les corsaires et explorateurs d'autrefois, reviennent en rapportant de nouvelles terres à l'Eglise. Ils sont membres à part entière de la communauté des croyants et ils sont l'expression de sa volonté de faire découvrir l'Evangile là où il n'est pas connu. Là où existe ce soutien, elles peuvent se développer en pleine union avec la hiérarchie comme avec les paroisses qui peuvent mettre à leur disposition un certain nombre de moyens pour accomplir leur tâche; quand ceux-ci leur font défaut, le risque est grand qu'elles se sentent coupés des communautés chrétiennes et ne donnent pas le témoignage de l'union de la foi et de l'engagement qui est essentiel à leur mission.

4. *Philosophie de l'action apostolique des professionnels catholiques et leurs associations*

Les professionnels catholiques et leurs associations dévoilent une vision alternative de l'existence face à celles, réductionnistes, de l'incroyance et des religions non chrétiennes. Leur message d'amour et de justice gagne en crédibilité chaque fois que les communautés chrétiennes s'engagent à leurs côtés[67]. Mis au contact d'incroyants ou de membres des religions

---

[66] JEAN XXIII, *Mater et Magistra* § 159.
[67] A. TERGEL, *Human Rights in Cultural and Religious Traditions* AUU Uppsala 1998 p. 154.

non chrétiennes dans des projets dont ils peuvent assumer la direction, ils montrent que la fidélité aux valeurs du christianisme ne fait pas obstacle à la poursuite d'objectifs communs.; ils découvrent en même temps que leur propre vision du monde peut être dépouillée des apports particuliers de leur tradition qui ne lui sont pas essentiels et comment celle-ci peut également s'enrichir d'une expérience de l'humain qu'elle n'a pas.

* * *

Les professionnels catholiques et leurs associations assurent la présence de l'Eglise dans un monde qui lui est étranger. Se détachant des préjugés de l'Occident, ils cherchent à établir une communion spirituelle avec les fidèles des autres religions en vue de s'approcher sur terre de l'idéal de justice et de paix qui est commun à tous. Messagers de l'Evangile sur des terres nouvelles, leur place dans l'Eglise doit être reconnue par les communautés de fidèles faisant ainsi du peuple de Dieu un peuple missionnaire.

L'un des dangers de la mentalité sécularisée et rationaliste est que les professionnels catholiques et leurs associations ne voient plus dans l'action ce qui les distingue des non-croyants comme des fidèles des autres religions. L'esprit analytique qu'ils tiennent de leur éducation ou de leur formation scientifique leur fait trop souvent considérer leur activité de recherche, d'enseignement ou d'assistance immédiate aux plus démunis comme n'ayant d'autre portée que leur activité même; or, s'ils n'y prennent garde, ils risquent d'oublier le sens chrétien qui donne sa finalité à leur action et d'adhérer alors à la vision dominante de la société ou de l'institution avec laquelle ils collaborent.

Le concours aux activités sociales doit être critique pour demeurer chrétien; c'est à dire que le professionnel catholique doit toujours garder présente à l'esprit la vision du développement et du progrès qui est la sienne. De même que les organisations humanitaires peuvent être amenées à se retirer d'un pays quand les conditions dans lesquelles on leur demande d'agir annulent le sens de leur mission aux yeux de l'opinion[68]

---

[68] J. JOBLIN, *Le droit d'ingérence* in *Gregorianum* 1995 76/1 pp. 119-122.

de même les professionnels catholiques peuvent devoir se dissocier des activités qu'on leur demande d'accomplir si elles sont à l'opposé de ce qu'ils tiennent pour une condition indispensable de la croissance humaine. C'est ici le lieu de rappeler l'affirmation de *Populorum Progressio*: «toute action sociale engage une doctrine»[69] c'est à dire que tout type de collaboration doit être évalué en tenant compte de la philosophie sociale de ceux qui en fixent l'orientation[70].

Il est de la responsabilité des OIC de donner une spiritualité appropriée aux professionnels catholiques comme aux membres des associations caritatives d'assistance; celle-ci doit leur faire prendre conscience de ce que leur mission est de témoigner dans l'actualité historique que le progrès matériel et spirituel de chaque être humain est lié à la place faite dans la société à la famille, à la nation comme aux institutions religieuses, ces «structures consacrées par l'histoire» (Pie XII).

La conscience de la spécificité de leur présence dans la société civile donnera des traits différents aux priorités des professionnels catholiques et de leurs associations selon qu'elles se trouveront face à l'incroyance ou aux religions non chrétiennes.

* Les sociétés qui font de la sécularisation la base de la paix sociale sont certes ouvertes à la fraternité universelle de tous les hommes mais elles n'offrent aucun contrepoids à la toute puissance de l'Etat. Lorsque celui-ci entraîne les populations à la poursuite d'un mythe terrestre, hier le racisme, le nationalisme, ou le communisme, aujourd'hui une certaine forme de libéralisme et ce que Jean-Paul II a appelé le consumérisme la dimension religieuse de l'existence est regardée comme un obstacle au progrès. Il s'agit alors pour les professionnels catholiques et leurs associations de renvoyer au sens vrai de la personne.

* Les religions non-chrétiennes sont peu ouvertes au pluralisme comme à l'universalisme. Il convient de leur faire perce-

---

[69] *Populorum Progressio* § 39.
[70] Il n'est pas possible de traiter ici les aspects divers de la collaboration avec les incroyants; sur l'interprétation nuancée de la collaboration des catholiques avec les communistes sur le terrain humanitaire cf. *Divini Redemptoris* §§ 57, 58 et son commentaire autorisé dans l'édition de l'Action Populaire Spes Paris 1937 p. 79 note 6.

voir que l'ouverture sur l'extérieur ne détruit pas la personnalité mais est condition de son progrès spirituel; c'est d'ailleurs ainsi que croissent les membres des familles et ceux d'unités plus larges comme la nation.

* * *

Les professionnels catholiques et leurs associations peuvent jouer une part considérable au XXIème siècle pour surmonter la division des blocs que leurs cultures opposent; ils doivent être conscients de ce qu'ils trouveront au sein des autres religions des hommes qui partagent leur soif d'universalisme; c'est avec eux qu'ils construiront un «pont spirituel» (Pie XII) grâce auquel sera dépassé le cloisonnement des blocs.

Il s'agit alors pour les professionnels catholiques et leurs associations de renvoyer au sens vrai de la personne.

Finito di stampare
nel mese di ottobre 1999

presso la tipografia
"Giovanni Olivieri" di E. Montefoschi
00187 Roma - Via dell'Archetto, 10,11,12